Contemporary Tourist Experience

This significant and timely volume aims to provide a focused analysis of tourist experiences that reflects their ever-increasing diversity and complexity, and their significance and meaning to tourists themselves. Written by leading international scholars, it offers new insight into emergent behaviours, motivations and sought meanings on the part of tourists based on five contemporary themes determined by current research in tourism experience: conceptualisation of tourist experience; dark tourism experiences; the relationship between motivation and the contemporary tourist experience; the manner in which tourist experience can be influenced and enhanced by place; and how managers and suppliers can make a significant contribution to the tourist experience.

The book critically explores these experiences from multidisciplinary perspectives and includes case studies from a wide range of geographical regions. By analysing these contemporary tourist experiences, the book will provide further understanding of the consumption of tourism.

Richard Sharpley is Professor of Tourism and Development at the University of Central Lancashire, Preston, UK.

Philip R. Stone is a former management consultant within the tourism and hospitality sector, and is presently employed as a Senior Lecturer with the University of Central Lancashire, Preston, UK.

Routledge advances in tourism

Edited by Stephen Page

School for Tourism, Bournemouth University

1 **The Sociology of Tourism**
Theoretical and empirical investigations
Edited by Yiorgos Apostolopoulos, Stella Leivadi and Andrew Yiannakis

2 **Creating Island Resorts**
Brian King

3 **Destinations**
Cultural landscapes of tourism
Edited by Greg Ringer

4 **Mediterranean Tourism**
Facets of socioeconomic development and cultural change
Edited by Yiorgos Apostolopoulos, Lila Leontidou and Philippos Loukissas

5 **Outdoor Recreation Management**
John Pigram and John Jenkins

6 **Tourism Development**
Edited by Douglas G. Pearce and Richard W. Butler

7 **Tourism and Sustainable Community Development**
Edited by Greg Richards and Derek Hall

8 **Tourism and Political Boundaries**
Dallen J. Timothy

9 **Leisure and Tourism Landscapes**
Social and cultural geographies
Cara Aitchison, Nicola E. MacLeod and Stephen J. Shaw

10 **Tourism in the Age of Globalisation**
Edited by Salah Wahab and Chris Cooper

11 **Tourism and Gastronomy**
Edited by Anne-Mette Hjalager and Greg Richards

12 **New Perspectives in Caribbean Tourism**
Edited by Marcella Daye, Donna Chambers and Sherma Roberts

13 **The Advanced Econometrics of Tourism Demand**
Haiyan Song, Stephen F. Witt and Gang Li

14 **Tourism in China**
Destination, cultures and communities
Edited by Chris Ryan and Gu Huimin

15 **Sustainable Tourism Futures**
Perspectives on systems, restructuring and innovations
Edited by Stefan Gössling, C. Michael Hall and David B. Weaver

16 **Advances in Tourism Destination Marketing**
Managing networks
Edited by Metin Kozak, Juergen Gnoth and Luisa Andreu

17 **Drive Tourism**
Trends and emerging markets
Edited by Bruce Prideaux and Dean Carson

18 **Tourist Customer Service Satisfaction**
An encounter approach
Francis P. Noe, Muzzafer Uysal and Vincent P. Magnini

19 **Mining Heritage Tourism**
A global synthesis
Edited by Michael Conlin and Lee Jolliffe

20 **Tourist Experience**
Contemporary perspectives
Edited by Richard Sharpley and Phillip Stone

21 **Sustainable Tourism in Rural Europe**
Edited by Donald Macleod and Steven Gillespie

22 **The Critical Turn in Tourism Studies**
Creating an academy of hope
Edited by Nigel Morgan, Irena Atelkevic and Annette Pritchard

23 **Tourism Supply Chain Management**
Haiyan Song

24 **Tourism and Retail**
Edited by Charles McIntyre

25 **International Sports Events**
Impacts, experience and identities
Edited by Richard Shipway and Alan Fyall

26 **Cultural Moment in Tourism**
Edited by Laurajane Smith, Emma Waterton and Steve Watson

27 **Contemporary Tourist Experience**
Concepts and consequences
Edited by Richard Sharpley and Philip R. Stone

28 **Future Tourism**
Political, social and economic challenges
James Leigh, Craig Webster and Stanislav Ivanov

Forthcoming:

Responsible Tourist Behaviour
Clare Weeden

Information Communication Technologies and Sustainable Tourism
Alisha Ali and Andrew J. Frew

Human Rights and Global Events
Rebecca Finkel

Tourist Experience and Fulfilment
Insights from positive psychology
Sebastian Filep and Philip Pearce

Contemporary Tourist Experience

Concepts and consequences

Edited by Richard Sharpley and Philip R. Stone

Routledge
Taylor & Francis Group
LONDON AND NEW YORK

First published 2012
by Routledge
2 Park Square, Milton Park, Abingdon, Oxon OX14 4RN

Simultaneously published in the USA and Canada
by Routledge
711 Third Avenue, New York, NY 10017

Routledge is an imprint of the Taylor & Francis Group, an informa business

British Library Cataloguing in Publication Data
A catalogue record for this book is available from the British Library

Library of Congress Cataloging in Publication Data
Contemporary tourist experience: concepts and consequences / edited by Richard Sharpely and Philip Stone.
p. cm.
Includes bibliographical references and index.
1. Tourism–Research. 2. Tourism–Psychological aspects. I. Sharpely, Richard, 1956- II. Stone, Philip.
G155.A1C6554 2012
338.4'791–dc23

2012001175

ISBN: 978-0-415-69742-2 (hbk)
ISBN: 978-0-203-13911-0 (ebk)

Typeset in Times New Roman
by Wearset Ltd, Boldon, Tyne and Wear

Contents

Contributors

Álvaro de la Rica Aspiunza (PhD, Economics and Business Administration) is Associate Professor in the Department of Tourism at the University of Deusto, Spain. Former Head of the School of Tourism at the Bilbao and San Sebastian campuses, he is currently Vice Dean for Bilbao Campus and for International Relations, Faculty of Social and Human Sciences. He lectures on business (financial management of tourism firms, administration and management of tourism firms, and other related subjects). He is a member of the Advisory Council of the journal *ROTUR* and also a member of the Leisure and Human Development research team, recognised by the Basque Government in the 2010 call for tenders. His specialist field of research centres on understanding tourism in the new leisure society from a business perspective.

Ali Bakir is Principal Lecturer at the School of Applied Management and Law, Faculty of Design Media and Management, Buckinghamshire New University, UK. He lectures on strategy and marketing in sport, leisure, tourism and music. He also leads the school's postgraduate programme in sports management and MBA (Sport). Ali's research interests lie in interpretive studies in strategy and the creative and cultural industries.

The late **Jim Bell** was Professor of International Business and Entrepreneurship at the University of Ulster, Magee Campus. His research interests were focused in the area of small-firm internationalisation and public policy in support of internationalisation. He published extensively in international journals and was a member of the executive committee of the UK chapter of the Academy of International Business. Jim was also Visiting Associate Professor in international business/marketing at the University of Otago, New Zealand.

Avital Biran is a Lecturer in Tourism in the department of Hotel and Tourism Management at Ben-Gurion University of the Negev, Israel. Previous to this she held a position as a Lecturer in Tourism at the University of Surrey, UK. Her main research interests are tourist behaviour and experience, visitor attraction management as well as the conceptual understanding of tourism. She is particularly interested in exploring these notions in to the context of heritage tourism, dark tourism and food tourism.

Peter Bolan PhD is Course Director for International Travel and Tourism Management at the University of Ulster in Northern Ireland. He holds an honours degree in Geography, a master's degrees in Tourism Management and e-Tourism and a PhD examining motivation, authenticity and displacement in film-induced tourism. His research interests and specialisms include film- and media-induced tourism, e-business, social media and mobile applications in tourism. Peter is currently involved in an EU-funded project to develop next-generation mobile phone apps for interpretive information at visitor attractions.

Stephen Boyd is Chair in Tourism at the University of Ulster. He is an ex-geographer who moved quickly into tourism, teaching tourism at Staffordshire University, England, the University of Otago, New Zealand, and now the University of Ulster, Northern Ireland. His research has covered many areas, but he is best known for his work on heritage tourism, marketing and managing world heritage sites and the relationship between national parks and tourism. He is currently researching political tourism and the interconnections between religious and political tourism. He is the Masters Coordinator of all taught programmes in his department, including International Tourism Development, International Hotel and Tourism Management and Event Management.

Barbara A. Carmichael is a Professor in the Department of Geography and Environmental Studies and the Director of NEXT Research Centre (Centre for the Study of Nascent Entrepreneurship and the Exploitation of Technology) in the School of Business and Economics at Wilfrid Laurier University, Waterloo, Ontario, Canada. Originally from the United Kingdom, she has a BA Hons in Geography from Bristol University, an MBA from Durham University Business School and a PhD from the University of Victoria, British Columbia. She lived in Kenya for six years during the 1970s and immigrated to Canada in 1987. Her research interests are in tourism entrepreneurship, quality tourism experiences, special events, casino impacts, market segmentation and residents' attitudes towards tourism.

Sean Doherty holds a Bachelor of Environmental Studies degree, a masters degree in Geography, and a PhD in Civil Engineering (Toronto). His research focuses on human activity/mobility patterns and decision-making, including tracking methods, modelling, and the impacts on health, safety and the environment. His current projects involve application of a global positioning tracking system to the study of diabetic patients, elderly home-care patients, children, tourists and immigrants. His partners in these projects include Bloorview Kids Rehab, Toronto Rehab Institute, Research in Motion, Telus, and Innovations at the University of Toronto.

Jennifer L. Erdely is an Assistant Professor of Communications at Prairie View A&M University, USA. Her research interests are in the performance and ethnography of touristic experiences. She also researches volunteer tourism, virtual tourism and museum tourism. She received her PhD in Communication Studies at Louisiana State University. She now teaches courses in ethnographic methods and virtual tourism.

Graham K. Henning received his PhD from the University of Calgary in Tourism Management. He is presently an Assistant Professor in Management at Adelphi University in New York. He has written on the nature of tourism, the ontology of the tourism experience, hermeneutical approaches to tourism, nature-based tourism, sustainable development, and cross-cultural relations in tourism. He is also undertaking the development of a new view of business, which has him immersed in philosophy, especially freedom/necessity, the nature of the corporation, the development of a hermeneutical ontology, dialogue and ethics. Prior to academia Graham worked as a lawyer, consultant, film producer and entrepreneur.

Aliakbar Jafari is a chartered marketer and Lecturer in Marketing in the Department of Marketing at the University of Strathclyde. While his overall research interests include areas such as interpretive consumer research, theories of globalisation and marketing theory, he is particularly interested in understanding how institutional forces shape market contents and structures as well as market-making practices. His work has appeared in *Consumption, Markets and Culture*; *Marketing Theory*; *Advances in Consumer Research*; *Journal of Islamic Marketing*; *International Journal of Management Concepts and Philosophy*; and *Iranian Studies*. He is guest co-editor of two special issues of *Marketing Theory* in 2012 and 2013.

Muhammet Kesgin is a PhD researcher and Associate Lecturer at Buckinghamshire New University in UK. He has a BSc and an MSc in Tourism and Hotel Management and a PGCE in Teaching and Learning in Higher Education. He became a fellow of the UK Higher Education Academy and Academy of Marketing in 2011. He worked in the hospitality industry for several years before he moved into education in 2005. He was a Lecturer at Akdeniz University, Turkey, prior to his current affiliation. He lectures in tourism, hospitality and event management. His current research areas include consumer behaviour in tourism and hospitality, destination management and marketing and mixed methods research.

Jacob R. Kirkegaard Larsen is a PhD candidate in the Department of Culture and Global Studies, Aalborg University, Denmark. His PhD thesis is based on qualitative research and relates to families with dependent children on holiday in a rented Danish holiday home. His research is centred on second-home tourism, family holiday and consumer behaviour with a particular interest in socio-psychological aspects of the tourist experience.

Lea Holst Laursen (PhD, MSc.Eng. Urban Design) is an Assistant Professor at the Department of Architecture, Design and Media Technology, Aalborg University. Her research is in the field of differentiated urban development and spatial restructuring, looking among other things into the term of shrinking territories. The research emphasises an action-oriented perspective investigating the role and potential of landscape, the potential of using tourism strategies and the potential in having a place-based starting point in territories undergoing spatial restructuring.

Maria Lexhagen received her PhD in Business Administration focusing on e-marketing and customer behaviour from the School of Business, Economics and Law at Gothenburg University. She is currently a researcher and lecturer at the European Research Institute (ETOUR) at the Department of Tourism Studies, Mid Sweden University. Her main research interest is customer behaviour and Internet-based marketing in tourism. Research interests also specifically include customer-perceived value, social media use and fans in pop culture tourism. She has published internationally on these topics in books and journals within the areas of tourism, marketing and information systems.

Darius Liutikas is a scientific researcher at the Lithuanian Social Research Centre, Vilnius. His research interests include modern and traditional pilgrimage, the sociology of tourism, forms of mobility, sacred places and sacred spaces, and the geography of religions. He has published around 20 articles in Lithuanian academic journals. The Community of Lithuanian Pilgrims published his monograph about manifestation of values and identity in the journeys in 2009 (in Lithuanian).

Christine Lundberg has a PhD in Business Administration from the School of Business, Economics and Law at Gothenburg University and holds a position as a researcher and senior lecturer at the European Tourism Research Institute (ETOUR) at Mid Sweden University. Her research focuses primarily on service encounters, employee relations, servicescapes and fan tourism. These topics have been under study in her internationally published works in journals and books.

Bridget Major is a Principal Lecturer at Newcastle Business School, Northumbria University. She has published in journals on specialist travel products and tourism education and is currently completing her DBA on the package holiday experience. Prior to academia, she worked in tour operating.

Fraser McLeay is Professor of Strategic Marketing Management at Newcastle Business School, Northumbria University, and co-chairs the Marketing, Travel and Tourism Management subject group. He has published over 50 book chapters, journal articles, and referred conference proceedings and has worked internationally for small and medium enterprises and multinationals in marketing and international business.

Yaniv Poria is a Professor of Tourism in the Department of Hotel and Tourism Management at Ben-Gurion University of the Negev, Israel. He holds a PhD in Heritage Tourism Management from Surrey University. His main research interest is the management of heritage in tourism.

Introduction

Experiencing tourism, experiencing happiness?

Richard Sharpley and Philip R. Stone

In a contribution to a recent collection of papers that explore the relationship between tourism and consumerism, in particular the emergence of the mass consumption of tourism and its subsequent social, economic and environmental consequences, Hall (2011: 301) concludes by asking the question: 'Why have so many people increasingly come to believe that consuming ... [leisure and travel] ... will somehow make them happier and improve their life?' In other words, he suggests that, although the specific reasons why people engage in tourism (that is, tourist motivation) have long been addressed in the academic literature, there remains more limited understanding of how or why tourism, as a specific and increasingly pervasive form of contemporary consumption, has come to be considered more generally as a potential source of happiness and well-being. This is not to say that this issue has been completely overlooked; for example, the link between tourism and the 'good life' is explored in a recent text (Pearce *et al.* 2011). However, by drawing attention to the assumed, or expected, contribution of tourism to personal well-being or happiness, Hall (2011) is not only asking a question of tourism consumption in particular that has long been considered by philosophers, sociologists, economists and others more generally – that is, can wealth be equated with happiness (Douthwaite 1999; Graham 2009)? He is also, albeit inadvertently, responding to the statement made some two centuries ago by Thomas Jefferson (1743–1826), the third President of the United States, that 'Traveling makes a man wiser, but less happy'.

Jefferson was, of course, writing at a time when tourism, as commonly understood today, did not exist. Leisure travel, if it could be described as such, was the preserve of a privileged minority engaging in activities such as the Grand Tour or, for the leisured classes, visits to European spas or seaside resorts that featured in the then social calendar (Towner 1996). Indeed, at the beginning of the nineteenth century, the socio-economic and technological drivers of the democratisation of tourism had yet to evolve, whilst travel for the purposes of recreation and leisure, as opposed to education, was still rare; only when an emerging middle class began to 'invade' the travel patterns of the aristocracy, for example, did an objective traveller's gaze come to be superseded by subjective sightseeing (Adler 1989).

Nor, perhaps, could Jefferson have imagined or predicted how 'travel' would evolve into the mass social and economic phenomenon that is contemporary tourism. Indeed, he could not have foreseen that tourism would become a barometer of individual and national wealth – it is, of course, no coincidence that tourism is nowadays growing most rapidly in those countries and regions enjoying the highest rates of economic growth – and, consequently, how experiencing tourism would become an accepted, expected and increasingly sought-after form of consumption. Nevertheless, his observation that an individual's sense of happiness may actually be diminished through participating in travel is as relevant, if not more so, today as it was then. Not only has tourism become a pervasive form of consumption in general, but consumption itself has both assumed a dominant role in postmodern social life (particularly in identity formation) and become an assumed source of happiness – the notion of 'retail therapy' reflects the broader belief that economic growth and increased economic activity enhances human well-being. In short, the tourist experience (or, more precisely, the consumption of tourism experiences) has come to be seen as a route to happiness (Hall 2011). Therefore, it is logical to suggest that, in order to understand more completely the phenomenon that is the tourist experience, it is important to consider it within the framework of the consumption–happiness debate.

The tourist experience itself is, of course, complex and multifaceted. Indeed, as we observed in the introduction to a previous collection of works on the topic (Sharpley and Stone 2011a: 2), 'understanding the nature of the tourist experience would seem to be a difficult, if not impossible task'. The tourist experience, or what people experience as tourists, is unique to the individual; thus, there are as many forms of tourist experience as there are tourists. Nevertheless, we suggested in that introduction there are two ways in which the tourist experience may be conceptualised. On the one hand, it may be considered to be the set of services or experiences consumed by the tourist during a holiday or time away from home. In other words, it may be seen as the collection of services and/or experiences produced or provided by the myriad businesses, organisations and individuals that comprise the tourism sector, as well as incidental or serendipitous experiences, that are defined temporally by the period of travel and that 'bring immediate but short-term satisfaction or benefits' to the tourist (Sharpley and Stone 2011a: 3). As such, these services or experiences may be subject to what Morgan *et al.* (2010: xv) refer to as 'experience management'; whereas tourism services were once produced and consumed on a price-utility basis, the advent of what Pine and Gilmore (1999) famously describe as the 'experience economy' transformed the destination into a stage where services are not produced but performed, and where added value (and, for tourism businesses and destinations, competitive advantage) is achieved through the provision of memorable experiences. Arguably, we have now moved into the era of the co-production of tourist experiences (Prahalad and Ramaswamy 2004), or a second-stage experience economy (see Chapter 1 in this volume) in which tourists play a more active role in creating their desired experiences, although Feifer's (1985) concept of the post-tourist, who recognises and adopts the role of a player in the inauthentic game that tourism has become, provides an interesting counterpoint. Nevertheless, the importance of effective experience management in tourism has long been recognised and, consequently, significant attention has been paid in the literature to the management of tourism experiences.

On the other hand, the tourist experience may be thought of as simply 'the experience of being a tourist, which results not only from a particular combination of provided experiences, but also from the meaning or significance accorded to it by the tourist in relation to his or her normal socio-cultural existence' (Sharpley and Stone 2011a: 3). This experience of 'being a tourist' embraces not only the actual period of holiday or travel as discussed in the preceding definition of the tourist experience, but also the bracketing periods of looking forward to and looking back on the holiday as experience; as the American novelist Edward Streeter once observed, 'Travel is ninety percent anticipation and ten percent recollection'. Putting it another way, the tourism consumption process may be seen as continual and cyclical, commencing with anticipation and continuing with memories which feed into and influence the anticipation of subsequent periods of tourism consumption. Moreover, this process is inevitably influenced by the people's socio-cultural existence in general and by their experience as tourists – or 'travel career ladder' (Pearce 2005) – in particular.

From this perspective, the tourist experience becomes a complex, multidimensional phenomenon; indeed, understanding the tourist experience is, perhaps, commensurate with the sociology of tourism, perhaps the first and certainly the most enduring perspective on the study of tourism more generally (Dann and Parrinello 2009). For this reason, the tourist experience is most usually considered in the context of specific constituent elements, such as motivation, perception/image formation, consumption, tourist–host relationships and so on and, implicitly, to understand fully the tourist experience is to understand the nature of and relationship between these constituent elements. To consider all of these is, inevitably, well beyond the scope of this introduction. However, Quinlan Cutler and Carmichael (2010: 8) usefully summarise them in a conceptual model of the tourist experience, which identifies two 'realms' – the 'influential realm', which includes factors external to the individual (for example, destination attributes, socio-cultural forces and tourism products), and the 'personal realm', or intrinsic factors such as motivation, knowledge, self-identity and so on – that come to bear on the nature of the tourist experience from anticipation to recollection.

Many of these factors in both the influential and personal realms have of course long been addressed in the tourism literature. To return to the initial theme of this introduction, however, an evident factor within the influential realm of the tourist experience is the significance of consumption in general and its influence on tourism in particular. That is, consumption has long been seen to play a defining role in contemporary (postmodern) society, no more so than in the context of tourism (Munt 1994; Pretes 1995; Sharpley 2008) whilst, more specifically, 'consumers are taken to have some prior needs or wants, which are fulfilled by consumption, leading to higher levels of satisfaction or happiness' (Dutt 2006: 1) Therefore, if increasing consumption (or, more precisely, the ability to consume more through increased wealth) can be equated with greater happiness, the question remains: are tourist experiences sought in the pursuit of happiness? And if so, does this pursuit end in success?

Given the uniqueness of the tourist experience to the individual tourist, definitive answers to both of these questions will inevitably remain elusive; indeed, to generalise about the pursuit and/or experience of happiness through tourism would be foolhardy. Nevertheless, it is possible to make a number of broad observations relevant to the understanding of contemporary tourist experiences and which, as noted shortly, provide a context for many of the chapters in this book. As Graham (2009) observes, philosophers and others have since time immemorial been concerned with what in general makes people happy whilst, following pioneering work by Easterlin (1975), the relationship between wealth and happiness in particular has come to be debated by an increasing number of economists, to the extent that it has become an identifiable and accepted branch of economics. Therefore, it is possible to draw on these debates to consider whether tourism, as a specific form of consumption, may be related to the pursuit or achievement of happiness.

The first point to consider is what is meant by the term 'happiness', particularly in the context of tourist experiences. Is it, on the one hand, the immediate pleasure or gratification resulting from, for example, visiting a particular site, experiencing a particular event, staying in an exclusive hotel or, more generally, enjoying a relaxing period away from normal home life – in other words, happiness that is 'of the moment'? Or, on the other hand, is it a more fundamental and longer lasting sensation that occurs not necessarily during but certainly following the holiday or period of travel? In fact, Grayling (2008) suggests that happiness is 'too vague and baggy a notion to be truly helpful. … Instead of talking about happiness, one should talk about satisfaction, achievement, interest, engagement, enjoyment, growth and the constant opening of fresh possibilities'. He goes on to suggest that happiness may not be experienced whilst undertaking activities that lead to satisfaction or achievement; rather, 'a person in the midst of doing something objectively worthwhile might not describe himself as happy … and only later will realise that what it is to be happy is to be absorbed in something worthwhile'.

According to Graham (2009), a similar perspective is revealed in economic research into happiness, with questionnaires most frequently asking respondents to assess their overall level of life satisfaction, or satisfaction with particular aspects of their (economic) life, such as employment or income. Thus, happiness (relative to wealth or consumption) is typically thought of as being commensurate with a sense of well-being, life satisfaction or perhaps contentedness, subjective human conditions that may also be influenced by a variety of non-economic factors such as an individual's relationships, health, aspirations, values and so on.

In the context of the consumption of tourism, therefore, this suggests that 'happiness' should be considered in terms of not the immediacy and intensity of pleasurable 'on-site' experiences, but of the longer-lasting, post-travel satisfaction that derives from particular tourist experiences which, at the time of consumption, may be more or less pleasurable. This, in turn, suggests that specific forms of tourist experience, such as volunteer tourism, physically or intellectually challenging experiences, those that demonstrate what Hall (2011) refers to as 'voluntary simplicity', or those that are instrumental as opposed to autotelic as in, for instance, holidays that are taken to enhance family bonds, may result in greater personal happiness or satisfaction than those experiences that represent more immediate conspicuous consumption. Indeed, it is perhaps no coincidence that, a time when there is increasing concern over social well-being rather than absolute levels of wealth, a current UK tour operator's (2011/2012) television advertising campaign promotes neither specific holidays nor destinations, but the opportunity to strengthen personal and family relationships. Moreover, a study by DeLeire and Kalil (2009) revealed that leisure is one of just two forms of consumption that, through enhancing social connectedness, lead to increased happiness.

There are also evident links between the definition of happiness as life satisfaction or a sense of well-being and the concept of tourism as a secular spiritual experience. In other words, it has long been argued that contemporary tourism is in general akin to a secular pilgrimage, a sacred journey that is not only physically but spiritually refreshing (Graburn 2001), whilst specific niche products, such as holistic or wellness tourism, explicitly embrace the spiritual dimension (Smith 2003). Whilst spirituality itself is variously defined (Heelas and Woodhead 2005) and whilst the spiritual dimension of contemporary tourism remains contested (Sharpley and Jepson 2011), it is not illogical to equate spirituality (commonly taken to represent a sense of connectedness, meaning or belonging) with happiness as well-being. Hence, certain tourist experiences that may be considered spiritual, or 'valuistic journeys' as discussed in Chapter 3 in this book, may be a source of happiness. Equally, those people actively seeking spirituality through tourism – perhaps Cohen's (1979) 'existential tourists' – may be thought of as seeking happiness though, if this argument is extended, recreational tourists seek only refreshment rather than spiritual 'happiness'.

The second point is that, since Easterlin's research in the 1970s, most economic studies of happiness have concluded that there is a limited correlation between wealth/levels of income and happiness, confirming what is known as the 'Easterlin Paradox'. That is, people with higher incomes in a particular country are more likely to say they are happy than those on low incomes (Oswald 1997); however, in cross-country comparisons, beyond a level of income necessary to meet basic needs, levels of happiness do not vary significantly according to income. Moreover, it has also been found that increases in national wealth not only may *not* be reflected in increased national happiness; as wealth increases, reported happiness and well-being may actually decline (Douthwaite 1999), suggesting that beyond a particular threshold, increased wealth is not reflected in increased happiness; in other words, happiness is recognising one has enough. Equally, increasing wealth may result in higher levels of aspiration, so that more is consumed to maintain a given level of happiness.

Of course, levels of wealth do not necessarily indicate levels of consumption. As Grayling (2008) notes,

> wealth is not so much what one has, but what one does with it. A man who has a thousand pounds and spends it on a wonderful trip to the Galapagos Islands is a rich man indeed: the experiences, the things learnt, the differences wrought in him by both, are true wealth.

Putting it another way, a rich person who can buy anything may never find happiness through consumption; conversely, a less wealthy person may find happiness in the consumption of a special object or experience, though the inability to consume more, particularly in comparison to one's peers, may also lead to unhappiness.

Nevertheless, studies focusing specifically on consumption typically suggest that consumption and increased material well-being are not related to happiness (DeLeire and Kalil 2009); that having more, or the ability (wealth) to have more, far from increasing happiness, may actually reduce it. Whether this generalisation is applicable to the specific context of tourism is unclear – reference has been made above to research indicating that leisure consumption may, for social reasons, enhance levels of happiness – though a number of observations can be made.

First, increased consumption of tourism, or enjoying more holidays or travel experiences, may not lead to increased happiness. The ability (to afford) to travel more may simply increase the desire to 'collect' more experiences, the focus becoming not the quality but the quantity of tourist experiences. Certainly, as opportunities to participate in tourism have become more numerous, diverse and, relative to income, affordable, there has been an undoubted trend, at last within wealthier nations, for people to participate in tourism more frequently; that is, although the proportion of people taking holidays has not increased markedly, those who do are taking more holidays each year. This has, perhaps, served to reduce the status of tourism from an object of consumption that is 'special' to one that is 'normal', no longer a luxury but an expectation or, as suggested in Chapter 2 of this book, a habit. And can habit be equated with happiness?

Second, the cost of a holiday may not be related to the level of happiness it generates; being able to afford a more luxurious holiday does not necessarily mean it will be a more memorable, rewarding or ultimately satisfying experience. It has long been argued that tourism is a form of compensatory consumption, often manifested in excessive levels of expenditure that inevitably result in only transitory happiness (Gottlieb 1982). However, deeper satisfaction may be generated by the application of voluntary simplicity (Hall 2011) – or involuntary simplicity – to the consumption of tourism; an 'anti-consumerist' approach to the consumption of tourism may inject more meaning to the experience and, hence, stimulate a greater degree of satisfaction or happiness.

Third, it is worth repeating the point made earlier that the tourist experience is unique to the individual, that there are as many tourist experiences as there are tourists. Similarly, of course, happiness is a deeply personal, subjective condition also unique to the individual. Thus, the tourism–happiness equation is infinitely variable; people consume tourism in numerous different ways and for a multitude of different reasons, whilst the source of happiness or contentedness undoubtedly varies significantly from one person to another. Therefore, there is no simple answer to the question: is to experience tourism to experience happiness? Nevertheless, it must be questioned whether the consumption of an experience that is principally driven by the desire to escape, to experience difference or 'the other', can ultimately increase people's happiness, for not only does this serve to highlight people' lack of satisfaction (or unhappiness?) with normality, but also it suggests that happiness is to be found in either anticipating or recollecting being elsewhere, not in the here and now. Consequently, just as Krippendorf (1987) once suggested that the solution to the 'problem' of mass tourism was to improve people's normal, day-to-day life so that they no longer felt the need to escape from it, so too might the route to happiness lie not in the consumption of tourist experiences, of going away, but in improved experiences of normality.

That being said, all the evidence nevertheless points to continued increases in the consumption of tourist experiences. Therefore, the need remains to understand better the concept and nature of the tourist experience as a basis for meeting more effectively the needs or expectations of tourists, for providing them with memorable experiences and perhaps even for contributing to their happiness. Thus, the purpose of this book is to make a further contribution to our knowledge and understanding of the tourist experience. It is structured around five themes, as follows:

Theme 1: Conceptualising tourism experiences

The tourist experience is complex, multidimensional and dynamic, inasmuch as it undoubtedly reflects or responds to transformations in the 'external' social worlds of tourism and tourists. Thus, despite increasing academic attention paid to the subject, there is a continuing need to enhance our understanding of the phenomenon. Fundamental to this is the development of a rigorous conceptual framework within which research into the tourist experience may be located.

Theme 2: Understanding dark tourism experiences

The concept of dark tourism continues to attract significant academic and media attention and is, arguably, one of the most popular contemporary issues within the area of tourist experiences. Much attention is focused on conceptual issues, such as the meaning or definition of dark tourism, although the importance of understanding how and why 'dark places' are experienced from a practical/management perspective is increasingly recognised.

Theme 3: Motivation and the contemporary tourist experience

Tourist motivation has long been the focus of academic attention. However, as the scope of tourist experiences increases, and opportunities for new experiences emerge, a more complete understanding of the motivation for such experiences is required in order to better inform their production and promotion.

Theme 4: Place and the tourist experience

Research into 'place', including place meaning, attachment and so on, is extensive. Yet, although the place or setting is fundamental to the tourist experience, and frequently the 'pull' factor in tourist motivation, the manner in which the tourist experience may be influenced and/or enhanced by 'place' remains relatively under-researched.

Theme 5: Managing tourist experiences

The tourist experience is not only a function of the relationship between the tourist and the object of consumption; the intervention of intermediaries (suppliers/managers of tourist experiences) may make a significant contribution to the nature of the tourist experience. Thus, research into the management of tourist experiences represents an important theme within the overall study of the tourist experience.

Inevitably, this thematic list is not exhaustive. Indeed, given the dynamic nature of tourism, its scope and scale and the apparently ever-increasing significance accorded to it as an object of contemporary consumption, it will continue to be a fruitful focus of new research. Nevertheless, it is hoped that this book will not only contribute to knowledge and understanding of a phenomenon that, in the early twenty-first century, continues to grow in social significance, but will also act as a catalyst for future research.

PART I

Conceptualising tourist experiences

To an extent, this section requires no introduction. In other words, not only does the tourist experience remain 'a complicated psychological process' (Quinlan Cutler and Carmichael 2010: 3) that is a function of a variety personal needs, perceptions and influences, but it is also dynamic inasmuch as it undoubtedly reflects or responds to transformations in the 'external' social worlds of tourism and tourists. Consequently, it is widely recognised that extant knowledge of the tourist experience is incomplete, that despite increasing academic attention paid to the subject (see Morgan *et al.* 2010) there is a continuing need to enhance our understanding of the phenomenon so that tourists' needs and expectations may be better met. Fundamental to this, of course, is the development of a rigorous conceptual framework within which research into the tourist experience may be located.

Within the contemporary literature, there is consensus that the tourist experience is no longer something that is 'supplied' by the tourism sector; rather, tourists 'co-create' their experiences in ways that reflect evolving meanings and modes of consumption with the so-called 'experience economy' (Pine and Gilmore 1999). It is from this perspective that the three chapters in this section conceptualise the tourist experience. In Chapter 1, the evolving relationship between tourists and those providing tourism services is considered by Ana Goytia Prat and Álvaro de la Rica Aspiunza. Identifying four distinctive periods, they argue that in the first decade of the twenty-first century we have entered a 'second generation experience economy' in which the tourism product/service value chain has been superseded by a tourist experience value chain.

In Chapter 2, Graham Henning sets out to challenge the very notion of the tourism experience, of tourists proactively seeking novel and meaningful experiences. Recognising that tourists' normal, contemporary lives are defined by inauthenticity and habitual rules, it is logical to assume that tourism represents the search for the authentic, the novel and the 'other'. However, introducing the philosophy of habit, he goes on to suggest that the consumption of tourism itself is habitual, if not an addiction. As a consequence, he concludes that tourism is perhaps an addiction to satisfaction and behaviour rather than the force for change and the place of deep experiences. Then, in Chapter 3, Darius Liutikas explores what he refers to as 'valuistic journeys'. Such journeys represent a means by which travellers (or pilgrims, in both the relgious and secular sense) reveal their personal values as well as creating personal and social identity. Reporting on research among traditional (religious) and modern (secular) pilgrim tourists in Lithuania, he identifies both difference and similarities between these two groups, thus developing a framework for understanding the significance of the experience of valuistic journeys.

1 Personal experience tourism

A postmodern understanding

Ana Goytia Prat and Álvaro de la Rica Aspiunza

Introduction

This chapter reviews and analyses, from a temporal or procedural point of view, the role granted to the tourist experience by tourism supply managers. The historical analysis is organised into three broad periods in each of which the evolution of the meaning given to experience, the tourism market approach and value creation in tourism supply are examined. The first period, which extends up to the 1990s, is characterised by the relocation of tourists to the centre of the tourism system. For the purposes of this discussion, tourists are understood as clients to whom products and services must be offered and given by providing as much added value as possible. The second period, referred to here as the 'design of emotional products for guests', occurs during the last decade of the twentieth century and responds to the so-called first generation experience economy in which tourist experience products and services are offered, and the creation of added value is achieved by selling memorable experiences. Finally, the third period, entitled 'co-creation of experiences and emotions', covers the first decade of the twenty-first century, when the tourist no longer has a passive role. It raises a 'second generation experience economy' characterised by a tendency to provide the opportunity for co-creating and living meaningful tourist experiences. The market focus has shifted from 'what I offer to you' to 'what you want to experience', so that the tourist is no longer a consumer and becomes a colleague, a partner, a friend who should be taken into consideration when producing tourist experiences. As a consequence, the tourist experience product/service value chain is superseded by the tourist experience value chain.

Up until the second decade of the twenty-first century, commentators have argued in favour of enhancing the humanistic angle of the experience's significance and of tourist experience management. Conversely, defining the experience as a holistic 'persona-centred' concept, in this chapter we focus attention upon the tourist experience's capacity for facilitating tourists' personal growth and self-development through immersion in the tourist experience. Understanding this capacity as the key issue in the tourist experience value-adding process, we pose the hypothesis of a new tourism business market-orientation led by an innovative tourist experience manager: the 'personal experiencer'.

The humanistic understanding of tourist experience management under suspicion

Ritchie and Hudson (2009) identify six broad categories which appear to reflect a current of thought and research concerning the tourist experience.[1] Of these six currents, this chapter will focus on the relationship between the first and the fifth; that is, on the understanding of what a tourist experience is when managing experiences in the tourism industry.

The study of the tourist experience emerged during the 1970s when it was understood as a modern phenomenon resulting from the democratisation of travelling for leisure purposes. The analysis of the nature and meaning of the tourist experience from a modern viewpoint was dominated by two competing perspectives. On one hand, authors such as Barthes (1972), Boorstin (1964) and Turner and Ash (1975) argued within a social criticism framework, viewing tourism as a new kind of colonialism and as a symptom of modern decadence. On the other hand, an opposing approach was represented by MacCannell (1973) who conceptualised the tourist experience as a meaningful modern ritual which involves a quest for authenticity. Nevertheless, both currents shared a modernist form of analysis that viewed societies and social facts, such as tourism, as totalities. In this respect, both standpoints have been unable to capture the existing variety in the practice of tourist experiences, instead offering a portrayal of the 'tourist' as a general type.

This modern homogeneous understanding of the tourist experience was first challenged by Cohen (1979: 180) who, in his seminal work on the phenomenology of tourist experiences, proposed that 'different kinds of people may desire different modes of tourist experiences'. Subsequently, from the early 1980s onwards, the tourist experience was increasingly understood as a postmodern phenomenon; that is, as a plural experience. Furthermore, the notion of a diverse and plural realm of postmodern tourism goes one step beyond Cohen's (1979) proposition as regards the variety of tourist experiences. While Cohen proclaimed that different people perform different tourist activities, Feifer (1985) characterised the 'post-tourist' according to their enjoyment of moving across the different types of tourist experiences.

Thus, whereas earlier theories of modern tourism homogenise the tourist experience as a general type, the postmodern understanding of the tourist experience is characterised by a multiplicity of tourist motivations, values, emotions, behaviour, preferences, interests and opinions. As a result, it is the person and their plural and unrepeatable nature that endow the tourist experience with sense and meaning. The question, therefore, is: to what extent do tourism managers recognise and respect the above mentioned humanistic and persona-centred understanding of the tourist experience?

In addressing this issue, the purpose of this chapter is to propose a humanistic tourism market approach that respects the concept of experience from a humanistic point of view. This main aim is achieved through the following objectives: to analyse from an historical perspective the evolution of the meaning given to experience; to review from an historical perspective the tourism market approach; and to discuss the value given to the offer of experiences and the configuration of the tourist experience value chain over time. As a result, we provide a contemporary, updated understanding of the tourist experience concept and offer a managerial proposal built on a humanistic perspective. In so doing, this chapter aims to provide a basis for helping tourism managers to better understand the role of the person, the tourist, in an industry characterised by continuous change.

The evolution of the tourist experience concept

From the 1980s to the 1990s. The tourist at the centre of the tourism system

Definition of experience

Up to the late 1980s, the supply or offer of tourism did not yet consider the experience as an aspect to be offered; rather, the value of the offering was that which was provided by the tourism product or service. The concept of tourism service was defined in comparison to that of a product, in the sense of a physical, tangible product (Rufino 1995). However, the need arose to consider the product at four distinctive levels: the generic product, the expected product, the improved or enhanced product and the potential product (Levitt 1980; Kotler *et al.* 2004). Among all these, the potential product is of particular interest in the tourism industry as it is based on the idea that the offer or supply of tourism services requires interaction with the purchaser of the service in a number of ways. First of all, tourists, as consumers of tourism services, have to interact with the service supply system, which means that the environment as the physical surrounding is a critical element of the services provided; second, the customer participates in the offerings of most tourism services, so there is therefore an interaction between the tourist and the service offered; third, in tourism settings, the service offer frequently involves or requires interaction amongst customers themselves; and finally, tourism services, as with other services more generally, are characterised by co-production, or the involvement of the tourist in the production of services on offer.

However, although these different product levels, particularly the concept of potential product, would, in the future, become an integral element of the concept of experience (LaSalle and Britton 2003), this was not the case in the late 1980s. In short, at this time a service offer was defined only from the perspective of production and not from the point of view of the tourist or their own needs.

Tourism market approach

The importance given to interaction with the customer led to a change in thinking on the part of tourism organisations. More specifically, from a production or transactional orientation, there was a shift towards a relational orientation or philosophy. Indeed, as Sainz de Vicuña (2006) points out, an important aspect to note is the confrontation between these two mentalities (the transactional orientation and relational orientation) when approaching identical problems. The new thinking that emerged during the late 1980s and into the 1990s consisted of focusing efforts on searching for a mutually satisfactory relationship between tourism companies and tourists. Establishing, maintaining and improving relations with tourists represent a completely different philosophy from the traditional approach, emphasising as it does the crucial role of those who are already customers of an organisation as opposed to searching for new customers. Authors such as Sánchez *et al.* (2000), Robledo (1998), Buttle (1996), Peppers and Rogers (1995) and Bitner (1995) identify the various factors behind the emergence and development of this relationship-based approach. These factors are: the need to cultivate the loyalty of increasingly sophisticated and demanding tourists; the influence of technology on almost all tourism products and services; the intensification of competition; and, the conception of markets as networks.

The paradigm shift from a transactional approach, based on the product, to a relational approach, based on resources and skills, is considered in detail by Grönroos (1996). This transformation is illustrated by Barroso and Martín (1999) in the figures in the following sub-sections. From the transactional perspective, the market is considered in terms of more or less anonymous customers and the company's offer basically consists of goods and services. Conversely, the relational perspective approaches the customers, be they tourists or tourism organisations, individually.

To summarise, the first period is characterised by tourists being relocated to the centre of the tourist system. The emerging importance of services as a feature in the value enhancement strategy for tourism products and of customer relationship management (CRM) are identified as key factors during this period, whilst business market orientation increasingly came to be based on relational marketing, such as considered in Berry's (1983) seminal work on 'relationship marketing'.

Tourism product service value chain

Exploring the concept of value more deeply, we can observe that, during this period from the late 1980s into the 1990s, the value of the overall tourism offer is provided by the product designed by the managers responsible for each subsector (transport, accommodation, restaurants, and so on) that collectively comprise the value system of the tourism product. What do we mean by this?

Essentially, the competitive advantage of the tourism sector is developed in a fragmented way, as each business or organisation considers only the value provided by its own product. Of course, this concept of competitiveness reflects the definition of the value chain proposed by Porter (1985). In his work, he states that a company is composed of a set of activities, the goal of which is to design, manufacture, commercialise, deliver and support their product or service, and that it is represented through the value chain. In the case of tourism, any

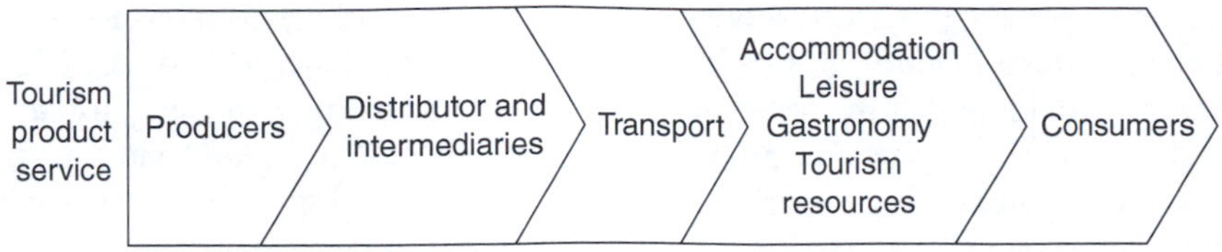

Figure 1.1 Tourism product service value chain.

company that is part of the tourism sector will have its own value chain with which it can create value for its customers.

However, Porter also asserts that any company is integrated within a larger flow of activities; that is, it is immersed in a value system. Consequently, it may be suggested that the value chain of the total tourism product can be considered as a value system. This value system means that we are not referring to the value chain of a specific tourism business or organisation (a hotel, a travel agency, an airport or museum) but, rather, and as can be seen in Figure 1.1, to the tourism product as a whole or, to use Porter's terminology, the, tourism 'value system'.

The reality of this first stage reveals the lack of a systematic approach to the concept of value and, therefore, to the competitiveness of the tourism product.

Last decade of the twentieth century: design of emotional products for a guest

Definition of experience

During the second period, covering the last decade of the twentieth century, Pine and Gilmore's (1999) writings on 'the experience economy' and articles such as 'The service experience in tourism' (Otto and Ritchie 1996) provided evidence of the importance of experiences in tourism. Indeed, it was not only in academic circles but also in the tourism sector that awareness of the critical role of 'experiences' in tourism began to emerge. However, things did not change overnight. The relational management paradigm remained dominant and the conceptualisation of the tourist experience continued to be based on the former so-called 'service dominant logic' (Vargo and Lusch 2004). The concept of experience considers tourists spending time in a personalised way as well as enjoying unforgettable events. Thus, the experience was fundamentally understood as an output of a production process from which, using facilities and services, a final experience is created.

This understanding of the nature of experience – nowadays referred to as the first-generation experience economy – had two main consequences. On the one hand, experience is defined on the basis of just one of its various characteristics: its emotional elements. It is understood as 'the emotional outcome of an individual as it is a culmination of a steady flow of fantasies, feelings and fun' (Holbrook and Hirschman 1982: 132; see also Murray *et al.* 2010). All remaining critical characteristics that shape the psychological nature of the leisure and tourism experience (Csikszentmihalyi 1975; Mannell 1980; Neulinger 1980; Mannell and Iso-Ahola 1987) were clearly avoided. This is particularly significant when talking about the personal nature of the tourist experience because the role of the tourist as an active protagonist is neglected. On the other hand, and as a result of the former, the experience is far from being understood from a humanistic perspective as a tourist's subjective, self-motivated phenomenon.

Tourism market approach

Within this context, the tourist becomes a guest for whom thrilling products are designed, but who still continues to be a mere consumer of 'experiential or emotional products' (Ferrari *et al.* 2005). In other words, tourism market orientation was based on a deeper approach to Berry's relational marketing (Grönroos 1996) and, furthermore, to 'experiential marketing', understood as the need to design and create experiences for tourists. The tourist experience is managed and served as a producer outcome whose value is still added at each stage of the tourism supply chain or tourism production process. As a consequence of this approach, the experiential tourism offer led to 'Disneyfication' where the offer must provide a strong sensory component focusing on the senses and emotions so as to provoke pleasure and excitement (Gentile *et al.* 2007; Shedroff 2008, 2009). When analysing the guidelines to be followed for developing tourism experiences during this period, it is worth reviewing Schmitt's (2000) Customer Experience Management (CEM) model covering five different aspects: the senses, feelings, acts, thoughts and relationships. According to each of these aspects, Schmitt proposes five kinds of tourist experiences: sensory experiences, emotional experiences, physical and lifestyle experiences, creative and cognitive experiences and social identity experiences. Similarly, Smith and Wheeler (2002) created the Customer Experience of the Brand Management model. In addition, LaSalle and Britton's (2003) seminal work considered the importance of understanding customers for creating valuable experiences. This first-generation experience economy conceptualises tourist experiences with a lack of consideration given to tourists as protagonists in the experience creation process.

Tourist experience value chain

However, as opposed to previous stages and in response to recognition of an emerging experience economy, a broader experiential nature of value is acknowledged. Based on Toffler's (1970) visionary proposal, experience is recognised as an economic value. Moreover, during this period and following LaSalle and Britton's (2003) point of view, the value of experience is considered as the interaction between customers and products, companies and all other stakeholders. Inevitably, these interactions result in some type of reaction; if positive, it will be recognised as a valuable experience-product. As Vargo and Lusch (2008: 7) argue 'value is always uniquely and phenomenologically determined by the beneficiary: Value is idiosyncratic, experiential, contextual, and meaning laden.' The experiential nature of value is reinforced by authors such as Holbrook (1999: 7), who suggests that 'value is an interactive relativistic preference experience' and Prahalad and Ramaswamy (2004: 137), who state that 'value is now centred in the experiences of consumers'. This shows a significant change compared with the former 'utility/exchange/use'-based meaning given to 'value'. However, because of the outlasting of the providers' role, the experiential value chain fell into the trap of being equated with the 'commerce travel experiences value chain' (see Figure 1.2 below).

As demonstrated in Figure 1.2, a perfect fit exists between the tourist product service value chain and the tourist experience service value chain. Both have a linear structure led by the producers. Although the experience of the 'guest' is being upgraded, this is supposed to be offered by the tourism industry. Aho's (2001) theory of the tourism experience is illustrative when it states that 'tourism can be characterized as a combination of those processes that are voluntary and purposely intended for producing experiences by means of moving people between places' (Aho 2001, cited in Ritchie and Hudson 2009: 114). The challenge is to attract, convince, feed, excite or entertain the customer who becomes crucial, though not as a subject of the action but as an indirect object. The attention of tourism managers is focused on how to increase the pull (attraction and inspiration) factors or motivators in each phase.

From the turn of the century onwards: co-creation of experiences and emotions

The third period, which covers the first years of the new millennium, allowed, thanks to 'tourism 2.0', a change in the tourist's role. The technological environment of the tourism system dramatically changed the system's organisation: the

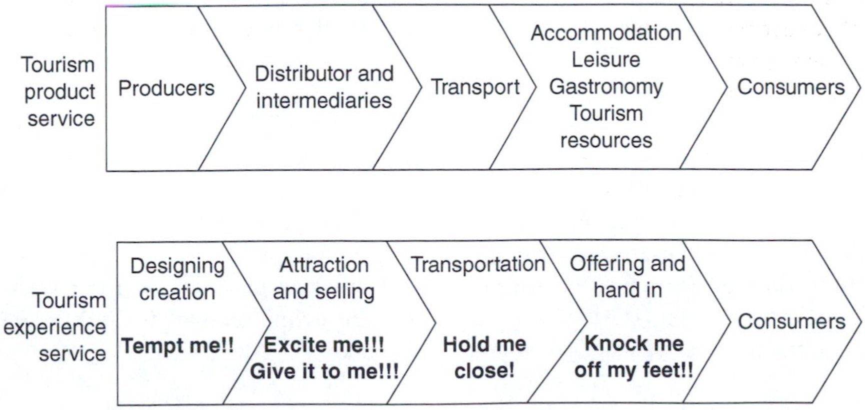

Figure 1.2 First-generation tourist experience value chain vs. tourism product service value chain.

tourist became the protagonist. Tourists can now travel and experience the journey not necessarily through or being dependent upon the tourism sector suppliers.

Therefore, the boundaries between producers and consumers have become blurred and the so-called tourist 'prosumer' (Toffler 1970) even takes part as an advisor (tourist adprosumer). The role of producers is reversed and customers become part of the experience design process. That is, not only – as in previous stages – do their expectations, preferences and tastes have to be fulfilled, but the tourists become the protagonists of the whole experience.

Definition of experience

Thanks to this prevalence of their role, the tourist began to be understood as a person, as opposed to a customer or even a guest. There was, in fact, a significant transformation in the understanding of tourist experiences that embraced the psychological humanistic narrative. This approach involves the understanding of the experience as a state of mind (Mannell 1984) of a meaningful nature, and has sometimes been considered as a European reaction to the American approach to the definition of experience. This European reaction to the experience economy tends to be one of warning against the creation of staged experiences that are considered too commercial, artificial and superficial and, therefore, not always suitable for attracting today's customers. The tourist experience today is fully understood as a personal experience in which the person is the main actor. Inspired by the ethnographic perspective, Binkhorst (2005), among others, proposes that the concept of co-creation deserves to be taken seriously. He argues that

> this means no separation between supply and demand, company and customer, tourist and host, tourism spaces and 'other' spaces but viewing tourism as a holistic network of stakeholders connected in experience environments in which everyone operates from different time spatial contexts.
>
> (Binkhorst 2005: 3)

This co-creation debate is led by European authors (Nijs and Peters 2002; Carù and Cova 2004; Binkhorst 2002, 2005; Boswijk *et al.* 2005) and institutions such as the European Centre for Experience Economy (NL) or the Tourism and Leisure research team at the University of Deusto (Spain).[2] Experience is a 'continuous interactive process of doing and undergoing, of action and reflection, from cause to consequence, that provides meaning to the individual in several contexts of his life' (Boswijk *et al.* 2005: 2). This definition implies the different nature of travel experience and tourist experience:

1 Travel experience
  Travel experience refers to the process in which the tourist is involved when travelling. The travel experience process has been recognised as a multiphased

rather than a single-step process (Chon 1990; Gunn 1989). Clawson and Knetsch (1966) provided evidence of the multiphase nature of leisure and tourism experiences, suggesting that these experiences involve five different and interacting decision phases: (1) anticipation; (2) journey to the site; (3) the on-site activity; (4) return journey; and (5) recollection. Gunn's (1989) later work identified a seven-stage process in the leisure travel experience: (1) accumulation of mental images of vacation experiences; (2) modification of those images by further information; (3) decision to take a vacation trip; (4) journey to the destination; (5) participation at the destination; (6) return journey; and (7) new accumulation of images based on the experience.

2 Tourist experience

The tourist experience is neither what is offered by producers once at the destination nor the participation in every step of the travel experience process. It refers to the tourist's own subjective experience. Therefore, the tourist experience cannot be equated to travel experience, since the former goes beyond merely travelling, acting, feeling and evaluating. It requires giving personal meaning or significance to actions. According to Shedroff (2008: 22)[3] 'meaning is a distinct level of cognitive significance that represents how people understand the world around them – literally, the reality they construct in their minds that explains the world they experience. Meaning is the deepest level of this understanding and is distinct from values, emotions, and functional or financial benefits.' So, tourism experience, understood as a meaningful experience, must include a personal attribution of meaning (one's sense of reality), which related to one's personal values (one's sense of identity) and emotions will become a meaningful and valuable trip.

Tourism market approach

Owing to the active role given to the tourist in attributing meaning to the tourism experience, a tendency emerges of offering the possibility of co-creating custom-made tourist experiences. Creating added value is no longer selling a memorable experience to customers but, rather, enabling individuals to live the experience with the help of the company. Therefore, the main aim of the tourism market is to facilitate leisure-tourism personal experiences rather than merely providing recreation and opportunities for fun. As opposed to former periods, the starting point of the experience economy is focused on understanding the significance and meaning for tourists themselves, their individual values, motives, desires, and understanding what an experience is. In Sharpley and Stone's (2011a: 7) words 'the tourist experience can only be understood by exploring specific contexts within which it occurs'.

Furthermore, as opposed to Schmitt's (2000) CEM model for promoting tourist experiences, today's frameworks point out that each individual has his or her various and dynamic 'experience networks'. That is why tourism experiences are means for co-creations with other stakeholders or other tourists, giving place to 'consumer to consumer' (C2C) experiences (Binkhorst 2005). Therefore, today's experiences management trends are aimed at facilitating an 'experience environment' (Prahalad and Ramaswamy 2004), a space where dialogue between company and consumer can take place. Boswijk *et al.* (2005) propose six fundamental principles for creating a meaningful tourist experience:

1. To consider things from the psycho-dynamic perspective of the individual and to try to contribute to his or her possibilities. To not forget that the individual can determine for him- or herself how much control he or she wants in the process of co-creation.
2. To consider the customer as a guest and to create a culture of hospitality.
3. To break through any dogmas and pre-existing notions.
4. To consider that the creation of a meaningful experience setting takes place in an interactive process between the individual and the offering party.
5. To show respect.

Tourist experience value chain

In this third period, the tourist experience value chain is no longer defined according to the role of the producers but according to the tourists who become the agents of added value. This approach to the travel experience is not new but, for the first time, it is being considered by the market. Various attempts have been made to supplant Clawson and Knetsch's (1966) phases of travel experience, such as Aho's (2001) proposal which defines the tourism experience value chain as including including: (1) orientation; (2) attachment; (3) visiting; (4) evaluation; (5) storing; (6) reflection; and (7) enrichment. As opposed to Clawson and Knetsch's (1966) travel value chain, which was defined from an objective point of view, the tourist experience value chain is subjectively defined, related to a self-individual process.

This persona-centred approach is reinforced by the technological tourism system environment. It affects the shaping of the tourism value chain because information technologies and new media contribute to the elimination of the strong distinctions between the different phases of the trip. Thus, the experience value chain is defined on the basis of a single experience during the trip, as illustrated in Figure 1.3.

This is a valuable approach since it considers the humanistic understanding of the experience and includes the personal attribution of 'meaning' in the value chain. The problem is, however, that authors such as Aho (2001) and others overlooked other important characteristics apart from the multiphase nature of the experiences (Lee and Dattilo 1994). More specifically, experiences are multidimensional (Kelly 1987; Tinsley and Tinsley 1986) so, during a trip, one can live a variety of experiences, including positive experiences as well as unpleasant ones. Furthermore, the tourism and leisure experience has a transitory nature (Kelly 1987; Mannell 1980; Tinsley and Tinsley 1986) as it takes place in short, interrupted episodes rather than occurring during the extended periods that a trip could take.

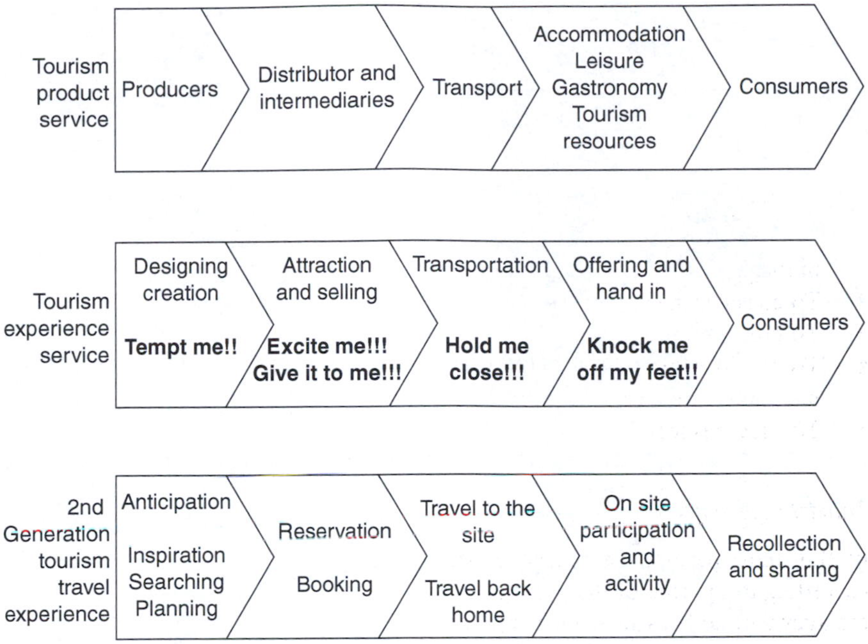

Figure 1.3 Second-generation tourist experience value chain vs first-generation tourist experience value chain and vs. tourism product service value chain.

Taking these characteristics into account, the conclusion may be reached that, as shown in Figure 1.4 below, the tourist experience value chain cannot follow the linear discourse shown in Figure 1.3. As an alternative, we propose the 'dolphin model' to explain the tourist experience value chain.

The three stages of the dolphin model can be explained as follows. The 'launch stage' includes three sub-stages: dreaming and planning; commitment (sometimes 'booking'); and anticipation stage. Subsequently, the 'immersion stage' includes two sub-stages. The first of these, the 'ongoing' sub-stage, is not always a synonym of 'en route' or 'en voyage'. Rather, it is a phase of the experience in which the tourist is emotionally ready. He or she makes headway in the sense that they are prepared for the transition from planning to acting and feeling the essence of the travel experience. The second sub-stage in the 'immersion' stage is engagement (involvement), and is at the heart of the tourist experience cycle. The engagement stage involves both behaviour and feelings or emotions. It implies occupation, involvement and enthralment; that is to say, a feeling of great liking for something wonderful (the experience) during the trip.

Finally, the reinterpretation and evaluation stage, in which the tourist evaluates the extent of meaningful experiences and satisfaction, closes the circle. It

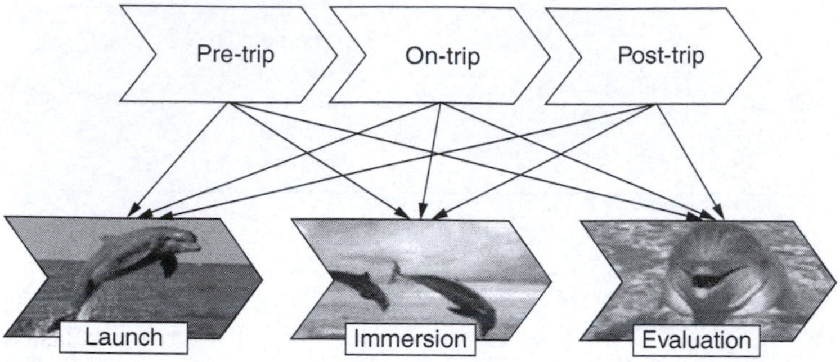

Figure 1.4 The dolphin model: tourist experience value chain.

equips tourists with reasons for continuing being engaged or not with the experience.

A persona-centred approach to the tourist experience management

Definition of experience

Looking towards the future and rethinking the 'persona-centred approach' to the tourism experience, we would like to go one step further – perhaps to a third-generation experience economy – as a basis for value and to promote the self-creation of experiences whose immersion process is closely related to the self and self-development. The experience is understood as the event created by the tourists themselves, where immersion has the ability to produce personal development.

Under this paradigm, the tourist experience intimately connects with transformational experiences that, though not necessarily new, exciting or exotic, nevertheless involve human development. This concept of experience is not necessarily applicable to all types of tourists. It requires the participation of creative tourists who are increasingly looking for more engaging and more interactive experiences where, by increasing their creative capital, they can achieve personal development and identity creation. Richards and Raymond (2000: 18) define creative tourism as 'tourism which offers visitors the opportunity to develop their creative potential through active participation in courses and learning experiences which are characteristic of the holiday destination where they are undertaken'.

Tourism market approach and tourism experience value

Interest concerning the operations that consumers undertake in their efforts to be submerged or immersed in the experience has emerged in recent years (Carù and

Cova 2004, 2006, 2007a). The results suggest that immersion in an experience is more progressive rather than being an immediate process, since immersion is not always easy to achieve during a certain trip. Furthermore, not all tourists have the necessary capacity nor the competence to do this. This means that the participation of an intermediary may be necessary. As a result, efforts are carried out in order to facilitate this progressive process.

These management trends pay attention to those service elements that could have an impact on the so-called 'operations of appropriation' (Carù and Cova 2006). Researchers point to three major operations of appropriation that could be involved in any immersion process: nesting or feeling at home; investigating so as to identify activities that develop points of anchorage and control; and lastly, attachment or personal attribution of meaning to an experience.

But we would like to propose a further step and propose a humanistic approach to 'experience design thinking'.[4] From this perspective, experience not only includes an emotional dimension, but requires a holistic understanding that considers an integral definition of human beings and human development. As a consequence, our experience design statement argues that tourism businesses and organisations can play a meaningful role in helping tourists to find their own way. This role does not refer to any of the 'personas or faces of innovation' that Kelley and Littman (2006) refer to,[5] but rather to a facilitator who carries out the function of accompaniment. This could well be a 'personal experiencer', understood as an experiential coach who helps tourists to reach their own potential, who assists tourists in setting their own goals, who provides feedback and perspective, who offers encouragement and new ways of tackling situations when travelling. It is like having someone running alongside you during the trip, giving you the extra input and insights that can really make a difference for the success of the tourist experience.

Summing up, and as Ladwein (2002: 61) suggests, 'there is nothing obvious or systematic about the access to the experience and it requires competences or aptitudes the consumer (tourist) does not necessarily possess', we propose that a 'personal experiencer' could make sure tourists really develop new skills and new habits in order to help them promote their self-development throughout their immersion in the tourism experience.

Finally, refrrence must be made to today's concept of 'tourist experience value'. As opposed to previous stages in which value was defined within the framework of the value chain, nowadays it is worth considering it as the experience in itself. In Bryant and Veroff's words, there exists a 'new model of positive experiences', so-called 'savoring experiences' because of their capacity for '*going beyond the pleasure experience to encompass a higher order awareness or reflective discernment on the part of the individual*' (2007: 3; our italics). That is to say, the value of experience, from the tourist's point of view, is based not only on co-creation but on human beings' capacity to promote their personal growth, relationships and altruism (Pearce 2011a). From our point of view, a humanistic understanding of tourist experience co-creation provides an incremental value thanks to its potential for personal and social development. This overcoming of the experience itself represents the unique value of the tourist experience.

Notes

1 (1) The essence of the tourism experience; (2) tourists' experience-seeking behaviour; (3) the specific methodologies used in tourism experience research; (4) the nature of specific kinds of tourist attraction experiences; (5) the managerial concerns related to designing and developing the tourism supply systems required to managed the delivery of basic/satisfactory/quality/extraordinary/memorable experience; and (6) the various levels or types of experiences that conceptually seem to form an evolutionary trail of experience thinking. This trail involves the basic experience, the quality experience, the extraordinary experience and the memorable experience.

2 Line of investigation in Leisure and Human Development, a team recognised by the Basque Government (Spain) in 2010.

3 The author claims that there are six dimensions to an experience: (1) duration; (2) intensity; (3) scope; (4) interaction; (5) meaning; and (6) graphical meaning or triggers.

4 Design thinking usually involves a period of field research to generate inspiration and a better understanding of what is needed, followed by open, non-judgemental generation of ideas. After a brief analysis, a number of the more promising ideas are combined and expanded to go into 'rapid prototyping,' which can vary from a simple drawing or text description to a three-dimensional mock-up. Feedback on the prototypes helps hone the ideas so that a select few can be used.

5 The Learning Personas (The Anthropologist, The Experimenter and The Cross-Pollinator); The Organising Personas (The Hurdler; The Collaborator; The Director); and The Building Personas (The Experience Architect; The Set Designer; The Caregiver and The StoryTeller).

2 The habit of tourism

Experiences and their ontological meaning

Graham K. Henning

Introduction

Tourism is a paradigmatic experience 'industry'; therefore, it is reasonable that it be a leader in conceptualising experience. Within tourism studies, the largest proportion of research on experience has taken it as subjective (Uriely 2005), which includes postmodern perspectives and psychology (for example, Mannell and Iso-Ahola 1987; McCabe and Foster 2006). There is also a stream of research that focuses on the so-called objective/object of experience (for example, Pine and Gilmore 1999). However, it is clear, today, that experience necessarily involves both subject and object; hence, any theory of and research into touristic experiences must address both. Indeed, there are those who have ventured views of experience that attempt to integrate subject and object (Haldrup and Larsen 2006), but have had difficulty in doing so without also siding with the subject or object as the locus of experience (Aho 2001; Jennings and Nickerson 2006).

This chapter provides a conceptualisation of experience that necessarily involves both subject and object, but posits a third realm – the in-between, the experience which arises in between all the elements involved in the experience. This conceptualisation is developed through the use of habit as an ontological feature of human being (Ravaisson 2008) within a dialogic framework using the concept of play (Gadamer 2003) as it has been developed in tourism (Henning 2006, 2008). The argument of this chapter first refers to some elements that 'precede' habit. It then addresses the concept of habit before finally integrating habit into a discussion of the in-between, dialogic experience.

One result of the view developed here is that experiences in tourism cannot be called tourist experiences (for that implies a subjective perspective). Additionally, another outcome of this chapter is that tourism can often be seen as addiction. There does not appear to be much agreement as to what constitutes addiction (Rotgers *et al.* 2003); however, when we take a meta-view of the research and add to it some modifications of Wallace (1999) we come to a view of the structure and course of addiction that serves our purposes. Addiction is, first of all, not a reflex action; addicts can and do choose otherwise. However, for whatever reason, and for the most part, they do not do so. The addiction fills a purported lack, whether that is a loss, a difference between value systems, or something else missing in their lives. Ultimately, the addiction does not give what it promises. Interestingly, this point coincides with work done in tourism where it has been found that tourism does not increase long-term happiness (Gilbert and Abdullah 2004; Milman 1998), nor provide authentic attractions (Wang 1999), escape (Moore 1997) or meaningful cross-cultural interactions (Henning 2011b). However, rather than go elsewhere to find the desired result, the addict 'returns'.

To better understand the nature of habit, addiction and the dialogic play of the tourism experience, we start with a contrast. In *The Human Condition*, Hannah Arendt (1958) valorises the idea of action.[1] Action is contrasted with behaviour, activity and habit, and has two main elements: it is about doing something freely and about doing something not done before. The person acting cannot be compelled to act, such as when someone holds a gun to your head or when you have to meet your tour bus at a certain time. The doing of something not done before is based on an objective measure (has this activity has been done by anyone?). Having not been done by anyone it has the character of beginning or natality, which reveals the beingness of humans, but it does not establish it (Henning 2011a). Repetition of action is necessary to found the beingness of humans (Ravaisson 2008).

Unfortunately, there is not much that is objectively new in tourism.[2] If there were, tourism would be called exploration. However, without some form of newness there is no experience, for experience involves the subversion of one's expectations or prior understandings (Gadamer 2003). That means experience is not the meeting of expectations, as so many working and writing in tourism assume (Henning 2006). Therefore, the structure of the touristic experience is that it is new to the individual but it is not objectively new. That suggests that tourism does not bring about social change, which involves the objectively new; it only brings individuals into the fold of socially sanctioned being. Even when one's expectations and prior understandings are subverted there is usually someone, for example a guide, or something, such as an interpretive plaque, to help tourists take on the 'correct' interpretation of what is going on (Edensor and Kothari 2004); that is, in encountering something subjectively new, tourists actually encounter and by their involvement reproduce a socially sanctioned repetition or habit.

This structure of tourism makes it an interesting endeavour. The lack of objective newness in tourism along with subjective newness means that concepts such as tradition, culture, history and authenticity are important in understanding tourism and the touristic experience. In every experience the past is implicated in the present. That further suggests that tourism is a conservative endeavour and necessarily involves interpretation, which also implicates language and meaning.

Precursors to habit

Newness to the individual provokes a sense of wonder (Ricoeur 1966), which is a familiar response in tourism. In fact, it might be argued that tourism gauges success and failure by the level of wonder it can provoke (the resulting activities that wonder provokes). This wonder 'expresses the irruption of the "other" into consciousness' (Ricoeur 1966: 260). Wonder indicates the difference between other and self, which makes it the starting point for experience given the subversion of expectations in wonder. Further, wonder does not distinguish between real and unreal (Ricoeur 1966), hence attempts to valorise the real via some sense of objective authenticity or the attempts to critique tourism for failing to provide actual escape (Moore 1997) are misplaced. As my previous research has shown (Henning 2006), in part people are seeking difference, not necessarily the objectively authentic. I experienced something of this on a recent trip to Turkey. Ephesus was too similar to Pompeii for me, so it was less interesting than Troy. I had never seen a ruin with nine cities piled on top of one another, so Troy was very exciting.

As Ravaisson notes, part of the reason for our sense of difference is that we are habitual creatures (Ravaisson 2008: 51). Our habits (Gadamer (2003) would include them in prior understandings)[3] impact our encounter with the touristic situation,[4] including our sense of newness and difference. Our daily lives are generally not authentic, as we are more concerned to fit in and do what we have to do than uncover our possibility (Heidegger 1962); hence, the habitual rules our daily lives (Gonzalez *et al.* 2008). Given this inauthentic and habitual way of being in the world, we rarely have a sense of wonder in our daily lives. As we engage in tourism we seek difference, we seek the authentic other, for difference from us (and hence a break from our inauthentic selves and our daily world) is supposedly ensured by authenticity. So, in seeking difference, tourists seek the authentic, even if that search is not for the objectively authentic (Wang 1999).[5] From this, we can suggest that the first step towards concluding that tourism may be addiction is the lack of authenticity and wonder in our daily lives. We seek out the authentic, which is actually the different, to fill that lack.

When wonder is provoked, the faculty of judgement comes into play, as wonder itself does not distinguish between good and bad; it only indicates something different (Ricoeur 1966). The faculty of judgement involves the determination of the desirable or undesirable (Ricoeur 1966). This determination is guided by one's passions (Ravaisson 2008). For instance, Troy is mostly piles of stones, rocks and bricks dug out of the hillside with only the occasional rebuilt object. In terms of its visual appeal, there is not much. For those on a bus tour that started on the site just in front of me it must not have been interesting, as I quickly lost sight of them. As for me, I had a long-time passion for Troy, born of a youthful encounter with Homer, but until an opportunity to see it arose along with a business trip, I never acted on that passion.

When passion is provoked, habits can form (Ravaisson 2008). And yet, passion and activity oppose each other (Ravaisson 2008). Passion is passive and is 'known only confusedly, barely distinguished from either the object or the subject of knowledge itself … [it] … appears to consciousness merely as obscure *sensation*' (Ravaisson 2008: 43; italics in original). It does not seek activity, for it already has its reward (the state of being in passion itself), and activity reduces passion (Ravaisson 2008); for example, my delay in going to see Troy. It is with habit that passion and activity are reconciled as the dance from passion to activity occurs; passion and activity meet on a middle ground of habit (Ravaisson 2008).

Engaging in activity in the attempts to satisfy desire/passion mobilises the illusion that we can necessarily obtain what we desire (Ricoeur 1966). Even though I was entranced by Troy while I was there, it did not satisfy – I did not obtain the answers to the questions I had. That has provoked a desire to explore the eastern Mediterranean basin. Hence, tourism to the extent it opens up passion, can, in a sense, fail on two levels: there may be the lack of gratification of the desired or expected (which most research and practitioners consider a failure); and there is the gratification of expectation. However, it is only the second that is actual failure; there is no experience and no lasting happiness beyond the trip and its short afterglow. Of course, from the perspective of providers, the lack of long-term happiness is not a problem but a positive for it means the potential for repeat business.

Where there is a subversion of one's expectations, two results can occur. A person may be provoked to travel more (until Troy I was starting to get bored by travel). And it is only when expectations and prior understandings are subverted in the encounter that experience can arise, with the resulting changes in understanding, and the potential for a change in the world and for long-term happiness (Gadamer 2003). This is not the happiness that is dependent on external circumstances (the funny joke, peace in the world, the immediate moment of seeing the waterfall, and so on), for that happiness does not last. Long-term happiness comes to the experienced person – the person open to the subversion of their expectations. In a sense, happiness comes with the wisdom that comes with experience. This experienced person (Gadamer 2003) is contrasted with the idea used in tourism of the experienced tourist; for example, the experienced tourist used by Pearce and Caltabiano (1983) in their tourism ladder theory is based on the number of trips a person takes. However, taking more trips does not necessarily mean encounters with the new, the subversion of one's prior understandings, and the dialogue that is experience. Further, only when tourism is willing and able to allow for the subversion of expectations will social change, such as poverty alleviation or cultural rapprochement, come through tourism, and that change requires the wisdom that comes from experience.

However, tourism is largely constructed to avoid the subversion of expectations. Providers are generally ill equipped to help those whose expectations are not met to reconcile their prior understandings to the situation; providers spend most of their resources on trying to meet expectations or provide socially sanctioned interpretations,[6] and researchers who work on expectations spend most of their time addressing expectation–experience congruency (for example, Pocock 1992). One reason for this scenario is that people generally prefer their expectations to be met when they decide to have tourism experiences (Henning 2006) even as they seek difference. A major reason for this, as Gadamer and others point out, is that people shy away from 'the burden of taking the initiative, which constitutes the actual strain of existence' (Gadamer 2003: 105). That is, tourists prefer not to work hard at understanding, but prefer to allow someone else to determine their understanding. In effect, tourists prefer to follow. Tourism supports this tendency by numerous means: guidebooks; guides; clearly marking attractions; tour operators working with hotels, restaurants, airlines and border officials; locals providing pseudo-environments for religious and cultural activities, and so on. Tourism, then, is a conservative endeavour – it agrees with the tourist that it should provide some difference but nothing that requires tourists to go too far from the world they know. There is very little in tourism that puts the existential self at risk, yet that is what is needed to have social change.

This low-risk nature of tourism gives tourists a reduced sense of empowerment, contributing to the addiction of tourism. Given our daily lives are filled with thwarted desires, failed achievements and monotonous habits, tourism is one place where we can confront the world of demons, dragons, space invaders, oceans and different peoples and come out feeling as though we were successful. Tourists can take a pseudo-authentic place, such as Troy, and imagine they defeat the Greeks, changing history. However, that success is purchased at a price. The tourism bubble ensures that one's success is not pure and the encounter with otherness is not authentic (there is no actual war with the Greeks, just as there is no *real* encounter with people of other cultures in tourism (Henning 2011b)). At best, there is the temporary adoption of a role that does not affect daily lives (Wickens 2002). The failure to have an authentic or successful experience means the conquering hero does not return to daily life, but the timid accountant does, for he knows that what was experienced was not changed understanding but simply a break. The person who learned elements of a new language returns to punch the same dials as before and forgets what they learned. In other words, the lack in daily life is not removed by tourism, leading the addict to continue the search.

Habit

When tourists return to their daily lives without being changed, with but the brief taste of temporary joy, it is reasonable they should want it again. Further, being embodied beings, our sensory organs 'seek' to be satisfied, and that also tends us towards activity (Ravaisson 2008).[7] However, the tendency to activity is opposed by the tendency of passion, which is to stay with the disembodied appropriation of the other. Passion, therefore, acts as resistance to the forces of activity (Ravaisson 2008). This passion is, however, transmuted into activity to the extent that there is sufficient force for the activity that it overcomes passion; and that requires effort on the part of the individual. This required effort is lessened when it is not action, as the individual does not have to initiate. Again, tourism is paradigmatic in this. The industry and tourists themselves seek ways to minimise effort on the part of tourists. This is the great virtue of guidebooks, guides and so on. It also leads to a valuing of repetition by providers and tourists.

This tendency to repetition is not necessarily a negative. Habit can be a positive. Habit as a positive comes from the view that being tends to the persistence of what it is (Ravaisson 2008). Basically, that means that habit is the form that human being takes, as habit is the tendency for humans to engage in a form of activity (or thought) repeatedly. Repeatedly returning to Hawaii for your winter vacation and following the guide are examples of habit. In effect, habit is ontological, not a problem (Ravaisson 2008). That is, who we are is obvious in our habitual ways of being in the world. Based on this definition, habit only becomes a problem if we find our being to be a problem. It is for this reason that Heidegger claimed that our inauthentic daily life is who we are, even as he sought to elevate humanity to the place of freedom to seek our potential (Heidegger 1962). This changes the critique of tourism from one of condemnation to one of sympathy, and suggests that claims for tourism as a force for change are misplaced utopian ideals. We engage in tourism, both as tourists and providers, in ways that recognise that we are habitual. We follow as tourists and we look for repetition as providers. And tourism itself is identified by the habits that we ascribe to tourism.

The habitual beingness of humans suggests a reason why passion is a hindrance to activity; it seeks to maintain its present state. However, once effort has overcome passion the person engages in activity. When we combine this idea with the idea that people do not like to initiate, we see why forms of tourism like bus tours are so popular and why researchers find the bulk of tourists to be other than adventurous. The level of effort necessary to engage in these bubble forms of tourism, such as bus tours, is much less than doing it on your own.

An interesting thing occurs with repeated activity: there is a diminishing of passion (Ravaisson 2008). This means that the most important factor in the provocation of activity is reduced and may even disappear as far as the person is concerned. It is with this diminishing that people develop the idea that habit is 'the epitome of inauthenticity, a simulacrum of being, an imitation of virtue. Pure mechanism, routine process, devitalization of sense, habit is the disease of repetition that threatens the freshness of thought and stifles the voice' (Malabou 2008: vii), for the question arises of how one can still have freshness when passion is diminished. I would argue that this is really the problem that tourism operators face; they want wonder and freshness but also want repetition, and both bring more business. But, as argued here, it is difficult if not impossible to have both. If a provider makes changes to provoke wonder, it may alienate those very tourists they are seeking to attract for return visitation. Seeking return visitation, which is the most efficient mode of marketing, works towards habit and ultimately addiction. Going in the other direction is more difficult, expensive and frustrating given the nature of humans, but it is the way to social change. This question, then, raises an ethical point, which I do not believe has been addressed in tourism.

With the diminishing of passion 'fatigue and struggle recede along with effort' (Ravaisson 2008: 49). That means that it becomes easier to redo something. When that occurs, there is a diminishing of the pleasure and pain associated with the sensation of passion (Ravaisson 2008).[8] As the sensation of passion diminishes, especially when pain diminishes in greater proportion to pleasure, the sensation of passion 'becomes more and more of a need' (Ravaisson 2008: 51). That is, the person needs the passion. At this point the line between habit and addiction appears.

Along with the diminishing of the passion that comes from repetition of the activity, there comes the strengthening of the activity (less effort is necessary to overcome the waning passion). With this strengthening, the activity becomes more of a tendency (Ravaisson 2008). In effect, the activity itself becomes easier, and since the activity is/was the means of achieving some relationship to the other/object, it becomes the focal point of consciousness (Ravaisson 2008). Through this elevation of activity and diminishing of passion, the sensation of passion itself is sought, not the other/object that first provoked passion. The activity becomes the anticipated source of passion rather than the other/object. So, tourists engage in more and more activity, never quite getting what they were initially seeking. We see this in tourists with the talk of another notch in the travel/experience belt.

The activity, having become a tendency, is

> a sort of obscure activity that increasingly anticipates both the impression of external objects in sensibility and the will in activity. In activity, this reproduces the [act] itself; in sensibility it does not reproduce the sensation, the passion – for this requires an external cause – but calls for it, invokes it; in a certain sense it implores the sensation.
>
> (Ravaisson 2008: 51)

In other words, the activity becomes the surrogate for the end originally sought. The activity replaces the will and the other. While the activity is still animated to some extent by the passion, the passion is deep within the individual (Ravaisson 2008). The activity becomes 'an unreflective spontaneity ... increasingly establishes itself there, beyond, beneath the region of will, personality and consciousness' (Ravaisson 2008: 53). This is habit.

At some point, habit can become an addiction; that is, when the activity becomes mechanical and irresistible. The 'ease, facility [and] power' that is present in the highest forms of habit (the athlete at the top of their game, the stellar lawyer in the courtroom) disappears as a 'machinic repetition' replaces the easeful ability (Malabou 2008: viii). The American who can navigate his own country with ease, leading to a certain level of riches and/or fame, and acts the same way outside the country leading to the moniker of the 'ugly American' is but one example.

Ultimately, the point at which something becomes an addiction is not precise or clear. But that determination may not be necessary. If tourism is a habit, then the wonder of the tourist and other good things sought in tourism, such as poverty alleviation or cultural rapprochement, are largely lost. At some point, those goals are lost as the activity that originally provided the way to those goals becomes more important than the goal – that is, by definition a habit/addiction. The failure to revitalise wonder and passion and the actual pursuit of noble ends bring money but no satisfaction. The way to alter matters is to provide experiences that satisfy one's passion – easy to say but not so easy to do for technical, ontological and monetary reasons.

While the idea that tourism is habit/addiction might seem to be more negative than positive, that is not all the story. Habit is our being and is also productive of change, just as it comes out of change. If it were not, the human world would eventually atrophy under the weight of habit. It is through experience, which starts with the subversion of one's prior understandings (including habits), that change comes.

Experience

While habit is not the experience, it is our starting point for an alternative view of experience. Habit is embodied activity in the world, coming from passion for something that is external, implying an interaction/dialogue with the environment/world; therefore, it suggests experience is a totality, not simply cognitive and subjective. The otherness indicated by the environment/world is not just other people but also the complete setting, which includes everything and everyone involved with the touristic situation (Henning 2008). In addition, since habit is intimately tied to time, change and continuity, an analysis of experience will necessarily involve an analysis of the history and culture of *all* that is involved in the experience. In other words, to research experience we have to understand the totality, which involves embodiment, history and the future, meaning, the social milieu, subjectivity and the objects and landscape involved. This even involves the study of the organisations that give rise to the experience (Henning 2006).

The dialogic nature of experience[9] is not exclusively a verbal dialogue (Ricoeur 1991). As Gadamer points out, we dialogue with people just by being around them when something that he calls festival occurs (Gadamer 1986a, 1986b; Henning 2008).[10] This festival is not the functional definition of festival used in tourism (see, for example, Getz 2007). It is the idea that there is a commonality that is shared when people are in the same situation, at least in situations like destinations/attractions in tourism. If one is at Disneyland there is a commonality that is shared by everyone there. Likewise, when one goes hiking there is a commonality with other hikers on the same trail, even if they do not meet each other. The sharing of the commonality is one form of dialogue.

Further, Gadamer develops an extensive analysis of the aesthetic experience (Gadamer 2003). The aesthetic experience is where the person beholding the work of art is dialoguing with the work, suggesting that dialogue not only occurs between people, but also occurs between people and objects.[11] A good example of this is how we interact with a movie or book, 'talking' to the characters, anticipating what will come, reforming our ideas as our anticipations are not always accurate, coming to the end with an understanding we did not have originally.

We can call this dialogue since it is always mediated through language, and the other makes demands on us we may not want to accept, leading to a give and take (to-and-fro) (Gadamer 2003).[12] In effect, we dialogue, or can dialogue, with the entire situation we find ourselves in, not just the people we speak to – experience is dialogic.

To more fully describe the idea of the dialogic experience, we turn to Gadamer's conception of play set out in Part 1 of *Truth and Method* (Gadamer 2003), which is a beautiful model for the dialogue we have in touristic situations and for the totality of experience. Play is not used as it has been rendered in tourism (Cohen 1985). It is not something the subject does. Play is something, ontologically, that engulfs me (Henning 2008; Gadamer 2003), so that I am dialoging within the play with all the elements involved in the play. I am absorbed into the play and the spirit of the play; I am part of the play. That is, I am not sovereign. I may try to do what I want or follow my habits, but there are others (people, rules, cultural norms and objects) that stand in my way. I am effectively played by the play (Gadamer 2003). In effect, the play is what arises in between all the elements. That is, play, as defined, is the same as experience. Experience is in between.

We see this clearly in sport. There is no ice hockey unless there is ice and players engaged in activity that is accommodated to the rules and others on the ice. There is no hockey if you only look at the rules or arena, and yet, without the rules, the people are not playing hockey. It is a necessary totality, and that totality is the experience; in the case of hockey it is the experience of hockey. In tourism, when we go to an attraction like Troy, we are not tourists for doing so, for we may be archeologists or locals going to work. It is when we engage the situation by paying for a visitor ticket, buying a guidebook from the locals, walking around the site taking pictures, refraining from excavating, fantasising about being a Greek or Trojan, touching the stone, scanning the horizon for a sense of its situation as a city exercising control over the Dardanelles/Hellespont, that we are tourists at Troy. As we do this, we necessarily interact with rules and the objects at hand in ways that are different from non-tourists. Then the experience is one of tourism at Troy, involving all the elements mentioned including the locals and archeologists.

When we go to Troy, we go with our habits (our prior understandings). Habits are like the skills of the hockey player. Those habits help us understand (navigate) Troy, but they may also hinder understanding, and it is here that dialogue becomes obvious. The sense that we can navigate the situation comes through our ability to navigate other situations (daily life and other tourism situations) with those habits when we do not see too much difference between those situations and Troy. Of course, where we suspect the latter is substantially different, we will have trepidation about our ability to navigate it – hence, one reason for the popularity of bubble forms of tourism. To the extent our habits hinder our understanding/navigation of the situation we have to dialogue with the situation to come to a better understanding, just as we did with the movie or book or to play hockey. That is, when our expectations and prior understandings are subverted we have to act. We are forced to decide whether we are going to dialogue or not. For instance, when I went to Troy I was expecting poor signage and just piles of undifferentiated rubble. So, I bought a guidebook to help decipher what was going on. To my great amazement, the site was much more obvious about the different layers of cities, there were interpretive signs and some reconstruction. I only occasionally consulted the book and concentrated on what I could see. Hence, the salutary nature of the subversion of expectations as opposed to attempts to satisfy expectations.

It is effectively in the dialogue that the experience occurs. And it is in the experience that understanding occurs. The three are intimately linked, but understanding is not the experience. What happens later, after the experience, when people talk about and share it with others, is the discursive and cognitive rendering of the experience which is akin to Weick's (1995) sense-making. So, it is in the dialogic experience where habits are reformed. Luckily, our habits are not rigid and so can be changed. Habit, whilst it comes from change and opposes change, also gives rise to change (Ravaisson 2008). The change in habit/understanding comes from the dialogue, as the person must take into account those elements that stand in their way of doing what they might otherwise do. That means that tourists are capable of change and of learning – tourists are not, as Bruner (1991) put it, immune to change. To the extent they are immune to change, tourists are addicted; addiction, then, is when our habits have become mechanical and are not reformable through our encounters in the world. We clearly see this in those unable to adjust to a foreign culture. But we also see it in those who have to travel to certain places repeatedly or travel in certain ways, without the ability to accommodate alternatives. When someone cannot change his or her habits in the face of a world that suggests he/she does not understand the situation – their understanding is inhibited and possibly wrong – there is no dialogue. In effect, when we are addicted to our way of being in the world, we do not change; there is no dialogue and no experience. Another way of saying this is that in addiction we impose our subjective habits on the situation. We know of many stereotyped examples of this, such as the ugly American or the rich Westerner. It also suggests that repeat visitors may not engage in experiences as others do. It further suggests that if people do not understand the tourism situation but take in uncritically the story told them by the providers, they do not dialogue as they simply allow the views of another to replace theirs. They do not bring themselves into the situation – they are basically ciphers. Dialogue is not uncritical acceptance of the other (Gadamer 1981).

To return to the sports analogy, we may wonder about those incredibly skilled athletes, such as Wayne Gretzky in hockey, and their apparent ability to impose themselves on the game. Is that not the same as addiction and should we not seek that out? It is not the imposition that comes with addiction, for it is skilled imposition. It is skilled dialogue or critical dialogue. Given the tendency of tourists to follow, this suggests that most tourists are not very skilled at being in a world they are not familiar with – they are not experienced. And tourism operators use that to their advantage to ensure dependency of tourists on the tour guides, guidebooks, return and so on. So, tourism is necessarily a world or experience of dependency. But one of the problems with dependency is that it more readily limits experience, as people are not having their expectations subverted and are not critically engaging the situation. That means that the parts of the tourism industry claiming to foster good outcomes such as poverty alleviation and cross-cultural understanding (both of which require the development of new habits by tourists and locals), is actually preventing those lofty goals. However, it must also be kept in mind that because people do not like to initiate, tourists and locals also participate fully in this delusional and habit-forming (and often addiction-forming) world.

In the dialogic experience, because of the interaction between all the elements of the experience, especially the habits of everyone, there is a to-and-fro that develops. This to-and-fro develops into the play noted above. When this occurs more than once, we can start to see a particular spirit or structure to the experience (Gadamer 2003; Ricoeur 1991). That is, we can identify the experience across different participants as being the same experience because the spirit of the situation is the same whenever it occurs and with whoever is involved. Troy is a touristic experience whenever there are tourists there doing tourist stuff. The to-and-fro is the dialogue of all the elements and is different for each experience. That means that experience is not the subjective sense one has of things like happiness or sadness, although these are an important part of the experience. That experience is more than the subjective suggests that, for the most part, tourism research has examined a part of the experience and considered it the whole. If we recall the story of the three blind men who examined a part of the elephant and decided it was different from what the others claimed, we see the potential danger of claiming experience is what goes on in someone's mind; that is only part of the story.

In effect, tourism is composed of habits as they are mediated through the dialogue of all participants in the touristic situation. In sharing these habits – going to the same places, taking toilet kits, using guides, travelling alone – we share a common humanity. This humanity may be less than the ideal human being we might imagine, but it is who we are flawed, afraid of being initiators, comfortable with our own, and curious. When we accept ourselves, we can discover the beauty of tourism in all its manifestations, even as an addiction. To each their own, but there is always company. We are, as Aristotle (1941) says, people who necessarily share our world with others and need that sharing. From this sharing, we divide the world into my tribe and others. Those others are people who do not share my habits. It is why we have such trepidation when we do things on vacation that are not congruent with our usual habits. For me, using a guide to see Ephesus was a challenge to my sense of myself as a tourist who does it alone. Even adventure tourists are subject to habits.

Conclusion

Tourism is habitual in character and design – we can say the habit of tourism. However, it appears that many of us engaged in tourism are also addicted. That suggests that to the extent there is no dialogue (addiction) there is a lack of tourism except in some sort of impoverished functional sense – it is tourism because people are walking around looking like tourists, but are in effect zombies. So, we can characterise tourism as less than fully functioning (some might say sick), but it is not only tourism where we are addicted; tourism is no different from any other human pursuit. That means, we can better understand the totality of our social world when we examine the totality of the tourism situation from the perspective suggested here, for as Ryan argues, tourism is a metaphor for the social world (Ryan 2002c).

The question that then arises is whether we can find ways that produce sufficient rewards for providers and, at the same time, provoke actual dialogic experiences; for now, they are dichotomous. As tourism stands today, it is not a force for change in the world; it is a work of dependency. We are beings that favour habit over the risk of the new and completely different. We seek small differences suggesting that any change will be gradual, not revolutionary. In spite of this, the view developed here suggests more charity towards those involved in tourism for they are no different from anyone else. Any condemnation of tourism is a condemnation of the beingness of humanity. However, this view also calls for more critical engagement in order to bring change to the world.

> Nothing is more impenetrable than the familiar.
>
> (Ricoeur 1966: 289)

Notes

1 In this chapter I will use the term action in accord with Arendt's meaning. The term activity will be used in distinction to action, as a term that includes habit, systematised work, and other ways of acting that are not free.

2 Natural attractions are things/places that were discovered previously. Almost all, if not all, constructed attractions are based on previously known elements; for example, Disneyland, which is often held out as being an innovation in amusement parks, was based on a cartoon mouse and other parks. To the extent that Disneyland was a new act of humanity in the world does not make tourism as a whole objectively new. The tourists who go to Disneyland are not doing something new, and theme parks since then are not new, except in some details.

3 Prior understandings, as used here, are not limited to cognitive elements, but are tied to the idea of being-in-the-world. Our way of being in the world is a total experience and prior understandings are composed of habits, culture, physical capabilities, etc.

4 I prefer the term situation to attraction or destination as it encompasses both. I realise that the latter terms have specific application, but for the most part, this chapter does not need to make that distinction; therefore, situation will be used unless one or the other term is more appropriate.

5 The argument set out here using authenticity is not limited to authenticity. It should apply *mutatis mutandis* to escape and other meta-motivations of tourists. It might be argued that all meta-motivations reduce to authenticity in that we seek something that is authentically other than us. The important point here is that our seeking is motivated by something that is real and different in comparison to our daily lives. This applies as well to the postmodern tourist who finds even constructed or kitschy attractions to be different from their daily life.

6 I am making a distinction between a socially sanctioned interpretation by a provider and a reconciliation of expectations with subverted prior understandings by a provider. The latter would entail more dialogue between tourist and provider; the former is satisfied by an authoritative statement with no opportunity for exchange.

7 Ravaisson (2008) argues that touch and smell are passive sensory organs not productive of activity, while sight and hearing are active and productive of activity, but that does not feel right to me. When I touch a fine material I want to run my hands over it; when I walk a mountain path the feeling of the ground (instead of concrete) beneath my feet provokes me to walk further on the path. A fine smell attracts me to move closer to it or to keep sniffing the air. Hence, I would argue that all our senses are productive of activity. Or, alternatively, activity is so ingrained in our senses that it is impossible to separate sense and activity. Only social grace trains out our natural tendency to want to continue to touch or sniff pleasant sensations.

8 Ravaisson (2008) uses sensation to refer to passion as well as the sensations that our usual senses engage. Ricoeur (1966) includes passion as an emotion. But Ricoeur misses Ravaisson's point. Passion is the sensation associated with desire for the object/other, which is why passion is satisfied with the disembodied appropriation of the other and hinders activity. One cannot easily separate perception, sensation and the object. Emotions can be separated from the object they relate to. Passion cannot be easily separated from its object, hence, its categorisation as a sensation.

9 The idea of experience being dialogical does not mean that any encounter between subject and environment will be dialogical. The strict equation of dialogue and experience is being made here. Where tourists do not dialogue there is no experience.

10 To understand experience as a totality that arises from habit we turn to Hans-Georg Gadamer. In tourism, Gadamer's work has been seen to be about the subjective – the idea that he is speaking of understanding and understanding is subjective or epistemological (e.g. Obenour *et al.* 2006). However, this is a misreading of Gadamer's opus (Schwandt 2000). Gadamer develops an ontological reading of understanding (Grondin 2003) that situates understanding within three non-subjective frameworks. First, understanding is our way of being in the world. Second, understanding is a dialogic process necessarily involving subject and object/other. Third, understanding is always carried out within what Gadamer calls tradition. In other words, understanding is an event within experience.

11 There is some debate as to whether the dialogue is with the object or with the meaning attached to or related to the object. To argue the latter, however, leads to an idealist interpretation of Gadamer, which flies in the face of his conception of being in the world and the nature of understanding. As Dunne (1997) notes, understanding, as Gadamer conceives it, is a practical event in the world. It is not the application of theory to practice but is itself a practice that necessarily affects the way we go about the world, in our embodied state. In effect, it is impossible to separate meaning from the other/object (Gadamer 2003), so the question of whether we actually dialogue with the object/other or with the meaning is irrelevant – in practice we do not distinguish the two.

12 Gadamer's view of language is similar to that of Heidegger. It is too complex to go into here. Suffice to say that language does not simply have a representative function as a tool of subjectivity; it is both representative and world-creating, while mediating the dialogue between subject and object.

3 Experiences of valuistic journeys

Motivation and behaviour

Darius Liutikas

Introduction

We live in a globalised, mobile and continuously changing world. At present, the most acceptable and popular form of mobility amongst people is tourism. According to the UN World Tourism Organization, over 900 million international arrivals were recorded in 2008 (World Tourism Organization 2009), a figure that rose to 940 million in 2010. However, it remains extremely difficult to analyse tourism as a homogeneous phenomenon because journeys differ from each other with regard to their motivation, objectives, means and forms. This chapter focuses upon and analyses the experience of so-called valuistic journeys. The term *valuistic journey* involves the concepts of both traditional religious and modern secular *pilgrimage*, and such journeys may be seen as a means of demonstrating the values of their participants as well as revealing their personal and social identity. For the purposes of this chapter, valuistic journeys are considered a separate and identifiable group of journeys or form of tourism.

The earliest known form of valuistic journey was the religious pilgrimage. However, according to Coleman and Elsner (1995), despite transformations in society in general and in the perception and construction of self-identity in particular, as well as advances in communication technologies, the religious pilgrimage has proved its ability to adapt to the innovations of secular modernity and even to appropriate them. Indeed, contemporary changes in society, such as globalisation and virtualisation, are increasingly enabling the blending of the *sacrum* and *profanum*, of the *valuistic* and *consumeristic* spheres. Pilgrimage is turning into a modern valuistic journey, its purpose being not only to travel to or visit a sacred place but also, in so doing, to achieve a sense of value, worthiness or identity from the place or event. Therefore, we define a pilgrimage or valuistic journey as a journey undertaken with the purpose of seeking or, indeed, expressing a valuistic ideal. During a pilgrimage, travellers/tourists go through different physical, emotional and spiritual experiences; the pilgrimage offers its participants the opportunity to consider the meaning of life or their own lives, their values and their relationships with other individuals. During the journey, their identity, outlook on the world and values are therefore expressed, demonstrated and consolidated.

To date, valuistic journeys and the meaning behind them have most typically been analysed from one particular perspective at a time. In other words, whilst the phenomenon of religious pilgrimage has been widely investigated by social scientists, this is commonly from a specific perspective or in a particular context. For example, the geographical aspects of religious pilgrimages have been explored by Rinschede (1986, 1990, 1992), Bhardwaj and Rinschede (1988), Bhardwaj (1973), Tanaka (1984, 1988), Nolan and Nolan (1989), and Jackowski (1996, 1998, 2000). Important insights in investigating the problems or challenges related to pilgrimage are provided by Turner (1967, 1969, 1973), Turner and Turner (1978) and their critics Eade and Sallnow (2000), whilst the concept of pilgrimage has been investigated by Morinis (1992), Coleman and Elsner (1995) and Coleman and Eade (2004). Similarly, the notion of the modern secular pilgrimage is addressed by Reader and Walter (1993), Clift and Clift (1996) and Margry (2008a). More specifically, links between pilgrimage and tourism have been proposed and developed by a number of commentators, most notably MacCannell (1999), Graburn (1989), Cohen (1972, 1979, 1992b, 2001) and Smith (1992). Moreover, work by Nolan and Nolan (1989), Rinschede (1992), Jackowski (2000), Swatos and Tomasi (2002) and Timothy and Olsen (2006) are of particular importance with regard to studies of religious tourism.

In this chapter, valuistic journeys are analysed from the point of view of one of the key categories of sociology – identity. The aim of this chapter is to reveal experiences of valuistic journeys and to explore the relationship between valuistic journeys and values of the individual tourist. Thus, the primary tasks of this chapter are to identify the main values of tourists, their journey motives and the values pursued during the journey and to assess the major tendencies of their behaviour as well as other factors that influence their experience.

Research on valuistic journeys in Lithuania is also the starting point for this chapter (Liutikas 2009). It summarises the results of several years of research carried out by the author and, therefore, draws on a variety of methods of research. Nevertheless, the principal methods utilised are those most typically found in the majority of social scientific research, including questionnaires and observation. Research data are analysed with the application of statistical methods such as factor analysis.

The quantitative research on Lithuanian pilgrims/valuistic travellers draws on theoretical insights developed by the author, and is based on the outcomes of a questionnaire survey which was carried out between July 2007 and May 2008. During the study, 700 valuistic travellers (400 Catholic pilgrims and 300 modern pilgrims) between the ages of 14 and 74 years old were interviewed. For the selection of respondents, non-probability purposive sampling was applied. Valuistic travellers were interviewed in organised groups going to places or events of religious or modern pilgrimage. In total, 30 groups of valuistic travellers were questioned.

In this research, pilgrims who travelled in an organised group outside Lithuania to other countries' religious pilgrimage centres or concerts, or travelled to religious pilgrimage places or sport competitions in Lithuania by a special bus in an organised group were interviewed. All the pilgrims had to cover a distance of at least 50 km from the departure to the destination point; that is, this was the shortest distance from their home to the sacred place or the event in which they participated.

The concept of valuistic journeys

Valuistic journeys today have become an expression of the identity of an individual, as well as an indicator of that individual's lifestyle and values. Within globalised space, which is particularly open to change, the desire to search for unalterable landmarks or to reinforce value systems is increasingly growing. And it is valuistic journeys which help to realise this desire. Journeys become not only a commercial commodity and a dynamic element of consumption, but also a cultural icon and a constituent part of cultural capital, the importance of which is continuously increasing (Shaw and Williams 2004).

One can define values as abstract beliefs which are culturally defined and serve as a guideline for views and behaviour. As Müller (1991: 57) notes, values 'govern a person's lifestyle and provide a direct and useful explanation of the multitude of interests, outlooks on life, consumption practices and activities that define a lifestyle'. In short, values are desired objectives, which predetermine the major principles of an individual's life. Truth and values may be valid for one person and false for another. However, changing beliefs about the nature of truth do not necessary contribute to the advance of modernism, since cultural and technological progress has often been propelled forward by a belief in an objective reality which could be discovered.

Morinis (1992: 4) defines pilgrimage in general as a journey undertaken by a person in quest for a place or a state that he or she believes to embody a valued ideal. This definition may be applied to all kinds of pilgrimage. The destination at the end of all pilgrimages shares the characteristic of being an intensified version of some ideal that the pilgrim values but cannot achieve at home. Clift and Clift (1996) present a broader notion of pilgrimage. According to them, pilgrimage is a journey, a ritual, a commemoration, a search for something, perhaps something the pilgrim cannot express in words, perhaps even something the pilgrim does not fully perceive (Clift and Clift 1996: 9). The goal of pilgrimage is individual: 'it's like the goal of your life' (female pilgrim, 38 years old).

Coleman and Elsner (1995: 214) argue that if we accept one aspect of a Durkheimian view of the sacred – the notion that the sacred is in some respects an embodiment and representation of societal ideals – we can argue that pilgrimage is currently taking on new forms that go far beyond standard religious practices. Pilgrims sacralise the space they worship in or through association with their experiences there, through decoration, through sight and sound, through entry rituals. The sacred space is not open all the time, it is often bounded with processes for entering and leaving, and pilgrims have to go on a pilgrimage to get into this space (Coleman and Elsner 1995: 214).

However, the places which are visited during valuistic journeys are totally different. They may include Graceland (the burial place of Elvis Presley), Liverpool (the city which was home to the Beatles) and the locations of TV shows, such as *Star Trek* or *Lost*, to sports matches or sports stadia (Gammon 2011). But valuistic journeys may also be to places of religious pilgrimage, such as Jerusalem, Mecca or Rome. Hall (2006) suggests that the meaning of a secular valuistic journey is identical to a religious pilgrimage:

> If one takes the religious humanist position that humans have created god, if a visit to Liverpool has a deep personal meaning that helps people explain their lives, then it is of equivalent value to a Christian's journey to Jerusalem.
>
> (Hall 2006: 73)

Following Morinis, Porter suggests that pilgrimage represents a quest for a 'place or state in which intensified ideals not attainable at home are embodied' (cited in Badone and Roseman 2004: 16). Starting from this assumption, she shows that for many *Star Trek* fans, convention attendance involves the pursuit of sacred ideals that are actualised in the convention itself. Significantly, these ideals coincide with those defined as sacred in the 'cult of man' that Durkheim predicted would become the religion of complex, industrialised societies: individualism, liberalism, freedom, justice, equality and tolerance of diversity (Badone and Roseman 2004: 16–17).

So we can define valuistic journey as an expression of valuistic ideals, as well as confirmation and demonstration of identity. Such journeys help to develop or change personal or social identity. The problems of providing meanings to the self and self-perception are potentially solved during the valuistic journey. Such journeys help to define self-identification features as well as one's outlook on the world and values. Values fostered by valuistic travellers can be related to religion or a quest for a personal spiritual path. They can also embody national, cultural or other collective ideals or the unique values of an individual. The destination of this kind of journey, which is carried out on the grounds of spiritual or valuistic motives, is sacred, estimable or a place related to personal values. Pilgrimage also means a journey to events significant for personal or social identity or to meet estimable persons or persons with authority as well as a journey searching for personal identity. The relationship between identity and valuistic journeys is conceptualised in Figure 3.1 below.

This clearly defined model of the concept of valuistic journeys permits the identification of two major groups of such journeys: a traditional (religious) pilgrimage and a modern (unrelated to religion) pilgrimage. A traditional (religious) pilgrimage is a journey to places related to religion while a modern pilgrimage is a journey to secular places not related to religion. However, the modern pilgrimage carries a kind of religiosity that overtakes traditional religious meaning and is built on immanent but universal values.

Modern pilgrimage can be divided into several types: sports fan journeys, for example, are related to supporting a team and/or an athlete during a competition

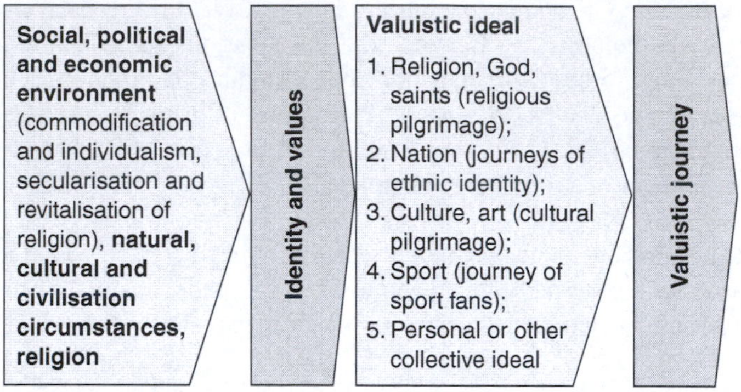

Figure 3.1 The relationship between identity and the valuistic journey.

outside their place of residence; cultural pilgrimages seek to express cultural values related to music, fine arts or other kinds of art; national identity journeys constitute travelling to a place or event of significance from the point of view of national history or statehood, seeking to pay tribute to political leaders or, if the place of residence is elsewhere, to visit the motherland.

So the main elements of the valuistic journey become a clearly defined geographical destination and valuistic motives impelling one to reach that destination. We can consider values a 'push' factor, and places in the space that symbolise values a 'pull' factor for the travellers.

Comparison between traditional and modern pilgrimage highlights similarities and differences between these kinds of journeys. Similar social and economic factors affecting the journey, forms of the journey, its phases, and willingness to give meaning to the destination point are characteristic of both traditional and modern pilgrimage. It is natural that religious and modern pilgrims differ with regard to their values of life and attitudes to religion. However, it is also important to note that structure and ritual are more characteristic of the traditional religious pilgrimage. Also, difficulties and privation are more appreciated on this kind of journey.

A relevant issue is the relationship between valuistic journeys and tourism. Contemporary research deals with the complicated relationship between these phenomena, including the economic, political, social, psychological, emotional and other aspects (see, for example, Cohen 1979, 1992b; Smith 1992). An analysis of the journey concept shows that, today, the terms *traveller* and *tourist* are often used synonymously although people engaging in certain forms of leisure travel such as backpacking often wish to distinguish themselves from tourists and hence refer to themselves as 'travellers'. Because of the complexity of tourist activities and difference in their interests, there is no definition of tourism which can be universally acceptable (Van Harssel 1994: 3). Officially, tourism is defined as the activity of persons who travel to places outside their traditional environment for leisure, business or other purposes and stay there without interruption for no longer than one year. However, because these official (or technical) definitions of tourism are used for statistical purposes, no consideration is given to the objectives of the journey. Moreover, as they include persons travelling not during their leisure time (for example, business travellers), ambiguity may arise in the concept of tourism.

In scientific publications, tourism is linked to a series of different factors: leisure time and a journey in this period, recreation, motives of travellers and journey experiences, acquisition of specific experience, as well as consumption of commodities and services (Burns 1999: 31). Lithuanian scientists often see tourism as a measure for meeting recreational needs (Grecevičius 2002). Quite often, social scientists (for example, Wang 2000: 4) define tourism as a voluntary and temporary journey carried out in leisure time seeking to experience novelty and changes. This notion, however, does not cover persons travelling for valuistic purposes (valuistic journey) or because of necessity or instrumental purposes, such as medical treatment, business travels, visiting relatives and so on.

Thus, bearing in mind these considerations, all journeys could be grouped in three major groups (Figure 3.2). This classification is based on the goal of the journey and motives of the travellers and includes: (1) recreational and cognitive journeys (usually described as tourist); (2) valuistic journeys (pilgrimages); and (3) necessary and instrumental journeys (business trips, travelling for medical treatment, etc.).

And yet, as has been mentioned above, the main difference distinguishing a recreational and a valuistic journey is the motivation of the traveller and his/her inner disposition. Religious or valuistic motives are primary in a pilgrimage, its basis remains the same; that is, reaching the objective (destination) of the journey and, at the same time, expressing personal identity and values, defining the features which identify the self.

The main difference between traditional pilgrimage journeys and other types of journey is that pilgrimage is a religious act in its own right and it is made for specific spiritual and religious purposes. This difference is clearly expressed by pilgrims:

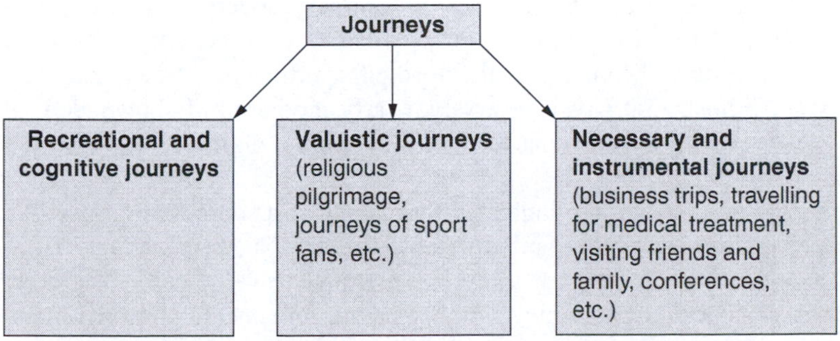

Figure 3.2 A classification of journeys.

> Pilgrimage, firstly, is a prayer. The difference is that you do everything in a different way. When you're going there with intention, prayer, with something, your inner disposition totally different. You can dance and sing, but the different dances, the different songs already.
>
> (Female pilgrim, 20 years old)

The difference between modern secular pilgrimage and modern tourism is more complicated than the difference between a valuistic journey and recreational or cognitive tourism in general. Of course, with regard to their external objectives and infrastructure, valuistic journeys today are becoming very close to the concept of modern tourism. On the other hand, the inner objectives of the traveller and the clear motivations and behaviours which express his/her identity separate these types of journeys. The distinction can be drawn that the goal for modern pilgrimage is particular and well-known in the preparation phases of the journey. The aim of the modern pilgrimage is to travel to particularly valuable places which are related to personal identity. This journey differs from tourist journeys that are made for general cognitive, recreational or other reasons. Modern pilgrims differ from tourists not only in the purpose of their travelling, but also at the level of ritualisation of the journey. Concerning the cultural configurations and symbolism of the places pilgrims seek out, a higher level of ritualisation is incidental to the modern pilgrimage. Specific behaviour during the journey and at the destination point is characterised by typical rites or models of behaviour.

In order to confirm the concept of valuistic journeys described above, it is important to find out how pilgrims themselves describe and evaluate their own journey. Here, multiple results emerged from the research in Lithuania. For example, over 60 per cent of religious pilgrims and one third of secular pilgrims define the pilgrimage itself as a spiritual journey to a sacred place. However, a quarter of secular pilgrims understand a pilgrimage as any valuistic journey, thus supporting the idea of the development of the pilgrimage concept as proposed in this chapter (see Figure 3.3).

When the pilgrims were asked to define their current journey, their opinions differed. Of the religious pilgrims, 90 per cent thought that their current journey was a pilgrimage or a valuistic journey. In general, modern secular pilgrims more often characterise their journey as *valuistic* and relate the term *pilgrimage* to religious travelling. More than one third of sports fans agreed that their journey was a valuistic journey. Conversely, nearly another third of them defined their journey as a way of spending leisure time without attaching any valuistic meaning to it.

Others (16 per cent) simply indicated that this was a journey to a match, a team support journey or simply 'an important journey'. Therefore, about half of sports fans evaluate their journey as exceptional and valuistic, while the other half of them consider such a journey simply as a way of spending leisure time or entertainment. Meanwhile, three-quarters of those travelling to concerts consider their journey as an entertainment, tourist or cognitive journey.

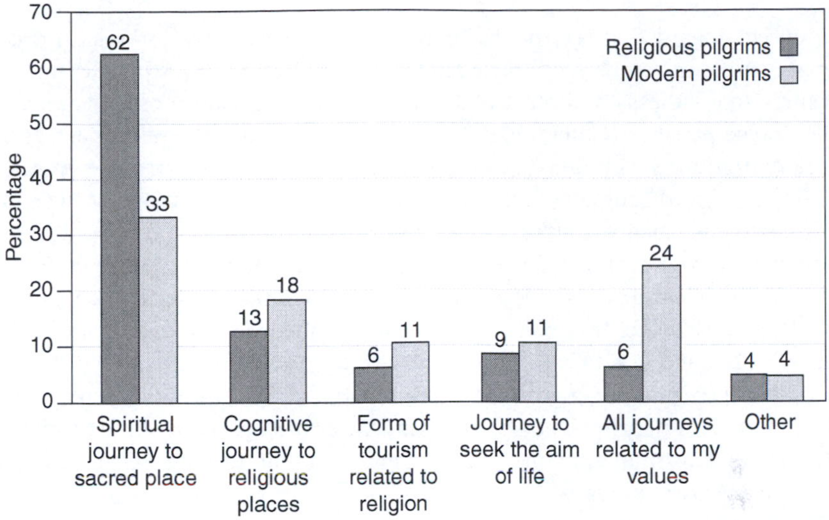

Figure 3.3 Understandings of the conception of pilgrimage.

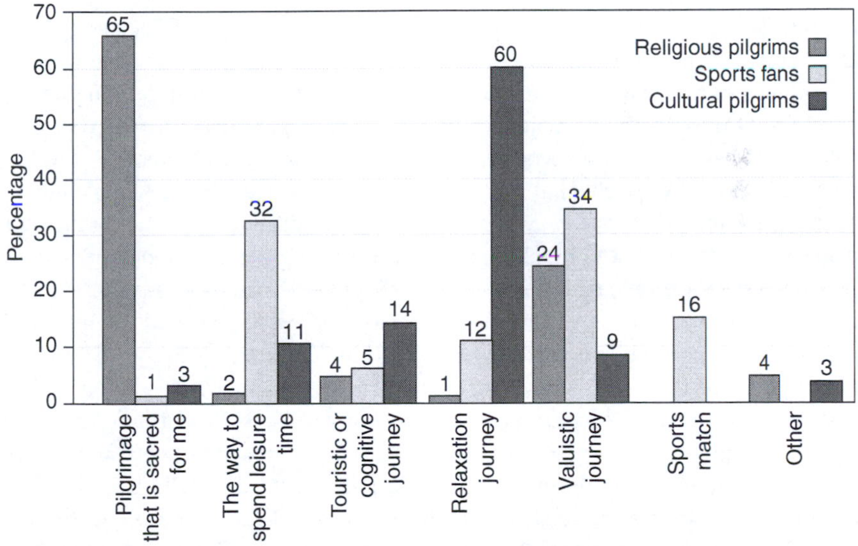

Figure 3.4 Characterisation of existing journey.

Motivation and values of valuistic travellers

All pilgrims regard the days of the journey as an opportunity to break out of normal routines and experience their faith or values. For religious people, this is in contrast to mindless conformity to the forms of religion that so often dominate in their home parishes (Galbraith 2000: 4). They experience the pilgrimage as a departure from the institutionalised expression of religion and a move toward a purer expression of religious faith. For modern pilgrims, it is an opportunity to demonstrate their identity, attitudes and true values. For both types of pilgrims, it is liberation from everyday society. Religious and modern pilgrimage is a rich context for both learning and reinterpreting cultural knowledge about the world.

As Rinschede (1992: 62) points out, the predominance of women among pilgrims can be found in all Catholic pilgrimage sites. In this research, 80 per cent of all the respondents among religious pilgrims were females. While analysing groups of modern pilgrims, the opposite tendencies are observed. Among sports fans, females constitute only one-fifth, while among cultural pilgrims, a balance between the genders prevails.

Pilgrims also differ in age. One-third of the religious pilgrims were over 60 years old, while among modern pilgrims, no persons of this age were recorded at all. The absolute majority of sports fans were young people, up to 29 years old. The prevailing age groups among cultural pilgrims were young people from 20 to 29 years old and midlife persons from 30 to 59 years old. A common feature of pilgrims is self-identification with the middle and upper group of society and the evaluation of their own material situation is as medium or higher than medium.

With regard to occupation, the composition of pilgrims differs depending on the objective of the journey. The majority (two-thirds) of religious pilgrims were schoolchildren, students and retired persons. These social groups typically tend to travel in organised groups by coach. Half of the interviewed sports fans were schoolchildren and students, the other half were persons working in different jobs while the vast majority (70 per cent) of cultural pilgrims were working persons (employees, civil servants, business people and self-employed persons). So, valuistic travellers (traditional and modern pilgrims) differ with respect to their gender, age and occupation.

In order to research the values of the pilgrims, the open question 'The main thing in my life is…' was presented to valuistic travellers. They were asked to complete this sentence. In all, there were 201 variations. These variations can be aggregated into 14 groups (see Table 3.1). A clear difference between the values of religious and modern pilgrims is observed. For one-third of religious pilgrims, the main things in life are related to faith, religion, and the will of God. Family and fellow men are the main value for modern pilgrims. The values related to helping others and human qualities are also characteristic of religious pilgrims. Some 10 per cent of religious pilgrims preferred such values. For modern pilgrims, especially for sports fans, it is important to identify themselves with a sport or a particular sports team, and also to choose values related to personal future and self-realisation. But the main thing in life for sports fans is family and fellow men. Family is associated with loyalty, devotion and partisanship.

Table 3.1 Scale of pilgrims' values (%)

	'The main thing in my life is…'	*Religious pilgrims*	*Modern pilgrims*
1	God and his will, faith, spiritual life, religion, Church	31	1
2	Family, fellow men	25	44
3	Personal future, personal goals and aims, self-discovery, realisation, self-development, myself	5	9
4	Communication with people, relationship, harmony in relationship	2	0
5	To be useful for others, to help them, to do good, to give happiness	3	0
6	Human qualities (honesty, honour, humanity, kindness, respect, modesty, heartiness, responsibility, confidence, justice, loyalty)	7	2
7	Common values (happiness, hope, wellbeing, truth, freedom, unity)	4	4
8	Job, learning, career	4	4
9	Spiritual and inner harmony, peace	4	4
10	Life itself, joy of life, fullness, sense	5	5
11	Love	6	1
12	Health	3	7
13	Sport, basketball, football	0	10
14	Other (material welfare, leisure time, nature, fatherland, music, cognition, etc.)	1	9

The motives of valuistic travellers depend on many things, the most important of which are the life experience of pilgrims, their lifestyle, as well as social and cultural influences.

In general, religious pilgrims vary in age, education and social position, but the purposes of their pilgrimage journey are the same – religious and spiritual:

> When you are going on cognitive journey, first of all, you are paying attention to the external world. But when you are going inside, you don't seek to know the world, you don't seek to know yourself, but to find something in the relation between God and you.
>
> (Female pilgrim, 24 years old)

Galbraith (2000: 66) provides similar reasons for going on a pilgrimage, based on interviews:

> We wish to renew our bond with God, and remind ourselves that we are all the children of God, who do not have an eternal home here, and through personal difficulty and prayer we wish to find the peace within ourselves, in order to pass it on to others.
>
> (Galbraith 2000: 66)

The research showed that the major motives of religious pilgrims, which were indicated by more than half of the respondents, were asking for God's grace, health, expressing gratitude to Jesus or the Virgin Mary and spiritual quest and renewal. It is interesting to note that 20 per cent of religious pilgrims are convinced that travelling to a sacred place is their religious duty (Figure 3.5).

Religious pilgrimage is the expression of religious identity attributable to its ritualistic dimension. Persons identify themselves with particular religious places, which become culturally constructed shrines. Strong religious identity is typical of Lithuanian religious pilgrims; however, they may choose whether or not to base this religious identity on Catholicism. We can define three factors in the analysis of pilgrims' ideological attitudes. The acknowledgement of a supernatural world which is not cognisable, is frightening and does not appeal to mundane laws, comprises the first factor. Its main features are a belief in an existing supernatural world, a belief in evil spirits and evil, a belief in life after death and a belief in miracles. Belief in God, in Redemption, in remission of sins and in apparitions of the Virgin Mary are the main features of the second factor, which we can call traditional religious features. The significance of religion in life is common to this factor. The belief in reincarnation, nature spirits, deities and fate make the third, oriental-pantheistic, factor (see Table 3.2).

Although religious pilgrimage continues to be, as it was in the Middle Ages, a spiritual journey to a sacred place, some contemporary pilgrims travel for cognitive or social reasons. Such persons choose the journey to diversify their holiday or weekend in order to experience new emotions or just for curiosity.

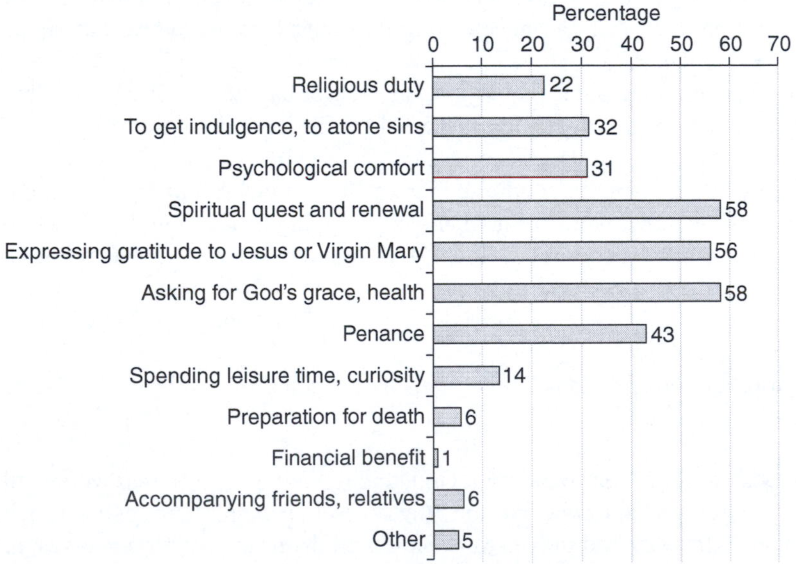

Figure 3.5 Main motives of religious Catholic pilgrimage.

Table 3.2 Results of factor analysis of religious beliefs (rotated component matrix, extraction method – principal component analysis, rotation method: Varimax with Kaiser normalisation)

	Factors		
	1	*2*	*3*
Do you believe in God?	0.009	0.804	0.013
Do you believe in supernatural world?	0.754	–0.092	0.152
Do you believe in reincarnation?	0.103	–0.134	0.817
Do you believe in life after death?	0.685	0.343	0.132
Do you believe in fate?	0.120	0.173	0.778
Do you believe in miracles?	0.662	0.377	0.120
Do you believe in redemption and remission of sins?	0.590	0.644	0.078
Do you believe in evil spirits and evil?	0.754	0.059	0.057
Do you believe in nature spirits and deities?	0.119	–0.104	0.796
Do you believe in apparitions of Virgin Mary?	0.482	0.693	0.084
Significance of religion in your life	0.080	0.786	–0.219

Occasionally, the choice of a journey could be predetermined by its lower price (especially travelling abroad) or seeking new social relations.

In order to get a better insight into the motives of religious pilgrimages and values of pilgrims during the pilgrimage, a factor analysis was carried out. Major group relations of analysed variables have been identified, which can be grouped in five components, see Table 3.3.

Further analysis shows that up to one-third of religious pilgrims associated the main values of the journey with good leisure time, another third with inner changes, and only the remaining one-third with its primary and actual sense, a religious act during which the priority is communication with God and prayer. Having carried out a factor analysis of the motives and values of modern pilgrims during a journey, we can distinguish one of the four models of the concept of a journey which is characteristic of all valuistic travellers. A journey is considered: (1) a way of spending leisure time; (2) an expression of values (religious or secular); (3) an opportunity for inner changes; and(4), an instrument for seeking other objectives.

However, not all the participants of valuistic journeys have valuistic motivations. In this respect, the concept of the pseudo-pilgrim could be defined. A pseudo-pilgrim is a person travelling with a group of pilgrims with motives different from the expression of values and identity. The motives of pilgrims are not fixed and stable. Other research (for example, Frey 1998) has revealed that some pilgrims form their motives or change them after their journey has started. There is rarely one reason for the journey; however, one major motive is often of principal importance for choosing the journey. However, investigations confirmed that the sacred dimension is not exclusive in religious pilgrimages. The wish to spend leisure time effectively, to have a satisfying holiday or to establish new social relations has an influence on the choice of a journey. Still, a common

Table 3.3 Motives of pilgrimage and values of the journey

	Component description	*Major motives and values of the journey*	*Description*
1	*Journey as means of spending leisure time*	Motives of the journey: spending leisure time, curiosity, psychological comfort; Important values related to the journey: new impressions, new environment, landscape, natural and cultural environment, good possibility to relax, to have a rest from the routine, possibility to express the self.	The journey is understood in a similar way as a tourist journey, a way of spending leisure time, seeking new impressions, new possibilities for expression.
2	*Pilgrimage as a religious act*	Motives of the journey: penance, asking for God's grace, health, expressing gratitude to Jesus or the Virgin Mary, seeking indulgence, redemption from sins. Journey as a religious duty, getting ready for passing away.	A journey the objectives of which are exclusively religious, which most of all expresses religious values.
3	*Pilgrimage in pursuit of inner changes*	Important values of the journey: possibility to change the self, community, inner motives, intentions of the journey, changes in the daily life after coming back home. The main motive of the journey is spiritual search and self-renewal.	The journey is aimed at changes of the inner life, new social relations are important.
4	*Pilgrimage as a specific ritual*	Important values of the journey: carrying out specific rituals or ordinances, satisfaction after the objective has been achieved, penance manifesting through physical difficulties and weariness.	The journey is understood as a ritual which requires physical efforts while, after the objective has been achieved, satisfaction is experienced.
5	*Journey as an instrument seeking other objectives*	Motives of the journey: economic benefit, accompanying close friends.	The journey simply has to be taken to overcome geographical space in order to accompany a friend or relative, or for economic reasons.

motive unites the majority of travellers. This common motive is the search for a better physical and spiritual life.

Behavioural features of valuistic travellers

A valuistic journey is a journey to a destination point which has been constructed from a cultural point of view and which occupies a central position in the identity of a person. It is important to emphasise the fact that the journey is used to provide meaning to specific places, thus forming the meanings of these places. Today, the focus of social sciences on the relationship between space, place and identity is increasing (see also Part IV in this book). *Who we are* is inseparable from *where we are*. All the aspects of our social life manifest themselves in material and symbolical space, which both is constructed socially and shapes sociality (Dixon 2008).

Identity, and the memory nurturing it, are not spontaneous actions, but rather are maintained by consistent attention and specific actions. Symbolically constructed places and events help to find external destinations, but rituals awaken internal spiritual forces. Of course, the level of ritualisation and structuralisation in modern pilgrimage and traditional pilgrimage differs. In contrast to the preferable formulas and rituals of traditional pilgrimage, modern pilgrims are often free to choose their behaviour during the journey. However, some exceptions do exist, such as sports fan rituals.

Religious pilgrimage is a spiritually motivated journey to a sacred place or shrine. The most important reasons for this journey are spiritual, such as penance, asking blessings, thanksgiving, spiritual quest and renewal, and worship. The analysis of the religious pilgrimages observed shows that pilgrims going on a journey for religious and spiritual motives devote their journey to prayer or meditation, to communication on religious topics and to the consideration of issues of the sense of life.

Rituals of a traditional religious pilgrimage often mingle with the general rituals of religious practice. Their form and structure are typically stricter. Rituals such as prayer, daily participation in Holy Mass and Confession of sins, acquire particular significance during traditional religious Catholic pilgrimages. In religious pilgrimages, prayer, which is an important element of the journey, manifests itself in different forms, such as personal prayer, singing, or prayers before and after meals.

Confession and penance for sins are typical components of a pilgrimage. Most of the major pilgrimage places in Lithuania (Šiluva, Samogitian Calvary (in Lithuanian, Žemaičių Kalvarija), Pivašiūnai) are visited during indulgence feasts. Penance (non-attachment to sin), as well as the sacrament of Confession, Eucharist, and a prayer for the Pope's intentions in the Catholic tradition are the main conditions for being awarded a plenary indulgence.

Another feature characteristic of pilgrimage is the leaving of something in the sacred or valuistic place, thereby endowing meaning to the journey or marking the journey and its motives. Religious pilgrims often leave their intentions (sometimes written on paper) and prayers whilst visiting sacred places; the Catholic tradition offers the potential, through confession and penance, to leave one's sins behind and to thank God for grace received. Votive amulets, which are signs of miracles of healing and grace (Latin *votum* means a vow, a promised donation; the amulets are golden or silver hearts, hands, legs, ears and other parts of a human body), used to be an extremely popular way of expressing gratitude for a grace received. When a large quantity of these votive amulets was gathered, they were often used for the production of coating for paintings, altar crosses and liturgical dishes. The votive amulets donated at the Dawn Gates (in Lithuanian, Aušros Gates) decorate the walls of the chapel. The tradition of donating votive amulets has survived up to the present day, although gratitude is, of course, also expressed in other ways. The simplest of these is lighting a candle, the flame of which is a symbol of the pilgrim's existence and his aspirations, or donating money.

In religious pilgrimages on foot, other features can be identified, particularly physical weariness and the influence of the landscape. The natural environment is of importance to pilgrims travelling on foot. Pilgrims state that the beauty of nature helps them to find or renew their relationship with God. Landscape changes can influence the experiences of their journeys. Many natural elements became particular symbols that can be identified by the pilgrims, such as a scenic landscape or spectacular natural objects (Liutikas 2003).

A clear disparity concerning the hardship of the journey exists between modern and traditional pilgrimage. Hardship is one defining element of a pilgrimage and, thus, traditional pilgrimage needs to contain a challenging physical element. Moreover, despite the sense of freedom that religious pilgrims experience on the pilgrimage, in practice they are happy to conform to many restrictions. Pilgrims regard these restrictions as a personal choice because they agree to abide by them when they decide to participate:

> Pilgrimage is particular offering, penance. The hardship is normal in it, your have to conquer yourself, your privation, all your discomforts and troubles. Your need to live through these things, and to sacrifice for God. And through it you get over your corporeality.
>
> (Male pilgrim, 39 years old)

However hardship is not necessary, and may even be unpleasant, for modern pilgrims. Perhaps as a consequence, travelling by foot, which is a common form of religious pilgrimage, is not the principal means of travelling to reach places of modern secular pilgrimage.

The research revealed other behavioural features typical of religious pilgrims at the destination. For example, half of the religious Catholic pilgrims receive the Holy Sacrament (Communion), one third donate to the Church, community or unfortunates, and a quarter partake in the Sacrament of Confession (Table 3.4).

The atmosphere of a modern pilgrimage is secular, resembling a tourist journey. At the destination point, pilgrims carry out different rituals which vary depending on the visited place, as well as the pilgrims' knowledge and experience. Thus, for

Table 3.4 Behaviour of religious Catholic pilgrims at destination place (%)

Feature of behaviour	*Confession of sins*	*Donation for Church, community, unfortunates*	*Going for Holy Sacrament*	*Buying religious souvenirs*
Always	26	35	51	16
Normally	32	29	21	37
Rarely	27	26	14	32
Never or not answered to the question	15	10	14	15

example, sports fans with national flags, symbols of their team, special clothing and, perhaps, travelling to distant places, share a number of similar rituals with religious pilgrims. For instance, the identity of sports fans is emphasised by the demonstration of particular clothing, slogans on banners, chants and so on.

At the same time, however, the rituals of a modern pilgrimage are looser, typically manifested in more individuality and most frequently without uniform structure and form. Both modern and religious pilgrims bring souvenirs and symbols of devotion from the journey, which are not only signs reminding them of the sights they have seen but also a confirmation to their friends that they have indeed visited that place and carried out the valuistic journey. Such souvenirs help in marking the change of the status of the person, their becoming an experienced traveller who has carried out a pilgrimage. Additionally, both religious and modern pilgrims take photographs of themselves, framing the extraordinary experience.

Social relations and the satisfaction of social needs during the journey are also of importance to both pilgrims and tourists. Such journeys provide a sense of community or *communitas*, thereby helping individuals to realise their hope or need for social interaction and togetherness. Family values can also be an incentive to carry out a valuistic journey; such a journey provides an opportunity to spend more time with family members. There can be no doubt that travellers on a valuistic journey become related to each other through a unifying experience and the sharing of common values. The community of the journey also creates an emotional link to the broader community (for example, all Catholics, all fans of the team, the nation). In such a journey, both social and self-conscious identity is consolidated because (particularly in the case of a successful journey), the participants' self-respect increases.

However, in contemporary culture, the formation of identity has come to be closely linked with the consumption of material and cultural goods. Pilgrimage itself and the pilgrim community may be considered as one commodity among many competing in the religious market. Indeed, Bauman (2001: 151) claims that identity owes the attention it attracts and the passions it stimulates to being a surrogate of community: of that allegedly 'natural home' which is no longer available in the rapidly privatised and individualised, rapidly globalising world.

Nevertheless, the outcomes of the research undertaken by the author contradict this argument. In a valuistic journey, the unifying experience and common values bring travellers together. The sense of community and solidarity experienced during the journey plays an important role in the experience of its participants. This creates conditions for the participants in valuistic journeys not only to satisfy their social needs but also, through establishing new social relations, to construct their own personal identity.

More specifically, if travelling takes place in an organised group, communication with other participants of the journey is inevitable. This communication, as well as shared experiences, allows travellers to develop and maintain a temporary community in which uniform identity manifests itself and where social differentiation and inequality disappear. According to Turner and Turner (1978), the group of pilgrims becomes a certain temporary community (*communitas*), a sense of social togetherness and equality experienced in unstructured or liminal contexts which is outside the general norms of society. Relationships between the participants of the journey, which typically reject traditional social markers, play an important role in their experience.

Fellowship and the collective experience have a huge significance in pilgrimages:

> The travelling ... when group of people go in an enclosed bus, if it's true these people have the same goal, the same faith ... they can share the experience of the faith and in this sharing a lot of things are uncovered personally.
>
> (Male pilgrim, 39 years old)

A religious community creates a memorable experience centred on religious doctrine and practice. Throughout the pilgrimage, participants' identity as believers of the same religion is validated and reinforced. According to Turner and Turner (1978), pilgrimage offers the liminal phase experienced in rites of passage. It liberates the individual from the obligatory everyday constraints of status and role and it equalises the status of participants during the ordeal. But, since pilgrimage is voluntary and not obligatory, Turner and Turner (1978) locate this social mechanism in the context of 'open' phenomena rather than the liminal. These theoretical considerations pertain to both types of pilgrimage.

Morinis (1992: 17) stresses that the interaction of individuals within their given structure of physical and psychological responses and cultural frameworks that incorporate a meaningful code, serves to induce specific, direct experiences. Communication with co-travellers and the non-trivial natural and cultural environment bring about a transcendent, emotional experience.

Therefore, four basic experiences of valuistic travellers going in organised groups can be identified:

1 *The experience of travelling.* A valuistic journey is about travelling in space and time for something in particular (to visit or experience a place or event). The journey has particular external and internal aims. These journeys also denote a breaking out of routine and liberation from everyday life.

2 *The experience of identity manifestation.* Identity is the perception of the self on both social and personal (self-consciousness) levels, with self-description and distinguishing factors enabling self-identification to arise in particular situations. A valuistic journey allows the expression of personal and social identity, both confirming and demonstrating it.
3 *The experience of community.* Pilgrims become aware that they are temporarily entering and becoming a member of the group which they are in *communitas* with. They imagine they are part of a greater community than they were before. Other members of the group influence their thoughts and behaviour. They go together, sharing common feelings and differences. They arrive together at the destination and then return transformed and enriched from a shared experience.
4 *The experience of the transcendent.* Encountering the divine, with enhanced consciousness of identity and in a state of high emotion, pilgrims are at the level of the transcendent. Transcendent experiences occur during the rituals close to their hearts, shared with fellow travellers and with a sense of sacredness; valuistic travellers say they are touched by 'something'.

Conclusions

Following a review of differing theoretical positions with respect to pilgrimage and having explored the outcomes of the empirical research, the following conclusions may be drawn.

An individual travelling in space with his/her personal valuistic attitudes, identity and motivation is one of the key elements of the journey. Therefore, for the purposes of this chapter, journeys are considered to be the context or place of the demonstration of these attitudes and the personal or social self. Having analysed the concept of tourism and journeys, and based on the objective of the journey and motives of the travellers, we can divide all journeys into three major groups: (1) recreational and cognitive journeys (described as tourist journeys in the vast majority of media and some academic writings); (2) valuistic journeys (pilgrimages); and (3) necessary and instrumental journeys (business trips, travelling for medical treatment and so on).

A valuistic journey is a journey carried out within a particular geographical space that expresses values and personal or social identity. The values fostered by valuistic travellers can be related to religion or the search for a personal spiritual path or embody national, cultural or other collective ideals, or they may be unique to the individual. The clearly defined model of the concept of a pilgrimage allows for the identification of two major groups of valuistic journeys: a traditional (religious) pilgrimage and a modern (unrelated to religion) pilgrimage.

From the evaluation of essential elements of the concept of a valuistic journey, four major features of such a journey can be identified:

1 a clearly expressed geographical destination of the journey, which embodies a certain value;

2. valuistic motives of the journey, internal attitudes impelling one to carry out the journey;
3. a strongly expressed link between the journey and the identity of the traveller, where the journey is an expression of personal or social identity or search for this identity; and
4. specific behaviour during the journey and at the destination point characterised by typical rites or models of behaviour.

The identification of the major elements that comprise a journey enables a complex and comprehensive analysis of the features of valuistic journeys. The following elements can be identified: a person expressing religious, national, cultural or sports fan identity, travelling from a home environment to a place of valuistic ideal and the geographical place itself, which embodies a certain value (from the cultural, symbolic and spatial point of view).

The motives for valuistic journeys depend on many things, the most important of which are the life experience of pilgrims, their lifestyle, and social and cultural influences. From the factor analysis of the motives and values of pilgrims during a journey, we can distinguish one of the four models of the concept of a journey which is characteristic of both modern and religious pilgrims. A journey is considered as: (1) a way of spending leisure time; (2) an expression of values (religious or secular); (3) an opportunity for inner change; and (4), an instrument for seeking other objectives.

Not all the participants of valuistic journeys pursue valuistic motivations. It should be noted that most (90 per cent) religious pilgrims emphasise the valuistic aspect of the journey, as do half of sports fans. Conversely, most of the cultural pilgrims who participated in the research consider a journey to be entertainment or a way of spending leisure time.

The constituent components of the specific behaviour model of pilgrims were identified during the research. Willingness to give meaning to the destination is characteristic of valuistic travellers (leaving inscribed petitions, votive amulets, candles, souvenirs, and so on) as is the carrying out of certain rituals. General rituals of religious practice – prayer, daily participation in Holy Mass or Confession – acquire particular significance during traditional religious pilgrimages. The identity of sports fans is emphasised by the demonstration of specific clothing and attributes, chants and so on.

The analysis of group pilgrimages reveals similarities in the experiences of travelling itself, the manifestation of identity, the sense of community and the feeling of transcendence. It is important to note the significance of the experience of community during the journey and at the destination. In a valuistic journey, unifying experiences and common values bring travellers together. The group of pilgrims becomes a temporary community which is outside the common norms of society. This creates the conditions for participants of valuistic journeys not only to satisfy their social needs but also, through establishing new social relations, to construct their own personal or social identities.

Part II

Understanding dark tourism experiences

Since the publication of Lennon and Foley's (2000) seminal work, though it was not first to coin the term 'dark tourism' – the same authors used the term in an earlier work (Foley and Lennon 1996) – the concept of dark tourism has attracted ever-increasing attention, not only within tourism studies but also in related disciplines and areas of study, from museum management to, perhaps not surprisingly, the academic study of death and dying. Numerous papers now explore the phenomenon from a variety of perspectives whilst, in a previous volume focusing on the tourist experience (Sharpley and Stone 2011b), there appear a number of chapters selected from one of the most popular themes (dark tourism) at the conference upon which that book was based. Nevertheless, it is probably true to say that, in some respects, knowledge and understanding of what is arguably becoming an over-used term (or, at least, an over-applied description of a specific form of tourism) still remains limited, though this may simply reflect the diversity of contexts to which the concept of dark tourism is of relevance. In particular, attention continues to be paid more to a supply perspective, whether identifying forms of tourism that can be described as 'dark' or considering more specific issues, such as the influence of political ideology, the ethics of displaying or 'promoting' the dead, or site management issues. Conversely, and as noted by Sharpley and Stone (2009a), rather less attention continues to be paid to behavioural, motivational or, more broadly, experiential aspects of dark tourism.

Therefore, the chapters in this section make an additional contribution to this less represented perspective on dark tourism. In Chapter 4, Avital Biran and Yaniv Poria set out to challenge what they consider to remain a fragmented and poorly conceptualised concept, asking whether in fact the innumerable sites and attractions labelled as 'dark' have anything in common. Concluding from a review of the contemporary dark tourism literature that our understanding is limited and contradictory, they argue that it is necessary to consider the notion of 'dark' experiences from a broader perspective, not necessarily related specifically to death. In so doing, they suggest that such touristic experiences are those which may be thought of as socially 'deviant', thus de-articulating dark tourism experiences from the specific context of places, sites and attractions associated with death and dying.

In Chapter 5, Philip R. Stone builds on previous work concerned with the thanatological dimensions of dark tourism experiences by exploring the ways in which visitors experience the 'traumascape' of New York's Ground Zero. Following a review of the events of 9/11 and the subsequent creation of Ground Zero as an arena of potential conflict between memory/mourning and its touristic consumption, he considers the outcome of empirical research undertaken amongst visitors to the site. Specifically, he suggests that, through their experiences of Ground Zero, visitors are able to develop what he refers to as 'mortality capital'; that is, through contemplating the death of others, visitors to Ground Zero achieve a form of capital which they can draw on to aid their own thanatopsis.

In the last chapter in this section, Richard Sharpley attempts to refute the claim that tourists who visit sites of genocide are nothing more than voyeurs gazing on the suffering and tragedy of others (Schaller 2007). Focusing on the Rwandan genocide, he explores the reactions and experiences of tourists visiting three of the principal sites that commemorate the victims of that genocide through an analysis of their web-based (blog) accounts. The research reveals not only that many, if not all tourists are drawn to these sites not by a ghoulish fascination but for a variety of 'positive' reasons, but that the experience elicits powerful emotions, the strength of which vary by the manner in which the genocide is depicted and interpreted. In particular, many tourists are left with a sense of hope for the future of the country.

4 Reconceptualising dark tourism

Avital Biran and Yaniv Poria

Introduction

Alongside the growing fascination of tourists and researchers alike with visits to sites associated with death and atrocity (Stone and Sharpley 2008), different terms (for example, black spots tourism, thanatourism or morbid tourism) have been keyed in the attempt to describe, define and conceptualise this social phenomenon. Scholars have commonly adopted the term 'dark tourism', first coined by Foley and Lennon (1996) (see for example, Cohen 2010; Mowatt and Chancellor 2011). Nevertheless, the common usage of this term does not suggest the existence of an accepted definition of this social phenomenon. Moreover, there is a general agreement that dark tourism still remains 'theoretically fragile' (Stone and Sharpley 2008: 575) and 'poorly conceptualized' (Jamal and Lelo 2011: 31). In line with Seaton and Lennon's (2004) observation that there are more questions than answers in relation to dark tourism, this chapter raises again the question of 'what is dark tourism?' (Jamal and Lelo 2011: 31). We attempt to challenge the current approach to dark tourism, asking whether experiences considered to be dark tourism, such as visits to Holocaust or slavery-related sites (Miles 2002; Dann and Seaton 2001), the favela of Rio de Janeiro (Robb 2009), Jack the Ripper walks in London (Stone 2006) and the Body Worlds exhibition (Stone 2011a) indeed have something in common?

The difficultly in conceptualising and defining dark tourism as a new and distinct tourism sub-group is not unique to this phenomenon. As disciplines develop and the level of research grows, a subject matter is often divided into sub-fields of interests (Poria *et al.* 2001, 2004). In the social sciences, disciplines such as geography, psychology and sociology have developed sub-fields or sub-groups which reflect sectorial divisions within the discipline. This growing disciplinary subdivision may, on the one hand, reflect the development of research and knowledge about a particular field. Yet, on the other hand, such subdivision may indicate uncertainty and a lack of conceptual development within the field. Such a situation may be particularly true in the context of academic tourism research which has been subject to rapid fragmentation (Poria *et al.* 2001). As long as two decades ago, Boyd (1991) identified over 100 tourism sub-groups, and more have appeared since then. These range from well recognised sub-groups, such as urban tourism and nature tourism, to more specific ones, such as cycle tourism and, as discussed here, dark tourism. Some of these sub-groups relate to a general area of interest while others to specific activities or behaviours.

Nevertheless, researchers need to consider whether such fragmentation serves academic purposes and contributes towards better understanding of tourism or, rather, indicates a lack of common theoretical ground. Are current studies able to distinguish dark tourism from other tourism types? Can they distinguish dark tourism from heritage tourism, historic tourism or other special interest tourism? Are visits to Auschwitz and Dracula tourism attractions part of the same social experience? As indicated later, we do not contend that dark tourism does not exist, but rather that the theoretical justification for the identification of this sub-group is limited (as has been mentioned by Stone 2011a). This limitation, in turn, leads to a simplistic understanding of tourism, dark tourism, and the tourist experience.

Thus, this chapter aims to enhance the theoretical conceptualisation of dark tourism. To do so the chapter commences with a discussion of the concepts of dark and darkness, followed by a review of the different approaches evident in the literature to the understanding of dark tourism. Finally, drawing on the post-modernist move in tourism research which emphasises the subjective and individual tourist's experience (Collins-Kreiner 2010; Uriely *et al.* 2011) as well as on Stone and Sharpley's (2008) thanatological framework, an attempt is made to offer an alternative approach to the conceptualisation of dark tourism. This attempt indeed differentiates dark tourism from other tourism sub-groups.

Lost in the dark

Drawing on the understanding that dark tourism is essentially 'tourism about darkness' (Hepburn 2010: 133), several authors have pointed to the need to step back and first clarify the notion of dark (or darkness) itself (for example, Bowman and Pezzullo 2009; Jamal and Lelo 2011). In particular, several issues are noteworthy as they reflect the complexity of conceptualising dark tourism.

The first and most apparent issue is the negative association attached to the term 'dark' or 'darkness', mainly in western cultures. Bowman and Pezzullo (2009: 190), for example, note that the notion of dark implies 'something disturbing, troubling, suspicious, weird, morbid, or perverse'. This negative connotation is reflected, for example, in the anxiety and moral panic reported over the practice of dark tourism (Stone 2009a; Lennon and Foley 2000; Seaton and Lennon 2004). Additionally, studies focusing on the dark tourism visitor experience have highlighted negative emotions such as rage and discomfort (Montes and Butler 2008), fear, horror, sadness, depression, and feelings of vengeance (Krakover 2005; Miles 2002) that are associated with visits to dark sites. Yet, while in purely linguistic terms, the word 'dark' is understood as 'devoid of light' (Bowman and Pezzullo 2009: 188), studies indicate that visits to such sites often lead to enlightened experiences with positive benefits, such as remembrance and commemoration, spiritual experience, demonstration and construction of one's identity or educational experiences (Austin 2002; Biran *et al.* 2011; Logan and Reeves 2009; Slade 2003). Additionally, Sharpley (2005) suggests that individuals visiting the graves of famous people, such as Jim Morrison or Elvis Presley, are interested in those people's lives and artistic creations rather than their deaths.

Second, and building on the above discussion, the idea that some forms of dark tourism may not be considered as dark suggests that darkness is a socially constructed concept (Jamal and Lelo 2011; Stone 2011c). For example, Jamal and Lelo (2011) ask provocatively whether a person attending a memorial service for a dead relative is a dark tourist. Similarly, one might ask whether a western tourist traveling to watch the Tibetan funerary practice of sky burial (in which the body of the dead is dissected and left for animals to feed on) is a dark tourist. Pezzullo (2009b) raises an additional challenging question when he ponders whether individuals volunteering to help in the aftermath of Hurricane Katrina are disaster tourists (see also Chapter 10 in this volume). These examples point to the importance of the social context in the construction of death and darkness in understanding the visitor experience at dark sites. In that context, Jamal and Lelo (2011), as well as Stone (2011c), have highlighted the need to consider the individual's racial, ethnic, or cultural background. Stone and Sharpley (2008) further suggest that dark tourism should be understood in light of the role of death in contemporary society. An outcome of these notions is the idea that while some may perceive visits to death-related sites as dark, others may not view them as such.

Finally, the literature review also highlights the variety of events and places that are considered dark. Studies have not focused solely on sites *of* death, disaster and depravity but also on sites *associated with* death, disaster and depravity (Miles 2002). For example, studies of dark sites broadly range from genocide sites such as Auschwitz-Birkenau (Miles 2002; Lennon and Foley 2000) and the death camps of Cambodia and Rwanda (Stone 2006; see also Chapter 6 in this volume) to plantation sites (Jamal and Lelo 2011; Dann and Seaton 2001) and Jack the Ripper walks in London (Stone 2006). In line with the variety of sites considered as dark, Robb (2009) broadens the definition of darkness to include destinations in which violence (rather than death per se) is the main attraction. Similarly, Jamal and Lelo (2011) suggest that the notion of darkness, and subsequently dark tourism, should be widened to include not only death but also other 'dark events' (Jamal and Lelo 2011: 40) such as segregation, crime, and war. Adopting such a wider understanding of dark tourism, scholars also include activities such as visits to Rio de Janeiro's favela (Robb 2009) and even bungee jumping and sky-diving, which put participants at risk of death (Bowman and Pezzullo 2009). Such examples imply that even activities and behaviours which are not necessarily associated with death may be considered dark.

To conclude, the above discussion highlights some of the difficulties and contradictions inherent in the current understanding of the term 'dark' and their possible implications for the understanding of dark tourism. Specifically, the conflict between the negative association and potential positive benefits of dark tourism, the recognition that the understanding of what is dark (or not) is socially constructed and subjectively determined, as well as the current use of the term 'dark' as an umbrella term to include many aspects of human behaviour and social life, rather than death per se, all serve to complicate the application of the adjective 'dark' to tourism. These observations suggest that what is currently understood as dark tourism may not always be dark, and that dark behaviours which do not involve death may be considered as dark tourism.

Deconstructing dark tourism

Numerous attempts have been made to define or conceptualise the phenomenon of visits to death-related sites. A review of the literature reveals two main approaches (supply and demand) that have been adopted in the attempts to understand dark tourism.

For the most part, present research has undertaken a supply perspective to the definition of dark tourism (Seaton and Lennon 2004). Lennon and Foley (2000), for example, perceive dark tourism as visits to sites associated with death, disaster, and depravity. Similarly, Stone defines dark tourism as 'the act of travel to sites associated with death, suffering and the seemingly macabre' (Stone 2006: 146). As reflected in these definitions, the supply perspective adopts a descriptive understanding (Apostolakis 2003), emphasising the individual's presence in spaces associated with death. This line of thought has led to an eclectic collection of studies exploring a diversity of death-related sites and experiences, all considered to be part of dark tourism. These experiences range from visits to *lightest*-entertainment and commercially oriented 'dark fun factories' (Stone 2006: 152) to *darkest* visits to sites of death and suffering characterised by higher political and ideological influences, offering education-oriented experience (Stone 2006).

While providing a starting point to the understanding of dark tourism, this approach leads to increasing dilution and lack of clarity (Sharpley 2009b). One could claim that this array of experiences challenges the actual existence of dark tourism as it seems that visits to any site that has something to do with death and suffering, even the weakest association, is considered as dark tourism. Dale and Robinson (2011), for instance, suggest that Las Vegas hotels, such as Caesar's Palace and Luxor (which Disneyfy death and suffering), are also examples of dark sites. So, is everything and anything dark tourism? Are the *darkest sites* noted by Stone (2006) not hosting heritage experiences? Can the supply approach differentiate between heritage tourism and dark tourism, for example? This descriptive approach arbitrarily combines different experiences, while ignoring the diversity of the individual's inner experiences and motives. Surely, the experience sought by tourists at death theme parks, such as the London Dungeon, might be different from the experience sought by tourists at the Hiroshima Peace Memorial. Moreover, studies indicate that visitors to the same site have different experiences (Austin 2002; Biran *et al.* 2011; Lisle 2004).

Though some scholars contend that focusing on sites' attributes alone offers a simplified understanding of (dark) tourism (Sharpley 2005, 2009b; Smith and

Croy 2005), this approach raises two meaningful issues relevant to the current attempt to conceptualise dark tourism. The first issue refers to the types of death on display. Some have suggested that dark sites do not present death per se, but particular kinds of death (Robb 2009; Stone 2011a; Walter 2009). Specifically, some have highlighted the focus of dark tourism on sudden and particularly violent death rather than 'everyday death' (for example, from stroke or cancer). Rojek (1993) who discussed the concept of dark attraction under the notion of 'Black Spots', considers examples such as sightseers flocking to the crash site of Pan Am flight 103 in Lockerbie, which was destroyed in a terrorist bomb attack, the annual pilgrimage to the site of James Dean's car crash, and the John F. Kennedy assassination anniversary. Additionally, as Walter (2009) claims, tourists do not tour psycho-geriatric hospitals or nursing homes where many people (in the western world) may end up dying. Walter (2009) also suggests that the death and suffering presented in dark sites are those, such as slavery or racism, which challenge the collective narrative of nation and modernity and raise questions such as 'How can this have happened?' Yet, it should be noted that Stone (2011a) highlights the appeal of everyday death, reflected for example in Body Worlds, an exhibition which displays cadavers of people who died due to smoking and alcohol consumption-related diseases.

The other issue highlights the timeframe in which the death on display has occurred. Robb (2009) contends that dark sites range from historical sites of atrocity which provide experiences from simply presenting past atrocities to re-enactments of past violence (for example, participation in a mock deportation at Stalin World in Lithuania, or re-enactments of the JFK assassination) to visits to sites where violence is still present, such as the slums of Rio de Janeiro. Drawing on Robb (2009), one can argue that sites which present past events of death and violence, such as Alcatraz, slavery sites, the Dungeon experience or torture museums, may be considered as socially acceptable. However, for example, traveling to watch a public execution or going to a hospital to watch dying people is generally not viewed as appropriate (at least not in most western societies).

The discussion about the type of death on display and its relation to the past or present not only highlights the variety of sites and activities classified as dark tourism under the supply perspective, but particularly suggests that while some types of death and violence are considered appropriate for the tourist's gaze (mainly unique death, occurring in past times), some forms of death are not considered appropriate and may even be deemed socially unacceptable (particularly, the present and everyday death). As will be discussed in the following sections, this notion is imperative to our attempt to reconceptualise dark tourism.

The second approach evident in the literature regarding the conceptualisation of dark tourism is the demand-oriented perspective, where dark tourism is defined in terms of visit motivation. This approach follows the common use of motivation as a means for defining and differentiating tourism sub-groups (McCain and Ray 2003). Indeed, Stone and Sharpley (2008) highlight that investigating why tourists are drawn to death-related sites or experiences is imperative to the understanding of dark tourism. As such, much attention has been devoted to tourists' motivation to engage in dark tourism (Stone and Sharpley 2008; Wight 2005). Given the wide range of sites classified as dark, the literature proposes diverse reasons for such visits. Dann (1998) suggests a comprehensive list of eight motives including: desire to overcome phantoms (childhood fears), search for novelty, nostalgia, celebration of crime and deviance, basic bloodlust and tourists' interest in challenging their sense of mortality. Seaton and Lennon (2004) identify two main motives: *Schadenfreude*, meaning pleasure in viewing the misfortune of others; and the contemplation of death. Ashworth (2002) emphasises motives as satisfying curiosity about the unusual, being entertained by horrific occurrences and the suffering of others, empathic identification (either with the victims or perpetrators), and, similar to heritage tourism, seeking of self-identification and understanding. In a later study, Ashworth (2004) notes that motives range from pilgrimage, identity search, search for knowledge, a sense of social responsibility (that is, lest we forget, never again) to darker and less 'politically correct' motives such as interest and indulgence in violence and suffering.

A prominent definition of dark tourism is that provided by Seaton who proposes that dark tourism is essentially a behavioural phenomenon 'wholly, or partially, motivated by the desire for actual or symbolic encounters with death' (Seaton 1996: 240). Seaton (1996) further argues that visitors' motivations exist on a continuum of intensity according to (a) whether interest in death is the single motivator or exists among other motivations and (b) the degree to which the interest in death is person specific (the dead is known to and valued by the visitor) or generalised (fascination with death is irrespective of the dead person or persons involved but rather focuses on the scale or form of the death). Hence, for example, a visit to the natural disaster site of Phuket, Thailand, in the aftermath of the tsunami (Rittichainuwat 2008) by a visitor who is not related to a victim is a 'more pure' (or darker) form of dark tourism. On the other end of the continuum, a visit to this site to commemorate a dead relative is classified as having a weak thanatourism element.

As reflected in Seaton's definition, the demand-oriented approach follows a hidden assumption that the presence of tourists at death-related sites reflects, at least to some degree, thanatouristic motives (Slade 2003). This approach overlooks the possibility that the reasons for visiting and the sought experiences at such sites might be completely devoid of interest in death. As noted by Seaton and Lennon (2004) and Wight (2005), one possible reason for this view could be attributed to the fact that the motives identified have often been drawn from theoretical research. In contrast, recent studies that adopt an empirical epistemology indicate a diversity of motives, not necessarily associated with death. Rittichainuwat (2008), exploring Thais' and Scandinavians' motivation in visiting Phuket in the aftermath of the tsunami, notes that most tourists were motivated by a willingness to help the recovery activities and the beautiful natural scenery. More recently, Thi Le and Pearce (2011: 461), focusing on the DMZ (demilitarised zone) battlefield in Vietnam, suggest that most visitors 'do not come across as particularly "dark" tourists' as they are mainly motivated by personal involvement, education, and novelty-seeking as well as convenience (that is, the site is located near or on the way to other tourist attractions). Similarly, in the context of Gallipoli, Hyde and Harman (2011) suggest visitors engage in a secular pilgrimage and leisure experience rather than a dark one, motivated by spiritual, nationalistic, family, friendship and 'must do' reasons.

As evident from the discussion in the literature, two main standpoints exist about tourist motivations to visit dark sites. On the one hand, there are those advocating the key role of fascination with death and dying (Ashworth 2004; Dann 1998; Seaton 1996). In line with this perspective, the engagement with dark tourism stems from less socially acceptable or politically incorrect motives, for example, the pleasure of viewing the misfortune of others, bloodlust, gore fascination. This approach regards dark tourism as a 'sectional pathology' (Seaton and Lennon 2004: 68), seeing it as a deviant or perverse behaviour. On the other hand, the second perspective emphasises a variety of motives for visiting, particularly highlighting that these reasons may be devoid of an interest in death (Biran *et al.* 2011; Hyde and Harman 2011; Slade 2003). The motives revealed under this notion are similar to those of visiting a 'regular', not-dark, heritage tourism attraction (Biran *et al.* 2011; Kang *et al.* 2011) or other special interest tourist attractions (Thi Le and Pearce 2011). This approach highlights the existence of socially acceptable motives and visiting experiences, such as visits to Holocaust sites (for example, Anne Frank's house in Amsterdam), war memorials (the Korean War Memorial in Washington) and battlefields (the site of the Battle of Waterloo in Belgium). It should be noted, of course, that some scholars have argued that a fascination with death or ghoulish curiosity were not revealed in empirical research owing to participants' reluctance to reveal or admit socially unacceptable emotions and motives (Ashworth 2004; Mannell and Kleiber 1997).

Towards a reconceptualisation of dark tourism

In contrast to the previously mentioned supply and demand approaches, which highlight the site's attributes or the tourist's motives, others have argued that a conceptualisation of dark tourism requires a more holistic view, one which clarifies the tourist experience (Biran *et al.* 2011; Seaton and Lennon 2004; Stone 2009a, 2009b, 2010a, 2011c; Wight 2005). This notion points to the first pillar of the reconceptualisation suggested here, namely the need for adopting an *experiential approach* (Apostolakis 2003) to the understanding of dark tourism. Specifically, this approach captures the experience as an interactive process involving both the visitor and the site's attributes (that is, an integrated supply–demand perspective), highlighting the symbolic meaning of the site. The experiential approach is consistent with the postmodernist move in tourism research which characterises the current development of a tourism body of knowledge (Belhassen *et al.* 2008). This approach stresses the diverse nature of the tourist experience and shifts the attention from the displayed objects to the visitors' subjective construction of the experience (Collins-Kreiner 2010; Uriely 2005).

Apart from a few notable exceptions, only limited attention has been given to the tourist experience in current attempts to conceptualise dark tourism. The most evident example is Sharpley (2005; also 2009b) who, in a conceptual paper, calls for clarifying the links between the site's attributes and the experience sought based on the extent to which tourists are motivated by fascination with death and the extent to which the site was initially created to satisfy that fascination and profit from it. Based on this, Sharpley (2005, 2009b) has identified four 'shades' of dark tourism experiences (black, pale, grey tourism demand and grey tourism supply), whereby black tourism represents a 'pure' dark tourism experience in which fascination with death is satisfied by purposeful supply (intentionally created to satisfy this fascination and profit from it). Thus, while narrowing the scope of dark tourism, Sharpley (2005, 2009b) stresses the possible existence of different experiences at death-related sites. Furthermore, and highly important for this study, he states that 'many forms of alleged dark tourism experiences are, in fact, alternative experiences' (Sharpley 2005: 226).

More recently and in line with the fact that many newly recognized dark sites are also often considered as heritage sites, Biran *et al.* (2011) have drawn on the experiential approach to further clarify tourist experiences at Auschwitz-Birkenau, the death camp considered to be the epitome of dark tourism. This approach emphasises the tourist's perception of the site (rather than the objective site's attributes) as a key element in understanding the tourist experience (Apostolakis 2003; Timothy and Boyd 2003). Specifically, Biran *et al.* (2011) base their study on literature which points to a link between one's perception of the site as personal heritage and a variety of behaviours, such as overall motivation to visit, specific reasons for the visit, satisfaction with the visit, willingness to revisit and preferences towards on-site interpretation (Poria *et al.* 2003, 2006); as well as studies which highlight the importance of the personal meaning assigned to death-related sites (Lisle 2004; Muzaini *et al.* 2007). Their findings indicate that whereas those who perceive the displayed heritage as personal are mainly interested in an emotional experience, those who do not mainly seek an educational experience. More importantly, these findings suggest that rather than being a tool for satisfying curiosity about death and dying, tourists' experiences at Auschwitz, the symbol of dark tourism, are similar to those at 'regular', non-dark heritage sites (that is, heritage tourism). This raises a question as to the existence of dark tourism. Specifically, it can be argued that the term 'dark tourism' is simply a new name for an old phenomenon (or an already existing tourism sub-group). Biran *et al.*'s 2011 study further highlights the need for a solid theoretical conceptualisation of dark tourism differentiating it from heritage tourism based on the tourist experience.

Of particular importance to the current discussion is Smith and Croy's (2005) conceptualisation of dark tourism. In line with the experiential approach, they emphasise the link between the display and the visitor, arguing that it is the *perception of the site as dark* which determines the nature of the visit experience. The proposed experiential approach, and particularly Smith and Croy's (2005) conceptualisation, draws attention to the possibility that not all visitors indeed seek or are engaged in a dark experience. This notion is supported by various studies which investigated the visit experience at dark sites. For example, studies highlight the educational experience (Austin 2002; Teye and Timothy 2004) and enjoyment of the scenery (Poria *et al.* 2004) as the core of the visit experience to such dark sites. Furthermore, studies of dark sites reveal that some tourists are not familiar with the site's attributes (Poria *et al.* 2004). As awareness is a pre-condition to perception (McClellan 1998), based on the experiential approach those visitors are, by definition, not dark tourists. Additionally, the focus on the perception of the sites as dark suggests that other sites (or behaviours) which are not necessarily associated with death per se could also be perceived as dark and yield a dark experience. Furthermore, highlighting the individual's perception of the site or activity as dark challenges the common assumption that death is necessarily dark.

An alternative conceptualisation of dark tourism

The previous sections challenged the current research practices relating to the conceptualisation of dark tourism, suggesting that it is not death or the dead that should be considered but, rather, visitors' perception of these concepts. Following the experiential approach, it is argued here that it is the individual perception of the site (or activity) as dark which is at the core of dark tourism. Namely, it is claimed that 'dark' sites and acts may not necessarily involve death per se, and death may not necessarily be dark. For example, as noted earlier, Auschwitz, considered as the darkest of dark tourism sites (Stone 2006), consists of a main-stream tourism experience – heritage tourism. This notion leads to the question raised at the beginning of this chapter, namely, what is 'dark'? Given the earlier discussion and following calls stressing the need to consider dark tourism within a wider socio-cultural context (Jamal and Lelo 2011: Stone 2011a, 2011c), we claim that 'dark' and subsequently dark tourism centres on the perverse and the socially condemned. Specifically, corresponding to Stone and Sharpley (2008) who emphasise the core role of the social construction of death in understanding dark tourism, we suggest that a wider perspective to the understanding of this phenomenon should be adopted, namely as contemplation of social norms rather than death per se.

Tourism environments allow people a break from daily routine and the opportunity to engage with deviant behaviours which may not be seen as socially acceptable if conducted in one's home environment, such as excessive drinking, smoking drugs, change in eating habits or sexual behaviour (Carr 2002; Uriely *et al.* 2011). Stebbins (1996) uses the term 'leisure deviant' to describe the existence of leisure behaviours which are, to some extent, tolerated in the home environment (for example, heavy drinking which has not turned to alcoholism, the use of light drugs). Following this notion, Uriely *et al.* (2011) suggest that tourism provides a social arena in which individuals can be involved in deviant leisure behaviours which are not viewed as legitimate and socially acceptable in one's home environment. They specifically rely on the idea that tourism is a domain of life which allows a temporary suspension of social norms and values, as it is characterised by a sense of anonymity. For example, Berdichvisky *et al.* (2010), in their study of women's sexual behaviours, indicate that tourism allows these women to engage with activities deemed as deviant and which they cannot be involved with in their normal place of residence (for example, anal sex, orgies).

However, it should be noted that deviant behaviours may lead to diverse social impacts for the individual. In this context, particularly relevant to the current conceptualisation is the notion of negative and positive deviance. Studies of deviant behaviour have largely linked it with negative reaction or social consequences (Ben-Yehuda 1990; Goode 1991). Nevertheless, it has been recognised that deviance may also lead to positive social reaction. Broadly defined, negative deviance refers to when deviation from normality is socially condemned (West 2003). Positive deviance is defined as when different (from normality) forms of behaviours bring about positive sanctions (Dodge 1985). Positive deviance figures or behaviours include those of saints, traditional heroes and geniuses, and positive and negative deviance may be thought of as existing on a continuum (West 2003).

We argue that, while dark tourism may be linked to death and violence, at its core are negative deviant behaviours in which one cannot engage (or even talk about) in one's home environments (as this will lead to social punishment), unless it is done 'in the dark' – hidden from one's home environment. Being involved in such deviant behaviours may trigger a sense of doing 'something wrong' or immoral and raise emotions of shame and embarrassment. It should be noted that this explanation is not valid for positive deviant behaviours. Tourists will not be afraid to inform those back home of their involvement in such positive deviant behaviours as they do not carry the threat of social punishment, and may even be praised.

Thus, dark tourism may involve activities or visits to sites, either associated with death or not, which the individual will avoid engaging in publicly or talking about in his/her home environment (see Figure 4.1 below). One example may be a person from the UK, a country which does not have the death penalty, who travels to watch a public execution. A western person travelling to China to eat dog meat or a monkey brain, or a very observant Jew or Muslim who travels to Europe to eat pork meat, may similarly be considered as a dark tourist. On the other hand, activities such as visits to dark sites like Auschwitz or the genocide camps of Rwanda and Cambodia may not lead to social punishment, as visiting such sites is not considered as deviant (or dark). Such visits may even be encouraged and socially rewarded, as they are seen both as educational and as commemoration of those murdered. For example, different agencies in Israel offer financial support to youths whose families cannot afford to pay for their children to travel to Auschwitz with the annual school trip. Similarly, participation in the Day of the Death Celebration in Mexico, in which family and friends remember their dead, is not regarded as a dark activity but rather a cultural tourism experience as it has no deviant components. Engaging in such an activity as a tourist is not likely to be associated with feelings of shame or have negative social impacts. The tourist is not at risk of being socially punished when talking about such experiences in his/her home environment. Thus, the conceptualisation proposed here considers the individuals' perception of their home social environment, the social context of the destination, the tourist's individual character and his/her dialogue with the social world. Namely, the same behaviour may be considered by one person as deviant and not by another, even in the same society, due to social or personal differences.

In line with the notion of positive–negative deviance, it is argued that visits to sites of death and violence range from positive to negative forms of deviance (see Figure 4.1). For example, in terms of positive deviance, a person visiting New Orleans or Phuket aiming to help the rescue and recovery activities following the disaster is likely to be seen as a hero and will be socially praised. On the other hand, a person travelling to watch a public execution or to experience cannibalism in another country would probably be considered a freak (that is, a negative deviance form of visiting death-related activities). It should be noted that nowadays, due to on-going legislative efforts, some negative deviant tourist behaviours (which are legal at the tourist destination) may involve legal punishment in the tourist's home country. For example, tourists have already been legally tried and penalised by their home country for engaging in child sex in another country (Ambrosie 2010). In the continuum between positive and negative deviant tourist behaviour, we can find visits to death-related sites and behaviours which are not seen as deviation from the norm. Stone (2006), for example, suggests that the London Dungeon offers a socially acceptable environment to gaze upon death and suffering. Similarly, visits to conflict sites such as battlefields, genocide camps such as those of the Holocaust and former sites of slavery are considered common and socially acceptable (even encouraged) tourism practices. Visits to such sites should, thus, be seen as heritage or educational experiences at sites associated with death, rather than dark tourist experiences. In line

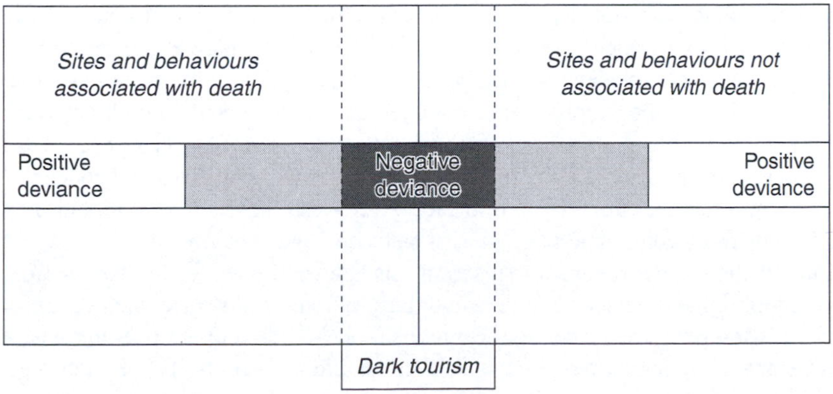

Figure 4.1 Alternative conceptualisation of dark tourism.

with this framework, we contend that dark tourism would then relate to visits to sites of death and violence in which the visitors are involved in negative deviant behaviours.

The approach to dark tourism suggested here corresponds with the notion previously highlighted suggesting that 'dark' may not necessarily be associated with death and that visits to sites and tourist attractions which do not present death can, in fact, be considered as dark tourism. It is argued here that even common mass tourism activities could be considered as dark tourism. One such example might be travel to another destination to experience sexual activities which are socially condemned in her/his home country, such as visits to the Red Light District in Amsterdam where tourists can observe and gaze at local prostitutes. These examples further stress the need to recognise dark tourism in a social context and in line with the individual's perception.

Conclusions

As the literature about tourism grows and as more researchers explore tourism-related issues, sub-groups of tourism have emerged. As indicated here, the definitions of these sub-groups appear to rely on fairly descriptive and superficial characteristics. Such simplified definitions do not contribute to the understanding of the enormous variety of tourism experiences. In light of the current fragmentation and theoretically loose conceptualisation of dark tourism (Jamal and Lelo 2011; Stone and Sharpley 2008), this chapter has identified the need for a type of conceptualisation which will differentiate it from other types of tourism experiences, particularly heritage tourism (which often presents death and violence). We propose that dark tourism should be defined based on the relationships between the visitor and the site attributes, namely the tourist experience. Specifically, it is argued here that the conceptualisation of dark tourism should be based on visitors' perceptions of the experience as negative deviance, such as that which involves a sense of social risk in one's home environment.

The focus on the social context of one's home environment suggests that other behaviours which are not necessarily associated with death should also be perceived as dark experiences. Thus, we suggest that dark tourism is the purposeful movement to spaces displaying acts and sights, which the viewing of or participation in may lead to negative social consequences for the tourist if such activities were revealed to those in his/her home environment. While Sharpley (2005: 226) argues that dark tourism 'is a relatively rare phenomenon', the proposed conceptualisation suggests that this may not in fact be the case; that is, dark tourism may also include more communal mass tourism activities and behaviours.

Finally, the current reconceptualisation raises several lines for future research. First, it highlights the need to understand dark tourism in different socio-cultural contexts. Moreover, the current conceptualisation of dark tourism presented here is not empirically supported. Future studies should aim to clarify whether dark tourism really exists or, as we claimed at the beginning of this chapter, it is the same old wine in a new bottle.

5 Dark tourism as 'mortality capital'

The case of Ground Zero and the Significant Other Dead

Philip R. Stone

Introduction

During the Middle Ages, a journey to gaze upon relics of the saints offered the only valid excuse for leaving home (Rufus 1999). However, while religious pilgrimages to view the sacrosanct dead or sacred places associated with their life or death have been common over the centuries, in an age of (western) secularisation, a new 'secular pilgrimage' is emerging (Hyde and Harman 2011; Margry 2008b). Arguably, these new types of secular pilgrimages involve the 'darker side of travel' (Sharpley and Stone 2009a), or what has commonly become known as 'dark tourism' (Lennon and Foley 2000; Stone 2005, 2006). From visiting Auschwitz-Birkenau, to the Killing Fields of Cambodia or to Chernobyl – the site of the world's worst nuclear accident – dark tourism is 'the act of travel to sites of death, disaster or the seemingly macabre' (Stone 2006: 146). Accordingly, dark tourism as secular pilgrimage is an activity that can constitute ceremonies of life and death which, in turn, have the capacity to expand boundaries of the imagination and to provide the contemporary visitor with potentially life-changing points of shock. Indeed, dark tourism may be perceived as a rite of social passage, given its transitional elements and its potential to influence the psychology and perception of individuals (Biran *et al.* 2011). Furthermore, dark tourism occurs within liminal time and space and, as such, locates the activity within constructivist realms of meaning and meaning making (Sharpley and Stone 2009a). Therefore, dark tourism provides a lens through which life and death may be glimpsed, thus revealing relationships and consequences of the processes involved that mediate between the individual and the collective Self.

Noting the distinction between dark tourism and the processes of (secular) pilgrimage, Reader (2003: 2) suggests 'the dynamics through which people are drawn to sites redolent with images of death ... and the manner in which they are induced to behave there ... [mean] that the topic calls out for discussion'. As part of that discussion, and despite the diversity of sites across the world, dark tourism has been advocated as *not* presenting death per se, but representing *certain kinds* of death (Walter 2009). Hence, dark tourism has been referred to as a contemporary mediating institution between the living and the dead (Walter

2009). Moreover, within a thesis of death sequestration, Stone (2011b: 25) suggests that 'dark tourism provides an opportunity to contemplate death of the Self through gazing upon the Significant Other Dead'. Whilst this hypothesis may form an integral part of a complex jigsaw of consumption, there is limited empirical evidence to support such a claim (but see Stone 2011b). The purpose of this chapter, therefore, is to address this gap in dark tourism knowledge and to augment the dark tourism literature by examining new times/new dark tourism sites and studies (Stone 2011c). In short, focusing upon the thanatological condition of society, that is, secular society's reactions to and perceptions of mortality, this research examines tourist experiences within the confines of a specific 'dark shrine/dark exhibition' (Stone 2006) and in particular, visitor experiences at Ground Zero and the Tribute WTC Visitor Center, in New York, the site of the former Twin Towers that were attacked on 11 September 2001 (9/11). In so doing, it critically evaluates the location as both a cognitive space and a contested place to explore contemporary death and dying. Ultimately, the chapter sets out empirical evidence to suggest visitors to Ground Zero may mediate death and dying as well as life and living and, thus, formulate a personal and contemporaneous 'mortality capital' whereby contemplative experiences of the Significant Other Dead provide an existential mortality saliency. First, however, an overview of Ground Zero and its touristification provides a context for the study.

The (dark) touristification of Ground Zero

Immortalised by artists, filmmakers and photographers, the twin towers of the World Trade Center had dominated the Manhattan skyline since the early 1970s. Officially opened in 1973 as part of a skyscraper complex of office buildings in New York's financial district and, at the time, the world's tallest buildings at 1,368 and 1,362 feet respectively, the towers soon became pivotal in New York City's iconography. As Glanz and Lipton (2003: 234) point out:

> The twins had become one of New York City's most popular postcards. It was not just CNN that featured the towers. Almost every time movie and television directors need an *embellishment shot* [original emphasis] of New York, it was to the Twin Towers that they turned … these steel boxes, in all their severity and grandeur, had become a shorthand symbol for New York.

The atrocity on 9/11 not only resulted in mass murder, but also confirmed a semiotic loss of the iconic Twin Towers for both New York as a city and for the wider country of America. Yet, the attack on the World Trade Center on 9/11 was not the first assault on the buildings. On 26 February 1993, a terrorist car bomb exploded in the underground car park beneath the World Trade Center's North Tower, killing six people and injuring over a thousand. Ironically, a broker, Bruce Pomper, who worked in the World Trade Center complex at the time, described the 1993 attack 'like an airplane had hit the building' (Pomper, quoted in BBC 2009). In 1995, a granite memorial fountain honouring the victims was unveiled, located on the Austin J. Tobin Plaza, directly above the site of the explosion. Along with the names of the six victims, the memorial inscription simply read:

> On February 26, 1993, a bomb set by terrorists exploded below this site. This horrible act of violence killed innocent people, injured thousands, and made victims of us all.

The memorial was later destroyed in the 9/11 attacks.These are well documented and do not need to be reiterated here. Arguably, however, of all the images of 9/11, it was the catastrophic structural failing of the Twin Towers and their disintegration, transmitted instantaneously and repeated *ad infinitum* through television and Internet media, which ensured the event became indelibly imprinted into the collective consciousness. Conceivably, however, *if* the World Trade Center towers *had* remained standing and the fires had been extinguished, with a much-reduced loss of life, especially amongst emergency personnel, the (western) cultural reaction to 9/11 and the American political-military response – 'The War on Terror' – might well have been less parochial. Nevertheless, the attack on the Twin Towers, as symbols of a (western) capitalist system and as icons of America's hegemonic power, up until the buildings' collapse, meant that America's hegemony, or at least its hegemonic image, was *wounded*. Crucially though, and speculation aside, the buildings did fail and the televised spectacle of the massive Twin Towers, constructed and maintained from modern techniques, disintegrating into dust amounted no less to a *mortal wounding* to the hegemony of the United States of America. Within a very short period of the buildings' collapse, creating a perception that America was under attack (Sturken 2004), the term 'Ground Zero' was extracted from history and appropriated by the media as an idiom to describe the former World Trade Center as a site of devastation and (attempted) annihilation (Tomasky 2003). Of course, the term Ground Zero has its origins inextricably linked to the destructive power of nuclear weapons and their point of detonation. Nevertheless, the term has now entered a contemporary lexicon to mean destruction and the mortal wounding of (American) supremacy, pride and assumed innocence.

However, the term Ground Zero also conveys the idea of a starting point, or a blank canvas, which allows not only a rebuilding of the physical edifices, but also a restructuring of local, national and global narratives. As Kaplan (2003: 56) notes, 'we often use *ground zero* colloquially to convey the sense of starting from scratch, a clean slate, the bottom line', a meaning she goes on to suggest 'resonates with the often-heard claim that the world was radically altered by 9/11'. Similarly, Sturken (2004: 311) suggests the idea of Ground Zero as a blank slate that enables a set of narratives about 9/11 to be formulated: 'both the narrative that the site of Lower Manhattan is the symbolic centre of that event and the narrative that September 11 was a moment in which the United States lost its innocence'.

Therefore, in the decade since the attacks, the iconography of Ground Zero as a site of destruction has been (re)constructed in political, religious and commercial imaginations as a sacred site. Consequently, the site has been imbued with immense emotional and political investments. In turn, this has resulted in a highly contestable space. Indeed, it is has become a place inscribed with numerous meanings and roles: as a neighbourhood of New York, as a commercial district of Lower Manhattan, and as a site of national and international memory and mourning. Hence, Ground Zero is a complex space, multilayered with diverse political agendas and intertwined with notions of grief, memorialisation and commerce. At the local level, there is contestation on how to maximise the space in a compact metropolitan environment, especially in relation to commercial interests and urban design (Hajer 2005). Moreover, Ground Zero, from a 'heritage that hurts' perspective (Sather-Wagstaff 2011), is influential in projecting and affirming national identity, certainly within the global context of exporting revitalised hegemonic images of the United States of America. Crucially, however, since 2001, the 'traumascape' of Ground Zero (Tumarkin 2005) has evolved into a place where tensions in the practice of memory and mourning have become apparent, especially in relation to the aesthetics and touristic consumption of death and disaster.

Indeed, (dark) tourism that has emerged and continues to evolve at the site often, but not always, takes the form of a secular pilgrimage in which prayers are uttered, votive offerings (for example, photographs, messages or gifts) are left on fences, and relics in the form of 'kitsch' commercialised tourist souvenirs are purchased (Sturken 2007; Frow 2008; Sharpley and Stone 2009b). However, many people, including locals, scholars, cultural critics and journalists, have lamented the commercialisation of the site and of the millions of tourists who have visited the site since 9/11 – even though the Twin Towers pre-9/11 were a major tourist attraction in their own right. For instance, in the early years after the atrocity, Blair (2002: 1) writes:

> Remember when it was just hallowed ground? Ground Zero is now one of the most popular tourism attractions in the city. ... The hustle of commerce hawking to the crush of sightseers has prompted some to call it September 11 World.

The attachment of reverence to the space through a mixture of media alchemy and Hollywood simulacra means that touristic consumption of tragedy at Ground Zero is perceived, to some at least, to be of questionable social value. Moreover, pre-text 9/11 narratives (i.e. the mounting factors leading up to the attacks) and post-text 9/11 narratives (i.e. the consequences of the resultant geopolitical response) are largely lost within current tourism interpretations at the site (Stone 2010). Hence, Ground Zero has been exploited, perhaps, for mercantile advantage as well as for the creation of a national memorial and mythology. Within dominant paradigms of tourism studies, this commodification and consumption are often considered deficient in social value, meaningfulness and authenticity.

Indeed, the very terms 'tourist' and 'tourism' often denote a negativity of a highly consumerist and commodified social practice (Tribe 2009). Thus, numerous media commentaries articulate tourists at Ground Zero as incidental outsiders within a persistent discursive construction of the tourist as the savage Other (for example, see Kendle 2008). As Jan Seidler Ramirez, chief curator at the September 11 Memorial Museum, which is due to open in 2012, points out:

> people have forgotten already. Everyone has heard of September 11; they don't have a sense of it ... [for many tourists coming to Ground Zero now] September 11 is a just a bumper-sticker word to them, and that's pretty scary.
>
> (Ramirez. quoted in Luongo 2011)

Evidently then, this perspective positions tourists at Ground Zero within a rudimentary framework of serendipity or just another sight to see on the tourist itinerary (Lennon and Foley 2000). Indeed, tourists have been portrayed as merely curiosity seekers who passively gaze and consume other peoples' tragedy and pain (Cole 1999). Yet this rather naively suggests that tourists are idle spectators of sites of death and tragedy, and that dark tourism at Ground Zero is highly questionable, if not socially inappropriate. Moreover, despite problematic protestations by Sather-Wagstaff (2011) of whether tourism at Ground Zero is actually 'dark' or not, Jamal and Lelo (2011) argue the conceptual and analytic framing of *darkness* within dark tourism is socially constructed, not objective fact. Furthermore, 'it is hardly an exaggeration to suggest that in the midst of many tourism forms of life, we are in death' (Seaton 1999: 132). Therefore, tourists at Ground Zero assume a central function in constructing 'dark' tourism and, as such, play a key role in both the literal and the symbolic creation and maintenance of the (death) site. Indeed, tourists at Ground Zero are integral participative agents in the socio-cultural production, consumption, performance and, ultimately, construction of a post-9/11 narrative.

For that reason, Ground Zero *is* a dark tourism site in the sense that historical saliency or, in other words, an event that witnessed brutality and death as well as heroism and selflessness, perturbed a collective consciousness and, subsequently, has been touristically produced and consumed. Of course, many tourists will have particular motivations for visiting Ground Zero, not least those that revolve around seeing the site for real rather than through the lens of the media. However, what is more important, perhaps, and regardless of the initial motivation to visit, is the sense of feeling and meaning that such visits can engender, particularly that which focuses upon a consequential deliberation of life, death and, ultimately, mortality. The idea of thanatopsis – that is, the reflection and contemplation of death and dying – and its role within dark tourism consumption is well rehearsed within the literature (Seaton 1996, 1999; Stone and Sharpley 2008; Stone 2009c, 2011a, 2011b). Yet, Sather-Wagstaff (2011: 74), in her ethnography of Ground Zero, argues that 'thanatopsis as the acceptance of death and dying is infrequently the result that visitation to such sites engenders'.

However, and rather perplexingly, she appears to contradict her own claim that contemplation of mortality is seldom engendered by dark tourism experiences. Particularly, she comments that one of her research interviewees *did* indeed reflect upon his life and death after visiting Ground Zero:

> He reflected on how his life and possible death were so closely linked to the events, not only making the World Trade Centre a national historical site and the events of 9/11 an important moment in his nation's history but also marking the event and the aftermath as having an even deeper emotional significance to him.
>
> (Sather-Wagstaff 2011: 75)

The contradiction is continued when Sather-Wagstaff states that 'tourists *are* [emphasis added] engaging in the contemplation of death and dying and memorialising the dead, and through doing so, they are situating emotional and politicised selves in an ongoing narrative of local, national, and international tragedy and its aftermath' (2011: 76). Therefore, in order to add much needed clarity as to whether tourist experiences at Ground Zero engender a degree of thanatopsis, this chapter now turns to empirical evidence. Particularly, the chapter now reveals dark tourism at Ground Zero does indeed allow a spatial and cognitive opportunity – at least for some visitors for some of the time – to contemplate, however briefly, mortality of the Self through consuming the Other dead. First, a brief discussion of the research methodology provides a framework for subsequent empirical findings.

Research methodology

This research arises from a simple yet fundamental interest in the social reality of death, and how mortality is not only manufactured within contemporary society but also how modern death and dying are contemplated. Thus, this study adopts an inductive phenomenological research philosophy with the overall aim of better understanding the consumption of dark tourism within contemporary perspectives of death. Using ethnographic methods of (covert) participant observations and semi-structured interviews in a progressive and sequential manner, the research was conducted between 17 and 23 February 2009 within the Tribute WTC Visitor Center – located at 120 Liberty Street, Lower Manhattan, New York City – as well as in and around Liberty Street (i.e. the area known as Ground Zero). The Tribute WTC Visitor Center, a project of the September 11 Families Association, is opposite the original Twin Towers and adjacent to 'Ladder 10' fire station, which sent the first wave of fire-fighters to the World Trade Center on 9/11. The Center houses a series of exhibitions depicting the events leading up to, during and after 9/11 (Table 5.1). Additionally, the Center organises guided walking tours around the perimeter of Ground Zero, culminating in a dedicated viewing platform area that provides tourists with a panoramic view of the construction site.

Table 5.1 Description of the five permanent galleries that comprise the Tribute WTC Visitor Center at Ground Zero

Gallery title	*Description*
Gallery 1 Experience the memory of the lively community that was lost	Examines the World Trade Center pre-9/11 attack, including retail, residential and commercial communities of Lower Manhattan.
Gallery 2 Journey through the events of 11 September 2001	Outlines a timeline of the events leading up to the attacks on the World Trade Center, and depicts the actual attacks themselves.
Gallery 3 Rescue and recovery	Highlights the initial rescue efforts by the uniformed services on 9/11, as well as subsequent recovery operations post-9/11. Includes hundreds of missing person flyers which friends and family posted in the area in an attempt to locate victims in the aftermath.
Gallery 4 Tribute	Exhibits symbolic objects of victims donated by family members, as well as photographs of the dead and a multi-media projection of the names of the deceased.
Gallery 5 Voices of Promise	Dedicated space for visitors to enter into a dialogue with the Tribute WTC Visitor Center, with an opportunity to write thoughts and opinions on postcards. Additional gallery space promotes narratives of tolerance and generosity, as well as highlighting experiences of people who were present in Lower Manhattan on 9/11.

Participant observation is an ethnographic method that seeks to understand context of everyday life and proved particularly effective for this research by highlighting tourists in relatively unstructured social interactions. Furthermore, by directly, and covertly, experiencing the activities under observation – what Scott and Usher (1999) identify as 'direct experiential value' – the participant observations provided opportunities to inductively build or guide explanations on the behaviour of people within a specific dark tourism environment. Meanwhile, the second stage of the research utilised semi-structured interviews which drew from a convenience sample of 16 adult respondents, all of whom were visitors to the Tribute WTC Visitor Center. Respondents were from the UK, USA, France, Australia, Ireland, Finland, Canada and Chile, with a ratio of four males to 12 females. Interviews were conducted within the spirit of 'co-authored narratives' and characterised by an appreciation for the interviewee's responses as a 'joint social creation' (Kvale 1996). In short, interviews were conducted within a context of narrative conception and flexibility, which sought to understand key informants within a complex social and cultural situation.

Of course, this research has particular limitations, not least that of a relatively limited female-centric sample size, as well as issues of respondent life stage, health status or religious/cultural nuances. Moreover, because of research design constraints, this study does not generalise its findings to all dark tourism experiences. Rather, the research suggests emergent findings be used as a context to frame future phenomenological research within a variety of socio-cultural environments, and to illustrate the level of support of dark tourism as a contemporary mediating institution of mortality. The research at Ground Zero highlighted a number of significant issues that have been translated under two broad themes. First, the theme of 'space, place and a mediation of mortality' suggests a contested sacral space at Ground Zero and its emergent restitution as a place of mediation between dead Others and the living Self. Second, the theme of 'semiotics: signs of life (through death)' reveals a semiology of Ground Zero which individuals consume to construct meanings of past death in order to comprehend present life and future living. Hence, it is to these two ethnographic themes that this chapter now turns.

Space, place and a mediation of mortality

Whilst Ground Zero is a location of mass murder, the actual site and its vicinity are largely a collection of analogous commercial buildings, or buildings under construction, that will serve as integral components of a broader service sector economy. Arguably, therefore, Ground Zero as an area is slowly evolving from a space of tragedy and destruction that is occupied by mourners, into a place of trade and construction that will be (re)occupied by merchants. Currently, however, a multitude of people coexist at Ground Zero, all with differing reasons for consuming and occupying the space at any particular time. Moreover, these disparate groups intermingle with one another within the geographical confines of Lower Manhattan: shoppers, tourists, office staff, relatives of the 9/11 deceased, emergency workers, street vendors, vagrants, commuters, and so on. Yet, this is a space designed not only for the living but also as a site of homicide, a place of commemoration. Thus, it is not only a space *of* death but also a place *for* the living.

Hence, an evident theme to emerge from the fieldwork data related to how the space, particularly the sense of scale of Ground Zero, appeared to act as mediator between the dead and the living. Particularly, the research revealed how consuming the place mediates between the past and the present, as well as providing a narrative for the future. Indeed, evidence emerged about how visitors triangulate their experiences between what they had previously heard, seen or read through media narratives of 9/11 with that of a 'feel for the place'. Consequently, emotional encounters within the public space of Ground Zero allowed individuals to construct private meanings. As a French male interviewee states:

> We've come to the Twin Towers, and really we didn't expect the site to be so big … its massive!! … it looked much smaller on TV … it is not until you get here [referring to the Tribute WTC Visitor Center] that you get a feel for the place. It's an extraordinary feeling, we went on the audio tour around Ground Zero, and listening to that and those recollections of that

> fateful day and the days that followed, you really get a sense of the sheer scale of the devastation and the amount of people killed that day.... I have found the whole experience deeply moving.
>
> (GZ Interviewee 1: Interviews 2009)

Ground Zero as an 'empty space' appears spatially great, perhaps not only because of potentially deceptive imagery of the original Twin Towers, but also because of the compact design of New York City generally. Obviously, urban planners have maximised the geography of Manhattan Island to include as many skyscrapers and other buildings as possible, yet this provides individuals, especially those visitors who are not from New York, with an ostensible perception of an overwhelming sense of 'structural dominance' (Observations 2009). Once the visitor enters the Ground Zero landscape which, at the time of writing, was a large cordoned-off construction site, the sense of scale and area of destruction in such a built-up and urbanised space are seemingly more pronounced than, say, in a more open-planned urban environment. Thus, an Australian female interviewee (a member of a group of four females) states:

> We're on a five day shopping trip, and we must admit we haven't visited this place on purpose [referring to Ground Zero] – we were actually going to Century 21 [a large retail department store on the east side of the Ground Zero site], but we walked out of the subway station and this vast space in the middle of the other skyscrapers just hits you ... it's a very chilling and surreal experience.
>
> (GZ Interviewee 2: Interviews 2009)

Of course, there is a notion of serendipity for the visit for this individual, as well as the spatial influence of the site, yet an American female interviewee suggested the (dead) space had to be formalised and reconstructed for the visitor:

> I have not been down here since last year [2008], and I heard on the radio the other day that the site is still a big hole in the ground. I know as a New Yorker that the authorities are pressing forward to see the construction completed as quickly as possible ... I know it looks a big mess now, but a place has to be built for the millions of us who want to see it and where those poor people were murdered.
>
> (GZ Interviewee 3: Interviews 2009)

It is here where the spatial (dis)junction of life and death becomes evident. Indeed, Ground Zero and its array of contested narratives may arbitrate between those who survived 9/11, or who witnessed the events unfold, and those who perished in the attacks. Consequently, the construction of a place for the untimely but significant dead, or in any case a place to remember their fate, must follow destruction (that is, death) of the living. Arguably, therefore, Ground Zero as a space is as much about mediation, contemplation and reflection of life and living, as it is about remembering and commemorating the dead. Indeed, a British female interviewee suggests:

> It is impossible to come here and not feel overwhelmed – by both the place and the actual size of it. My entire family fought back the urge to just stand in there [referring to the Tribute WTC Visitor Center] and sob as we read the names – we looked at the photographs and all those little personal items of the victims. ... We've come out here [outside the Center and across from Ground Zero] and took turns to peek through the holes in the fence at the building site. ... We've also been peeking inside the fire station doors [referring to Ladder 10 fire station adjacent to the Tribute WTC Visitor Center] and looking at the memorials inside the fire station. ... Then we walked around and looked at the bronze mural on the wall and all the names and photos of the firemen who died ... got to say, we leave New York on Friday [20 February 2009] with an eternal imprint on ourselves. ... It's a really sad place, and it's made me think what I would have done if I had been stuck up there [referring to the Twin Tower buildings].
>
> (GZ Interviewee 4: Interviews 2009)

Of course, peeking inside the perimeter of the construction site or inside the fire station is, perhaps, simply a way of attempting to access the space and comprehend what was before, what is now, and what will follow. Conceivably however, Ground Zero for this individual and her attempt to access it intercedes with her reflective account of what she would have done if she had been faced with a similar fate as those trapped in the Twin Towers on 9/11. It is here that her spatial experience of Ground Zero arbitrates in her own life-world reflections, in her own sadness of the event, and her personal pondering of a hypothetical mortality moment – that is, *if* she had been in the World Trade Center on 9/11.

An Irish male interviewee also indicates this reflective theme by suggesting an attachment of sacrality narratives to Ground Zero which are generated by a sense of spatial awareness and locational authenticity:

> It's really interesting being here ... its certainly worth a look just to see how horrible 9/11 really was, and the Center [referring to the Tribute WTC Visitor Center] really put things into context for me ... but out here [Ground Zero] I can't believe how many buildings are still under renovation. I guess if people are interested in seeing the site, then they had better hurry, because I imagine this place will soon be full of skyscrapers again.... Our guide said that they are not rebuilding on top of the World Trade Center directly since its now sacred ground.
>
> (GZ Interviewee 5: Interviews 2009)

Whilst the redesign of Ground Zero has been protracted, especially during the planning stages in 2003 and 2004 (Jacobs 2008), the so-called footprints of the former Twin Towers, that is, the actual ground space of the original buildings, have taken on extra significance. Indeed, the September 11 Families Association campaigned for the actual footprint space not to be commercially developed because to them this constituted a gravesite and, thus, sacred ground. Consequently, as part of the official WTC Memorial 'Reflecting Absence', which partially opened on 11 September 2011, and is due to be fully open by mid-2013, the footprints of the original Twin Towers will be filled with water. Hence, the artistic rendering of the memorial will create a symbolic and reflective mediating space where individuals may reconcile the events of 9/11 within their own psycho-social life-world, and where the dead, or at least a commemoration of the dead, are interfaced with everyday living. Importantly, however, it is this notion of sacrality of space that allows, for some individuals at least, the process of arbitration between the dead and the living. In short, the public space of Ground Zero allows for the private contemplation of relationships between a 'dark legacy' and its transformation into a 'dark heritage' within the confines of (dark) tourism. However, at the time of this research, there appeared to be a sense of frustration amongst some visitors generated by restricted access to Ground Zero and a desire to 'get up close and personal' to the actual site of death – that is, the actual building footprints. The mitigation of any potential mediating effects is noted by a female Finnish interviewee:

> We've come here [Ground Zero] expecting to see the imprint area of the Twin Towers, but didn't realise that the entire area would be fenced off … it's pretty difficult to see anything through the fences [that surround the perimeter of the building site] … this is such a historic and hallowed place and we really haven't experienced the impact of the site, which is a bit disappointing … I think it will be better to visit the site again when they've completed the building work … and will be more suitable to pay your respects when it's completed.
>
> (GZ Interviewee 6: Interviews 2009)

Thus, perceptions of the space as a 'hallowed place' and subsequent notions of sacrality are again apparent. Yet, also evident are frustrations at the current state of the (building) project and disenchantment amongst some visitors at being denied access to the actual 'traumascape', that is, the actual site of destruction, the point of collapse, the 'true' ground zero (Obs 2009). As a Canadian male interviewee noted:

> I know we cannot get to the actual site, but to be honest, this is close enough for me … I think we'll return when the Freedom Tower [the main building currently under construction] is completed and see the water features … but, today it's been great being here just to soak up the sadness of the whole place and reflect on what happened … its really put my life and my own mortality into perspective … I know we all have to go at some point some day, but the way these guys died is just horrible … horrible … I would hate to be faced with the same fate.
>
> (GZ Interviewee 7: Interviews 2009)

Evidently then, the spatial aspect of Ground Zero does provide a contemporary mediating place to contemplate and reflect upon how people were killed, why they died and what their deaths may mean, both individually and collectively. Additionally, visitors appear to be locating themselves within the imagination of the tragedy and, consequently, pondering their own mortality and life-worlds. Ultimately, however, the present condition of Ground Zero, both as a physical place of (re)construction and also, and perhaps more importantly, as a psycho-social space with attached emotional and contested narratives, is a site of mediation between the dead and the living. However, it is a site currently in flux through its emergent restitution, both as a mercantile place for the living, and also as a memory space for the dead.

Semiotics: signs of life (through death)

The issue of various emotional, cultural and political narratives invested in 9/11 as an historic event, both individually and collectively, together with a great deal of available 'signage' of the atrocity, either through a variety of texts, audio accounts or images, ensure a particular semiology of Ground Zero. Thus, an evident theme emerged from the ethnographic data that focused on how individuals seemingly both provide and are provided with 'emotional markers' in order to utilise a tourist site of death. In short, visitors appear to consume Ground Zero and its inherent symbolism to construct meanings of past death in an attempt to comprehend present life and future living. Related to the theme of Ground Zero as a place of mortality mediation, as previously discussed, the theme of semiotics revealed how visitors reflect upon touristic signs and heritage interpretations of death and tragedy. These interpretations have largely been formalised by the Tribute WTC Visitor Center, though what is important for this study is how the visitor experience at the Center engenders a sense of life and death by gazing and consuming the macabre and mass murder.

For instance, a particular exhibit at the Tribute WTC Visitor Center which depicts heroism and courage, especially from the emergency services who attended the 9/11 attacks, also narrates tales of gallantry from ordinary civilians who were caught up in the events. Specifically, in Gallery 2, which takes the visitor through a timeline of 9/11 events, visitors are provided with evidence of how ordinary people helped and supported one another in an extraordinary situation. Consequently, the Center offers emotional markers to visitors through its (re)presentation of tragedy. Moreover, the visitor experience engenders a sense of embodiment by accounts of valour and intrepidness, especially by those 'ordinary' people who faced adversity and death. In turn, these tales of tragedy inspire a sense of munificence, as an American female interviewee who lived in New York states:

> My son has just graduated from the fire academy here in New York … so for me, this place is very emotional. My whole family and I were down here last anniversary … and all day people kept coming up and thanking my son

> for being a fire-fighter ... the people of New York City are wonderful ... they come up on the street or in the subway while he [her son] was in his uniform and wanted to shake his hand ... I think this place [Tribute WTC Visitor Center] is such an important reminder, and I'm glad we can come and recover ... it's important to have a place set up to pay tribute to all the lives lost and never forget.
>
> (GZ Interviewee 8: Interviews 2009)

To help construct a sense of tribute, images and memorabilia of the Fire Department of New York (FDNY) are strategically deployed within the Tribute WTC Visitor Center to invoke a sense of gallantry of those who directly confronted the atrocity. Whilst visitors do undoubtedly want to pay respect to the uniformed emergency services, there are also indications that images of the disaster and subsequent narratives of heroism are manipulated to provoke (national) pride and a sense of duty. Particularly, the widely publicised photograph of three FDNY fire-fighters raising the USA flag on rubble at Ground Zero in the immediate aftermath of 9/11, which echoed the famous photograph of American marines planting the USA flag on Mount Suribachi on Iwo Jima in 1945 after defeating the Japanese, is displayed prominently within the Tribute WTC Visitor Center. Consequently, the iconic image that has become metaphorical of a contemporary stoic American spirit plays a central role in (re)constructing official representations of (national) grief, hope and recovery from acts of terrorist atrocity and murder.

It is here, encapsulating in celluloid the moment when 'ordinary heroes' reclaim Ground Zero by planting a flagstaff, a ritual often reserved for marking the capture of enemy terrain, where triumph or, at least the notion of a future victory, is signified. Thus, the Tribute WTC Visitor Center describes narratives, displays symbols through various artefacts, videos and photographs, and, overall, recites tales of a group rescue effort on 9/11. However, the emphasis of American military might is transferred to the 'common man' (to a large extent, the fire-fighter) who works in concert with his neighbours and where 'victory' will ultimately prevail. As an American female interviewee stated:

> the presentation [referring to the Tribute WTC Visitor Center] did a beautiful job of telling the story of 9/11 through its videos, photos, the recovered articles and all those personal stories.... I really feel sorrow for all the families who lost loved ones and for the rescue people who had to endure such horrific conditions to do their job ... I tell you, I will sleep more soundly in my bed tonight knowing those guys [referring to the emergency services] are out there.
>
> (GZ Interviewee 9: Interviews 2009c)

As well as providing emotional markers of those who survived the events, which are essentially an assimilation of real-life (heroic) stories of people who faced death, or had to deal with the dead, the Tribute WTC Visitor Center also offers signage of the actual dead. Specifically, the Center displays hundreds of 'missing person' posters and flyers that relatives and friends spontaneously put up around Lower Manhattan in the immediate aftermath of the attacks in an attempt to locate missing individuals (Figure 5.1). In particular, Gallery 3 displays a montage of amateur flyers, clearly compiled in haste, all with various photographs of the victims, contact information and details of their last known location. The visitor is not only provided with symbolic signs of hope (of finding the missing), but also real signs of anguish from loved ones and friends whose purpose in originally displaying the flyers was to help locate missing people. Invariably, however, many of the missing person flyers, which now have morphed into a collective epitaph, allow the visitor to gaze paradoxically upon despair and desperation, yet also hope and optimism of those who sought those missing.

However, it is in Gallery 4 which is simply entitled 'Tribute', where visitors realise that many of those who are depicted in the missing person flyers are in fact dead. The Gallery comprises a wall inscribed with almost 3,000 names of people killed on 9/11, as well as those killed in the earlier attacks in 1993. Additionally, a roll call of victims' names, ages and occupations is presented on a large television screen on a continuous four-and-a-half-hour loop, paying a perpetual tribute to the victims. Solemn piped music is also played quietly in the

Figure 5.1 Missing person flyers displayed in Gallery 3 at the Tribute WTC Visitor Center, New York (photograph: © P. R. Stone (2009)).

Figure 5.2 'Tribute' (Gallery 4) with tissue boxes at the Tribute WTC Visitor Center, New York (photograph: © P. R. Stone (2009)).

background which creates a reverent atmosphere, and with tissue boxes strategically placed around the gallery space, the visitor/viewer is essentially 'emotionally invigilated' into sentimental reflection of those who died (Figure 5.2).

Perhaps the most striking feature of Gallery 4 is the hundreds of photographs and personal items of the victims donated by their families and displayed against two walls. The photographs portray the dead in routine day-to-day activities and ordinary situations. For example, there are images of a father playing ball with his son, a young woman in her graduation gown, a family on holiday on a beach, and a grandmother posing next to a Christmas tree. Additionally, tangible items belonging to the victims, such as baseball gloves, football shirts and other personal trinkets, add to a sense of loss. One of the most poignant 'emotional markers' displayed in the Gallery is a small hand-made heart-shape card which had been designed and coloured with crayons by a pre-school boy called Kevin Hagg. His father, Gary Hagg, aged 36, was Vice President for Marsh and McLennan, a US based professional services and insurance brokerage company, located in the North Tower of the World Trade Center. Marsh and McLennan offices suffered a direct hit when American Airlines Flight 11 crashed into the building. Gary Hagg died instantly. The emotive message on the card from his young son simply reads:

> To Daddy, I hope you are having a great time in heaven. I Love You. Love, Kevin.

It is this sense of the ordinariness of the victims, that is, ordinary people in ordinary situations who faced an extraordinary event, and of victimhood and innocence, that provokes sentiment in the visitor. Indeed, the average age of those who were killed on 9/11 was just 40 years old. While the majority of visitors viewed the Tribute Galley in a sombre and respectful silence, there were visitors who were crying, some openly, whilst they looked at photographs and read personal messages, although whether these particular individuals had a relationship with the deceased was not clear. Nevertheless, whilst emotional responses from a diverse range of people will invariably be different, the representation and signage of the ordinary but significant dead, in this particular exhibit at least, does seemingly engender some reflection of mortality, as well as reactions and responses to personal life-worlds. As a female British interviewee states:

> This place [referring to the Tribute WTC Visitor Center] is both heart-warming and heartbreaking at the same time … it's very informative and seeing all the visual stuff of debris, memorabilia and photographs of the many people who passed away made me appreciate more the Ground Zero site, and I must admit of my own family.… But those missing person flyers and pictures of those who died with the names did it for me … I couldn't look at the missing person flyers on the walls for some reason. It was too hard for me and brought tears to my eyes. I had to turn away. To see that many people die was too hard … I kept thinking of what I would have done if my husband went missing – would I put a flyer up? I don't know, but it makes you wonder, which perhaps is the hardest part of it.
>
> (GZ Interviewee 10: Interviews 2009)

Similarly, another female interviewee (from Chile) suggested her visitor experience reminded her of the recent death of her father, who had not been killed on 9/11, but simply died of natural causes. She goes on to state:

> The whole thing, all those photographs and trinkets and that, just reminded me of my father; I don't know why, but looking at the people who died, I just kept seeing his face.
>
> (GZ Interviewee 11: Interviews 2009)

While official interpretations provide 'memory markers' of the deceased, visitors locate and imagine themselves in the same or similar situations as those ordinary people who have died, or moreover, reflect upon general mortality within their own psycho-social life-world. This reflection is formalised in Gallery 5 where an official space is provided to record visitors' own 'signage' in the form of individual comment cards. These postcards, in turn, have come to represent a kind of 'moral marker'. Specifically, once the visitor leaves Gallery 4 and its portraits of the dead, they descend downstairs to Gallery 5 through a plethora of origami paper chains, donated by the Japanese government as symbols of healing and peace. The origami chains and their inherent symbolism valorise Gallery 5, which is entitled 'Voices of Promise', and, consequently, the space is officially opened up to promote peace and understanding. Thus, whilst the dead are left behind in the galleries upstairs, the living descend to begin the act of communication of moral tales about the 9/11 atrocity and its consequences.

Once inside Gallery 5, visitors are invited to read a collection of postcards left by other visitors that provide a brief indication of personal views and opinions. To contribute and continue the 'moral conversation', visitors are invited to write down their own views, to express how they feel and, ultimately, to leave personal moral markers for other visitors to read (Figure 5.3). Indeed, since 2006, 72,000 cards in 46 languages from 118 countries have been left at the Center. Approximately 200 of these cards have been 'selected' by the Center and are displayed on a wall against an official message of tolerance and peace (Figure 5.4).

It is here that moral conversations are not only sanctioned but encouraged as the living attempt to come to terms with life through death (and the dead). As a result, personal messages litter the gallery space, signifying and anticipating a better future. During observations, an opportunity presented itself to undertake

Figure 5.3 Visitors gather in Gallery 5 inside the Tribute WTC Visitor Center, New York, to record 'moral judgements' on postcards (Photograph: © P. R. Stone (2009)).

Figure5.4 Visitor 'postcards of morality' inside the Tribute WTC Visitor Center, New York, (Gallery 5) (photograph: © P. R. Stone (2009)).

a rudimentary content analysis of 50 individual comment cards, located in a file in Gallery 5. Out of the 50-card sample, all written in English, 11 keywords were extracted against a simple criterion that a single word had to appear at least five times in order to confer a greater sense of validity through its repetition. The frequency of these keywords, as they appeared within the sample of comment cards is illustrated in Figure 5.5, whilst Figure 5.6 shows the percentage of keywords utilised.

Of course, this content analysis is limited in its design, simply due the opportune discovery of the comment cards during covert participant observations and the fact that the cards were bundled and presented in a file for public viewing, thus providing ease of access. Hence, the researcher only had concealed scrutiny of them for a very limited period. Despite these limitations, the results do indicate a majority of comments are positive in nature. In particular, words such as 'hope' (82 per cent), 'peace' (74 per cent) and 'love' (54 per cent), used in a visitor centre which showcases the murders of thousands of people, suggest visitors are constructing a meaning of mortality that focuses not on the actual death itself, but on life, and on future aspirations of both individual and collective harmony. Of course, visitor comments illustrate a great deal of 'sadness' (72 per cent), but 'anger' (30 per cent) as a corresponding feeling is less pronounced.

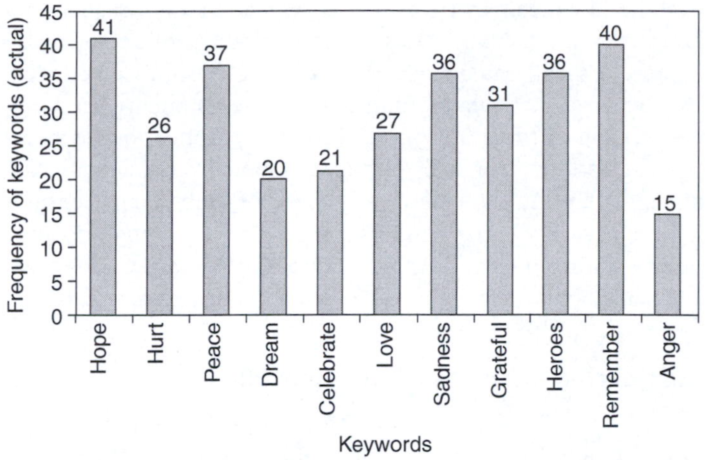

Figure 5.5 Graph showing the frequency of times a keyword appeared on visitor comment cards at the Tribute WTC Visitor Center (n=50).

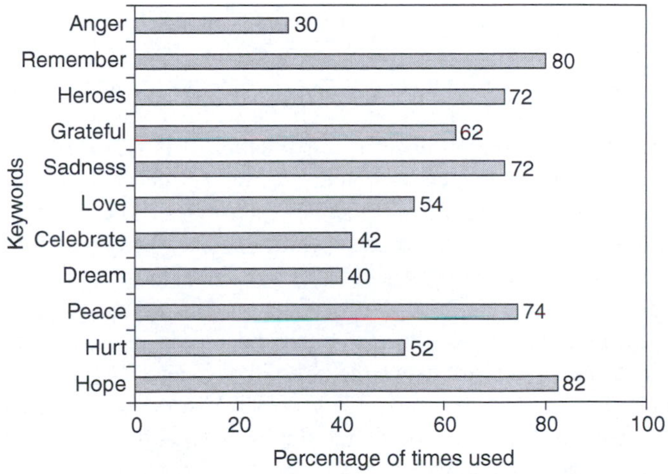

Figure 5.6 Graph showing the percentage a keyword appeared on visitor comment cards at the Tribute WTC Visitor Center (n=50).

Additionally, comments that commemorate the dead through the word 'remember' (80 per cent) offer a paying of respect to the deceased and their families. However, the term 'remember' also suggests, perhaps, the notion of remembering events pre-tragedy and post-tragedy, subsequently informing cultural and political responses, not only of how to deal with the atrocity but, importantly, for the atrocity not to occur again. Significant, however, and certainly within this theme of semiotics, are the positive words that provide signage for other visitors which, consequently, allow a conveying of messages that signify broader concepts of peace, hope and understanding. Despite potential issues of censorship or moderation of visitor comments cards by the Tribute WTC Visitor Center, what is apparent is the Center's interpretative philosophy of communication, commemoration and education of (tragic) death. Evidently then, individual visitors play an engaging and performative role through emotional embodiment with official representations of 9/11. Ultimately, this sense of embodiment ensures that the significant dead (victims) provide signs for the ordinary living (visitors), which, in turn, allows for aspirations of hope, peace and tolerance, as well as brief but important thanatoptic contemplations of death, dying and mortality.

Ground Zero and dark tourism: mediating mortality moments

Death is a fundamental underpinning to life and to the order of life. As Metcalf and Huntington (1991: 2) aptly note, 'life becomes transparent against the background of death'. In other words, death (and its thanatological analysis) can reveal the most central social and cultural processes and values and, consequently, becomes a catalyst that, 'when put into contact with any cultural order, precipitates out the central beliefs and concerns of a people' (Kearl 2009: 1). On an individual level, however, exposure to death events, especially events such as 9/11 that create a collective effervescent moral conversation about mortality moments, can crystallise and invigorate the Self's own life pathway (Kearl 2009; Stone 2009a). Hence, for the purpose of this chapter, it is assumed that individuals' death anxiety and experience of grief are strongly structured by their own social environment and personal life-worlds (Tercier 2005). Thus, the logic moves from the cultural order, that is, the broad realm of social reality that augments and shapes our collective cognitions, emotions and behaviours, to that of the institutional orders, such as religion, politics, mass media or indeed dark tourism. It is these institutions that (in)directly filter and mould our mortality experiences and actions and directly influence the individual order.

With this in mind, Ground Zero and the Tribute WTC Visitor Center as an institution of dark tourism display death and dying: the 'dark legacy' of 9/11 and its dead are recreated and packaged up within a 'dark heritage' exhibitory memorial experience and consumed within socially sanctioned confines of 'dark tourism'. Hence, a number of significant themes have emerged from this study. These themes address how the dead co-habit a world with the living through their continued exhibitory existence and how the space of Ground Zero acts as a reflective place where visitor experiences are inextricably connected with mortality moments. However, the research also revealed how the exhibited dead take on significance, giving consequence to the reality of 9/11 which surfaces when visitors consume the ordinariness of the dead and, in turn, reflect upon broader conceptions of life and living as well as death, and dying. Consequently, this brings up notions of mediation and the Significant Other Dead.

The role of the Significant Other Dead

Throughout history, religious rituals have provided an ontological link between the dead and the living. In turn, religion, which has evolved from ancient practices of praying to ancestors and gods, has constructed ecclesiastical mechanisms that promote public and spiritual 'traffic with the dead' (Walter 2005). In particular, mourning rituals and subsequent prayers for the deceased provide intercession, for many, between those who have passed away and those who are yet to pass away. A Christian perspective suggests God 'is not the God of the dead, but of the living (Matthew 22: 32); 'for there is one God, and one mediator between God and men, the man Christ Jesus' (1 Timothy 2: 5). However, an increasingly prevalent secularised ideology suggests the 'dead have no spiritual existence, so communication with the dead soul is not so much wrong as impossible' (Walter 2005: 18). Thus, secularism, as a feature of contemporary society, may be considered a 'barrier ideology', cutting the living from the dead soul (Walter 2005). Indeed, Strobe and Schut (1999) argue that the contemporary (western) individual has little choice but to reconstruct a life without the (their) dead. This is particularly the case when the institutional sequestration of death is taken into account, whereby an apparent 'absent/present' death paradox exists within the public realm (Giddens 1991). In short, real death of the Self has been sequestered (or made absent) from the public gaze during the past 60 years or so, through processes of medicalisation, professionalisation of funerary practices, and a reduction in the scope of the sacred that has given rise to privatisation of meaning (Mellor 1993; Mellor and Shilling 1993; Willmott 2000). However, in its place is (re)created death, where the Significant Other Dead co-habit the living world (or are made present) through a plethora of mediating channels, including literature, architecture, monuments, the media, and so on (Harrison 2003). Stone (2011b) augments this sequestration thesis, advocating that mortality has been relocated from the family and community gaze to a back region of medics and death industry professionals to create a *bad* death (also Kellehear 2007). However, the modern Self still hopes for a 'death with dignity' or a good death, as depicted by quixotic ideals of Romanticism, which, arguably, still pervade a consciousness of modern-day mortality (Howarth 2007). Consequently, this apparent institutional sequestration of death raises notions of dread and potential issues of ontological security and personal meaningfulness for the individual Self within secular society (Giddens 1991). By way of 'de-sequestering' death, and making absent death present within the public realm, Stone and Sharpley (2008) suggest that (significant) modern-day death is revived through a substitute of recreated situations and memorialisation, including those found within dark tourism (re)presentations (also Stone 2009c).

Therefore, to suggest contemporary western society is wholly cut off from its dead, with no traffic between the two domains, is not entirely accurate. Indeed, Walter (2005) advocates there is considerable traffic, with several professions making a living out of the dead. In his 'mediator death-work' analysis, Walter examines those who work within the death, dying and disposal industry, including spiritualist mediums, pathologists, obituarists, funeral directors, and so on. Arguably, those who produce dark tourism (re)presentations may join this mediator death-work list, such as, for example, the Tribute WTC Visitor Center. Walter goes on to note Philippe Ariès' claim of modern unfamiliarity with the dead and states, 'if Ariès is right that it is lack of familiarity that makes death dangerous and wild, then mediator death workers re-tame it and enact this taming in public ritual' (2005: 19; also Ariès 1981). It is this notion of mediation/mediator and the 'taming of death' within public spaces, making absent death present, and its relationship with dark tourism consumption that this chapter has revealed. Indeed, the empirical research at Ground Zero suggests, albeit to varying degrees, evidence of a meaning of mortality for individuals, or at least the construction of mortality meaning within a dark tourism context. The empirical analysis also indicates mortality meaning was mediated by dark tourism (re)presentations of Other death, either through spatial and locational authenticity or specific symbolism that take on particular levels of significance to individuals.

Hence, the Other of Death as a defining feature of dark tourism (Seaton 2009) is important in the role of mediating between the living and the dead. Consequently, consuming dark tourism provides a potential opportunity to contemplate death of the Self through gazing upon the Significant Other Dead. As Harrison (2003: 158) notes:

> The contract between the living and the dead has traditionally been one of indebtedness. ... The dead depend on the living to preserve their authority, heed their concerns, and keep them going in their afterlives. In return, they help us to know ourselves, give form to our lives, organise our social relations, and restrain our destructive impulses. They provide us with the counsel needed to maintain the institutional order, of which they remain authors...

Thus, the 9/11 dead take on a level of significance bestowed on them by the living and, in turn, the Significant Other Dead help maintain an institutional order of death that can mediate contemporary mortality moments. Therefore, dark tourism becomes a mediating institution within secular death sequestered societies, which not only provides a physical place to link the living with the dead, but also allows the Self to construct contemporary ontological meanings of mortality. Ultimately, dark tourism experiences at sites such as Ground Zero allow the Self to reflect and contemplate life and living, as well as to engender a sense of mortality through consuming the Significant Other Dead.

Conclusion

To be faced with a mortality moment is not necessarily the same as facing imminent death. Mortality moments exist whenever we have a sense of enquiry affecting our existential being; from learning of health maladies, to the loss of a loved one or the (tragic) demise of ordinary, but faraway people with whom we develop a pseudo connection with our own life-worlds. For many, the events of 9/11 created such mortality moments, not only for those who were caught up in the tragedy but also for those who consumed media images of the atrocity. The evolution of the event from a global live televised spectacle to a touristically produced sight allows for mortality moments to be relived and for our sense of being and finitude to be brought back into focus. Of course, to live is to die, yet within a secularised contemporary society many of us have become divorced from the social reality of death and dying. Instead, we have become enveloped with an almost ubiquitous (re)creation of death, where Other death is consumed at a distance and mediated through popular culture and the media. In lieu of traditional religious structures that offer guidance, control and, ultimately, a social filter to our sense of finitude, contemporary mediating institutions of mortality now offer (re)presentations of tragedy and death that have perturbed our individual and collective consciousness. Dark tourism is such an institution, and Ground Zero and the touristic consumption of the 9/11 atrocity has become part of dark tourism.

As such, the visitor experience at Ground Zero can engender a sense of thanatopsis and subsequent meanings of ontology, whereby visitors may reflect and contemplate both life and death through a mortality lens. Of course, it remains to be seen whether dark tourism experiences invoke a greater or lesser extent of ontological (in)security, and whether packaged-up death provides reassurance or threatens an individual's life-world. Moreover, as the space of Ground Zero matures into a memorial place, this study has simply captured the evolution of dark tourism at a particular 'product life cycle' stage. Nevertheless, individuals may formulate a personal and contemporaneous 'mortality capital' whereby contemplative experiences of the Significant Other Dead at Ground Zero provide for an existential mortality saliency. In other words, against a contemporary secular backdrop of death sequestration, the 9/11 dead have brought death, or at least a *certain kind* of death, back into the public domain. In turn, the touristic production and consumption of the 9/11 dead have become significant in allowing the Self a socially sanctioned mechanism in which to explore death and dying, both the death of others and the mortality of oneself. Consequently, this mediated mechanism provides a capital from which the Self may draw on to aid thanatopsis. Therefore, dark tourism experiences as mortality capital allow for the construction of a contemporary social filter, in which the dead communicate with the living, but the living are protected from the dead.

Inevitably, dark tourism as a mediating institution of contemporary mortality raises further questions and, thus, future research avenues, about the role it plays in broader social practice and cultural dynamics, as well as in the ideation of tourism ethics, authenticity and identity of place. Specifically, future research should address dichotomic social scientific-religious tensions of how dark tourism not only provides for mediation of mortality for the individual Self, but also can cast a critical reflection upon the collective Self and how secular societies deal with death. This is particularly so if the resurrected Significant Dead Others are conceived to represent various dichotomous socio-cultural or technological relations that may collide within secular society and, thus, contest narratives of both living and dying. Nonetheless, this particular study has specific implications, not least for the management and governance of 9/11 memorials and museums in particular, but dark tourism sites in general. Crucially, those who are responsible for the management and (re)presentation of 'Other death' at dark tourism sites need to recognise the role of particular sites as potential receptacles of mediation between the lives of visitors and their perspectives of mortality. This is particularly important considering the institutional sequestration of death, which to some at least, may instil a sense of ontological insecurity. To that end, dark tourism, which makes absent death present, is not so much about presenting narratives of death, but about representing narratives of life and living in the face of inevitable mortality. Ultimately, these narratives form the crux of a mortality capital in which the Significant Other Dead play a central role in our existential saliency.

Acknowledgements

The author wishes to express his gratitude to Carley Sutton from the University of Central Lancashire (UK) for her much valued research assistance during the field visit to New York.

Participant observation and interview data cited in this chapter may found in Stone 2010b.

Dedication

This chapter is dedicated to all those who perished on 9/11 and to the families who still mourn their tragic loss, and to all visitors to Ground Zero who feel that 9/11 'made victims of us all'.

6 Towards an understanding of 'genocide tourism'

An analysis of visitors' accounts of their experience of recent genocide sites

Richard Sharpley

Introduction

On 6 April 1994, the president of Rwanda, as well as the president of neighbouring Burundi, died when the plane in which they were travelling was shot down above Kigali airport in Rwanda. To this day, it remains uncertain who was responsible for the rocket attack that brought down the aircraft. Some claim that it was the rebel Rwandan Patriotic Front (RPF), a group of Tutsi refugees who were seeking to overthrow the president, a Hutu; others suggest it was Hutu extremists seeking a pretext to exterminate the Tutsi community. What is certain, however, is that the death of the Rwandan president almost immediately triggered a campaign of mass murder across the country, the great majority of victims being Tutsis and most of those who perpetrated the violence being Hutus (BBC 2008; Alluri 2009). In the 100 days that followed, an estimated 800,000 Rwandans were killed, the genocide only coming to an end when the Tutsi-led RPF captured Kigali, the capital of Rwanda, and established a multiethnic government. Subsequently, some two million Hutus, fearing retaliation, fled into neighbouring countries.

Since then, the country has remained relatively peaceful and, as a consequence, has experienced, amongst other things, the remarkable revival of its tourism industry. Indeed, it is has been suggested that the redevelopment of tourism has in fact made a significant contribution to the benefits the country has experienced from post-genocide peace and reconciliation, (Alluri 2009). Prior to the events of 1994, Rwanda had become an established tourist destination but the economy in general and the tourism sector in particular were devastated by the genocide. However, in the years that followed, tourism grew rapidly; receipts increased from just US$6 million in 1995 to US$202 million by 2008 (Nielson and Spenceley 2010) whilst total tourist arrivals amounted to 826,374 in 2007, increasing to 980,577 in 2008 (NISR 2010).[1] Moreover, whilst its contribution to Rwanda's GDP remains limited, tourism has become the country's largest source of foreign exchange earnings. For international non-African leisure tourists, mountain gorillas have, as they were prior to the genocide, once again become the main attraction.

However, the 1994 genocide itself has, in a sense, become a tourist attraction. In other words, not only have a number of sites associated with the genocide, including mass graves and places where massacres occurred, been developed as memorials to the victims. At the same time, these sites have also become 'dark' tourism destinations. In tourist guides they are frequently listed, along with the country's national parks and other natural and cultural sites, as 'things to see', and they are often included in the tours offered by local tour operators (Schaller 2007). Moreover, although no accurate figures with respect to visitor numbers are available, there is no doubt that many international tourists visit these genocide memorial sites during their stay in Rwanda. As Schaller (2007: 514) suggests, they have become a 'must see' for every visitor to the country; they are visited because they are famous for being famous or, from a semiotic perspective, because they have come to signify or be symbolic of contemporary Rwanda.

It is not surprising, therefore, that significant debate surrounds the memorialisation and re-presentation of genocide, both in Rwanda and elsewhere, for tourist consumption or the development of what some refer to more generally as 'genocide tourism' (Beech 2009). More specifically, for survivors, relatives of victims and other people directly affected by genocide (including, perhaps, the perpetrators), such sites fulfil the vital purposes of not only remembrance but also education and reconciliation (Sharpley 2009a; Williams 2004, 2007). However, their promotion, exploitation and commoditisation as tourist attractions are more controversial both from an ethical point of view and, in particular, with respect to tourists' motivations. As Schaller (2007: 514) observes, 'it is, after all, the great demand for trips to former concentration camps and killing fields that makes genocide tourism possible in the first place'. Many, including Schaller, consider genocide tourism to be little more than voyeurism yet, in reality and as with the consumption of dark tourism more generally, relatively little research has been undertaken into how and why tourists experience genocide sites.

The purpose of this chapter is to address this gap in the literature. Focusing on the Rwandan genocide, it considers the results of an analysis of tourists' experiences of the principle genocide memorial sites in the country as revealed in their travel blogs. In so doing, it attempts to reveal the meaning of and, indeed, motivation for such visits and the subsequent implications for the management of genocide tourism more generally. The first task, however, is to locate 'genocide tourism' within the context of dark tourism more generally before reviewing briefly how the Rwandan genocide is presented and memorialised.

Genocide tourism: darkest tourism?

Travel to and visiting 'dark sites', or so-called dark tourism, is by no means a new phenomenon. As long as people have been able to travel, they have been drawn, purposefully or otherwise, towards places or events that are associated in one way or another with death, disaster and suffering (Sharpley 2009b). For example, the gladiatorial games of the Roman era, attendance at medieval public executions and even travel to witness warfare, as in the case of visits to the battlefield of Waterloo from 1816 onwards, are early examples of what Seaton (1999) refers to as 'thanatourism'. Similarly, visits to the morgue were a regular feature of tours in nineteenth-century Paris (MacCannell 1989). Moreover, there is little doubt that, over the last half century or so and commensurate with the remarkable growth in tourism more generally, dark tourism has become both widespread and diverse. Not only has there been a rapid increase in the provision of such attractions and experiences, including genocide sites, but there is also evidence of a greater willingness or desire on the part of tourists to visit dark attractions and, in particular, the sites of dark events.

It is surprising, therefore, that it is only relatively recently that academic attention has focused on the phenomenon of dark tourism. The term 'dark tourism' itself was coined by Foley and Lennon (1996) in a special issue of the *International Journal of Heritage Studies*, although research into the interpretation of war sites (Uzzell 1989) and the presentation of the heritage of atrocity (Ashworth 1996), as well as Rojek's notion of 'Black Spots', predate the development of the dark tourism concept. The publication of the now widely cited *Dark Tourism: The Attraction of Death and Disaster* (Lennon and Foley 2000) introduced dark tourism to a wider academic and popular audience and, since then, it has become the subject of more extensive academic research and media interest.

A complete review of the dark tourism literature is beyond the scope of this chapter (see, for example, Sharpley and Stone 2009a). Of fundamental relevance, however, is the point that dark tourism, which may be defined as the 'act of travel to sites associated with death, suffering and the seemingly macabre' (Stone 2006: 146), is a broad concept that embraces an almost infinite variety of both dark tourism consumption and dark tourism sites and attractions. In other words, although a morbid fascination or curiosity about death, voyeurism or *Schadenfreude* may be principal drivers of tourism to certain dark sites – for example, Cole (1999: 114) argues that 'there can be little doubt that an element of voyeurism is central to holocaust tourism' – in other cases an interest in death may be minimal or non-existent, or the association with death may be of little relevance. Thus, there may exist different 'shades of darkness' with respect to the intensity of a tourist's interest or fascination in death, which in turn may be related to the nature of the attraction or site being visited (Sharpley 2005). Visitors to Graceland, the home of Elvis Presley, for example, undoubtedly celebrate not his death, but his life; conversely, those who visit murder sites are more likely to possess a morbid fascination.

Similarly, there also exist various forms of dark tourism sites or supply. As Stone (2006: 150) observes, the adjective 'dark' cannot 'readily expose the multi-layers of dark tourism supply'. Different sites or attractions may be located at different positions on a 'dark tourism spectrum', from darkest to lightest, their position being determined by a variety of factors such as the authenticity of the site, its spatial and temporal proximity to the event it represents or commemorates, the extent to which it focuses on history/fact/education rather than heritage/stories/entertainment, the degree of political influence or ideology it conveys, and so on. For example, Miles (2002) suggests that a distinction exists between 'dark' and 'darker' tourism reflecting the temporal and spatial distinctions between sites. Thus, he argues that Auschwitz-Birkenau, a place *of* death and atrocity, is darker than Washington's Holocaust Memorial Museum, a place *associated* with death and atrocity. Stone (2006) proposes a typology of seven 'dark' suppliers of different shades on the spectrum. The 'lightest' he refers to as 'dark fun factories', or purpose-built attractions which, presenting real or fictional accounts of death and the macabre, focus predominantly on fun and entertainment. Such attractions include 'ghost tours' and 'houses of horror' (Stone 2009b). Conversely, and of particular relevance to this chapter, the 'darkest' he refers to as 'dark camps of genocide', or places where murder and atrocity occurred on a mass scale and, in one way or another, are represented, interpreted and commemorated for public consumption.

In terms of supply, therefore, genocide sites, such as those in Rwanda, may be thought of as the darkest manifestation of dark tourism supply; located at sites where mass murder occurred, certainly (in the case of Rwanda) in the recent past, focusing on history, education and authentic interpretation though with a strong political message, they undoubtedly conform to the criteria suggested by Stone (2006) at the darkest end of the dark tourism spectrum. However, whether genocide tourism, or visits to such sites, constitutes the darkest form of dark tourism consumption, as suggested by Schaller (2007), Cole (1999) and others, remains unclear. Indeed, as the next section suggests, with the exception of the Holocaust, there is a paucity of research into genocide tourism in general, and into the motivations and experiences of tourists who visit genocide sites in particular.

Genocide tourism

In his editorial on genocide tourism, Schaller (2007: 513) expresses surprise that an organised form of tourism based on genocide could exist: 'the idea seemed just too bizarre and macabre to be true'. Similarly, Beech (2009: 207) observes that the pairing of the words 'tourism' (usually signifying fun, escape, holidays and hedonism) and 'genocide' may seem unlikely. Nevertheless, genocide tourism is an identifiable (and flourishing) sector of the overall tourism market. For example, the site of the Auschwitz-Birkenau concentration camp in Poland, one of numerous sites associated directly or indirectly with the Holocaust, attracted over one million visitors in 2007, over 750,000 being international tourists. In this case at least, therefore, it is also big business.

As noted shortly, it may be appropriate to distinguish Holocaust tourism from other forms of genocide tourism though, to consider genocide tourism, it is first necessary to define genocide itself.

What is genocide?

Although there is evidence throughout history of mass violence against particular groups, the term 'genocide' is relatively recent. It was first coined in 1944 by a Polish-Jewish lawyer, Raphael Lemkin, to describe the systematic destruction of European Jews, and in 1948 was subsequently adopted and formally recognised as an international crime by the United Nations Convention on the Prevention and Punishment of the Crime of Genocide (CPPCG). Article 2 of this Convention defines genocide as 'acts committed with intent to destroy, in whole or in part, a national, ethnical, racial or religious group'. This definition remains contentious, however, not least because it is not applied to the mass killing of people on either social or political grounds. Perhaps as a consequence, the Convention has been applied in only two cases since 1948: in 1998 to Rwanda following the 1994 genocide and to Serbia in 2007 in connection with the crimes committed against the people of Bosnia-Herzegovina, specifically the Srebrenica massacre of 1995. More recently, a third case has commenced against the president of Sudan related to crimes against humanity in Darfur.

This arguably restricted definition of genocide means that certain events, such as the mass killings of Armenians by Turkey during and after the First World War, are not formally recognised as genocide, although the systematic destruction of the Armenian population in the then Ottoman Empire is widely considered to be the first modern genocide. Also missing from the official list, though again widely thought of as genocide, is the death of over two million Cambodians during the four-year Khmer Rouge period in that country and brought to wider public attention by the 1984 movie, *The Killing Fields*. Nevertheless, both have become, according to Beech (2009), genocide tourism destinations, having experienced the systemic and deliberate killing of large numbers of people. In particular, the Tuol Sleng Museum of Genocide and the Cheung Ek Genocidal Centre in Cambodia are becoming increasingly popular attractions amongst the rapidly growing number of international tourists to that country.

Genocide tourism in Cambodia has also attracted increasing academic interest (Hughes 2008; Williams 2004), as has the development of genocide-related tourism in Bosnia (Johnston 2011; Simic 2008) although, for the most part, the relevant literature remains limited. Not surprisingly, the majority of work related to genocide tourism has focused on the Holocaust, though not under the specific heading of genocide tourism and more usually in the context of the management, development and interpretation of sites associated with the Holocaust. For example, a major theme in Tunbridge and Ashworth's (1996) exploration of dissonant heritage is the interpretation of the Holocaust at the concentration camps, whilst Ashworth and Hartmann (2005) subsequently devote significant attention to the development of Holocaust-related sites. More generally, one of the most common themes within the dark tourism literature remains the Holocaust – for example, much of Lennon and Foley's (2000) text, referred to above, focuses on sites related to the Holocaust, whilst Auschwitz in particular has proved to be a fruitful topic for academic research (Cole 1999; Miles 2002; Poria 2007). It is for this reason that, as suggested earlier, Holocaust tourism is perhaps best considered as distinct from other forms of genocide tourism. Not only are there numerous sites around the world associated with the Holocaust, but it is in a sense becoming an historical event whereas other genocides, particularly Rwanda and Bosnia, remain more 'contemporary'.

In contrast to the relatively extensive literature on Holocaust tourism, research into tourism related to other more recent genocides is, as noted previously, limited. Moreover, in the case of both Holocaust tourism and tourism to other genocide sites more generally, little attention has been paid to the consumption of genocide tourism, or how tourists experience such places. Therefore, this chapter now turns to genocide tourism in Rwanda, a subject which, with the exception of a recent working paper (Alluri 2009) and a study of tourists' images of Rwanda (Grosspietsch 2006), has been largely overlooked.

Rwanda: commemorating genocide

Following the 1994 genocide in Rwanda, a number of memorial sites were established at sites of specific atrocities or where mass graves are located. For the purposes of this chapter, a brief description of the four principal sites (that is, those most commonly visited by tourists and referred to in their descriptions of their experiences) follows:

Figure 6.1 Map of Rwanda.

Kigali Genocide Memorial Centre

The Kigali Memorial Centre was opened in April 2004, on the tenth anniversary of the Rwandan genocide. Located on the site where over 250,000 victims of the genocide are buried, it is intended as a 'permanent memorial to those who fell victim to the genocide and serves as a place for people to grieve those they lost' (KGMC 2010). The Centre offers a permanent exhibition of the genocide, as well as an exhibition of other genocides around the world. in addition, it also has a memorial garden and a wall of names. Whilst intended primarily as a memorial, the centre also focuses on education:

> One of the principal reasons for the Centre's existence is to provide educational facilities. These are for a younger generation of Rwandan children some of whom may not remember the genocide, but whose lives are profoundly affected by it.
>
> (KGMC 2010)

According to its website, in the three months following its opening the centre attracted over 60,000 visitors, many being survivors of the genocide. However, over 7,000 were international tourists.

Nyamata

When the genocide started in April 1994, many people from surrounding areas came to gather in the town of Nyamata, about 35 kilometres south of the capital, Kigali. The church and nearby houses belonging to the priests and nuns became havens for the frightened people who fled there hoping to escape death. They used the church as a refuge, thinking the militia would not enter and kill them in a place usually thought of as a sanctuary. However, according to the testimonies given by survivors, about 10,000 people were killed in and around the area of the church. People from all around congregated in the church and locked the iron door with a padlock to protect themselves; however, the door was broken down and all those in the church were massacred.

Today in the church itself, bloodstains can be seen on the walls and the altar cloth, whilst bullet holes can still be seen in the roof. In the crypt are bones and skulls of some of those in died in the massacre, whilst outside the church visitors are able to enter mass graves where they can view the remains of hundreds of victims.

Ntarama

The Ntarama Genocide Memorial is located about 30 kilometres south of the capital city of Kigali, and is close to Nyamata. Formerly a tiny parish church peacefully situated in the countryside, it is a site where some of the most brutal killings of the genocide occurred. The church was seen as a safe haven by almost

5,000 people, including many children and women. However, they were barricaded in and grenades were thrown in; any survivors were then killed with clubs and machetes.

The walls and ceiling rafters of the tiny church are now covered with victims' clothing, and a trunk full of children's schoolbooks is located near the front of the church. Lined up on racks at the back of the church are hundreds of skulls, most of them revealing how the victims died.

Murambi

The Murambi Memorial Centre, located in what was once a technical school near the town of Gikongoro, close to Butare in southern Rwanda (see Figure 6.1), perhaps epitomises the horror of the genocide in terms of both the atrocities that occurred there and the manner in which they are represented. When the killing commenced in April 1994, over 65,000 Tutsis had fled to the school, believing they would be safe as French troops were stationed there. However, the troops allegedly left the Tutsis to defend themselves and, in the space of just three days, over 40,000 people were slaughtered.

The school has been developed as a memorial to the victims of the massacre and as a permanent exhibition of the genocide. Visitors to the Centre follow a pathway which leads them first to an exhibition describing the context of the genocide, then into so-called burial rooms. Here, the preserved bodies of some 800 victims, men, women and children, are laid out on tables for visitors to gaze upon.

From these brief descriptions, it is evident that the presentation, memorialisation and interpretation of the genocide at all four sites is powerful, stark and uncompromising. Whilst more conventional means, such as storyboards, photographs and written testimonies of survivors, are employed, particularly at the Kigali Centre, the display of the preserved bodies of victims which reveals the violence and horror of their deaths, collections of skulls and bones, and the bloodied clothes of victims not only bring the genocide into the present but also personalise it; they are overtly intended to shock. Moreover, survivors of the genocide now act as guides at each site, adding a human, living and personal account to visitors' experiences and, in a sense, keeping the genocide 'alive'. It is against this background that the research into tourists' accounts of their visits is now considered.

The research

As stated earlier, the purpose of the research was to develop an understanding of how tourists experience genocide sites in Rwanda. More specifically, its purpose was to identify what motivates tourists to visit such sites, their responses to their visits and the consequential meaning of their genocide tourism experiences. In so doing, it sought to explore the extent to which tourists are simply engaging, as some suggest, in voyeurism or are motivated by a morbid fascination in death, or whether there exist more complex reasons for and responses to their experiences.

An online search identified approximately 50 travel blogs posted by international (English-speaking) tourists following their visits to some or all of the genocide sites described in the previous section. A number of these blogs were 'hosted' by dedicated travel blog sites, such as travelpod.com or travelblog.org; others were found on personal sites whilst a small number of relevant comments were found on the Tripadvisor site (www.TripAdvisor.co.uk). Those blogs that were simply factual accounts of the visits were discounted; the content of the remaining 35 was analysed to identify common or key themes with respect to the tourist's experience of or response to their visits. It is around these themes that the results of the analysis are now structured, with quotations from blogs highlighted in italics.

Tourist experiences of genocide sites: key themes

I Motivation

The genocide memorial sites in Rwanda are listed in most tourist guides to the country and are included in tours provided by many local tour operators. Moreover, the genocide is the most significant event in Rwanda's recent history and something that is immediately associated with the country:

> it's hard to visit Rwanda and not spend a lot of time thinking about the genocide … you realise that everyone over the age of 16 has lived through a total nightmare.

Therefore, it might be assumed that tourists, rather than being motivated by a positive desire to learn about and understand the genocide (or even by a negative, ghoulish fascination), passively visit the genocide sites simply because they are there; they are a 'must see' part of Rwanda.

It is immediately evident, however, that this is not the case. In other words, implicit in many tourists' accounts is the assertion that the sites should be visited for the purpose of learning about, experiencing or understanding the genocide, that it is, in a sense, a visitor's duty to visit the sites

> somehow you can't (and shouldn't) forget what happened here in 1994.

For example, one tourist states that

> while in Rwanda, a macabre but necessary tourist attraction are the genocide memorials

whilst for another,

> there are tourist attraction sites such as the Kigali memorial centre that is a must-visit for insights into the worst genocide in history.

More specifically, some tourists refer to seeing the 2004 movie *Hotel Rwanda*, which tells the true story of a hotel manager who protected over 1,000 Tutsis from the Hutu militia, as the inspiration for wanting to visit the country and the genocide memorials in order to learn more about the events portrayed in the movie. Others have more direct reasons for visiting:

> The Rwandan genocide … fascinated me as the most blatant example I have heard of people, regular people, going horribly wrong seemingly overnight. Ever since I have been trying to understand what could possibly bring people to turn on … and kill people who had yesterday been their friends, colleagues … even husbands and wives. So it was appropriate, if a bit disturbing, that Rwanda was one of my holiday destinations.

What is clear from the travel blogs, however, is that tourists do not adopt a passive approach to visiting the genocide sites. Nor, indeed, are they motivated by morbid fascination; many reveal that they approached their visits with trepidation, knowing that what they would see would challenge their belief in humanity, whilst one blogger recounts how he did not want to take photographs of corpses, but was encouraged to do so by his guide:

> I guess it makes sense – they did this [displaying preserved corpses] so it would be seen. Anyway, thinking about them as photographic subjects was easier than thinking about them as people.

The majority of travel blogs either implicitly or explicitly reveal positive motivations to visit the genocide sites: to learn, to try to understand, to assuage guilt (that the rest of the world let it happen), but perhaps also, as discussed below, to satisfy a personal need to be shocked, to be horrified, to be shaken out of complacency or to feel and share hope in humanity.

II Site experiences

Unsurprisingly, tourists' accounts of their visits to the genocide sites (all those in the sample of blogs analysed had visited the Kigali Genocide Memorial Centre and many had also visited at least one, if not all, of the other sites described above) both provide a factual description of the sites and reveal their emotional responses to the experience. From the analysis, a number of clear themes emerged with respect to these experiences:

Shock/horror

A dominant theme within many blogs is the intense feeling of shock, horror and revulsion experienced and described by most visitors to the genocide sites. However, it is not clear from the narratives whether this sense of shock is an immediate response to being confronted by the sight of innumerable bodies in mass graves, the preserved corpses laid out on tables, the piles of human bones and skulls and the bloodstained clothes of victims (a graphic and uncompromising form of display and interpretation that undoubtedly challenges most visitors' moral and ethical values), or an indirect response to the scale, violence, horror, inhumanity and tragedy of the genocide as a whole. Certainly, many comments revealed an immediate reaction to what was seen. For example:

> When I reached the doorway, my entire body went cold. I froze, a few steps from the entrance. I could see, along the back wall of the church, stacks upon stacks of human skulls ... I felt a wave of nausea come over me.

> It was ... the most uncomfortable I have ever been in my entire life. It was shelves and shelves of bones from floor to ceiling.

> This was the most harrowing experience I've ever had: hundreds of bodies had been exhumed from mass graves and covered in lime to preserve them in their contorted, broken states.

> One step forward; look to the right. Skulls with bullet holes, machete slashes and other obscure death signs. Two steps forward. I can't do this. How do you process this?

At the same time, however, the display of human remains has, for some, a numbing or negative effect. In some accounts, the sheer volume of skulls and bones is described as having a dehumanising effect; the evident scale of the tragedy depersonalises it, there is too much to take in and the remains of any single person lose their individuality. Moreover, as one visitor describes it:

> it is clear that the memorial has the intent to shock. It does. But at the same time, it is so macabre that it was hard to feel any grief when seeing the bodies.

For another, the shock value is too great:

> it didn't make me reflect on the genocide as much as it made me offended by the showing of these bodies.

For this reason, perhaps, some visitors experience greater emotion when seeing the clothing of the victims, specifically in Ntarama church:

> having the colourful but mouldy cloth of the victims hang over their bones increased the intensity of the grief and despair we felt for these people we had never met.

So too did the children's schoolbooks, the last entries in which are dated around the time of the beginning of the genocide. In other words, for some it is these symbols of life – clothing and schoolbooks – rather than the dehumanised, preserved remains that are the more powerful emblems of lives cruelly lost.

Nevertheless, the great majority of accounts describe in some detail the preserved bodies, the crushed skulls and the piles of bones which, as intended, evoke shock and horror amongst visitors. These emotions are translated more broadly into questions of how the genocide could happen: for one visitor,

> seeing all this makes understanding genocide and what happened even more impossible to comprehend.

for another,

> I have never felt such shame and anger at what humans are capable of doing.

However, the manner in which their experiences are described suggests that it is primarily the displays themselves (enhanced by the smell of preserved bodies that a number of accounts refer to) rather than what they represent that visitors find most shocking.

Focus on children

> The saddest sight in the middle of all the horror was the small tops of skulls of children ... these small bones were stacked in little piles. ... We all wondered mute at the stunning cruelty of which we human beings are capable

A common theme amongst tourists' narratives is the violence wrought against children. Most draw attention to the large numbers of children's corpses, some evidently being protected by their mother, making frequent reference to the manner in which they were killed. Significantly, however, it is not the corpses and the bones of child victims that many visitors find most distressing, but pictures and details of children who died. For many:

> the most difficult exhibit was the photos of young children with a short summary of their age at death, their favourite food and games and, very distressingly the manner of their murder. Like most people with young children, my mind's eye kept drifting to them.

Two points emerge from this. First, the horror of the genocide is, for many visitors, encapsulated in the violent death of innocent children, epitomising as it does the cruelty and savage violence of the perpetrators. More significantly, perhaps, it is not the anonymous, depersonalised remains of children, their bones or preserved corpses, that visitors find most distressing, but the personalised, individual stories and accompanying photographs of young victims. In other words, as horrific as the corpses and bones are, it is the photographs and stories that emphasise a young life lost that provide a personal, human perspective and that, in a sense, inject a reality to the genocide that, for some visitors, is lost in the numbing displays of mass graves:

> to read about once vibrant children being 'hacked by machete' or being blown up by a grenade while hiding in their home's shower is deeply saddening.

Inability to comprehend

Though not often directly stated in the accounts of their experiences, visitors imply within their narratives an inability to comprehend the genocide. Though the memorials provide stark evidence of its horrors and tell what happened and why, visitors are left wondering how it happened. For example, one tourist writes:

> Afterwards, it occurred to me that it was probably the first time I could remember desperately wanting to pray. The need to explain the unexplainable … to fill that thick, dark silence with a higher power, someone who I could call out to, to blame.

Tellingly and uniquely, another visitor writes:

> In a lot of ways, I felt like I didn't have the right to understand what I had seen, because there were stories that were being told that were not mine – and never will be mine.

In other words, unlike the majority of other tourists who do not question their right to visit the memorial centres and to attempt to share the horror and memories of the genocide with those who lived through it, this visitor hints at an inherent dilemma in genocide tourism more generally: whilst the victims of genocide may benefit from having their story told, what right do outsiders have to share that story with the victims?

The impact of stories

Just as the photographs and written stories of child victims elicit a more emotional response on the part of visitors than the shock of gazing upon innumerable preserved corpses, so too do the stories and accounts of survivors of the genocide. Many visitors refer to the fact that they are guided around the memorials by survivors of the genocide, who sometimes recount stories of their survival or escape. For these visitors, it is the story of survival that provides an insight into the genocide, the story of death being recounted by the living. For example, one visitor to Ntarama was shown round by Eugene, one of just ten survivors of that massacre:

> This was such an important experience, one that few visitors to Rwanda and the memorial get to witness. After, I spoke with Eugene and thanked him for sharing his story with us. It was the hardest thing I have ever had to hear someone tell me … I will always remember this day.

Hope

The final theme evident in the travel blogs is hope. Many refer to the peace and calm of Kigali, the friendliness of local people, how the country is evidently coming to terms with the events of 1994 and is looking to the future. As one tourist observes:

> Visiting Rwanda has been an emotionally confronting experience. I have never felt such shame and anger. … Yet, seeing how far the Rwandan people have come, I have never felt so much hope.

Or, as another concludes her account:

> I couldn't believe the contrast. We are standing in front of a genocide memorial with its horrible past … and here are the kids – the new generation – carefree, uninhibited, friendly – young humans – the future of Rwanda.

Conclusions

What, then, does this analysis of tourists' accounts of their visits to genocide memorial sites in Rwanda reveal about their experiences and about the touristic consumption of genocide sites more generally? As observed in the introduction to this chapter, genocide tourism is becoming increasingly recognised as a specific form of dark tourism, perhaps in its 'darkest' manifestation in terms of both supply and demand. Consequently, it is suggested by some that it is little more than opportunistic voyeurism, that tourists who visit genocide sites are responding to a ghoulish fascination in the (mass) death of others.

The review of tourists' blogs discussed in this chapter suggests that this is clearly not the case. Indeed, the research suggests that, far from being a negative process in which tourists satisfy their morbid fascination by gazing upon representations of mass murder and atrocity, genocide tourism in Rwanda is, in many respects, a positive experience for both visitors and, perhaps, local communities.

First, it is evident from the research that most tourists are proactive in deciding to visit genocide sites, and for positive reasons. Many state their desire to learn about the genocide, to try to understand how it could have occurred, to witness how the country is recovering, or perhaps to assuage the guilt they feel as affluent citizens of countries that did little or nothing to stop the genocide. In other words, rather than engaging in voyeurism or, as Lennon and Foley (2000) generalised as the motivation for dark tourism more generally, visiting the sites simply because they are there (that is, genocide tourism being supply driven), tourists decide to visit the sites for identifiable reasons and in the expectation of positive outcomes.

Second, visitors' emotional responses to what they encounter at the genocide sites similarly point to a deeper emotional engagement with the sites and what they represent and memorialise rather than shallow gazing or voyeurism. On the one hand, most tourists report vividly their shock and horror, particularly when encountering preserved corpses and piles of bones. Certainly, this contrasts with the emotion they feel when they see images and read stories of children who died in the massacres, suggesting that it is being confronted with broken and mutilated corpses that shocks them rather than the scale of the genocide and the cruelty of the perpetrators. Indeed, it may be that visitors have a need to feel a sense of shock (Hughes 2008), that they visit the genocide centres to challenge the security of their own worlds, to experience, as one tourist put it:

> the overriding feeling ... not that there was a group of awful people doing terrible things at that time, it's that we, as human beings, have the potential to do it. You don't have to have an evil disposition to get involved in the horrors of something like this.

In other words, the experience of the centres challenges the visitors' own social worlds.

On the other hand, the reality of the genocide is most starkly exposed through the death of children, their photographs, stories and schoolbooks, and through the testimonies of survivors. Though they shock, the anonymous and impersonal corpses do not tell the story of the genocide; the images of victims and tales of survival do and are, perhaps, the more effective means of highlighting the horror of genocide.

Third and finally, both the stories of survivors and, more generally, the contrast between the events of 1994 represented and memorialised in the genocide centres and the contemporary world of Rwanda outside the centres provide visitors, both implicitly and explicitly, with a sense of hope; that despite the horrors of the genocide which they will never forget (as perhaps visitors to the centres will also never forget it), the people of Rwanda are rebuilding their lives and their country. Thus, the study of genocide tourism, as has been suggested about dark tourism more generally (Sharpley and Stone 2009c: 251), 'may tell us more about life and the living'.

Note

1 Care must be taken in interpreting arrivals figures. In 2007, for example, 80 per cent of tourists were from other African countries, whilst 34 per cent were travelling on business, 40 per cent were visiting friends and relatives and 18 per cent were transit passengers. Conversely, less than 3 per cent were on holiday. Thus, the number of 'international', or non-African leisure tourists remains low; in 2008, just 20,000 visits were made to Rwanda's national parks, 17,000 of which were to see the mountain gorillas. and it is likely that the annual total number of international tourists is similar to pre-genocide levels of around 35,000.

Part III

Motivation and the contemporary tourist experience

The tourist experience is a complex and multidimensional experience, related as it is to not only the activities and experience of 'being there' at the destination but also the complete spectrum of the tourism consumption process. In other words, the nature of the tourism experience cannot be divorced from broader processes and influences, both particular or intrinsic to the individual tourist and also within the tourist's external world, which may ultimately dictate the extent to which the experience is 'successful' or otherwise. For example, most if not all people engage in tourism in anticipation of hoped-for outcomes; there is a future-focused influence on the tourist experience. Similarly, the tourist experience is typically subject to retrospective analysis, which may subsequently inform future choices and expectations with respect to tourist experiences, suggesting that the tourism experience is difficult to distinguish from a continual, cyclical and complex tourism demand/consumption process. As Pearce (1992: 114) suggests, the demand for tourism is 'discretionary, episodic, future oriented, dynamic, socially influenced and evolving'.

Key amongst these factors that influence the tourist experience is motivation (see also Quinlan Cutler and Carmichael 2010). As noted widely in the tourism literature, it is motivation that inspires or pushes people to participate in tourism in the first place; it is the process which translates identified needs into goal-oriented behaviour (that is, tourism), the goals being particular experiences that are anticipated to meet or satisfy the tourists' needs. Thus, understanding the tourist experience demands a consideration of its relationship with tourist motivation or, putting it another way, as the scope of tourist experiences increases, and as opportunities for new experiences emerge, a more complete understanding of the motivation for such experiences is required in order to better inform their production and promotion.

The purpose of this section, therefore, is to explore the relevance and influence of motivation with respect to the tourist experience. First, in Chapter 7, Muhammet Kesgin, Ali Bakir and Eugenia Wickens discuss the outcomes of research that sought to identify the motivations of British tourists on holiday in Turkey. They hypothesise that holiday choice and, hence, anticipated experience will reflect a combination of both push and pull factors; that is, both felt needs and destination attributes will be influential. However, their research reveals that not only are push factors dominant, but also that price is a key filter in destination choice, with significant implications for those who supply destination experiences. In Chapter 8, Karina Smed considers the potential relationship between motivation, identity seeking and the tourist experience. Reviewing the transformation of the study of motivation from a behaviourist to a more anthropocentric perspective which embraces critical and reflexive thought on the part of the individual, she develops a conceptual model, based on an empirical study, of the manner in which the tourist experience is defined over time (that is, throughout an individual's travel career) by the process of identity construction.

This section concludes with Chapter 9, in which Christine Lundberg and Maria Lexhagen explore the motives of so-called pop culture tourists, specifically those who are fans of the Twilight Saga and who consequently travel to places, events and attractions associated with Stephenie Meyer's successful book series and subsequent movies. Recognising that the motives of such tourists may be more complex than those of 'traditional 'tourists when considered in terms of desired experiences, the authors draw on a variety of literatures, particularly that related to sports-fan tourism, to develop an online study amongst 'Twilight Tourists'. The outcomes of this research are presented in this chapter, which also considers implications for the management of Twilight destinations and the experience of visitors to these destinations.

7 Being away or being there?

British tourists' motivations holidaying in Alanya, Turkey

Muhammet Kesgin, Ali Bakir and Eugenia Wickens

Introduction

Tourism scholars have produced many explanations as to why holidays are seen as significant periods for people: 'the need to escape' (Dann 1977); 'for well-being and recurperation' (Wickens 2002); 'for having fun' (Bakir and Baxter 2011); 'anticipation' (Parinello 1993); 'having something to look forward to' (Sharpley 2003); and 'necessary part of life' (Gibson and Yiannakis 2002). The literature reveals competing accounts of motivation and, often, conflicting interpretations (see Bakir and Baxter 2011) of what motivates tourists. Others draw our attention to the difficulties in investigating why people are motivated to visit coastal destinations, such as Alanya in Turkey. For instance, scholars stress that holiday makers may not be willing to reveal to the researcher their travel motives, or what the tourists say may be only reflections of deeper needs of which they are not fully aware (Dann 1981; Lundberg 1971).

A major criticism of motivation studies in the tourist behaviour field (Gnoth 1997) is the prevalent confusion, contradiction and ambiguity over the definitions of key related concepts. As Dann (1981: 198) has observed, there is a 'definitional fuzziness' regarding tourist motivation. This lack of clarity is caused by, among other things, the interchangeable use of terms, such as motives and motivation. And although some psychologists advise against the synonymous use of words, such as 'motives, 'needs', 'urges', and 'drives' (Bayton 1958), others are content with this use. However, as Giddens has argued:

> Motives do not exist as discrete psychological units … needs are not motives … because they do not imply a cognitive anticipation of a state of affairs to be realised – a defining characteristic of motivation. … We should regard motivation as an underlying 'feeling state' of the individual.
>
> (1991: 64)

It is also important to recognise that motivation is both socially and psychologically determined in that the holiday makers' home environment plays a considerable role in influencing the reasons for holiday making (Bright 2008; Jamal and Lee 2003; Pearce 1992).

The purpose of this chapter is to present and discuss findings derived from an empirical study designed to examine tourists' motivation and behaviour. The study employed a questionnaire survey consisting of both closed and open-ended questions and an interview guide. A convenience sample of 505 British tourists is employed in the analysis to assess the underlying 'feeling states' (Giddens 1991) and/or 'goal states' (Fodness 1994) as manifested in the push, pull, and constraining/facilitating factors.

This chapter commences with a review of studies pertinent to the topic and continues with an explanation and justification of the methodological framework. Following this methodological account, the chapter provides some background information about the setting; it then presents and discusses the key findings. It should be noted that the study's findings are part of a broader investigation into British holiday makers' behaviour and experiences of Alanya. Further publications should be anticipated, in particular, on the qualitative aspects of the study.

Literature review: an analysis of tourist motivation

A number of writers (Pearce 2011b; Bakir and Baxter 2011; Uysal *et al.* 2008; Hsu and Huang 2008; Bowen and Clarke 2009; Wickens 2006; Ryan 2002b; Goodall 1991; Gilbert 1991) highlight the significance of tourist motivation for understanding tourist behaviour. 'Being a tourist' is viewed as part of modern life, and the past 50 years or so have seen several contributions to our understanding of this phenomenon from a variety of disciplinary perspectives (Cohen 2008).

An examination of the literature reveals that classifications of tourists' motivations have been influenced by Maslow's hierarchy of needs (Maslow 1970). The themes of escape, relaxation, isolation, social status, nature, self-actualization, self-enhancement, self-development and novelty appear in these studies as core tourist/travel motives (for example, Pearce and Lee 2005; Ryan and Glendon 1998). Furthermore, motivations based on demographic criteria, personality characteristics of travellers, as well as values and lifestyles, have also been put forward by researchers in market segmentation studies (Mehmetoglu *et al.* 2010; Gretzel *et al.* 2004; Sirakaya *et al.* 2003; Thrane 1997; Fodness 1992). In recognising the complexity of travel motivation, a number of researchers have devised and developed their own tourist typologies for shedding light on this phenomenon; for example, Wickens (2002), Gibson and Yiannakis (2002), Plog (2001, 1974), Smith (1977), Cohen (1972, 1974) amongst others.

Motivating factors have also been classified into two broad categories: (1) those factors that motivate an individual to take a holiday, and (2) those that motivate an individual to take a holiday to a particular resort, such as Alanya (Bowen and Clarke 2009; Uysal *et al.* 2008; Bright 2008; Swarbrooke and Horner 2007). These are often referred to by analysts as push and pull factors. Crompton (1979: 410) stated that, in tourism, 'push motives have been thought useful for explaining the desire to go on a vacation while pull motives have been thought useful for explaining the choice of the destination'. Push factors have also been variously described as socio-psychological motives: 'person's specific motivations', 'internal', 'primary', 'escape from', 'being away', amongst others. Pull factors which are external to an individual, are often represented as the destination's specific attributes (Goodall 1991). The literature thus acknowledges that push factors are motives and one of the motivational forces for tourists, while pull factors are associated with tourists' expectations (Sharpley 2003; Jang and Cai 2002; Turnbull and Uysal 1995); one reinforces the other (Dann 1981).

Furthermore, tourism is by its very nature 'mediated' (Ooi 2002); 'what the individual is seeking is in part what she or he has been led to believe is desirable in personal identiy formation: she or he is varyingly versatile within the mediated structure of experience' (Prentice 2004: 261). Thus, Prentice rejects the structural distinction between push and pull factors and suggests that 'in the practical sense of destination promotion, it is often more useful to start from the product base of the destination, and the motivations this product base can meet' (2004: 261).

Several studies acknowledge, however, that most motivational situations are in reality a combination of push and pull conditions (for example, Reeve 2005; Petri 2005; Cofer and Appley 1964). There are several empirical studies privileging the interplay between push and pull factors over the view that these factors operate entirely independently of each other (Prayag and Ryan 2011; Uysal *et al.* 2008; Klenosky 2002).

Other scholars also claim that it is pointless to argue whether push or pull factors are more important (Witt and Wright 1993) because the importance will vary according to tourists' motives and the type of holiday, as well as tourists' perceptions (or awareness) of places (Uysal *et al.*, 2008). Nevertheless, push and pull are still treated as two sets of factors; one focusing on whether to go on holiday, the other on where to go (Klenosky 2002).

The decision of 'where to go' is also associated with tourists' perceptions of a destination or a resort with regard to its attractiveness for those tourists (Uysal *et al.* 2008; Crompton 1979). Van Egmond (2007: 46) argued, 'the decision-making process does not start anymore with the question: "Are we going on holiday or not?" but rather "Where are we going for the holiday(s)?"' Therefore, it may be suggested that the real battle is on the question of 'where to go?' both from the tourist perspective in their decision-making and from the destination perspective in attracting tourists.

Furthermore, 'when to go?' and 'how much?' also play an important role in this decision-making process, in particular at times of global financial and economic crisis (Papatheodorou *et al.* 2010; Dwyer *et al.* 2006). These questions, amongst others, represent the enabling/facilitating or constraining factors (Pearce 2011b: Carneiro and Crompton 2010; Silva and Correia 2008; Raymore 2002; McDonald and Murphy 2008; Uysal 1998; Dellaert *et al.* 1998). In support of this argument, Ryan (2002c: 61) stated: 'for some tourists, especially those using package holidays, the destination was secondary to factors such as price, timing, departure airport and other convenience factors when the main needs of sun and "being away" were met'. The prevalence of push factors as antecedent to pull factors is especially visible in the sun-seeking holidays of the Mediterranean destinations. This type of holiday is characterised as price-sensitive, and is constrained by vacation time, disposable income, and a destination's image and attributes (Goss-Turner 2000).

As such, the push/pull framework can serve as an appropriate model for examining tourists' motivation and behaviour. Price sensitivity, as we shall discuss later in the chapter, is a major facilitating factor. So far, however, there have been few empirical studies which compare the effects and consequences of price sensitivity in tourists' behaviours (Ryan 2003). Moreover far too little attention has been paid to the linkages of tourists' motivations and holiday activities. Therefore, an understanding of the choice of holiday activities at the destination and its linkages to tourist motivation may have theoretical and managerial implications.

However, in recent years, studies looking at tourist behaviour and motivation at seaside resorts, such as Alanya, have been particularly neglected, as the focus shifted from mass tourism to alternative forms of tourism. The association of seaside with mass tourism (Knowles and Curtis 1999), and the polarised view of mass tourism as 'an evil' and mass tourists as gullible and passive consumers of places, shifted scholars' attention to other research areas (Marson 2011; Aremberri 2010) such as backpacking (Paris and Teye 2010). Moreover, several studies have revealed that even mass tourism has the ability for meaningful experiences (Pons *et al.* 2009; Jacobsen and Dann 2009; Therkelsen and Gram 2008; Wickens 1999). From a slightly different point of view but relevant to our study is Sharpley's (2003: 5) emphasis that 'the study of tourist motivation is of most relevance to the category of what may be described as holiday tourism; that is tourism that is generally non-essential and for pleasure'.

Although a considerable number of studies have produced empirical evidence on tourist behaviour at the seaside, many questions remain unanswered for lack of sufficient data. Furthermore, studies on tourists' behaviour visiting Turkey are very rare and to our knowledge, no studies have been conducted on British tourists' motivation and behaviour in Alanya. The latter is the focus of this chapter, not least because Alanya is host to many types of tourism, for example; mass and alternative types of tourism.

The study setting

Turkey as a main destination and Alanya as a tourist resort attract millions of tourists each year. Whilst there is a large body of empirical studies on motivation, little has been written on what motivates British holiday makers to visit Alanya. Alanya welcomed more than 1.5 million tourists yearly in the last five years, mostly from Germany, Scandinavia, the Netherlands and Russia. It, like many other resorts in Turkey, offers low-price package holidays; however, Alanya is not among the popular British holiday list of resorts.

Alanya, a district within the Antalya province, is situated approximately 135 kilometres east of Antalya's metropolitan city centre. It is one of the major tourist resorts located in the so-called Turkish Riviera that stretches for approximately 60 kilometres on the Mediterranean coast of Turkey. The area comprises the main city centre and a number of smaller towns and villages nestled between the coastline and mountains, with a population of 250,000. Alanya enjoys an almost sub-tropical climate suited to an all-year destination, and possesses typical characteristics of Mediterranean beach holiday resorts. It is also often described as a naturally beautiful destination with much to offer tourists (Pike 2008; Facaros and Pauls 1986). Alanya's most popular attraction is Alanya fortress, overlooking the city, which features in the UNESCO World Heritage List of nominees. Some other major attractions in the city centre include: the old town around the castle area, Ickale (the inner castle), the bastion tower in Tophane district, a Byzantine church, Darphane (the mint), the pirate's cave, Tersane (the naval dockyard), the Kizilkule (Red Tower), several historical mosques (Suleymaniye, Emir Bedruddin, Aksebe), an ethnographic museum, and Damlatas (asthma-curing) cave. Other important attractions in the neighbourhood of Alanya include: Sarapsa caravanserai, Alara Inn, Dim cave and Dimcayi (brook valley) and several ancient sites (Hamaxia, Leartes, Syedra and Iotape).

Methodology

The aim of the study was to assess tourists' motivation and behaviour using a theoretical model of the push and pull factors. In addition, constraining and facilitating factors influencing tourists' behaviour were utilised in the analysis of both quantitative and qualitative data collected during the summer period, 2010, in Alanya, Turkey. This theoretical underpinning guided the methodological design of this study.

This chapter employs an embedded 'mixed methods research' approach. The main instrument was a structured questionnaire comprising both closed and open-ended questions. A total of 58 items (30 pull, 18 push, and ten constraining/facilitating) derived from the literature were measured using a five-point Likert-type scale. The push motivation scale of this instrument is a derivative of the leisure motivation scales (Pan and Ryan 2007; Mohsin and Ryan 2007; Ryan and Glendon 1998); however, it should be noted that 'fun and enjoyment' was not previously distinctly identified in these scales. Although the pull items are destination specific, in this case Alanya, they were also in part derived from other similar studies. A convenience sample of 505 British holiday makers was used for the purpose of the study. In addition, an interview guide based on the questionnaire was employed with 42 volunteer participants from this sample, using a digital recorder. Respondents chosen for this study were staying at a number of hotels throughout Alanya; the collection of data both for the questionnaire and the interviews was conducted within two days prior to their departure. The length of the interviews varied from 20 minutes to one hour.

Data analysis

Quantitative analysis

Predictive Analytics SoftWare 18 (PASW) for quantitative data was used for the analysis. Before proceeding with the quantitative data entry, 44 questionnaires were eliminated from the initial sample size of 549 due to high missing ratio or inconsistencies. Factor analysis was employed for data reduction purposes and to determine the dimensionality of measures. Principal component analysis (PCA) was conducted on the 18-item scale of push motivation, the 30-item pull motivation and the ten-item constraints/facilitators with orthogonal rotation (varimax). Varimax rotation was chosen as suggested by Hair *et al.* (2010). The Kaiser–Meyer–Olkin (KMO) measure verified the sampling adequacy for the analysis. Initial analysis was run to obtain eigenvalues for each component in the data. Factor loadings over 0.40 appear in bold and the reliability of measures were determined using Cronbach's alpha.

Qualitative analysis

All interviews were recorded with the consent of the respondents, and transcribed. First, the qualitative data was organised using the software package, NVIVO 9. One of the advantages of this package is that the researcher can simultaneously listen to the transcribed material and look for similarities and differences in participants' responses. The analysis then proceeded manually, selecting significant statements which were then coded in terms of theoretical concepts and themes found in the literature (for example, escape, novelty, and price).

Results

Profile of respondents

Table 7.1 shows the profile of respondents. A close examination of this table reveals that a small majority of respondents were females (57.8 per cent). A quarter (24.6 per cent) of the respondents were between the ages of 18 and 24; one-third (33.3 per cent) between the ages of 24 and 44; and one-third between the ages of 45 and 77. This shows a fair distribution of age amongst the study's respondents. Married respondents were 39.6 per cent of the total. The majority (70.09 per cent) were from the UK. Almost two-thirds (64 per cent) of the respondents were employed, and only one in five was a student. Respondents' profiles reveal that they were from a wide range of occupations. A big majority of respondents were first-time visitors to Alanya (87.5 per cent). However, it is interesting to see that 42.4 per cent of respondents had previous experience of Turkey (twice to 28 times). The majority of them (79.2 per cent) reported previous holiday experiences in other Mediterranean countries. Almost all respondents

Table 7.1 Profile of respondents

Gender	n	%	*Package holiday*	n	%
Female	292	57.8	Yes	473	93.7
Male	213	42.2	No	32	6.3
Age	n	%	*Accommodation type*	n	%
11–17	54	10.7	Self-catering	47	9.3
18–24	124	24.6	Bed and breakfast	106	21.0
25–34	69	13.7	Half-board	163	32.3
35–44	99	19.6	All-inclusive	189	37.4
45–54	94	18.6			
55+	65	12.9			
Marital and family status	n	%	*Length of stay*	n	%
Married	200	39.6	7 days	160	31.7
Others	305	60.4	10 days	23	4.6
Children in family	273	54.1	14 days	307	60.8
Employment status	n	%	*Past experience*	n	%
Employed	327	64.8	First time in Turkey	286	56.6
Student	92	18.2	Repeaters to Turkey	219	42.4
Retired/housewife/ unemployed	36	7.2	First time in Alanya	442	87.5
			Repeaters to Alanya	63	12.5

were travelling either with family or friends. More than half (60.8 per cent) were on a two-week holiday; the vast majority of them (93.7 per cent) were on a package holiday; with 37.4 per cent on an all-inclusive package and 32.3 per cent half-board. Furthermore, it should be noted that travel agents promote Alanya as a two-week holiday destinations. This finding is supported by the fieldwork (see Table 7.1).

Quantitative analysis

Importance ranking of motivation items

An examination of the ranking of all 58 items (Tables 7.2, 7.3 and 7.4) indicated that, in general, respondents were highly motivated by push items, with the top eight shown below:

1 enjoy myself
2 have fun
3 enjoy good weather
4 have good time with family/friends

5 relax physically
6 relax mentally
7 get away from it all
8 experience different places.

Two pull motivational items followed:

9 it has a pleasant climate
10 it is a new place for me.

It is important to note that the mean scores of all these ten items were above 4.10 (see Tables 7.2, 7.3 and 7.4).

Moreover, an examination of the top 20 items revealed that the mean score of each was above 3.48; half of those were push items, and the other half included eight pull items and two price-related constraining/facilitating items, namely: holiday in Alanya is 'influenced by price' (ranked 14, with a mean score of 3.78), and 'taken because it was a good deal' (ranked 17, with a mean score of 3.70). The rankings of the next 38 items can be seen in Tables 7.2, 7.3 and 7.4.

The 58 items is reduced to 16 push, pull, and constraining/facilitating factors using principal component analysis, as shown below.

Push factors (Table 7.2)

The KMO measure of sampling adequacy was 0.77 ('good') and all KMO values for individual items were >0.68, which is well above the acceptable limit of 0.5 (Field 2009). Bartlett's test of sphericity χ^2 (153)=2,308.387, $p<0.001$, indicated that correlations between items were sufficiently large for PCA. Six components had eigenvalues over Kaiser's criterion of 1 and in combination explained 61.98 per cent of the variance. Communalities were fairly high for each of the 18 items, with a range of 0.412 to 0.870. The grand scale had high reliability of 0.796. Corrected item-total correlation ranged from 0.256 to 0.770 and Cronbach's alpha ranged from 0.448 to 0.870 among the six factors.

The first component, namely 'Factor 1: learning and exploring' (eigenvalue=2.31) accounted for 12.85 per cent of variance and had three items ('experience different cultures', 'experience different places' and 'increase my knowledge'). The second component, 'Factor 2: fun and enjoyment' (eigenvalue=2.02), accounted for 11.22 per cent of the variance and had three items ('enjoy good weather/sunshine', 'enjoy myself/ourselves' and 'have fun'). The third component, 'Factor 3: excitement and relationship' (eigenvalue=1.94) accounted for 10.80 per cent of the variance and had five items ('have thrills and excitement', 'experience holiday romance', 'challenge my abilities', 'do things I find personally meaningful' and 'make new friends'). The fourth component, 'Factor 4: relaxation' (eigenvalue=1.90), accounted for 10.60 per cent of variance and had two items ('relax physically' and 'relax mentally'). The fifth component, 'Factor 5: escape' (eigenvalue=1.50) accounted for 8.35 per cent of the

Table 7.2 Summary of push items and factor loadings from PCA

I came to Alanya to	*Component loading*							
	1	*2*	*3*	*4*	*5*	*6*	*Com*	$\bar{x}^a$
Factor 1 learning and exploring								
experience different cultures	**0.728**	0.034	–0.038	0.106	0.202	0.192	0.622	3.84 (12)
experience different places	**0.708**	0.261	0.026	0.214	–0.063	0.058	0.623	4.19 (8)
increase my knowledge	**0.662**	–0.099	0.215	–0.044	–0.009	0.112	0.509	2.42 (53)
Factor 2 fun and enjoyment								
enjoy good weather (sunshine)	0.043	**0.765**	–0.033	0.097	0.142	–0.063	0.621	4.69 (3)
enjoy myself/ourselves	0.117	**0.748**	–0.062	0.081	0.219	0.218	0.679	4.73 (1)
have fun	–0.098	**0.661**	0.236	0.255	–0.019	0.105	0.579	4.71 (2)
Factor 3 excitement and relationship								
have thrills and excitement	0.086	0.343	**0.664**	0.119	–0.125	0.201	0.637	3.62 (19)
experience holiday romance	–0.112	–0.077	**0.660**	0.103	0.108	0.070	0.481	2.03 (57)
challenge my abilities	0.539	–0.025	**0.580**	0.039	0.002	–0.040	0.631	2.44 (52)
do things I find personally meaningful	0.461	0.031	**0.479**	0.091	0.301	0.006	0.541	2.96 (43)
make new friends	0.270	0.021	**0.469**	–0.019	0.230	0.255	0.412	2.83 (44)
Factor 4 relaxation								
relax mentally	0.106	0.092	0.069	**0.903**	0.158	0.064	0.870	4.56 (6)
relax physically	0.016	0.167	0.057	**0.900**	0.159	0.066	0.870	4.57 (5)
Factor 5 escape								
do nothing	–0.248	0.043	0.024	0.131	**0.728**	–0.026	0.611	3.37 (29)
get away from it all	0.165	0.228	–0.023	0.147	**0.622**	0.176	0.519	4.26 (7)
have a chance of time for reflection	0.329	0.045	0.322	0.213	**0.493**	–0.030	0.503	3.41 (24)
Factor 6 family/friend togetherness								
build relationships with family/friends	0.118	–0.150	0.229	–0.015	0.095	**0.813**	0.759	3.38 (28)
have good time with family/friends	–0.016	0.345	–0.081	0.155	–0.032	**0.734**	0.690	4.65 (4)
								Total
Eigenvalues	2.31	2.02	1.94	1.90	1.50	1.46		11.13
% of variance	12.85	11.22	10.80	10.60	8.35	8.15		61.98
α (Cronbach's alpha)	0.645	0.673	0.679	0.869	0.448	0.491		0.796
$\bar{x}$(composite mean scores)	3.48	4.71	2.77	4.56	3.68	4.01		3.70
Number of items	3	3	5	2	3	2		18

Note

a Importance ranking of 58 items.

variance and had three items ('do nothing', 'get away from it all' and 'have a chance of time for reflection'). The sixth component, 'Factor 6: family/friend togetherness' (eigenvalue = 1.46), accounted for 8.15 of the variance and had two items ('build relationships with family/friend' and 'have good time with family/friend').

Pull factors (Table 7.3)

The KMO measure of sampling adequacy was 0.91, 'superb' (Field 2009), and all KMO values for individual items were >0.85, with the exception of 'it is a new place for me' (=0.522). Bartlett's test of sphericity χ^2 (435) = 6,851.844, $p<0.001$, indicated that correlations between items were sufficiently large for PCA. Seven components had eigenvalues over Kaiser's criterion of 1 and in combination explained 61.47 per cent of the variance. Communalities were high for each of the 30 items, with a range of 0.433 to 0.768. The grand scale had high reliability of 0.924. Corrected item-total correlation ranged from 0.261 to 0.801 and Cronbach's alpha ranged from 0.364 to 0.893 among the seven factors.

The first component, 'Factor 1: culture and sightseeing' (eigenvalue = 4.42) accounted for 14.74 per cent of variance and had five items ('of its heritage', 'of its history', 'of sightseeing', 'of cultural activities' and 'of Turkish culture'). The second component, 'Factor 2: hospitality and accommodation' (eigenvalue = 3.40), accounted for 11.36 per cent of the variance and had six items ('of its friendly locals', 'of its calm atmosphere', 'of its local life', 'of its hospitality', 'of its Turkish cuisine' and 'of its good accommodation'). The third component, 'Factor 3: convenience and facilities' (eigenvalue = 2.92) accounted for 9.75 per cent of the variance and had five items ('of its cleanliness', 'of its safety and security', 'it offers good facilities for children', 'it offers good facilities for elderly' and 'of its reasonable prices'). The fourth component, 'Factor 4: activities and shopping' (eigenvalue = 2.76), accounted for 9.20 per cent of variance and had four items ('it has an active nightlife', 'of entertainment', 'of sports activities' and 'of shopping'). The fifth component, 'Factor 5: nature and weather' (eigenvalue = 2.16) accounted for 7.21 per cent of the variance and had five items ('it has nice beaches', 'it has a pleasant climate', 'it has beautiful scenery', 'it has an exotic atmosphere' and 'it has many attractions'). The sixth component, namely 'Factor 6: novelty/familiarity and prestige' (eigenvalue = 1.46), accounted for 4.87 per cent of the variance and had three items ('it is a new place for me', 'it is a place that I can tell others about' and 'it is a familiar destination'). The seventh component, 'Factor 7: popularity' (eigenvalue = 1.29), accounted for 4.31 per cent of the variance and had two items ('it is not popular in my own country' and 'my friends have not been here before').

Table 7.3 Summary of pull items and factor loadings from PCA

I am visiting Alanya because	*Component loading*								
	1	2	3	4	5	6	7	*Com*	$\bar{x}^a$
Factor 1 culture and sightseeing									
of its heritage	**0.826**	0.136	0.182	0.123	0.008	–0.035	0.084	0.757	3.05 (41)
of its history	**0.824**	0.239	0.097	0.107	0.102	0.029	–0.009	0.768	3.17 (37)
of sightseeing	**0.757**	0.169	0.079	0.268	0.208	0.091	0.012	0.732	3.39 (26)
of cultural activities	**0.750**	0.092	0.239	0.254	0.013	–0.028	0.122	0.708	2.97 (42)
of Turkish culture	**0.656**	0.391	0.213	–0.047	0.080	0.092	0.063	0.650	3.35 (32)
Factor 2 hospitality and accommodation									
of its friendly locals	0.265	**0.737**	0.173	0.141	0.137	–0.021	0.027	0.682	3.48 (20)
of its calm atmosphere	0.077	**0.654**	0.152	0.225	0.119	–0.084	0.131	0.545	3.36 (30)
of its local life	0.306	**0.598**	0.032	0.399	0.147	–0.058	0.086	0.643	3.22 (35)
of its hospitability	0.268	**0.590**	0.302	0.085	0.196	0.111	–0.100	0.579	3.71 (16)
of its Turkish cuisine	**0.459**	**0.557**	0.121	0.127	0.093	0.027	0.040	0.562	3.17 (38)
of its good accommodation	0.088	**0.553**	**0.472**	0.069	0.169	0.149	0.035	0.594	3.68 (18)
Factor 3 convenience and facilities									
of its cleanliness	0.200	0.219	**0.720**	0.046	0.213	0.115	0.182	0.701	3.47 (21)
of its safety and security	0.252	0.266	**0.695**	0.011	0.174	0.003	0.206	0.690	3.36 (31)
it offers good facilities for children	0.208	0.181	**0.689**	0.308	–0.030	–0.009	–0.140	0.666	2.72 (45)
it offers good facilities for elderly	0.164	0.114	**0.600**	**0.509**	0.030	–0.064	0.014	0.664	2.41 (54)
of its reasonable prices	0.313	0.286	**0.362**	–0.277	0.201	0.049	0.209	0.474	3.30 (33)
Factor 4 activities and shopping									
it has an active night life	0.017	0.202	–0.031	**0.655**	0.273	0.042	0.126	0.563	3.13 (39)
of entertainment	0.215	0.291	0.140	**0.576**	0.189	0.075	0.090	0.531	2.69 (46)
of sports activities	0.312	0.079	0.335	**0.533**	–0.100	–0.066	0.175	0.545	3.24 (34)
of shopping	0.283	0.147	0.108	**0.526**	0.090	0.135	0.127	0.433	3.39 (27)

continued

I am visiting Alanya because	*Component loading*								
	1	*2*	*3*	*4*	*5*	*6*	*7*	*Com*	$\bar{x}^a$
Factor 5 nature and weather									
it has nice beaches	0.056	0.137	–0.070	0.112	**0.721**	–0.047	0.152	0.584	3.79 (13)
it has a pleasant climate	–0.021	0.201	0.247	–0.028	**0.591**	0.093	–0.091	0.469	4.18 (9)
it has beautiful scenery	**0.503**	0.054	0.156	0.259	**0.572**	0.015	0.046	0.677	3.76 (15)
it has an exotic atmosphere	0.234	0.158	0.159	**0.414**	**0.544**	0.116	0.010	0.586	3.40 (25)
it has many attractions	**0.441**	0.155	0.209	0.377	**0.454**	–0.106	0.021	0.622	3.21 (36)
Factor 6 novelty/familiarity and prestige									
it is a new place for me	0.037	–0.037	0.058	0.060	–0.002	**0.830**	0.043	0.701	4.10 (10)
it is a place that I can tell others about	0.104	0.420	0.170	0.203	0.157	**0.534**	0.042	0.568	3.99 (11)
it is a familiar destination	0.090	0.392	0.270	0.280	0.022	**–0.462**	0.044	0.529	2.69 (47)
Factor 7 popularity									
it is not popular in my own country	0.124	0.030	0.122	0.105	0.076	–0.121	**0.783**	0.675	2.67 (48)
my friends have not been here before	0.023	0.096	0.036	0.236	0.003	0.331	**0.606**	0.544	3.43 (23)
									Total
Eigenvalues	4.42	3.40	2.92	2.76	2.16	1.46	1.29		18.41
% of variance	14.74	11.36	9.75	9.20	7.21	4.87	4.31		61.47
α (Cronbach's alpha)	0.893	0.841	0.788	0.720	0.814	0.470	0.364		.924
$\bar{x}^a$(composite mean scores)	3.19	3.44	3.05	3.11	3.67	3.59	3.05		3.31
Number of items	5	6	5	4	5	3	2		30

Note

a Importance ranking of 58 items.

Constraining/facilitating factors (Table 7.4)

The KMO measure of sampling adequacy was .73, 'good', and all KMO values for individual items were >0.63. Bartlett's test of sphericity χ^2 (45) = 1,311.106, $p < 0.001$, indicating that correlations between items were sufficiently large for PCA. Three components had eigenvalues over Kaiser's criterion of 1 and in combination explained 60.33 per cent of the variance. Communalities were fairly high for most of the 10 items, with a range of 0.385 to 0.760. The grand scale had high reliability of 0.761. Corrected item-total correlation ranged from 0.310 to 0.605 and Cronbach's alpha ranged from 0.668 to 0.754 among the three factors.

The first component, 'Factor 1: recommendation and information' (eigenvalue = 2.38), accounted for 23.87 per cent of variance and had five items ('influenced by recommendation of friends', 'influenced by recommendation of family/

Table 7.4 Summary of constraining/facilitating items and factor loadings from PCA

In choosing a holiday in Alanya the decision was	*Component loading*				
	1	*2*	*3*	*Com*	$\bar{x}^a$
Factor 1 recommendation and information					
influenced by recommendation of friends	**0.778**	0.150	–0.003	0.629	2.24 (55)
influenced by recommendation of family/relatives	**0.744**	0.216	–0.166	0.627	2.46 (51)
influenced by media (e.g. brochure, TV, etc.)	**0.680**	0.052	0.092	0.473	2.13 (56)
influenced by recommendation of travel agent	**0.588**	0.098	0.169	0.384	2.64 (49)
influenced by reviews on travel blogs/Internet	**0.582**	0.019	0.401	0.500	2.64 (50)
Factor 2 time and children constrains					
influenced by available time for holiday	0.089	**0.835**	0.236	0.760	3.07 (40)
influenced by the time of year	0.075	**0.779**	0.331	0.722	3.46 (22)
influenced by children	0.236	**0.611**	–0.138	0.448	2.00 (58)
Factor 3 price and deal					
taken because it was a good deal	0.078	0.046	**0.858**	0.745	3.70 (17)
influenced by price	0.079	0.273	**0.814**	0.744	3.78 (14)
					Total
Eigenvalues	2.38	1.83	1.81		6.03
% of variance	23.87	18.36	18.09		60.33
α (Cronbach's alpha)	0.729	0.668	0.754		0.761
$\bar{x}$ (composite mean scores)	2.42	2.84	3.74		2.81
Number of items	5	3	2		10

Note
a Importance ranking of 58 items.

relatives', 'influenced by media', 'influenced by recommendation of travel agents' and 'influenced by reviews on travel blogs/Internet'). The second component, 'Factor 2: time and children constraints' (eigenvalue=1.83), accounted for 18.36 per cent of the variance and had three items ('influenced by available time for holiday', 'influenced by the time of the year' and 'influenced by children'. The third component, 'Factor 3: price and deal' (eigenvalue=1.81), accounted for 18.09 per cent of the variance and had two items ('it was a good deal' and 'influenced by price') (see Table 7.4).

There were minor issues regarding cross-loadings and reliability (see Tables 7.2, 7.3 and 7.4). Low inter-item correlations ('do nothing', 'it is a new place for me' 'it is not popular in my own country' and 'my friends have not been here before) decreased the reliability of a number of factors; however, elimination of these items did not improve the reliability of these scales. Therefore, for the purpose of this chapter all items were retained and no further steps were taken to further improve the validity and reliability of the measures. For representing the factors the mean scores of subscales (summated) scales and surrogate (or reference) variables were used in further analysis (Hair *et al.*, 2010).

Importance ranking of extracted factors

The factor analysis of responses shows that 'fun and enjoyment' (mean score of 4.71) and 'relaxation' (mean score of 4.56) were the most important. The 'escape' factor (mean score of 3.68) consisted of three items; the reference item, 'get away from it all' (mean score, 4.26) placed escape as the third most important factor. Similarly, 'nature and weather' has a mean score of 3.67; its reference item, 'weather' (mean score of 4.18) by itself placed this factor as the fourth most important pull factor/destination attribute. Furthermore, 'novelty/familiarity and prestige' factor (mean score, 3.67) was made up of three items: 'familiarity' (mean score, 2.69), 'novelty' (mean score, 4.10) and 'prestige' (mean score, 3.99). Closely linked to novelty, the learning/exploration factor consisted of three items: 'experience different places', 'experience different cultures', and 'increase my knowledge'. However, only 15 per cent of respondents agreed with the last item. The factor analysis indicated that the majority of respondents were motivated by the variety of experiencing different cultures and places rather than by deep engagement in learning about Alanya. Discarding the third item, the mean score of 4.03 of the first two items followed the novelty and prestige items. Family/friend togetherness was also one of the most important factors (mean score, 4.01) for holidaying in Alanya.

Price with a mean score of 3.73 is an important facilitating/constraining factor, as shown by the analysis. However, it is interesting to note that two pull factors, namely: 'hospitality and accommodation' (mean score of 3.44), and 'nature' (mean score of 3.44) were equally important. The remainder of the pull motivational factors were least important as their mean scores were much lower. However, of the full 16 factors the least important were two constraining factors: 'time and children' (mean score of 2.84), and 'information and recommendation' (mean score of 2.42), and one push factor, 'excitement/relationship' (mean score of 2.77).

Qualitative analysis

Analysing data from the interviews produced themes which fitted into the push/pull factor framework. The following extracts from interviews demonstrate the importance of holidaying in Alanya:

Push factors

> I go on holidays to relax [relaxation] ... but I also travel to see the world [novelty], to explore or learn about different cultures' [learning].
>
> (Male, 25 years old)

> We just want to see the world really [novelty] and for holidays [relaxation, fun, enjoyment].
>
> (Male, 52 years old)

> Just to have a holiday, to get away from work, to see something different, to relax, just to do nothing, just to read our books, so just lie by the pool.
>
> (Female, 27 years old)

> My holiday is the only thing that keeps me going [escape] (laughing). ... Because the work is difficult and I like to have a break from the greyness of England [escape, sun] and go and see other places [novelty] ... so it is important ... very much so.
>
> (Female, 40 years old)

Pull factors

> Because I like to see blue skies, blue seas [sun, sea].
>
> (Female, 40 years old)

> Because I wanted to go to Turkey for the hot weather [sun and sea] and we found a nice hotel in Alanya [accommodation].
>
> (Female, 27 years old)

> For the sun [sun] ... we are retired, we do not work no more so we go away every month...
>
> (Female, 61 years old)

> To experience different culture [novelty], the weather ... what I particularly like about Turkey you know is, lovely climate [weather]. Every single time we have been it has always been perfect.
>
> (Female, 47 years old)

Constraining/facilitating factors

> This year I think the euro was a big influence because ... because holiday in Alanya was cheaper than holiday in Tenerife [price].
>
> (Female, 46 years old)

> There are many places that I have not been in the UK, because ... it is actually cheaper for me to come abroad to Alanya for holidays than to go maybe to Scotland for the same length of time ... it would cost me twice as much money to go to Scotland for two weeks than to come to Alanya.... I cannot afford a holiday in England [price].
>
> (Female, 40 years old)

> Time of the year [time constraint] and the price [price] again ... I think. And also because it's sunny.
>
> (Female, 18 years old)

> I got very good value for money ... I think it was with Thomas Cook [information, recommendation]. ... It was just advertised at the last minute ... I booked about four weeks before I came ... I decided to take it and you know I am glad I came [price].
>
> (Male, 40 years old)

> The travel agent, Thomas Cook ... recommended it.... We told them our budget and they came up with a list of hotels in Alanya [recommendation, information, price].
>
> (Female, 18 years old)

Discussion

Overall, the quantitative analysis of this study suggests that fun and enjoyment, relaxation, escape, novelty and prestige, exploration and family/friend togetherness are core motivational factors, which support the findings of previous studies (Jacobsen and Dann 2009; Uysal *et al.* 2008; Pearce and Lee 2005; Jang and Cai 2002; Ryan and Glendon 1998). Furthermore, fun (pleasure) or enjoyment, as seen in the above analysis, empirically confirms the theoretical argument that it is a major human need (see Avery *et al.* 2010; Holbrook and Hirschman 1982). This finding is consistent with recent empirical studies conducted by Bakir and Baxter (2011) and Ryan *et al.* (2010).

The findings on pull motivational items identified weather, nature, hospitality and accommodation as most important destination attributes for holidaying in Alanya, which are also consistent with those of other studies in the same context (Jacobsen and Dann 2009; Prebensen 2005; Kozak 2002). For instance, Kozak (2002) studied British and German tourists' motivations visiting Mallorca and Turkey and found that relaxation, culture and pleasure-seeking/fantasy were most important factors. Prebensen (2005) examined Norwegian tourists' motivations in visiting Turkey among other countries and found that 'stress reduction', 'sun/bathing' and 'culture' were identified as the most important factors.

Furthermore, the findings from the qualitative data analysis triangulate with the quantitative findings and with the above studies. The fieldwork shows that the push motivations include relaxation, escape, novelty, learning, fun and enjoyment, amongst others. The study also found that the pull motivational factors that emerged from this study are similar to other studies (Prebensen *et al.* 2010; Kozak 2002; Jacobsen 2002). It is evident that most of the pull factors that emerged in this study, such as, sun, sea and weather, are found in most of the Mediterranean countries, and are not unique to Alanya. However, it was the pricing, the perceived value for money, that was the facilitating factor in the respondents' selection of the resort.

Taken together, the analysis of motivational factors lends support to the theoretical argument of the dominance of push factors over pull factors, an empirical finding which appears to support past studies (Pearce 2011b; Bogari *et al.* 2003; Lee *et al.* 2002).

Conclusion

Past studies have measured the relationships between push and pull factors using mainly quantitative research instruments and some have explored these relationships using qualitative techniques. It should be noted that the Alanya study is one of few studies that uses mixed methods in the analysis of tourist motivation and behaviour. However, the study has some limitations as have already been mentioned in the methodology section, as well as the fact that the fieldwork has taken place in only one resort in Turkey. More research is required to improve our knowledge on tourist motivation and behaviour in other Turkish resorts.

It is also equally clear from the above analysis and discussion that push factors are more dominant motivational factors for holidaying in Alanya than the resort's pull factors. Further, a striking finding to emerge from this study is the high importance of price in the selection of Alanya. For this resort, 'price' functions as a facilitating factor rather than as a constraining factor as has been suggested elsewhere (for example, Nyaupane and Andereck 2008; Raymore 2002; Pennington-Gray and Kerstetter 2002). Taking into consideration the limitations, the findings suggest that 'being away' is more important than 'being there' for the study's respondents as long as the destination, in this case Alanya, guarantees sunny weather and the 'price is right'. The study thus makes a contribution to the field and has important implications for destination marketing and planning of tourism products.

8 Identity in tourist motivation and the dynamics of meaning

Karina M. Smed

Introduction

Tourist motivation is logically the underlying reason for people engaging in tourism and arguably the starting point of all tourist activities (Crompton 1979; Iso-Ahola 1982; Fodness 1994; Pearce 2005). Understanding tourist motivation is therefore fundamental in trying to understand tourism and its role in modern society. However, it is no secret that tourist motivation is a complex and intangible phenomenon, something which is also reflected in the number of attempts made to theorise it. Research into tourist motivation seems to be complicated by at least three factors, namely: that tourists may not be conscious of their motivations at all levels and, thus, they are unable to express them; that tourists may not want to reveal their motivations, owing to perceptions of the acceptability or status of certain motivations over others; and, that motivations are most likely to change over time due to both internal and external circumstances in the life of the tourist (Smed 2009). Therefore, an exploration of underlying meanings rather than actual behaviour, which seems to have been the point of departure for many motivational studies in tourism, is attempted throughout this piece of research. However, it needs to be stressed that only a fraction of potential meanings can be addressed here, whilst the reasons underlying the focus on identity constructions that has been chosen here will be considered as these meanings are unfolded throughout the text.

As a starting point, identity and self and tourists' relation to the context in which they exist – arguably determining desired identities and self-constructions – are addressed for the purpose of generating in-depth insights into the meanings of tourism to modern tourists by applying a perspective in which the individual tourist and his/her accumulated travel experiences are in focus, as these are seen as expressions of change at several levels. The concept of a travel career as suggested by Pearce and Caltabiano (1983) becomes central in terms of adding the all-important dynamics to the understanding of tourist motivation, which often seem to cause difficulty for researchers of tourist motivation. Moreover, this is intended to add to the understanding of identity and self as dynamic constructions and expressions of meaning.

It is, therefore, the purpose of this chapter to develop an understanding of the different meanings of tourism as constructed identity. This will be approached through an exploration of tourism, understood as modern-day consumption, in which displays of identity and the construction of self can take place, and eventually linking this to a meaningful tourist experience. This is undertaken through the application of a dynamic approach that explores the travel career as accumulated tourist experience, its context, and constructions of identity and self as a reflection thereof.

The chapter is structured as follows: the first section presents a review of tourist motivation research as well as introducing the perspective from which the author is addressing the key issues relevant to the focus of the chapter. The second section then moves in the specific direction of identity as a meaningful component of tourist consumption, functioning as a component for creating coherence, whilst the third section attempts to place these perspectives in a dynamic context, thereby searching for potential explanations for the relationship between dynamic contexts and meanings and, subsequently, tourists' motivations. The last section includes the development of an exploratory framework for tourist motivation studies and, finally, the conclusion suggests an alternative view of tourist motivation as a complex and dynamic area of tourism studies. It is not the intention that this will offer another theory of tourist motivation (although this would be a successful outcome for the author!), but it is the intention to offer a way of exploring the meanings of tourism to modern tourists from a dynamic point of view.

Perspectives on tourists' motivations

A brief review

One of the main critiques in relation to much tourist motivation theory and research is that it easily becomes overly simplistic and static (see, for example, McCabe 2000), primarily because the outcome frequently consists of typologies of tourists based on particular behaviours or derived motivations. Moreover, this often occurs without regard to the dynamic influences that move tourists back and forth between different types or locate tourists in between different types; that is, there is generally a failure to reflect upon the relationship between the individual tourist and these different types (Pearce and Caltabiano 1983). For example, a tourist may well consider very specific factors of motivation when individual travel is concerned, such as the possibility of pursuing particular interests, visiting a particular site or using particular types of accommodation. Conversely, travelling in a group may trigger other concerns, such as reaching a compromise in terms of where one would want to go and where to stay or considering the possibilities for engaging in activities together. This indicates that this one tourist may fall into different categories of tourist types depending on the context, including social and individual contexts, from which motivations derive – an issue that will be addressed in more detail later on.

It is assumed that developments within tourist motivation research reflect and potentially derive from those in motivation research within psychology. There, the behaviourist school of thought dominated early thinking within the field; for example, the work of John Watson and Ivan Pavlov was mostly concerned with readily observable aspects of motivation evident in behaviour (Evans 1975). As a consequence, mental processes were disregarded as objectively or scientifically valid explanations of motivation, on the grounds that they were not readily observable. Subsequently, however, the cognitive revolution brought a paradigmatic turn away from this school of thought into a more cognitive understanding of human motivation and behaviour (Reeve 2005). Abraham Maslow, for example, termed this turn an 'anthropocentric' rather than an 'animalcentric' approach to motivation (Maslow 1970). That is, it was concerned with humans rather than animals, thus contrasting with past experiments with test animals, such as Pavlov's dogs, which implied a condition of animal instinct and reaction rather than critical and reflexive thinking that sets humans apart from animals.

Although this turn indicates an increased focus on internal mental processes related to motivation in general and to tourist motivation more specifically, it seems that some aspects of behaviourist thought may still reside in later research (for example, Cohen 1974). It is evident that typologisations of tourists, as mentioned above, exist because they serve a purpose that may very well be related to the criticism made earlier, namely, the challenges of simplifying a highly complex concept whilst maintaining its usefulness and contribution to understanding of that concept. The challenge thus lies in developing a conceptual framework for a highly complex concept, such as tourist motivation, that can be generalised to the extent that makes it relevant in terms of theorising while, at the same time, taking these complexities into consideration rather than oversimplifying them. Perhaps because there has been limited success to date in overcoming this challenge, and also perhaps owing to the relative success and acceptance of earlier perspectives on the nature of human behaviour and thereby motivation, it appears that static theories still, to an extent, dominate discussions of this sort. Moreover, is likely that this is the case not only because static or fixed typologies are a simple representation of motivation, but also because they are compatible with the previously dominant behaviourist approach to research. At the same time, typologies represent a tangible and understandable approach for tourism practitioners relying on market research of various sorts to implement in their daily work.

The aim of this study is not to attempt to propose an all-encompassing theory of tourist motivation that takes all these complexities into account. Indeed, it is likely that this would only further contribute to the over-simplification of conceptualising tourist motivation. Rather, it aims to contribute a more dynamic and rather specific perspective on the field of tourist motivation. In so doing, it may stimulate or provide the basis for new methods of exploring those mental processes related to behaviour and tourist motivation which have previously been overlooked and, to a great extent, undermined as a result of arguments surrounding the potential subjectivity and intangibility inherent in this type of approach. However, it is a main contention of this study that subjectivity and process are necessary and essential components of tourist motivation, because the nature of such motivation is not readily observable but lies 'hidden' in mental processes.

The travel career: adding dynamics to tourists' experiences

The discussion followed above builds to some extent on ideas that have already been explored in existing research, although within slightly different frameworks, the best example of which is perhaps Philip Pearce's travel career concept (see Pearce and Caltabiano 1983; Pearce 1988, 1992, 2005; Pearce and Lee 2005). The travel career may be defined as the accumulation of travel experiences that any traveller may have, the fundamental proposal of the concept being that motivational changes within the individual tourist may be directly related to the level of travel experience possessed by that tourist (Pearce and Caltabiano 1983). This idea furthermore builds on the underlying argument that a travel career is constituted by motives relating to the individual tourist's present age and state of mind, as well as past experiences (Pearce and Lee 2005).

Initially, the travel career concept was developed from Maslow's well-known hierarchy of needs (Maslow 1943), which prescribes a hierarchical order of motivations based on an individual's personal physiological, social and intellectual needs. However, the built-in hierarchy in the initial travel career ladder (TCL), as proposed by Pearce and Caltabiano (1983), was subsequently revised and transformed into the so-called travel career pattern (TCP) (Pearce and Lee 2005). This advanced the concept of the travel career from a still somewhat static view of human motivation, aligning it more closely with the notion of a dynamic approach to tourist motivation discussed above.

The nature of dynamic, mental processes in tourist motivation remains, as already suggested, relatively unexplored within the tourism literature. However, the travel career concept may offer a foundation on which to consider the tourist's qualitative construction of experiences. Moreover, the travel career concept suggests a direct relationship between transformations in motivation and context, inasmuch as the personal context of the individual tourist (age, experience and so on) is taken into consideration. However, it is the aim of this chapter to also add the social context of the individual tourist to this idea of a travel career, because it is assumed that social relations are just as important, if not more so, to tourist motivation as personal preferences. This particular way of framing tourist motivation will be elaborated further and explored in more detail throughout the following sections.

Identity and meaning

Symbolic consumption and the tourist experience

The significance of identity in the context of tourist motivation as considered throughout this chapter is significant for at least two reasons. First, it is through communicated constructions of identity that understandings of tourist motivation are assumed to become tangible, at least to the extent that they can be analysed. Second, it is through identity constructions that tourist motivations are contextualised and give meaning to the individual tourist's life. In the field of consumer studies, symbolic consumption is a well-known concept and, when transferred to the specific context of tourism, symbolism in the consumption of various tourism-related activities may be a means of identity construction that reflects underlying motivations. Such a suggestion is supported by the following passage which addresses consumer experiences and their meaning:

> the consuming individual is conceived as a *tourist* [original italics] who is looking for new experiences via consumption. This is not done due to a need for it or due to a need for fulfilling wants to get beyond a cognitive dissonance. Instead, it is based on a *desire* [original italics] for a meaning in life (Østergaard 1991) because the consuming individual, in this approach, uses the consumption of products and services as bricks in the construction of a meaningful life. It is an ongoing project for the consuming individual to construct meaning, and it is based on emotions and feelings where the single consuming individual tries to create a coherent life.
>
> (Østergaard and Jantzen 2000: 17)

Here, the purpose of consumption going beyond mere functionality is articulated, and so too is the contention that the various experiences entailed in consumption to a great extent facilitate this symbolic purpose of constructing meaning. At the same time, this points to a link between consumption and life in general – as consumerism verifies – in which consumption potentially adds meaning to life through added symbolic values. Consumption in tourism serves that same purpose and, moreover, presents, sometimes in a very literal and direct way, the opportunity for meaningful experiences. It is for this reason that the tourism product may be assumed to entail features obviously well suited for constructing identity.

The following may illustrate more explicitly the usefulness of tourist experiences in such constructions: When someone goes travelling, they may undertake their journey in many different ways but, inevitably, they always make choices as to where, when and how to go, what to do and so on. Collectively, these choices add up to a particular experience related to travelling, and this is often the explicated reason for travelling; that is, to experience things. Upon return, this experience is constructed in a certain way so as to communicate the consumed experience and, thereby, to construct oneself as a traveller as well as a consumer and an individual with a particular identity. Because the product consumed is by nature experience-oriented, it seems natural for the tourist-consumer to put into words the experiences that this type of consumption has provided (Noy 2004), and which has now become part of them. This then renders the product functional in terms of experiences, though heavy in symbolism as well. In other words, an experience-oriented product, such as tourism, offers the opportunity for tourists to consume and communicate experiences which are evident tools for identity construction, in that experiences can be perceived as tangible activities to engage in at the same time as they become internalised by the individual engaging in them; that is, involved in constructing identity.

This suggests that the tourist experience includes both tangible and less tangible features which are connected and, thereby, potentially become more explicit in their construction and use by the individual tourist for identity-related purposes. Indeed, when considering the relationship between the travel experience, in both a tangible and a less tangible form, and identity construction, the usefulness of the travel career concept referred to above becomes apparent. The travel career is, in effect, an accumulation of travel experiences containing both forms of experience that are conceptualised here as two different yet interdependent notions. These two notions may be defined as follows: notion A, experience that is understood as an actual, specific activity that gives a certain, and to some extent instantaneous, experience at a particular moment in time (*Erlebnis* in German); and notion B, experience that is understood as a mental state of accumulating knowledge through an inherent experiencing of different situations, events and so on, such as those implied within notion A (*Erfahrung* in German) (Smed 2009). Larsen (2007: 9) provides a similar explanation: 'One could probably say that *Erlebnis* is something people have in a "here and now" fashion, whereas *Erfahrung* is something the individual undertakes, goes through or accumulates'. Since the notion A experience is directly related to tangible action, it is naturally the one most obviously related to when communication of tourist experience takes place. However, the interdependence of the two inevitably causes indications of notion B in this communication as well. Figure 8.1 illustrates relationship between these two notions, and adds identity construction to the mix, the implications of which are be explained in more detail shortly.

The travel career, which embraces both notions of the tourist experience, forms the core of this model. Both notions are instrumental in shaping the travel career, in that notion A represents touristic action and notion B the internalisation of action, with reciprocal evaluations of the action eventually forming a basis for future action. This means that notion A is a prerequisite for accumulating tourist experiences of any sort, whilst notion B is an inevitable effect of engaging in notion A experiences and will inevitably influence notion A experiences in the future. That

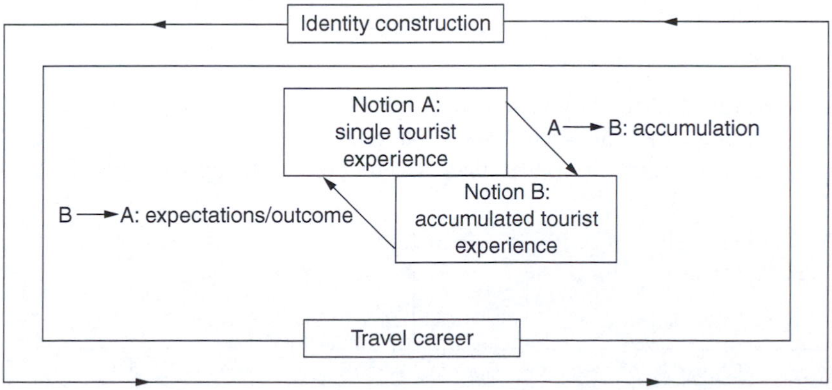

Figure 8.1 Relationship between experience, travel career and identity construction.

is, notion A experiences are carried with the tourist through notion B, and vice versa. Identity construction is assumed to take place on the basis of these tourist experience notions, because they are both contributions to constructions stemming from the tourist's actions and reflections on actions communicated to the surroundings by the tourist and of the tourist.

The significance of context

At first sight, and given its component feature, Figure 8.1 may appear to be a relatively simple conceptualisation of identity construction through tourism. However, closer inspection suggests that it is rather more complex given the implicit dynamics that it entails. For example, it is complicated by the fact that context plays a role in the outcome. That is, the touristic action taken, how that action is evaluated and how identity is subsequently constructed may reflect the particular context upon which it is based. First, it is important to stress that identity construction only relates to the present, as it is assumed to be dynamic in nature and, thus, directly linked to the surroundings in which it occurs. This does not mean, however, that the past and the future are not part of the process, since identity construction is also dependent on past constructions and how they are related to the present and, eventually, to the future. Specifically in relation to tourist experience, Mossberg (2003) suggests that there is always a 'before' and an 'after' that precondition the tourist to make certain choices, and that these may involve identity-related considerations, whether these consciously affect choices or not. The dynamics of this have to do with the fact that 'after' is turned into a new 'before' over time and, thereby, new – or revised – evaluations are made, providing a new basis for choices being made. Figure 8.2 shows this temporal relationship.

Thus, there is a direct link to the contention that context shapes how certain experiences engaged in in the past are evaluated in the present and acted upon in the future, as what is experienced is constantly being revised according to a new context. That is, it is revised in terms of both personal-individual and social-collective contexts, whereby motivations are affected by these changing views.

A social dimension of identity

One proponent of identity as a social construct is Jenkins (2008), who claims that identity has often been subjected to static interpretations in which it is addressed as 'something that simply is' rather than a 'process of "being" or "becoming"'

Figure 8.2 Accumulation of travel experience.

(Jenkins 2008: 17). Jenkins' own view is that it is 'never a final or settled matter' (ibid.: 17). Similarly, Tajfel and Turner's (1979) social identity theory suggests that, although traditional psychology perceives identity as a personal matter, there might also be a social side to it that makes it much more dynamic than previously assumed. This means that there is a personal, individual dimension to identity which is to do with one's personal sense of who 'I' am; that is, one's perception of self. At the same time, however, there also exists a social, collective dimension which has to do with one's sense of who 'I' am on a larger scale, in a group and in the surrounding world; that is, in relation to others and how they perceive the individual. In this respect, Maffesoli (1996) speaks of tribe membership, indicating that the individual desires to fit into a group and, therefore, behaves according to group conventions, particularly when communicating. Likewise, Douglas (1986) suggests that although people in modern, western societies live in what are thought to be highly individualised societies, they may be more dependent on the thoughts and opinions of others than might be assumed or imagined, not least in that we are all affected by social environments and institutions which shape our specific ways of thinking and behaving. Referring to Durkheim's work (1912) on the social origin of individual thought, from which she gained much inspiration, Douglas observes that:

> Classifications, logical operations, and guiding metaphors are given to the individual by society. Above all, the sense of a priori rightness of some ideas and the nonsensicality of others are handed out as part of the social environment. He [Durkheim] thought the reaction of outrage when entrenched judgments are challenged is a gut response directly due to commitment to a social group.
>
> (Douglas 1986: 10)

Thus, so-called individual experiences may have strong social connections. However, these may be somewhat hidden to the individual, hence the contention made in the introduction to this chapter that social relations may be even more important than individual preferences. In addition, Douglas (1986) speaks of a thought style, or a frame of reference for making certain value judgements. She then moves on to pose the argument that, on this basis, there must be some kind of common experience shared within a social group. Likewise, Ryan (2002c) speaks of tourists as social beings, as they are part of a particular social history – and a history of tourism – in which constructions are made of themselves as well as the meaning of holidays in light of the context of which they have been part. In this way, the context becomes a component of identity construction in any type of relationship that it is put into, owing to the fact that the social dimension of identity is always present, even though we may not think so. In addition, tourist motivation is significantly influenced by what is socially constructed as desirable. Therefore, identity, from this perspective of becoming expressions of social norms as interpreted by the individual, becomes highly central to these understandings of meaning. Thus, this social dimension also plays a central role in the research discussed below.

When this social constructivist approach to identity is linked to the travel career concept with all the dynamic features that it potentially involves, it is assumed that ascribed meanings of the tourist experience will become more explicit through communication. Therefore, an analysis of such meanings of the tourist experience will give access to the mental processes deemed important for understanding human motivations. Moreover, underlying motivations related directly to the specific contexts of the tourist will be revealed, as will the actual meanings ascribed to specific tourist experiences. This will be addressed and exemplified throughout the next section.

Dynamics of tourist experiences

Developing an exploratory framework

The exploration of these proposed connections deserves some exemplification, and therefore, draws on a set of data in which motivational factors appeared to be an inevitable focal point.[1] The data comprised the outcomes of qualitative interviews with 21 British and 21 Danish travellers/tourists. These interviewees, defined as 'ordinary' people, represented a wide variety of tourist activities, as well as life circumstances which are talked about openly and at a thematic level in the interviews.[2] Some general characteristics of the group of interviewees were defined. First, an underlying assumption was applied that, in order to explore context as part of the dynamics in tourist experiences, it would be relevant to consider the frequency of travel at various life stages. Therefore, interviewees of a certain age and life experience were chosen. Consequently, all interviewees were between 50 and 65 years of age at the time of interview. Moreover, they were selected on the basis that they did travel frequently, and also had some experience of travelling in the past. It was assumed that members of this particular generation[3] have had opportunities to travel throughout most of their lives, individual life circumstances aside, and that they were perhaps the first generation in the two countries involved to have enjoyed that opportunity. In other words, it was assumed that they would have travel careers to talk about and relate to. Second, the issue of the individual as a social being was addressed by including interviewees from different cultural contexts as well as interviewees with different family statuses. The purpose of this was to embrace different social environments in general as well as the concept of thought style as an influence on individual thoughts, experiences and preferences, suggested by Douglas (1986), in particular.

This group of interviewees thus provides an interesting focus for addressing the issue of tourist motivation within the framework of dynamic meanings explored through identity constructions. The idea is that, through a hermeneutic process of change between this data and theory in various combinations, a holistic framework for analysis can be proposed, which suggests an exploratory approach to studying tourist motivation. This framework is illustrated in Figure 8.3, and is explained in the following section.

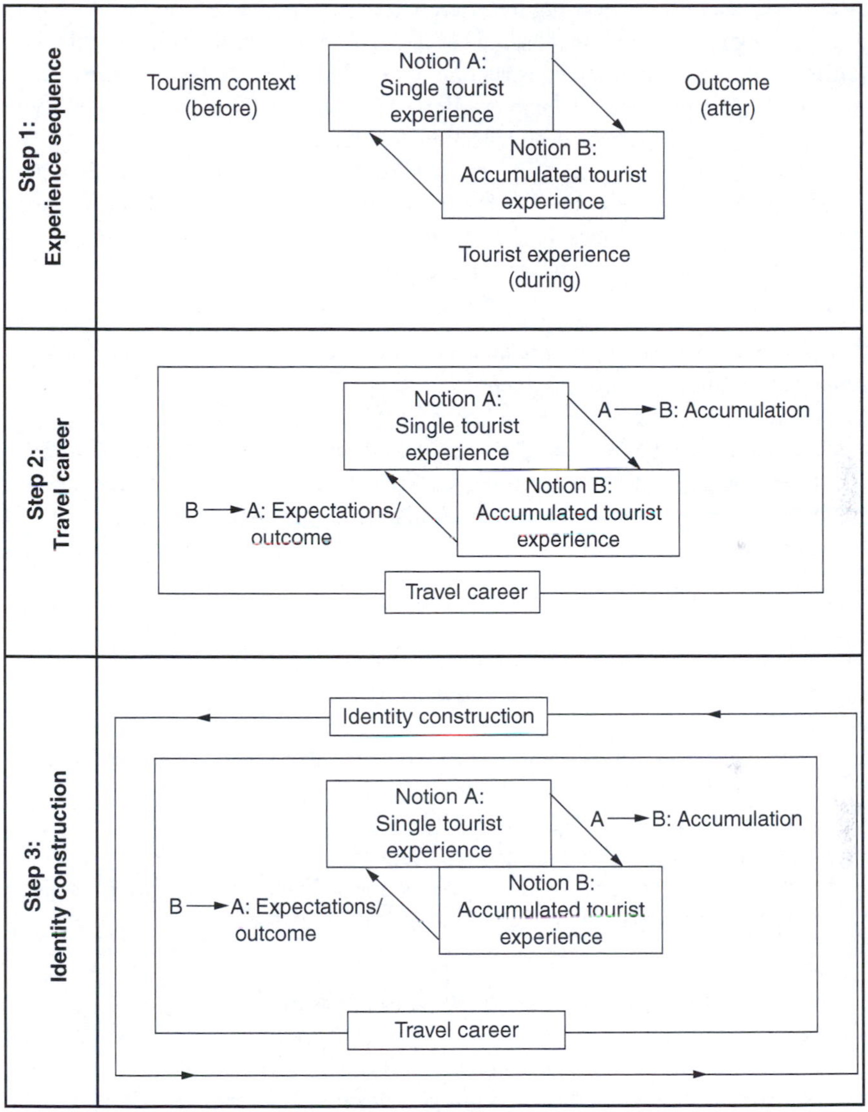

Figure 8.3 Framework for the analysis of tourist motivation.

Exploring the travel career as a component of context

A central part of this framework relates to the travel career and the two notions of the tourist experience earlier illustrated in Figure 8.1. The travel career is perceived as an expression of tourist experiences, both in terms of the actual experiences that people have engaged in (notion A) and are conscious of having experienced to the extent that they are able to talk about them, and the accumulated experience from engaging in different tourist experiences (notion B) which, to a great extent, may be unconscious and, thus, implicit in the stories told about tourist experiences, thereby constructing a coherent travel career and subsequent identity. Therefore, the travel career offers a framework for exploring identity in relation to tourist experiences and also underlying meanings.

Based on the interview material, some core themes have been extracted which reflect the topics raised by the interviewees. These are not factual descriptions of what has taken place in terms of tourist experiences, but communicated descriptions as they have been constructed in the interviews.

Theme 1: the tourism context (defined as issues that surround a specific tourist experience and, thus, influence it)

- Individual circumstances, for example, practical considerations (finances, time, compromises, etc.) forming a particular frame for the experience;
- Collective influences, for example, historical developments such as travel opportunities and norms which at a particular point in time may point in a particular direction.

Theme 2: the tourist experience (defined as issues related to the tourist experience itself – both notion A and notion B)

- Approach to the tourist experience (focus on the number of different experiences vs. details of one experience);
- Adventure (risk and danger vs. trivialisation);
- Novelty (as opposed to familiarity);
- Atmosphere – underlying the experience as a frame of reference (nostalgia, ideals and dreams).

Theme 3: outcome (defined as issues that relate to what is gained from the tourist experience in retrospect)

- Memories and togetherness (forming bonds based on experience);
- Recharging: relaxation and escape (getting away and preparing for everyday life).

It is thus assumed that at the core is the tourist experience itself, but surrounding it are aspects of context and outcome that have a significant influence on the way the experience is constructed and ascribed meaning. There is a high correlation between these empirical themes and the theory presented previously, in that Mossberg's time/space dimension of an experience involves a before, a during and an after, which may very well correspond to the above themes. Aspects of the tourism context may be said to relate to the *before* dimension, since practical considerations, historical developments and so on are part of the considerations about and influences on any given holiday and the choices that precede it, and hence the upcoming tourist experience.

The purpose of the first two steps of this framework is to create an overview of the travel career, the different contexts of travelling that it involves, and eventually how these contexts relate to each other. The family life cycle (FLC) is often used in consumer studies, as it is widely considered to underpin different needs, demands, motivations and derived consumption patterns. At the same time however, the FLC is criticised for similar issues as tourist typologies, such as a lack of consideration of demographic and psychographic trends and broad generalisations. Therefore, the FLC has not been applied directly in this framework, although it serves as inspiration for the development of the travel career stages that will be presented below. The relevance of a stages approach here is that it is not only a widely used approach to capture the consumer, but it is also related to the line of thinking implied in Pearce's travel career concept. Different ways of capturing the travel career stages have therefore been explored, while the relationship between travelling and the general life situation of the tourist, which may have an impact on travelling, is also considered. The travel career concept was originally developed to focus on the level of travel experience and its possible influences on the tourist, and not necessarily on the significance of surrounding circumstances for the individual, that is, the social, collective context. Therefore, when researching aspects of the travel career, the intention is to broaden the context within which the tourist is situated and, by doing so to expand the understanding of the tourist's world and the tourist within it. This is approached through the use of a travel unit model, developed on the basis of the need that occurred when this set of data was processed. The term 'travel unit' has been suggested as a reference to the group of people travelling together and, thus, the people that are all taken into consideration when travel decisions are made, although some may have more decision-making power than others. The centre of the unit is, however, the individual tourist, regardless of the power of the individual in the travel unit. The general idea is that, no matter what, individual travel behaviour will be influenced by the travel unit and, implicitly, by the social context surrounding the individual tourist. Table 8.1 illustrates the different stages of a travel career, as introduced by the group of interviewees.

Evidently, each of the travel units mentioned above may appear at different times throughout an individual's travel career, hence the dynamics that they are assumed to illustrate. Although one type may dominate at a given point in most interviewees' lives, the idea is to be able to discover dynamic relationships between the social contexts within the individual tourist's travel career as an expression of change in life and, therefore, tourist motivations and subsequently tourism behaviour.

Table 8.1 The stages of a travel career

Travel unit	*Description*
+ Parents	The interviewee travelling as a child with his/her parents
+ Friends or relatives	The individual is travelling without a partner but with friends or relatives. Examples are: an adolescent travelling around Europe with a friend, a divorcee travelling with a brother or sister, or someone travelling without their partner for specific interests, e.g. golfing, rock climbing or work
+ Partner	Couples travelling just the two of them. It needs to be stressed though that a partner appearing at one stage of an interviewee's travel career may not be the same partner appearing at other stages, e.g. in the case of divorce
+ Partner and friends or relatives	A couple travelling with another couple or a couple travelling with parts of their family
+ Family	Travelling with a partner and one or more children – your own, your partner's or your children together
+ Family and friends or relatives	Travelling with the family and with others outside the immediate family, e.g. another family or grandparents
By oneself	This is used relatively, as opposed to the other stages, and indicates someone setting out to travel without any travel partners that they already know. This does not mean, however, that they are necessarily isolated while travelling by themselves, e.g. they may join some sort of group travel or visit friends or family along the way

Types of tourist experiences within the travel career

Now that the travel units have been addressed as a means of defining different stages of the travel career, the next issue to address is the tourist experiences that each stage may entail. The purpose is to describe different types of tourist experiences that illustrate connections between the individual tourist as a member of a travel unit, and related tourist experiences. The assumption is that, by identifying different types of tourist experiences based on the empirical data for each travel unit, the notion A tourist experiences that tourists undertake at different stages of their lives and travel career will become more tangible. This will facilitate illustrations of a travel career and its relations to surrounding life circumstances and, eventually, the construction of identity. It is important to stress that the aim is not to generalise to the extent that there is only one type of tourist experience for each travel unit, which is not the case. Rather, the aim is to try to capture some of the tendencies that can be found in the available data without disregarding the unique character of every single tourist experience mentioned by the interviewees. However, this gives a clear impression that some similarities exist within these unique experiences and the way they are communicated by the interviewees.

Table 8.2 Travel units and related tourist experiences

Travel unit	*Types of tourist experiences* *Tourist experiences (notion A)*	 *Accumulated tourist experience (notion B)*
+ parents	Travelling by car to a domestic seaside destination, camping for a week during the summer, swimming, sunbathing, etc.	Novelty – a sense of adventure as a change from everyday life Togetherness – as a family
	Visiting family and friends at a domestic or international destination for a couple of weeks during the summer, swimming, sunbathing, social gatherings, etc.	
+ friends or relatives	Travelling by car or public transportation to an international destination, usually moving around, using cheap accommodation along the way, sometimes working, 'roughing it' for 2–4 weeks, in some cases months	Education Adventure – through independence and a sense of freedom
	Travelling domestically or internationally for 1–2 weeks, engaging in specific hobbies, staying at accommodation appropriate for the activity at hand	'Doing what I like' Togetherness – a sense of community
	Going on a package tour to an international/European destination, by plane, for 1–2 weeks, doing typical beach activities, most often combined with organised tours	Novelty – change from everyday life Relaxation
+ partner/+ partner and friends or relatives	Flying to a remote international destination for 2 or more weeks' holiday, staying at cheap hostels, B and Bs or hotels doing cultural activities, sightseeing and relaxation	Novelty – experiencing new, unfamiliar cultures and places Adventure Relaxation Togetherness – as a couple or group
	Going on a package tour abroad for 1–2 weeks, staying at a hotel, doing typical beach activities, sometimes combined with organised tours, or going by car or public transport to a domestic destination for short breaks, staying at B and Bs, cottages	Relaxation Comfort Togetherness – as a couple or group
	Visiting family and friends at a domestic or international destination for a couple of weeks during the summer, swimming, sunbathing, social gatherings, etc.	
+ family/+ family and friends or relatives	Travelling by car or public transport to a domestic seaside destination, staying at a B and B or camping for a week or for day trips during the summer, swimming, sunbathing, etc.	Togetherness – as a family and sometimes with other travellers (particularly the children) Relaxation Novelty – change from everyday life
	Going on a package tour to an international destination, by plane, bus or train, for 1–2 weeks, staying at a hotel or camping, doing typical beach activities	Togetherness – as a family and sometimes with other travellers (particularly the children) Relaxation Novelty – change from everyday life Education
By oneself	Flying or going by public transport to an international destination, backpacking, usually moving around, staying at anything from cheap hostels or camping to regular hotels, walking, climbing, swimming, sunbathing, reading, for 2–4 weeks	Novelty Adventure Togetherness – with other travellers
	Flying, driving or going by public transport to an international or domestic destination, visiting friends and family for a couple of weeks or more, mainly engaging in social and cultural activities.	Togetherness – as a group/family members Relaxation
	Going on a package tour abroad for 1–2 weeks, staying at a hotel, doing typical beach activities, sometimes combined with organised tours	Relaxation Comfort Togetherness – with other travellers

These types may, therefore, serve the purpose of illustration whilst, equally importantly, revealing some level of tangibility that may provide more clarity in the conclusions obtained. The purpose is, thus, to create an overview of the material in terms of expressions of tourist behaviour and the relation to these, that is, when identity is constructed on this basis. The types are constructed by looking closely at the data material and categorising the different tourist experiences presented by the interviewees according to different variables, such as domestic or international travel or modes of transportation, in order to suggest the most prevalent tendencies at each travel unit stage. Each travel unit stage and related types of tourist experiences are presented in Table 8.2.

Based on Table 8.2, it is suggested that, by taking travel units representing tourists' social contexts and constructed notion A experiences into account, notion B experiences will appear and, thereby, inadvertently function as expressions of tourist motivations in context. In addition, the final factor of identity construction surrounding this process will add to the understanding of motivations as they are communicated in the interviews, that is, in the way in which they are made sense of by the interviewees. In order to illustrate and summarise the usefulness of this framework, the conclusion presents some key points in relation to the application of this framework to the data material.

Conclusion

The theoretical before, during and after dimensions of the tourist experience are to a great extent fluid. This is primarily because the experience is not only a marked point in time, but also because it has two dimensions, notions A and B, that function on several levels in terms of approaching the experience, which is a state of mind within the individual tourist. Therefore, notion A may be said to be part of the 'during' phase, and notion B part of the 'after' phase, which then together form the basis for a different 'before' phase. This means that overlaps are frequent and fairly difficult to manage in terms of research. Nevertheless, it appears that these different phases are distinct when it comes to the themes extracted from the data material. Before, during and after are all brought up throughout these themes – the tourism context mainly concerns before, the tourist experience mainly before and during, and outcome relies on all three and, to the greatest extent, draws the after dimension into it all. The two different notions and the three dimensions in time indicated by the experience sequence, Step 1, of the analytical framework operate on slightly different levels and, as such, they are not equivalent but interconnected and relatable, as Table 8.3 illustrates.

Table 8.3 Relation between theory and analytical findings

Theme	*The tourism context*	*The tourist experience*	*Outcome*
Time	Before	Before + during	Before + during + after
Notion	Notion A + B	Notion A	Notion B

A complex picture consequently emerges from all of these factors being dependent on each other, and none of them being distinctively separable from the rest. Logically, only a very rough description of the complexity in these connections can be provided, as attempted in Table 8.3. Nonetheless, a simple illustration may support further understanding of such connections.

With respect to identity in this connection, the idea of the 'other' seems central in the sense that it directs how experiences are communicated to the surroundings. Therefore, the experience sequence above entail social contexts and everything inherent in these, whereas the 'other' becomes a means of navigation in terms of defining and expressing who one is and is not or, in other words, applying underlying meanings of what is good or bad in a touristic sense to define oneself. The other depends on the tribe memberships to which the individual subscribes. The data material indicates that some agreement exists among these tourists in terms of what is desirable and what is not, which is in full accordance with Douglas' thought style. Indications within the data material reveal a pattern as shown in Table 8.4.

Although agreement thus exists at a fairly general level, it is less obvious at a more detailed level where personal preferences as well as social influences, or the two dimensions to identity construction, are more influential Within the data material, specific focal points appeared around four different dimensions of the tourist experience, namely, approach, adventure, novelty and atmosphere, presented earlier as theme 2. Since the purpose here is not to explore the specifics of these but to relate these to underlying meanings and motivations, Figure 8.4 is presented to exemplify ways in which constructed experiences relate to identity,

Table 8.4 Relationship between the tourist 'self' and 'other'

Tourist other	*Touristic self*
Cultural insensitivity	Cultural sensitivity
Passivity	Activity
Travelling in herds	Independence
Ignorance/inability	Knowledge/ability

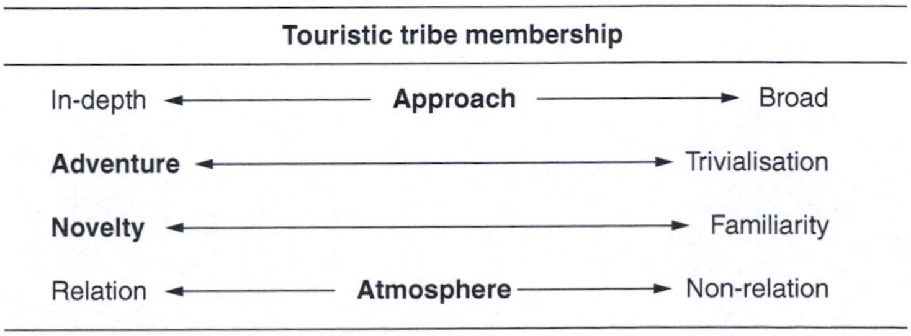

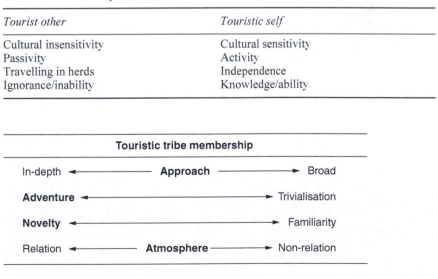

Figure 8.4 Constructed experience and identity.

and the ways in which the interviewees for this study tended to lean in one or the other direction, thereby displaying a certain identity.

In conclusion, it is assumed that, by combining a complex, in-depth approach to tourist experience, taking into consideration both its two different notions and a social identity approach which depends on contexts in various forms, the underlying meanings of tourism will appear as reflections of the identity that is sought. Tourist motivations are instrumental in this search and, thus, are expressed through communicated identity. Therefore, it is proposed that studying identity in tourism may facilitate access to evaluations of the acceptability of certain types of tourist activity as well as to the entailed contextual changes on behalf of the tourist.

Notes

1 The data set stems from the author's PhD work – see Smed (2009).

2 More detailed methodological considerations and approaches have not been included due to the focus and purpose of this chapter, in which other issues were deemed more important.

3 All interviewees are born between 1942/1943 and 1957/1958, and all data were collected in 2007–2008.

9 Bitten by the Twilight Saga

From pop culture consumer to pop culture tourist

Christine Lundberg and Maria Lexhagen

Introduction

More than a quarter of a million fans have travelled from all over the world to the small town of Forks, Washington, on the North Olympic Peninsula after it was selected as the key setting for Stephenie Meyer's highly successful book series the Twilight Saga. Before Twilight hit the town of only 3,175 inhabitants, the city's economy was dependent on the timber industry, which was in decline. The Twilight Saga changed this town forever. As a result of the town's proximity to the Olympic National Park, it has gained popularity among sport fishers and hikers but the number of tourists that the town has attracted as a result of the Twilight Saga is unparallelled (*Destination Forks*, DVD).

The Twilight Saga tells us the story of the young heroine Bella Swan who moves from sunny Arizona to the rainiest town in continental US – Forks – to live with her father, the town's police chief. At school she meets the handsome 'vegetarian' vampire Edward Cullen and falls in love with him. Her best friend, Jacob Black, turns out to be a werewolf; according to legend, vampires and werewolves are mortal enemies and, thus, a feud between the two is unleashed (www.stepheniemeyer.com). The Twilight Saga books have sold a total of 226 million copies worldwide (*Twilight*: 47 million, *New Moon*: 52 million, *Eclipse*: 58 million, *Breaking Dawn*: 69 million) (http://wiki.answers.com/). The first four films (out of five) which have been released on the big screen and DVD/Blu-ray have grossed over US$3.1 billion worldwide. The fourth movie in the series (released on 18 November 2011) grossed over US$500 million worldwide during its first week of screening (www.the-numbers.com/). Its readers and movie goers are varied, although a majority are female fans between the ages of eight and 80, contrary to the media perpetuated image of Twilight fans as young, screaming, obsessive, ready-to-faint teenage girls. Its contradictory messages have been used as an explanation for its massive and mixed audience:

> a series that presents neither a subversive nor a conservative view of larger social contexts but is an ambiguous mixture of both … provides such narrative pleasure because it is able to offer different things to different readers. It is like a Vegas buffet – there is something for everyone.
>
> (Wilson 2011: 8)

There are several destinations around the world that attract Twilight tourists. These destinations can be divided into *settings* (Riley *et al.* 1998), that is, destinations associated with books, films or TV series, or *locations* (Tooke and Baker 1996), that is places where films or TV series are shot. In the case of Twilight, there are mainly four different *settings* – Forks, La Push and Port Angeles, Washington, US, and Volterra, Italy. The Twilight *locations* that attract tourists are Portland, Oregon, British Columbia (for example, Vancouver, Squamish and Tofino), and the city of Montepulciano in Italy (Lundberg *et al.* 2011).

Regardless of whether these are settings or locations, they attract substantial numbers of Twilight tourists and illustrate what has been described as *location dissonance*, which is the difference between the place where the movie is filmed and where it is set (Frost 2006, 2009). In addition to this, there are a number of promotional events, conventions and fan-organised get-togethers around the world, not specifically associated with the Twilight Saga, that attract thousands of travelling Twilight fans (Lundberg *et al.* 2011).

Tourism to places associated with popular culture media such as literature, film and TV series, is not a new phenomenon. This is illustrated, for example, in Frost's (2006) historical review of film tourism where he pinpoints this form of tourism to the early twentieth century. However, it is primarily during the last decade that interest in how this form of tourism contributes to attractive destination images and affects the flow of tourists has been documented (Hudson and Ritchie 2006b; Lee *et al.* 2008). One explanation for the growing interest in this

Figure 9.1 Welcome sign at the borderline (aka Treaty Line) between the Twilight destinations Forks and La Push, Washington, USA (source: the authors).

form of tourism can be found in the emotional tie that is created between the pop culture consumer and the dramatic events, places or characters that are portrayed in a book, film or TV series (Kim and Richardson 2003; Müller 2006). These ties are related to so-called constructed realities, which mean that they are based on both authentic and purely fictitious foundations (Frost 2009). In addition, this form of tourism entails a significant degree of storytelling, which is a powerful and popular tool used in the production of experiences (Mossberg and Nissen 2006).

This form of travel is of particular interest from a research perspective as it is highly demand-driven (Müller 2006) and grows rapidly, thereby often surprising the receiving destinations (Lundberg *et al.* 2011). As a result of this, it is difficult to predict and it may also create a capacity problem at these destinations. Furthermore, problems in balancing the book- or film-constructed aspects of the place and the authentic elements have been documented (Shandley *et al.* 2006). The fact that the source of some of the these destinations' attraction is not primarily created for tourism but, rather, as works of art is problematic in terms of usage and exploitation owing, for example to copyright ownership. A few examples exist, such as Walt Disney's Disneyland and Disneyworld Resorts (Frost 2006; Marling 1997), but collaborations between the tourism industry and other creative industries are rare. In addition to this, the sustainability of this form of tourism has been questioned (Connell and Meyer 2009). However, Frost's (2006) historical overview of film tourism destinations around the world demonstrates the long-term potential of it.

This form of tourism is defined here as popular culture tourism (hereafter, pop culture tourism) as it originated from a pop culture phenomenon in film and literature. Pop culture has been defined as a collection of accessible artifacts or cultural expressions within film, literature, music, clothes/fashion, TV, radio and social processes (Strinati 2004). There are a number of criteria that have been used to define the pop culture phenomenon. First, it is liked by 'the many' (i.e. a volume criterion), it is set against 'fine culture' (i.e. an ethical value criterion), it is mass produced, mass consumed and commercial. It has further been defined as 'the people's culture' (by the people, for the people) and it is easily accessible, sometimes seen as trivial and dumbed-down (Lindgren 2005; Strinati 2004). As the pop culture phenomenon has strong impacts on attitudes, values and behaviours (Lindgren 2005), it is useful as a concept formation and theoretical frame of reference when researching tourists' motives for participating in tourism originating in cultural expressions such as film and literature.

So, what motivates tourists to participate in pop culture tourism? It has been suggested in film tourism research that these tourists' motives are made up from a complex combination of factors. These factors include traditional tourists' motives such as escapism, searching for identity, nostalgia, learning and attractiveness of the destination. But in addition to this, film-specific motives such as content of the movie, emotional ties to a place where a film is set, experiencing an enhanced emotion in the cross-road between fiction and reality, and celebrity spotting have also been cited (Beeton 2005). The research questions addressed in

Figure 9.2 Twilight tourists dressed up as characters from the films during their visit at the Twilight destination Forks, Washington, US (source: the authors).

this chapter are: What are pop culture tourists' travel motives, in the case of the Twilight Saga, and do they differ from traditional tourists' motives? What is the perceived value for these tourists and to which extent does motive and perceived value impact future pop culture travel intentions among these tourists?

Fan tourists' motives and perceived values

Tourists' motives have traditionally been described as continuums of seeking–escaping, push–pull and personal rewards–interpersonal rewards. On one side of the first spectrum, seeking–escaping, we find intrinsic motives where the tourist aims at satisfying internal needs. On the other side of the continuum, the tourist attempts to find release from everyday life by engaging in touristic activities. The second well-documented travel motives continuum is push–pull. The former entails psychological and social tourist characteristics which drive the tourist to partake in travel while the latter refers to destination specific characteristics which steer tourists' destination choice (Crompton 1979; Dann 1977; Uysal *et al.* 1993). The personal rewards–interpersonal rewards continuum focuses on rest, relaxation and ego enhancement (personal rewards) on the one hand and social interaction with family and friends (interpersonal rewards) on the other (Uysal *et al.* 1993).

However, when attempting to understand the travel motives of Twilight fans, research on fan tourism (in particular sport tourism) provides a more complex and usable frame of reference. One explanation for this complexity is that fans' travel is motivated by substantial investments in time, money and energy, sometimes bordering on an addictive, obsessive behaviour: 'it cannot be reduced to a few basic drives and needs' (Smith and Stewart 2007: 156). Fan tourists have been described as 'remarkably loyal, but they can also be fickle and critical ... [and] travel long distances to secure a special experience' (Smith and Stewart 2007: 157). In Smith and Stewart's (2007) review of sports fan tourism, they conclude that fans who identify themselves strongly with the object are more likely to partake in touristic activities related to their interest: 'Fans with stronger identification have sport more deeply embedded in their self-concept, and are more likely to attend games and travel greater distances to do so, purchase merchandise, spend more on tickets and products, and remain loyal' (Smith and Stewart 2007: 162). Twilight fans can be described as a highly involved fandom. For example, in our web survey of Twilight fans, they graded their interest and involvement in Twilight very highly ($\bar{x}$=6.43 on a scale of 1–7). In addition to this, the Twilight fandom is described, by the fans themselves and others, as having a strong sense of community and high level of fan productivity. The latter is an expression of fan involvement and, in the case of Twilight, takes the form of, for example, the creation of blogs, fan-pages, fan-art and fanfiction, which are fan-created stories about the characters and settings portrayed in the original work, often shared online with other fans (Lundberg *et al.* 2011). An example of the productivity expressed through the medium of fanfiction is that a search of Twilight-related fanfiction stories on one of the online forums for fanfiction publications generated almost 24,000 hits (this excludes several of the dedicated Twilight fanfiction sites). As many as 52 of these stories have been published by traditional publishing houses (however, revised in order not to cause copyright infringement) such as Omnific, The Writer's Coffee Shop Publishing House, and The Wild Rose Press (http://published.thetwilightawards.com).

Fan motivations have been divided into three dimensions: psychological, socio-cultural and social belonging. Examples of psychological motives are eustress (positive stress or arousal or stress release), escapism (diversion from daily life), aesthetic pleasure (enjoyment of the beauty of the activity) and drama and entertainment (intense enjoyment) (Crawford 2004; Fink *et al.* 2002; Smith and Stewart 2007; Trail and James 2001; Wann 1995; Wann *et al.* 2001; Weed and Bull 2004). Socio-cultural motives include spending time with family, friends and like-minded people (social interaction) and cultural connections such as 'mythical images', icons and symbols (Segrave and Chu 1996; Smith and Stewart 2007; Trail and James 2001). Social belongingness motives consist of tribal connections and vicarious achievement and self-esteem. The former entails being a part of a 'tribe' with norms, routines, symbols, rituals and language. Vicarious achievements are reached by being associated with a success(ful) person/team and, by this, attaining some form of empowerment (Morris 1981; Sutton *et al.* 1997; Trail *et al.* 2000). There are a number of moderating factors that influence fan travel motivation. Many of these are demographic variables such as age, education, income, gender and race (Armstrong 2002; Bilyeu and Wann 2002; James and Ridinger 2002; Wann 1995).

The concept of perceived value is close to the concept of motivation since it is also about understanding why people choose to participate in experiences. Also, the motivations behind a decision to purchase and participate in a tourist experience will likely influence the type and level of perceived value (Babin *et al.* 1994). Research has also shown that the motivation to consume hedonic types of products, such as travel and tourism, is based on the direct linkage between attribute-based value and the individual's enduring higher order values. The consequences of consumption are less important as an explanation for the formation of motivation (Mort and Rose 2004).

The definition of perceived value used here is based on Woodruff and Gardial (1996) and Holbrook (1996, 1999, 2006). The value of a product/experience is different depending on whether that product/experience contributes to an end-state or the pure possession of it is an end in itself. Value is a trade-off between negative and positive consequences from using a product/experience, and it is context dependent. Perceived value is also interactive (product/experience–customer), relativistic, comparative, situational, personal and a judgement of preference. Value can be perceived at different stages of the search, purchase and consumption process. If it is measured during the search and decision phase, it is said that it can be used as an approximation of what customers want and what they believe they will get (Woodruff 1997), linked to the formation of motivation. Furthermore, research has shown that it is important to measure satisfaction, loyalty and customer perceived value since these concepts have a comprehensive and complex effect on behavioural intention (Cronin *et al.* 2000), such as intention to purchase and recommend (Al-Sabbahy *et al.* 2004). For example, Duman and Mattila (2005) found that affective benefits positively influence future vacation choice.

Experiences, such as tourism experiences, are believed to be subjective, intangible, continuous and highly personal phenomena (O'Dell 2007). Satisfaction can be viewed as a general outcome of tourism experiences (Quinlan Cutler and Carmichael 2010). However, customer-perceived value dimensions of utility and hedonic value can also be used to evaluate outcomes of tourist experiences. Utilitarian value is focused on functional benefits and sacrifices (Zeithaml 1988), and hedonic value is focused on experiential benefits, such as enjoyment, escapism, pleasure, status and esteem (Babin *et al.* 1994; Holbrook 1999). In an attempt to uncover the essence of memorable tourism experiences, Tung and Ritchie (2011) found that affect, expectations, consequentiality and recollection enable the formation of memorable experiences. Clearly, these are linked to the concepts of perceived value and satisfaction. Based on this, it also appears to be important to further research perceived value in the context of specific types of tourism, in this case pop culture tourism.

How to figure out pop culture tourists' motives and perceived value

In order to understand pop culture tourists' motives, perceived value and travel intentions, an international web survey was published in September 2010 (and is still running). Forty Twilight-related online blogs, forums and communities were contacted (selected because of their large number of visitors, geographic location, position as online community nodes, and listed affiliated sites on these by employing a so-called snowball sampling), of which six posted the survey and urged their readers to participate in the study. The reason behind the decision was that the only known characteristic of the population was that many of them visited Twilight-related websites, blogs or forums, and as a result of this the sample frame was the online Twilight community. An unexpected outcome of these postings was that the link was picked up and tweeted (that is, reposted by users) on Twitter. As a result of this outcome, we contacted a total of five 'Twilight celebrities', which included actors in the series and so-called 'fandom super people' (that is, people in the fandom who are celebrities themselves due to their involvement in Twilight, such as Twilight fanfiction writers, Twilight charity organisers) on Twitter and asked them to tweet about our web survey link. One of them posted the link on her Twitter feed.

The total number of questions included in the web survey was 38, covering respondent characteristics, trip characteristics (for example, travel companion, mode of transport, length of stay), motives for travelling, experienced value and future travel intention as well as online involvement and behavior. A Likert-type scale was used for all questions related to motives, value and intention. A literature review covering the research themes was used in order to develop the questionnaire. In addition to this, a number of pilot tests were conducted among friends and colleagues to test the survey.

A total number of 863 respondents had completed the survey by February 2011, of which 64 per cent (n=753) stated that they had participated in Twilight Saga tourism at one or several points in time.

In Table 9.1, the descriptive distribution of the sample is presented. Due to the placement of background variables at the very end of the survey, the number of respondents on these questions is lower than that of the rest of the questionnaire.

The measurement items included in the survey concerning travel motives and experienced value are presented in Tables 9.2 and 9.3.

In order to evaluate the sustainability of pop culture tourism, a measure of intention to participate in this type of tourism in the future was implemented. The measure was developed by the authors and was expressed as 'To what extent is it likely that you would participate in a Twilight related event/trip in the future?'

Table 9.1 Respondent characteristics

Sample descriptives	*% of* n = *402–427*
Gender	
Men	1
Women	99
Age	
Between 12 and 67; median: 20	
Country of origin	
Sweden	70
North America	14
Other (South America, Asia, Europe, Australia)	16
Family status	
Single with/without children	49
Married with/without children	19
Other	32
Education	
Less than high school	29
High school	27
Undergraduate	38
Postgraduate	6

Twilight travelling: trip characteristics

A majority (64 per cent, *n*=753) of Twilight fans reported that they had previously travelled to a Twilight destination or participated at a Twilight event. Sixty-three per cent (*n*=487) of those who had participated in Twilight tourism activities one to three times had Twilight as a primary motive for their trip, while 89 per cent (*n*=283) of those who had travelled one to three times had Twilight as a secondary motive. Of those who had Twilight as a primary motive for their previous travels, 68 per cent (*n*=465) had partaken in one to four domestic trips and 32 per cent (*n*=470) in one to four international trips. On the question regarding their most recent Twilight-related trip, 95 per cent (*n*=354) stated that Twilight was the primary motive for their journey; 90 per cent (*n*=278) of Twilight fans' most recent trips could be categorised as event tourism and 5 per cent as destination tourism (that is, settings and locations).

With regards to the trip characteristics, 66 per cent (*n*=314) stated that their most recent Twilight trip lasted for one day and 24 per cent that it lasted two to four days. The primary mode of transportation was car for 48 per cent (*n*=313), 22 per cent travelled by train and 11 per cent reported going by plane. The Twilight tourists mostly travelled with 'real-life' friends (51 per cent, *n*=315) compared to online friends (2 per cent,), family (21 per cent), and a combination of family and friends (15 per cent). When searching for information to plan their trip they primarily used Twilight websites (61 per cent, *n*=308) and other

Table 9.2 Operational measures for motives

Motives measurement items	*Developed from previous research*
To experience a sense of belongingness to Twilight and/or the Twilight community	Crompton and McKay 1997
To experience a 'Twilight atmosphere'	Faulkner *et al.* 1999
To participate in activities that are fun	Formica and Uysal 1998
To experience new and different things	Kim and Chalip 2004
To get away from the usual routine	Mohr *et al.* 1993
To experience excitement	Scott 1996
To party and drink	Smith and Stewart 2007
To be with people who are enjoying themselves	Trail and James 2001
To meet old friends	Uysal *et al.* 1991
To meet new friends	Uysal *et al.* 1993
To share the experience with the people travelling with me	Wann 1995
To have fun with my friends and/or family	
To participate in other activities that are not Twilight related	
To visit an attractive destination	
To have an opportunity to visit this particular destination	
To watch people and be a part of the event/trip	

Table 9.3 Operational measures for perceived value

Perceived value measurement items	*Developed from previous research*
The event/trip had a consistent quality	Babin *et al*. 1994
Relative to other events/trips I have participated at, this event/trip had an acceptable level of quality	Overby and Lee 2006
The result was expected	Petrick 2002
The event/trip exceeded my expectations	Sánchez *et al*. 2006
The event/trip was a good purchase for the price paid	Steenkamp and Geyskens 2006
The event/trip purchased was reasonably priced	Sweeney and Soutar 2001
The event/trip was well worth the time and effort spent	
The price was the main criterion for the decision	
By participating at a Twilight-related event/trip I accomplished just what I need	
I am comfortable with the event/trip I purchased	
I enjoyed the event/trip	
The event/trip made me feel good	
During the event/trip I felt absorbed by the experience	
The event/trip was an escape	
The event/trip gave me a chance to learn about new information and trends	
The event/trip made me excited	
Compared to other things I could have done, the time and effort spent on this event/trip was truly enjoyable	
Participating at this event/trip helped me to feel acceptable	
This type of event/trip is taken by many people I know	
Participating at this event/trip improved the way I am perceived by others	
People who participate at this type of event/trip obtain social approval	
I participated at this event/trip to make a good impression on other people	
I participated at this event/trip to be able to interact and communicate with other people	

websites (17 per cent). It is noteworthy that only 4 per cent used travel operators or agencies as a source of information when planning their trips.

Twilight as a tourist attraction: Twilight attractiveness versus destination attractiveness

It is notable that 63 per cent (n=332) of Twilight tourists reported that they would not have travelled to the destination if it had not been for their interest in the Twilight Saga. Based on this finding, a split between a so-called Twilight Attractiveness group and a Destination Attractiveness group was made. The former consisted of those 63 per cent who would not have visited the destination if not for Twilight. The latter consisted of tourists (37 per cent) who would have travelled to the destination at the same point in time even if it had not been associated with Twilight. For example, they travelled to London in order to participate at a Twilight fan event but would have travelled to London even if there had not been a Twilight event held there at that time.

An independent sample t-test was conducted to identify differences in mean scores for motives and perceived value for these two groups. A significant difference was found between the Destination Attractiveness group (M=5.07, SD=1.92) and the Twilight Attractiveness group regarding *belongingness* (M=5.65; SD=1.73, t (255)=–2.486, p=0.01 (two-tailed)). The magnitude of the difference in the mean (mean difference=0.58, 95 per cent CI: 1.00 to 1.20) is small (eta squared 0.024) according to Cohen's (1988: 284–287) recommendations for eta squared levels. Also, a significant difference was found between the Twilight Attractiveness group (M=3.09; SD=2.19) and the Destination Attractiveness group regarding *to visit an attractive destination* (M=3.71; SD=2.32, t (242)=2.113, p=0.03 (two-tailed)). The size of the difference in the mean (mean difference=.62, 95 per cent CI: 0.04 to 1.20) is small (eta squared 0.017). Another difference was found for the motive *to participate at non-Twilight related activities* (Twilight Attractiveness group M=2.17; SD=1.82 and Destination Attractiveness group M=2.91; SD=2.08, t (241)=2.912, p=0.00 (two-tailed)). The effect size for this was also small (mean difference=0.74, 95 per cent CI: 0.24 to 1.24, eta squared 0.031).

Table 9.4 Significant differences between the Destination Attractiveness and Twilight Attractiveness groups

Most important motive/perceived value	*Destination Attractiveness group*	*Twilight Attractiveness group*
Motive: Belongingness		✓
Motive: Participate in non-Twilight-related activities	✓	
Motive: Visit attractive destination	✓	
Value: Comfortable	✓	
Value: Enjoyed	✓	

A few significant differences were also found for perceived value between the two groups. *Perceived enjoyment* is less important for the Twilight Attractiveness group (M=6.39, SD=1.40) than for the Destination Attractiveness group (M=6.72; SD=0.66, t (211)=1.940, p=0.05 (two-tailed)). The size of the difference in the mean (mean difference=0.32, 95 per cent CI: 0.005 to 0.649) is small (eta squared 0.024). Furthermore, the Twilight Attractiveness group perceived *comfort* to a significantly less extent (M=6.02; SD=1.57) than the Destination Attractiveness group (M=6.37; SD=1.05, t (206)=1.745, p=0.08 (two-tailed)). The magnitude of the difference in the mean (mean difference=0.34, 95 per cent CI: –0.045 to 0.743) is small (eta squared 0.017).

Groups of Twilight tourists

In order to find relationships between the motives and perceived types of value respectively, factor analysis was used. The dataset was prepared and cases considered as outliers were removed and the data were also evaluated in terms of normality, linearity and homoscedasticity. Bartlett's test of sphericity shows 0.000 (significance $p<0.05$) for motive and value measurements, suggesting that the intercorrelation matrix contains sufficient common variance for factor analysis to be worthwhile. Also, the Kaiser–Meyer–Olkin measure of sampling adequacy is .773 for motive measures .906 for value measures which are both above the suggested minimum value of .6 (Tabachnick and Fidell 2007). The factor analysis, with 16 items from the motive scale and 23 for the perceived value scale, was run using direct principal components to extract factors and oblimin rotation to allow for factors to be correlated.

The results revealed that there are five underlying components with eigenvalues above 1.0 explaining a total of 65.60 per cent of the variance for motives. The screeplot suggested the retention of two components, a parallel analysis suggested three components, the component matrix suggested the retention of four components, and the pattern matrix five components. The results for the perceived value scale suggested four underlying components with eigenvalues above 1.0 explaining a total of 62.48 per cent of the variance. The screeplot suggested the retention of two of the components, parallel analysis three components, the component matrix four components, and the pattern matrix suggested that four components could be retained since they all have three or more items loading above 0.3 on each component.

Based on the results of the parallel analysis, two three-factor solutions were chosen with a 52.5 per cent total explained variance for the motives scale (component 1 contributing 27.7 per cent, component 2 contributing 16.3 per cent, and component 3 contributing 8.5 per cent) and 57.8 per cent total variance explained for the perceived value scale (component 1 contributing 36.6 per cent, component 2 contributing 15 per cent, and component 3 contributing 6.2 per cent).

The three-factor solutions are presented in Tables 9.5 and 9.6. The first group – 'atmosphere and fun-seeking fans' – included the factors of fandom atmosphere and belongingness as well as party and drink. The second group

Table 9.5 Factor analysis of Twilight tourist motives

*Factor/item**	*Factor loading*	*Variance explained (%)*	*Communalities*
Atmosphere and fun-seeking fans		27.7	
Twilight atmosphere	0.835		0.677
Party/drink	–0.661		0.518
Belongingness	0.651		0.460
Traditional tourists		16.3	
Opportunity to visit this destination	0.875		0.732
Visit attractive destination	0.863		0.743
Participate in non-Twilight activities	0.756		0.602
Community-seeking fans		8.5	
Meet old friends	0.792		0.602
Be with people enjoying themselves	0.768		0.621
Have fun with friends and family	0.592		0.464
Share experiences with others	0.508		0.444
Cronbach's alpha of the total scale		0.809	
% Variance explained		52.473	
KMO:		0.773	
Bartlett:		1,381.983	
Significance:		0.000	

Note
* Only items with loadings above 0.5 are used in the results.

Table 9.6 Factor analysis of Twilight tourist perceived value

*Factor/item**	*Factor loading*	*Variance explained (%)*	*Commonalities*
Sensible experience seekers		36.6	
Feel good	0.909		0.820
Enjoyed	0.864		0.740
Well worth time and money	0.844		0.720
Compared to other things	0.840		0.718
Good purchase for price paid	0.826		0.700
Comfortable	0.818		0.667
Absorbed	0.797		0.631
Consistent quality	0.743		0.580
Excited	0.740		0.551
Exceeded expectations	0.710		0.528
Relative acceptable quality	0.694		0.541
Accomplishment	0.661		0.516
Reasonable price	0.652		0.431
Result as expected	0.549		0.327
Social success seekers		15	
Social approval	0.827		0.677
Improved the way I'm perceived	0.811		0.724
Good impression	0.648		0.478
Feel acceptable	0.632		0.554
Many people I know do this	0.582		0.351
Trendy price-conscious escapist*s*		6.2	
Escape	0.744		0.537
Learn new things/trends	0.709		0.694
Price main criterion	0.569		0.397
Cronbach's alpha of the total scale		0.874	
% Variance explained		57.845	
KMO:		0.906	
Bartlett:		2,746.183	
Significance:		0.000	

Note
* Only items with loadings above 0.5 are used in the results.

resembled to a great extent traditional tourists' travel motives and was thus titled 'traditional tourists', and included typical motives such as visiting an attractive destination and participating in activities not specifically focused on Twilight. The third group, 'community-seeking fans', consisted of motives that focus on the fellowship with other people such as meeting and having fun with family and old friends and sharing this experience with others.

The factor analysis also resulted in three perceived value groupings. The first of these was 'sensible experience seekers', which consisted of values related to good value for time and money spent and enjoyment. The second group – 'social success seekers' – included perceived values which focus on social acceptance from others. The third and final group – 'trendy price-conscious escapists' – consisted of values connected to price and trends and escapism.

Future Twilight travel intentions

One of the main criticisms put forward regarding tourism related to, for example film and literature tourism, from a destination perspective, is regarding its sustainability. The focus on the investment costs in relation to its possible short-term life-cycle has been the heart of the matter (Connell and Meyer 2009). The main argument for this criticism is that the main attraction of film and literature tourism is based on pop culture phenomena whose nature is fugacious. One way of estimating the perishability of this form of tourism is to ask tourists about their future travel intentions and recommendations to others. Of the Twilight tourists questioned, 48 per cent (n=492) stated that it was likely to extremely likely that they would partake in Twilight travel in the future, of which 39 per cent stated extremely likely. Just 13 per cent stated that it was not likely at all. In addition to this, 41 per cent (n=496) reported that it was likely to extremely likely that they would recommend others to participate at a Twilight-related event or trip; 32 per cent stated that it was extremely likely that they would do so. Only 15 per cent responded that it was not likely at all. Since these findings are based on tourists who have already participated in Twilight-related travel, it can be concluded that Twilight tourism is not a once-in-a-lifetime experience for tourists but represents a potential for repeat travelling and long-term development for destinations.

A multiple regression was conducted in order to assess which motives and types of perceived value affect future Twilight-related travel. The dependent variable was future intention to participate in a Twilight-related event or trip and the independent variables were all of the motives and perceived value items used in the survey. No multicollinearity problems were detected from the assessment of the tolerance (low values below 0.10) and VIF-statistics (no values above 10). The combination of motive variables entering the regression explain 37.1 per cent (R^2) of the variance in future intention to participate (F-value 7.120; Sig.=0.000; $p<0.0005$). Significant contributions, in order of size of beta value, to the regression model were observed for the following motives: Twilight atmosphere, an opportunity to visit the destination, to share the experience with others, to visit an attractive destination, to participate in non-Twilight-related activities, to get out of the usual routine, and to have fun.

As regards the types of perceived value that affect future Twilight-related travel, again no multicollinearity problems were detected (low values below 0.10 for tolerance statistic and no values above 10 for VIF-statistic). The combination of types of perceived value variables entering the regression explain 48.5 per cent (R^2) of the variance in future intention to participate (F-value 7.281; Sig. = 0.000; $p < 0.0005$).

These findings not only pinpoint which motives and perceived value might explain future travel intentions but can also be used in order to understand how a destination can develop their product in order to attract future Twilight tourists.

Lessons learned on Twilight Saga tourism

It has been suggested in previous research that fans' travel motives are more complex than tourists' motives in general. This conclusion is based on the fact that this form of tourism is founded in a strong interest in and knowledge about a particular phenomenon. Furthermore, it is based on a strong emotional tie between the traveller and the characters, stories and places portrayed in for example films, TV series or books. From a pop culture destination perspective, the main attraction is made up by constructed realities which mean that it is based on both authentic and purely fictitious foundations. This in turn adds to the complexity of fans' travel motives and perceived value.

Our findings support this sentiment. Results showed that there are a clear majority of travelling fans who are attracted to Twilight rather than the destination per se – a group titled Twilight Attractiveness group. These are contrasted to those travelling fans who are attracted to the destination as well – Destination Attractiveness group. For the former group, the motive of belongingness is significant while for the latter, participation in non-Twilight activities and visiting the destination are important motives. Furthermore, perceived value as comfort and enjoyment is important for this latter group. In addition to this, the results showed that a majority of motives are linked to perceived values. For the Destination Attractiveness group, the strongest correlation was found between escapism motives and values of routine and escape. For Twilight Attractiveness Group, the strongest correlation was found between interaction motives and values, such as meeting new friends and interacting and communicating.

These results have implications for travel operators and receiving destinations. For example, the Destination Attractiveness group exhibit more traditional tourist motives where the attraction of the destination and escapism constitute the base for their travel motivations. The Twilight Attractiveness group on the other hand is made up by tourists who are focused on living out their Twilight experience with other Twilight fans at the destination. A division between those who travel with Twilight as a primary and a secondary motive can also be inferred from the results. Those travelling with Twilight as a primary motive are likely to be found within the Twilight Attractiveness group and those with

Twilight as a secondary motive within the Destination Attractiveness group. Noteworthy is that in order to continue to attract tourists with Twilight as a primary motive, destinations need to understand and create opportunities for these fans to exercise their need for belongingness with other Twilight fans, for example by meeting and interacting with their peers. For the Destination Attractiveness group, destinations need to satisfy these tourists' needs to visit an attractive destination with a supply of interesting and fun non-Twilight-related activities in order to continue to attract this group. However, Twilight is the core attraction for both of these groups and without the destinations' association with Twilight, none of these groups would travel to them.

The findings related to the Twilight tourists' travel motives and perceived value groupings showed three groups respectively. The motive groupings consisted of atmosphere and fun-seeking fans, traditional tourists and community-seeking fans. These results picture social belongingness and social-cultural motives as most important. However, destination attributes and attractiveness are also important. The perceived value groupings showed groups of sensible experience seekers, social success seekers, and trendy price-conscious escapists. The most important perceived values are social approval/impression and enjoyment. In addition to this, price, value for money and quality are also important.

This analysis supports our previous findings on different Twilight tourist groups (for example, Destination Attractiveness versus Twilight Attractiveness groups, Twilight as a primary versus secondary travel motive) but, in addition to this, it also provides destinations with a more versatile view of the travelling fans' motives and perceived values which need to be met in order for them to travel to these destinations.

As regards the impact of these results on estimating future travel intentions, both motive and perceived value are important factors that affect Twilight tourists' travel intentions. Beyond this, the degree of measured future intentions suggests a long-term impact of Twilight tourism. These findings are in stark contrast to previous criticisms put forward in research regarding the sustainability of this form of tourism (cf. Connell and Meyer 2009).

As this research shows, fans' travel motives and perceived value are complex. At the core of this form of tourism is the experience which often is difficult to predict and plan, for the reasons described above. The fact that these experiences are based on the emotional ties between fans and the characters, events, story or places portrayed in pop culture phenomena poses a special demand on receiving destinations as regards how to develop products based on constructed realities that satisfy fans' needs of such experiences featuring both purely fictitious and authentic elements. As such, one of the biggest challenges for pop culture tourism development lies in the collaboration between tourism and other creative industries in order to develop sustainability, for example regarding copyright ownership. As discussed, this form of tourism is highly demand-driven (fan-driven), it grows rapidly and as a result of this, often surprises the receiving destination. Due to the explosive nature of development for this form of tourism, collaboration between the industries could assist in generating proactive destination development strategies rather than the dominant standard in the industry of reactive behaviour in order to meet the travel motives and experienced value of pop culture tourists. The copyright owners in the creative industry could benefit from such collaboration by for example a strengthened bond between fans and their object of interest through touristic experiences, which in turn can generate increased sales in terms of movie-goers, DVD/Blu-ray, books and other merchandise.

Examples of future research can be drawn from these findings. For example, more research is needed as regards which pop culture tourist destination attributes generate different types of value. Our research shows that the relationship between fans' travel motives and perceived value is one key to understanding this form of heightened tourist experiences in a postmodern experience economy.

Acknowledgements

The authors would like to thank Stavroula Wallström at the University of Borås for insightful ideas in the development of the survey instrument. In addition to this, we would like to thank Mid Sweden University and the European Union Structural Funds for their contribution to the funding of this study.

Part IV

Place and the tourist experience

Simply stated, tourism involves the movement of people to and their temporary stay at places away from their normal place of residence. Quite evidently, therefore, the place or setting of tourism, whether the destination in general or more specific locations within the destination area, is fundamental to the tourist experience. Not only is the attraction or 'pull' of the destination a key factor in the tourism demand process; every tourism place possesses a set of 'destination-specific attributes' (Goodall 1991: 59) which influence destination choice. At the same time, the extent to which tourists' images, perceptions or expectations of the destination are met or verified will dictate how the tourist interacts with the destination and, ultimately, has a satisfying experience.

Of course, academic attention has long been paid to 'place', such as the construction or meaning of place, particularly within the human geography literature (Manzo 2003). Thus, it is commonly recognised that a space only becomes a place when people attach meanings and values to it, and when they use or interpret it in particular ways (Tuan 1977). In other words, the meaning or identity of a place to an individual is typically a function of the tangible characteristics of the place, the (usually socially constructed) meanings attached to it, and the ways in which he or she uses or interacts with it. Nevertheless, within the tourism literature, the relationship between place and experience or, more specifically, how the tourist experience may be influenced or enhanced by place, remains relatively unexplored.

The chapters in this section begin to address this gap in the literature. First, in Chapter 10, Jennifer L. Erdely presents an ethnographic account of how volunteer tourists in post-Hurricane Katrina New Orleans experience the city. She demonstrates, first, how volunteer tourists attempt to understand the city by comparing it with other places that have suffered tragedy and disaster before going on to consider the way they view the landscape and conditions of the city as a place to live. With an intimate look at New Orleans through the homes, lives and situations of its residents, volunteer tourists notice aspects of New Orleans leisure tourists do not get to see; they experience what cannot be physically seen through talking to local people, visiting their homes, spending time in neighbourhoods and working with them to rebuild the city. Consequently volunteer tourists develop their own sense of place of New Orleans.

Research into theuse and experience of the holiday home place by families with children is the focus of Chapter 11. Drawing on the results of a qualitative study amongst groups of tourists staying in Blokhus and Hals, two popular destinations in northern Denmark, Jacob Kirkegaard Larsen and Lea Holst Laursen explore the importance of place in relation to the family experience in a holiday home. Deconstructing the holiday destination into different places/spaces, they discuss the outcomes of the research which reveals that certain places do not equally meet the needs of both older and younger family members, but that opportunities exist to create what they term 'hybrid' places for satisfying family-wide experiences. This is followed in Chapter 12 by a conceptual consideration of the emergence of experiential consumption and the consequential implications for the provision of tourism and leisure experiences in general, and for enhancing visitors' experience of and engagement with museums in particular. Specifically, Babak Taheri and Aliakbar Jafari argue that the leisure experience is no longer passive; people seek to engage in or 'co-create' their experiences of places, frequently within the spirit of playfulness. Thus, museums need to respond to this transformation in consumption to meet the expectations of contemporary consumers and hence both to remain competitive in tourist markets and to continue to fulfil their wider social role.

10 Volunteer tourists' experiences and sense of place

New Orleans

Jennifer L. Erdely

Introduction

The floods of Hurricane Katrina brought many aspects of New Orleans to the surface. Volunteer tourists – that is, tourists who travel to a destination to work there without pay in response to a perceived social or environmental need – seek to understand the sense of New Orleans through its cultural traditions and engage with these cultural traditions to understand the city, its people and its landscape on a deeper level. Volunteer tourists examine the cultural traditions of New Orleans, such as what it means to be from the southern United States, multigenerational living, community, the role of levees, family and land, to understand the city. By becoming familiar with New Orleans through talking to residents, spending time in neighbourhoods and rebuilding homes, they understand more than what they can see. These experiences allow volunteer tourists to understand not only the city but also its sense of place. As witnessed by the stories presented in this chapter, many volunteer tourists gain a holistic sense of New Orleans and become advocates for the community's continued rebuilding.

Volunteer tourism and place

As in this chapter, some research within the study of volunteer tourism focuses on volunteer tourists' relationships with locals. Nancy McGehee and Kathleen Andereck (2008), for example, compare the relationship between residents and volunteer tourists in McDowell County, West Virginia, and Tijuana, Mexico. In Mexico, volunteers are responsible for building homes and schools, while the volunteers in West Virginia help at the local food bank and assist with building projects (McGehee and Andereck 2008). McGehee and Andereck discuss the 'othering' of residents by volunteer tourists through the recitation of a 'God talk' in exchange for work (McGehee and Andereck 2008: 21).

Harng Sin (2009) joins Action Africa, a group from the National University of Singapore. Her research cites the desire to travel, to help others, as a personal challenge, and a convenient way to travel as reasons volunteer tourists travel to South Africa to learn about the local culture. Wearing and Ponting discuss how volunteer tourists self-identify and discuss that 'members of the host community can then play a valuable part in determining the "identity" of the destination through the value that they have for particular places, events, and traditions' (Wearing and Ponting 2009: 261). They argue that residents guide tourists, pointing out cultural values. However, although these studies help us understand how volunteer tourists interact with the community, they also invite a more in-depth study of the relationship between volunteers and residents and between volunteers and place. Because New Orleans residents are tied to the city despite its struggles, my study seeks to understand how volunteers interpret the ties between residents and New Orleans and also to show how volunteer tourists develop ties to the city. Additionally, this chapter utilises volunteer tourists' descriptions of their interactions with locals to explain how they come to understand post-Hurricane Katrina New Orleans.

Sense of place

To understand the cultural traditions of New Orleans we have to understand that the space in which they occur is both the context and the reason for those cultural traditions, acting both as a mobiliser and a limitation. Christopher Tilley also sees space and events as related, and he explains:

> a humanized space forms both the medium and outcome of action, both constraining and enabling it. ... Socially produced space combines the cognitive, the physical and the emotional into something that may be reproduced but is always open to transformation and change. A social space, rather than being uniform and forever the same, is constituted by differential densities of human experience, attachment and involvement.
>
> (Tilley 1994: 10–11)

As Tilley states, all sites/spaces stem from the actions of people, or all space/sites are created by individuals. The existence of New Orleans is a demonstration of its relationships between the elements interacting with it. One element of New Orleans is the city's newest set of tourists, volunteer tourists. Interactions between volunteer tourists, residents and the landscape affect the culture of New Orleans and the culture of volunteer tourism.

Additionally, aspects of New Orleans are conveyed through bodies of residents and bodies of the landscape to bodies of volunteer tourists. Volunteer tourists understand New Orleans through their bodies. Volunteer tourists interact with New Orleans through their bodies by spending their time and money and working in the city. Tilley discusses how meaning involves people and talks more specifically about bodies. He defines space, stating, 'an experience of space is grounded in the body itself; its capacities and potentialities for movement' (Tilley 1994: 16). Tilley suggests that the body's limits and capacity are the medium through which aspects of the locations are conveyed. Volunteer tourists demonstrate Tilley's idea of movement by changing their perspectives about the city as their bodies interact with it.

Volunteer tourists understand New Orleans because of the stories told about it by other volunteer tourists, residents, workers, friends, and so on. Through the stories told by others, New Orleans becomes a living thing that is dynamic, engaging and changing. Elizabeth Bird talks further about the process of understanding a place, stating, 'Through stories, people continue to make aesthetic and moral sense of places, at the same time endowing these places with a sense of their own cultural identities' (Bird 2002: 544). Bird asserts that individuals understand locations on multiple levels through telling stories. She also discusses how telling stories helps people to understand who they are.

Volunteer tourists also not only make sense of how New Orleans looks, but how the politics of the city play out in its appearance and the spirit of the residents. The stories volunteer tourists tell also help them understand who they are and how they fit into the city in a dynamic phase of its existence. Through the stories residents tell volunteer tourists and volunteer tourists then retell, a connection to New Orleans' unique landscape and residents forms. Moreover, volunteer tourists' relationship to the city not only forms a temporary connection with New Orleans, but prompts many to come back annually.

Method

To understand the culture of volunteer tourism, I participated with volunteer tourists and conducted this study as ethnography. I did preliminary research from February to May 2008, and my concentrated research period stretched over seven months, from November 2008 to June 2009, during which I gathered data through participant observation, in-depth interviews and spontaneous conversations. I spent Thursday through Saturday weekly with volunteer groups shadowing and participating in volunteer activities. In January and February 2010, I resided with a volunteer tourism group for four days.

I spent some time at the site working; in addition to rebuilding activities, sometimes we spent time together at lunch or dinner. I would ask if a few co-workers would be willing to be interviewed about their experience as a volunteer in New Orleans. I videotaped 50 interviews with volunteer tourists. In addition to videotaped interviews, I also include notes from conversations.

A place like any other?

The complicated issues of New Orleans are highlighted as volunteer tourists compare New Orleans' situation to locations that face or have faced tragedies. Most commonly, volunteer tourists compare New Orleans to developing countries and to New York, another American city that faced great tragedy on 11 September 2001. Also, volunteer tourists try to understand New Orleans through the way people live in the city: the attitudes of people who deal with death on a daily basis and the condition of the city. By comparing New Orleans to other places that experience tragedies, volunteer tourists demonstrate their understanding of the plethora of issues facing New Orleans post-Hurricane Katrina. Also, volunteer tourists understand that the issues facing the city also face the entire New Orleans community.

In this section, Brenda compares New Orleans to India, Wayne relates it to his homeland of Jamaica, and Amy and Liz to New York City.

Garrett, a man in his seventies from Wisconsin who was shining the wood-panelled walls in Ms Vera's home, sent me to Brenda. Brenda sits on the newly lacquered floor of Ms Vera's home, painting the baseboards. I timidly enter the room and tell her that her colleague, Garrett, suggested I talk to her.

She says 'Come on in'.

I sit on the floor and Brenda starts talking. She talks about everything: her background, feral cats and New Orleans, to name a few topics. At a break in the conversation, I interject, 'Last night at the group reflection, you mentioned something about a puppy at your work site. I was wondering if you could tell me more about that.'

She says:

> In the morning, we had come in and the puppy was sleeping at this house and the people at the house had moved the day before and the puppy was on the doorstep. Later on we didn't see the puppy. So I asked the boys that we had seen playing with it, 'Where's the puppy?' And they said this one kid had him. So later on in the day Garrett noticed a *whole* crowd of people on the doorsteps of the house that the family had moved out of, and there was the puppy. Also they had three toddlers. The toddlers were throwing things at the puppy who was chained and so I went over and tried to just, you know, play with the puppy. Over the course of the two weeks, we've seen children act afraid of this puppy who would follow people all around; it wasn't on a chain or anything. And you know he's had a lot of people throw things at him so I went over and I was playing with him. He's a puppy so he chews and he was chewing on my hand. I know the trick where you stick your hand in farther and they can't bite down. But then when he was getting rougher I would say, 'Now, don't bite.' And I was trying to teach this whole family by modeling behavior. Well, they thought I wanted to buy it. So they said it would be $75 and then they started bickering among themselves about how they would divide up the money.
>
> (Brenda)

Brenda, fearing the puppy would become aggressive, attempted to show the neighbourhood children how to treat a puppy. The adults, seeing her interact with the puppy, thought she wanted to purchase it. She unpacks the situation for me:

> It reminded me of the stories I've been told about India. I've never been to India. Beggars will cut off a child's limb in a family so that tourists will feel more sorry for them and give them money because they have a child without a limb. It's not my concept at all, and it almost seemed like that's what they

> were doing with the dog. [They were] saying, 'Ok, here's an opportunity or if you don't want to do it our way which is to train this dog to be an aggressive dog that we don't bond with but maybe will be a guard dog or something. Either buy it or leave us alone.' I don't know. That's sort of how I felt.
>
> (Brenda)

Brenda talks about the treatment of the puppy, comparing it to how some humans are treated in India. Relating the scenario to what she has heard about India, Brenda tries to understand why these residents are doing this.

By using the lens of India, Brenda views the situation as survival, not animal abuse. She relates the complicated situation of people sacrificing a loved one's limbs in India for survival and the residents' attempt to sell her the dog. Linking India to New Orleans shows that New Orleans is a desperate place in a desperate situation and residents make decisions based on those situations. In complicating the situation in New Orleans by likening it to situations in India, Brenda reveals the complexity of residents' struggles. By revealing her understanding of residents' struggles, Brenda relays her understanding of the community of New Orleans and her revised understanding of New Orleans through her experience in the city. She understands New Orleans through the way these residents treat the puppy.

Like Brenda, Liz and Amy understand New Orleans through comparing it to another place. I listen as Liz and Amy attempt to understand New Orleans by comparing it to New York City as we sit on the front steps of Ms Claire's house. With strawberry blond curls at the top of her head, Liz doesn't look 30, much less all 40 years she admits to. Liz works in a theatre in New York City and her tone is excited and passionate. Amy, a Unitarian Universalist pastor intern and about the same age, is careful and articulate. Her black hair is straight, tied in a neat ponytail at the base of her neck. Careful about her words and her tone, Amy is serious and speaks slowly. The two volunteer tourists discuss New York City, as it is close to where they reside in New Jersey. In trying to understand New Orleans, Liz and Amy debate why New Orleans was ignored by the government following the storm.

> Liz states, 'New York City is so important it cannot be replicated, it cannot be moved, so we do what we can to protect it. For some reason the will to do that with New Orleans was absent . . .'
> '. . . because it's not a financial city,' Amy retorts.
> Liz agrees, 'Right. It's not Wall Street and also . . .'
> '. . . it's a very insulated, very particular culture. Which is not understandable by the rest of the world let alone the rest of the country,' Amy states.
> Liz adds: 'And I do think there's this puritanical streak in our country that doesn't understand people who make different choices, you know. Living in New Orleans there's a lot less of keeping up with the Joneses. People don't really care if they have the latest model whatever. You know your iPhone is

> really not going to impress many people. They put their energy into family and food and music and other places that the rest of the country sees as …'
>
> '… frivolous.' Amy states.
>
> Liz continues: 'Frivolous, an expendable vacation, "It's a good time but I couldn't live in that space," and of course there's a downside to that, the streets don't get fixed, all the things that the people who live here roll their eyes at. It's a different way of life and I don't think that a lot of the rest of the country, at least where I've lived, understand those values, those choices.

Liz and Amy speak to perceptions of the city that could have slowed the post-Hurricane Katrina governmental response. Although this was Liz's fourth trip to New Orleans, this is Amy's first. Their perspectives are nuanced and speak to the place of New Orleans – its makeup including the people, the environment and the aesthetic of New Orleans. Liz and Amy understand New Orleans through the priorities of residents in relation to the priorities of the government.

Liz and Amy's dialogue moves from the financial aspects of the city to the overall values and uniqueness of the culture. Liz contends that many people don't see the value in the culture, and she asserts that the infrastructure suffers because of the laissez-faire way of life. She also brings up the opinion of some visitors that New Orleans is dispensable or only serves one purpose – as a place to have fun. Discussing the conflict between New Orleans' reputation as a party town and how people live in New Orleans, Liz and Amy conclude that people live here because residents prioritise their lives differently than in other places. These volunteers observe residents' priorities as family, food and music, and working around the infrastructural items that do not function. Liz conjectures that outsiders see New Orleanians as lazy because of this attitude. The richness in New Orleans comes with a price – improvements don't happen efficiently. Outsiders do not understand how people live with this attitude from local government. Because New Orleans is a place known for its relaxed environment, the government does not see it as productive and did not respond to its residents accordingly.

Amy and Liz understand the complexity of the response to New Orleans by highlighting the finances, race and sense of community in the city. Liz and Amy come to an understanding about New Orleans' and New Orleanians' way of life through comparing the city to New York City. In comparing tragedies, they understand the repercussions of New Orleans' lack of financial stature. By understanding New Orleans' lack of financial stature, they then understand the struggles of the community to rebuild.

Like Amy and Liz, Wayne also compares New Orleans to a place with which he is familiar. In an unheated community centre on a cold January morning in the Lower Ninth Ward, Wayne, a volunteer from the Caribbean, and I are talking. His presence is notable. He is tall and his dark skin is a sharp contrast to the majority of Caucasian volunteers in the city. A student at Florida State University, Wayne explains his understanding of New Orleans:

> I'm originally from Jamaica, and the US is supposed to be that place that everybody can come together. This is supposed to be a wealthy country and look at the houses. It really breaks my heart. These are Americans and they're living like they're less than Americans, like they're second-class citizens. They don't have houses; people are still living in trailers. It's really ridiculous.

Although most volunteer tourists are considered 'outsiders', Wayne understands New Orleans as a non-American. His expectations of how Americans are supposed to live are violated as he sees people living in substandard housing. A tension exists between how Americans are 'supposed' to live and how New Orleanians actually live post-Hurricane Katrina. His perception of New Orleans and how New Orleanians live is not consistent with the way he has seen other Americans live.

Wayne's views show how complex his feelings are about New Orleans. His description of New Orleans and comparisons to his home nation of Jamaicia demonstrate that New Orleans has characteristics of a developing nation. By this comparison Wayne highlights that the issues in New Orleans are greater than rebuilding flooded homes. His observation that New Orleanians are living like 'less than Americans' reveals his understanding of the community's plethora of issues. He understands the community through his experiences with the community and seeing the way members of the community live. New Orleans is seen as a diminished place, a devastated place, but also as a place that seems comfortable how they treat their poor.

By understanding the city in comparison with other cultures, volunteer tourists better serve New Orleans. The contributions volunteer tourists make to the community of New Orleans are more significant because they have an understanding of New Orleans in the context of other places throughout the world. The struggle to understand New Orleans manifests itself in how volunteer tourists talk about it in comparison to other places, the government, conditions in New Orleans, the landscape, race and culture. Volunteer tourists also gain an understanding of New Orleans through the government's immediate response following Hurricane Katrina.

A landscape suitable for habitation?

Volunteer tourists attempt to understand New Orleans through its landscape, particularly the levees. Conflicting feelings of being secure in a community and insecure with the government's system of levee protection are central to New Orleanians' mindsets. Through understanding the system of protection of New Orleanians, volunteer tourists understand the community. As demonstrated in this section, the levees serve as not only a measure of protection but also a reminder of the storm to both residents and volunteer tourists. Haley discusses levee repairs, Brenda relates her discussions with her Wisconsin neighbours, Ethan discusses the connection to the land, Helen talks about New Orleanians' connections to family, and Brett relates information he communicates to younger volunteer tourists.

First, Haley talks about how it must feel to be a New Orleanian, with the constant confrontation of a possible levee breakage post-Hurricane Katrina. Sitting on the newly built steps on a house in the Lower Ninth Ward, Haley discusses the conditions of the levees stating:

> When I go up to the levee and see where they've patched the wall, and it's caulked. It's not caulked well enough that you would even want it in your bathroom. That's what makes me really angry. When I'm at the levee and I realize that the people that are rebuilding on the other side don't have any more protection than they did before and that we haven't solved any problems.

The government's treatment of the levees helps Haley understand New Orleans. The condition of the levee and the level of risk residents endure because of it disturb her. Additionally, Haley expresses anger that the structures the government built to protect people in New Orleans haven't been properly repaired. Although her anger is not directed at the residents, Haley attempts to understand how people live with these structures as their only protection if a storm comes. Haley understands the complexity of the community through the constant tensions between being part of a place and the government's faulty protection system. Through Haley's understanding, she better sympathises with the community's difficulties in deciding to stay in this area.

As Haley vents her frustrations, other volunteer tourists adopt the role of advocate for the rebuilding of New Orleans. I ask Brenda, 'What do you take back from these trips?' Brenda relays some of these conversations acquaintances have had with her:

> I think one is, living in Wisconsin, when I talk to other people in my social network from other places as well, they say, 'It's in a flood plain. It should just be abandoned. Those people should move somewhere else.' [They] have a really hard, crass attitude about it. I can see that point of view. The first time I came down here, last year, it hit me how wide the Mississippi flood plain is because it is such an old river. If you did that, you would have all the people from Mississippi, Arkansas, and Louisiana move somewhere else. Where? And then you'd have to start with California, New York, and Delaware, and Florida. You know everyone's going to be lined up in a lump in tornado alley in some, I don't know where, Colorado maybe, and chase out the Native Americans again. So it's too simplistic to say, 'Well, some of it's under water, get rid of it.' That doesn't make any sense.

Brenda deconstructs the argument that New Orleans should not be rebuilt and responds to critics who question living in New Orleans, given its low elevation. Other volunteers relate that they have to justify coming to New Orleans to their friends and relatives because of these same reasons. In discussing the low elevation of New Orleans, she also highlights many people's belief that the city should never have been developed. Volunteer tourists have invested physically, mentally and emotionally in the rebuilding of New Orleans and reject the focus on its vulnerabilities. Volunteer tourists confront the city's perceived lack of worth and statements that efforts to rebuild it are futile. In Brenda's responses to questions as to why not abandon New Orleans, she confronts the complexity of New Orleanians' situation with her friends. In understanding the community through her own physical and financial investment in the city, Brenda advocates for its rebuilding despite its location. An essential part of New Orleans' sense of place is the defence of it.

Like Brenda, other volunteer tourists also struggle with tensions about whether New Orleans should have been built, and what should be done with the city now. Ethan, an African American man originally from Illinois and now living in California, states:

> I've heard some question why people live here. I grew up along the Mississippi River. Every year there's a flood, and every year people say why don't those people just move away? They know the flood's coming again next year, and people have an attachment to the land in a very significant way. Your parents grew up here. Your grandparents grew up here and your great grandparents and on and on and on and on. For some that is very significant. And I actually feel a little guilty that I moved so far away from my roots. Who knows, maybe as I get older maybe I'll feel more compelled to be closer to them. But right now, I feel the movement from my roots has given me the ability to even do this work and other work that I do because it exposes me to a much broader community and a community I have some currency in. I can navigate it, I can work in it, and bring something to it, you know?

Ethan refutes discussions that New Orleanians should move. He attributes living near family to the development of a strong sense of family that exists in the city. Talking of the arguments that people should relocate, he discusses how people are connected spatially. Ethan highlights how the place affects the person. He concentrates on the bonds people have to land through the culture of family existing in these areas, and attributes the connection to the landscape, to part of New Orleans as a place. Through self-reflection and understanding residents' relationship to the land, Ethan is able to understand the sense of the city that keeps people there. As Ethan understands the relationship between people, their land and the landscape, he understands the community and the reasons members of the community live with the constant risk of hurricanes or floods.

Unlike Ethan, who uses his own experience to understand how New Orleanians live, Helen uses residents' experiences to understand the city. A volunteer in her seventies from New Hampshire, Helen relays a story about the family-oriented culture in New Orleans over the whirring generator and table saw. She states:

> The guy who told the story about his home was visiting some people across the street from the house we were working in. What it gave me is that I'm listening to somebody whose family for generations back has lived in that same place. It helped me feel why people live here. Why would they stay in a place that is subject to hurricanes? That was very humbling actually.

I pressed Helen, 'How so?' I asked.

Helen continues:

> It's an appreciation that he has for handing things down – for family to have someone be able to say, how far back did they go, how many hands did the house pass through. The second year, no, the first year when we were fixing up Barbara's house, there was a home next door where the father and mother cleaned up the front yard and put a flag in the yard. That was very moving. I walked over and I talked to them about it. That home had been in the mother's family back to her great-grandmother. It was her grandmother's, then it was her mother's, then it was hers, and now it was their daughter's. How many times does that happen where I'm living? It doesn't. It doesn't. And that felt good; it felt good that in parts of America that still happens.

Helen processes how residents deal with the struggle of breaking family tradition to live in a less flood-prone area. Homes pass from family member to family member with multiple generations living together in single-family homes. Helen understands family ties are often why residents live with the risks associated with hurricanes. Through understanding this resident's experience, Helen is able to understand why people remain in this community. She understands New Orleans as a place through the resident's experience of living in the same home as her ancestors. The passing down of homes demonstrates the sense of family in New Orleans, and Helen understands this through her interaction with this resident.

Although Helen later tells me about relaying information when she gets home, Brett discusses how he relays information about New Orleans while he is volunteering in the city. Brett, a man in his mid-forties from New Jersey, is accompanying a group of 14- to 18-year-olds who are also helping with rebuilding in New Orleans. Brett relates his understanding of New Orleans through a conversation he had with the adolescents accompanying them on the trip. He states:

> Some of the youth were wondering why they were fixing up this enormous house. 'Well, because there's not just one family living there. And there are not ten kids in their family. The house has been around for generations.' So

> it's not like they built this big house; there are a lot of people living in there. It is a different style of living.

This volunteer informs the adolescents that owning a big house does not mean the resident is wealthy but that multigenerational living is part of New Orleans' culture. Not only does Brett understand the community of New Orleans, but he also passes the information on to young Unitarians.

As volunteer tourists explain, New Orleans' residents have to decide between living near their families and original communities and living in a less flood-prone area. The volunteers notice that New Orleanians are constantly defending their decision to live in the city. Volunteer tourists listen to the stories, view the landscape and gain an understanding of New Orleans as a place. In fact, many volunteer tourists see the benefits in the way New Orleanians live, particularly in creating a strong family culture. However, when discussing the conditions of New Orleans, volunteer tourists feel the city suffers.

Conditions of New Orleans

Volunteer tourists realise that New Orleans is handicapped through the post-Hurricane Katrina conditions of New Orleans. Not only were homes destroyed by the storm, but so were businesses and infrastructure. Part of understanding New Orleans is coming to terms with its post-Hurricane Katrina state. Previously semi-functional aspects of the city are now non-existent. Through their understanding of New Orleans' post-Hurricane Katrina state, volunteer tourists understand that New Orleans' issues are more pervasive than the damage to homes. Some volunteer tourists express frustration when residents do not have enough money to buy all the supplies they need to finish a project; others are frustrated on behalf of the residents that their needs are not being met by the limited resources available. Still other volunteer tourists relate the conditions of New Orleans to their hometowns and either empathise or express disappointment. Through understanding the city, volunteer tourists understand that the issues facing New Orleans affect not only select homeowners, but the community as a whole.

In this section, I discuss the tensions between what New Orleans looks like and what people think it should look like this long after the storm. Donna talks about the recreational facilities, and Barbara and Carol talk about money. Additionally, Haley and Tammy talk about the remnants of death, and Izzy discusses how people make money out of the disaster.

Donna from the Philadelphia Unitarian Universalists discusses volunteering at one of the city's baseball fields:

> You know it was funny, they had tractors and heavy equipment and all before the storm and now all they have is shovels and rakes. And they have to do it if they want the kids to play ball. And here we are doing this, you know, heavy physical labor. I almost thought well maybe we should protest

> and not do it so then they have to get equipment, but it's not going to happen either. So that was a real low point for me. I thought, 'That ball field apparently is used by the high school team, so they haven't had a ball field for four years and they got people, volunteers and city workers, doing it with rakes and shovels.'

Donna attempts to understand the complexity of the New Orleans Recreation Department and what they, as volunteer tourists, can do about it. She realises that coming to New Orleans is not only about rebuilding homes. Additionally, she expresses frustration at not having adequate supplies to repair the baseball field. Disturbed with the lack of progress, Donna contemplates protesting to provoke change. Donna contemplates standing up for what she feels is right versus helping with the limited resources available. She evaluates whether protesting will be an effective mode of action. Given the city's condition four years after the storm, Donna realises that not only are homes impacted, but children's lives are impacted as well. Because of the effect on the children, Donna understands that the influence of the storm pervades to the entire community.

Like Donna, Barbara and Carol were also frustrated with their project. Although volunteers donate labour, the residents buy supplies for the projects. Some volunteer tourists express their disappointment that they can only do so much with the little amount of money residents have to buy supplies. Barbara from Montana explains their project in the Lower Ninth Ward, '[The resident] only had $500 to spend so we purchased what we could.'

Carol adds, 'With sheetrock [plasterboard], you can only go so far with that amount of money, and you're done unless there's extra money available.'

I ask Barbara to name a disadvantage in coming to New Orleans. She responds,

> Just the lack of money to complete a project. I think that's been the most discouraging, that, you know, we'd love to walk away knowing we've made a home ready for someone to move into, and so the funds are the biggest thing.

Barbara and Carol wish the resident had more money so that *they* would feel better knowing they were able to provide a completed home for her to move into. However, that amount of sheetrock makes it easier for the resident to live in part of the home. Barbara talks about the limits of charity, or the tensions between helping and feeling like one is not helping enough. The feeling of not helping enough is contingent on the amount of money the resident has to spend on supplies. Barbara and Carol understand the complexity of New Orleanians' issues through the supply shortage experienced at their current job. However, these volunteer tourists only understand the supply shortage to the degree that it affects them. Barbara and Carol do not discuss how the financial issues affect the homeowner who has lived in a house with just studs and concrete floors for the past four years. Barbara and Carol do not understand how financially taxing it must be to continue to work to support a home while trying to rebuild it, one panel of sheetrock at a time. Although these volunteer tourists have some understanding of the financial issues, they only understand them to the extent that they are not able to complete the project.

Like Barbara and Carol, many volunteer tourists want to see immediate change in New Orleans; however, as Tammy and Haley explain, change in New Orleans is incremental. Tammy and Haley put themselves in the place of residents to gain a better understanding.

> Tammy begins, 'It makes me sad that tomorrow when we go home, Monday we're back into our lives again and these people will wake up with the same thing. Not the same thing because there is growth and improvement but ...'
> 'It's a long road,' Haley says.
> Tammy adds, 'We just talked to a lady at the community center that is somehow connected to the school system, she said, when these kids look out the window they probably see floodwaters and bodies floating. That statement really affected me today. Even when it's all cleaned up these children, for the rest of their lives, are going to have this image.'

Tammy and Haley relay that New Orleans will still represent death to many people regardless of how many years have passed. Also, the images of the storm will remain as representations of the city to many residents. The volunteers also adopt these images into how they understand New Orleans. As volunteers, Tammy and Haley came to New Orleans to help rebuild and change the images of New Orleans. Despite the efforts of the volunteers, the residents' lasting impression from the storm is the fear accompanying water engulfing their home, their neighbourhood and their lives. Through understanding residents' struggles to forget the horrific scenes immediately following the storm, Tammy and Haley understand the community's continued difficulties to deal with the past.

Izzy discusses the issue of the once-devastated neighbourhoods becoming a tourist attraction. She talks about the buses and vans of organised tours that bring paying tourists to view the neighbourhoods. These tours take three and a half hours and are conducted in anything from a 15-passenger van to a 50-person charter bus (see Pezzullo 2009b). Izzy, a college student from Maryland, relates a story a homeowner told her:

> One of the home owners was telling us that there are tours through the Lower Ninth Ward as a tourist attraction and people pay money to come and see the disaster. None of the money comes back here; it doesn't help rebuild their homes or their community. They want their homes back; they don't want to be a tourist attraction.

Izzy discusses how residents don't like being a spectacle; they don't want their misery on display and other people making money from their unfortunate circumstances. By listening to the stories of residents, she understands that the community is not only trying to rebuild, but is also struggling with their new role as an attraction. Izzy is appalled that people are paying to take a tour through a devastated neighbourhood, yet, she is also a tourist in a devastated neighbourhood. Even though Izzy understands New Orleans through the shift in tourist attractions in the post-Hurricane Katrina environment, she does not understand that she also is a part of that shift. She realises that the damage throughout the city becomes a tourist attraction, but she does not understand that she is similar to the tourist on the bus but is framing her touring as a volunteer.

Conclusion

As volunteer tourists relate stories about what they've seen and experienced in New Orleans, they are simultaneously inscribing and creating a sense of place. Through their stories, they come to an understanding of the city by comparing it to other places and the post-Hurricane Katrina conditions of the city.

As volunteer tourists visit the city, they adopt an understanding of New Orleans and why events unfolded in the way they did. Volunteer tourists also become advocates for the rebuilding of New Orleans during their short stays and spread this knowledge when they go back to their home towns. Through their experiences in the community they convert the media's stories into their own stories. These experiences give the volunteer tourists a sense of New Orleans, its community and its residents' struggles. Volunteer tourists' understanding of the stories residents tell and their experiences in New Orleans contribute to the community. Understanding these experiences gives volunteer tourists not only a way to understand the community, but also a way to explain their experiences and the experiences of residents when they return home to increase understanding of New Orleans.

Despite volunteer tourists' understanding of New Orleans, there are aspects of being a tourist in post-Katrina New Orleans they do not understand. Volunteer tourists are clear that the reason they come to New Orleans is to volunteer, but they do not state explicitly that they would not be in New Orleans were it not for Hurricane Katrina. Thus, Hurricane Katrina is the 'attraction' that brings these individuals to New Orleans; volunteer tourists being in New Orleans because of the disaster and to help with the disaster problematises their role in the city. However, if volunteer tourists were not in New Orleans because of the disaster and were not learning about the city through local people, their understanding of New Orleans would not be as complex as they have expressed. Therefore, volunteer tourists still contribute to the city and have a multifaceted understanding of New Orleans despite being here because of the disaster.

Tourists contribute to the places they visit by seeking to understand the culture and people of the place. They also help the location by advocating for it when they return home, just as the volunteer tourists in New Orleans advocate for the city and have a clearer understanding of why people live below sea level. Tourists contribute to the places they visit through vocalizing this support once they have left the place.

11 Family place experience and the making of places in holiday home destinations

A Danish case study

Jacob R. Kirkegaard Larsen and Lea Holst Laursen

Introduction

In his seminal book, Tuan (1977: 102) states that space and architecture are related and that the physical elements within spaces can facilitate the psychological emotions that create a place experience. While extensive tourism research involves the notion of place, particularly in the form of spectacular landscapes, sites and constructions being a destination's 'pull factors' (Crompton 1979; Dann 1977), the interactions between tourists and the physical structures *in place* seem to be partly neglected. The purpose of this chapter, therefore, is to explore place experience within holiday home destinations and to scrutinise how the making of place may happen as an interactive process between its tourists and the architecture of space. The empirical foundation focuses on the region of North Jutland (Denmark), a tourist destination sold for its scenic landscapes of swaggering woodlands, blossoming meadows and harsh coastlines. Accounting for 59 per cent of all foreign overnight stays in 2010 (Danmarks Statistik 2011), the rental of holiday homes situated along the coastlines makes up the main leisure tourism accommodation within the region, the primary target group being families with dependent children (VisitDenmark 2005). Existing research (Haldrup 2004; Larsen and Therkelsen 2011) has shown that, although combining their stay with excursions to attractions, renters spend a significant part of the holiday within the holiday home and the nearby natural surroundings, notably the beach, whilst several other studies of the family holiday show the importance of spending time together, having accessible fun and exciting activities, and the possibility of children meeting other children (Fodness 1992; Gram and Therkelsen 2003; Thornton *et al.* 1997). However, while the external supply of experiences during the summer might fulfill children's need for activities, the holiday home and its surroundings are characterised by small-scale suburban structure and architecture that lack space for adventure and activities, thus limiting the immediate place experience (Dirckinck-Holmfeld and Selmer 2006; Laursen 2011; Nørgaard and Clausen 2004). Hence, it seems relevant to examine how the family with children in fact experience place within the spaces of a holiday home destination.

Based on both site registrations and qualitative interviews with families with children on holiday in a rented holiday home in two holiday home destinations – Blokhus and Hals, North Jutland, Denmark – this chapter provides a renter perspective on the place experience and making of place within the holiday home, the holiday home area and its close surroundings (for example, the beach and towns), taking both parents' and children's experiences into consideration. The point of departure for the research is the argument in the literature that architectural making of space is in fact a crucial factor for place experience. However, experience of place cannot be determined without considering it from the perspective of its users (Canter 1977; McCabe and Stokoe 2004); thus, it is the perspective of holiday home tourists that is scrutinised in this chapter.

Theories of place

From a philosophical point of view, a dualism between 'space' and 'place' can be established; the former entails the abstract and absolute category while the latter is imbued with social meaning (Pocock 2006). Accordingly, Tuan (1977: 6) describes space as movement, while place is a pause in movement which may transform space into place. Hence, 'space' becomes 'place' only when it means something to us (Ringgaard 2010; Suvantola 2002) – that is, when we experience it. In the same vein, Canter (1977: 158–159) argues that a place cannot be fully identified until we know the behaviour associated with a given location, the physical parameters of that setting, and the descriptions or conceptions people hold of the behaviour in that physical environment. Accordingly, Canter presents the meaning of place as a result of relationships between actions, conceptions and physical attributes (Figure 11.1).

In order to understand place experience, the following theoretical framework builds upon Canter's (1977) three elements of place.

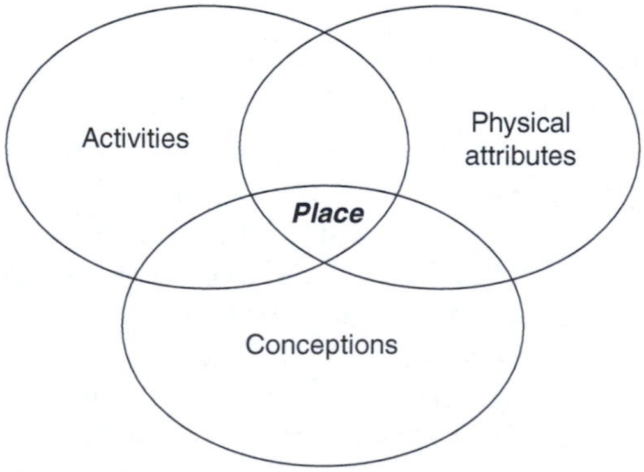

Figure 11.1 Dimensions of 'place' (drawn freely after Canter (1977))

The physical place and its architecture

Entrikin (1991 in Suvantola 2002: 30) stresses that, in order to explain the experience of place, one has to acknowledge the physical elements, as we often refer to places as a cluster of things. Architectural structures are a central part of these physical elements as architecture determines the specific place and its physical qualities (Solá-Morales 1997). The architecture brings an aesthetic dimension to space; the architectural intervention with its composition of landscape, use of materials, textures, surfaces, furniture and so on can create an experience in itself as it may add a certain expression to space which can be enjoyed and turned into a place (Laursen forthcoming). Thus, the architecture of space matters in the making of place experience inasmuch as a specific work with architectonic structures can influence such experiences and an architectonic restructuring of existing space can even create new meanings for its users – making new places. However, when working with the design of place structures, the inherent potentials of space have to be considered a decisive element and incorporated as an active and acting partner (Stenbro and Christoffersen 2008). Consequently, dealing with the architectonic structures of place implies that the architectural building of 'interventions', as well as the inherent potentials of the existing landscape, are dominant aspects.

The architectural work of place is born into a difference between landscape and urban, historical and social contexts (Stenbro and Christoffersen 2008) and in this chapter, the physical place and its architecture are understood in the broadest of meanings; from the design of a holiday home to the construction of the public square or the structure of landscapes. Hence, architecture and the design of buildings, landscapes and towns may contribute to a tourist destination in creating different spaces, each with different architectural qualities that may *potentially* accommodate different experiences or, in other words, creating several places (Suvantola 2002; Ringgaard 2010).

Conception of place

Aesthetic and architectonic design and structure do not, however, imply that places are fixed and non-changeable; on the contrary, place is never to be seen as a finished composition unable to change, but consists of a past, a present, and a future (Hvattum 2010). Accordingly, places and 'tourist places' are not clearly defined entities just waiting to be visited but emerge when the physical surroundings are appropriated, used in different ways by people engaged in embodied social practices, imbued with meaning and made part of memories (Bærenholdt *et al.* 2004; Ringgaard 2010; Shaw and Williams 2004; Squire 1994; Vestby 2009). Hence, the making of place depends on individual conceptions.

Conceptions draw on memory and inscribe the place experience in circles of anticipation, performance and remembrance (Bærenholdt *et al.* 2004). *Anticipation* as part of the 'pre-conception' of place is based on images (Gartner 1993) whereby previous experiences in the same or similar places play a central part.

These images form the expectations we have of a particular location and, therefore, make up part of the overall place experience (Jensen 2005; Mossberg 2007b). When being physically 'in place', the bodily and social *performances* or activities are influenced by these prior anticipations although they may be contested and adjusted by present experiences (Bærenholdt *et al.* 2004; Ek *et al.* 2008). Finally, *post-conception* is formed by memories which may turn into emotions that establish routines in the preference of specific experiences (Jantzen and Vetner 2007) and, thus, affect tourists' choice of holiday places. Memories and associations thereby reinforce anticipation of present places. Hence, expectations of future, attention to present and memory of past (Bærenholdt and Simonsen 2004) are continuously interconnected in a place experience.

Activities and performance 'in place'

The performance 'in place' depends on the individual's conception, the anticipation of being there and, thus, the capability to live out the activities offered by the physical architecture and social parameters in a given space and time. Hence, activities involve interaction between the lived body and the particularities of place which creates a range of sensations (Cassey 1996 in Pocock 2006: 96). These sensations are subjectively evaluated as positive or negative emotions (Jantzen and Vetner 2007; Jantzen 2007); that is, good or bad experiences. So, even though the physical attributes and architecture of a given space – or the 'experience room' (Mossberg 2001, 2007b) – may create emotions, the settings only enhance the *possibilities* of an experience establishing the frame for appropriate activities. However, it will always be the subjective conception and capability to enjoy a certain location that determine whether the activity within place is pleasurable or not (Jantzen *et al.* 2006; Jantzen 2007; Ooi 2005). 'Conception' and 'activity' are, thus, closely interrelated in the formation of a 'place experience'. Consequently, 'activity' should be understood in the broadest of senses insofar as it covers a continuum from exciting and physically active experiences to relaxing and recreative ones (cf. Csikszentmihalyi 1997; Yiannakis 1992) and a particular space may, therefore, foster activities with opposed agendas. Hence, not only do multiple places within a destination provide different characteristics such as hedonic, utilitarian, social and novel places (Snepenger *et al.* 2007) but also hybrid structures of place may provide different experiences within the same space and time.

Furthermore, tourism consumption is a social action and includes the travel unit (for example, the family) and other tourists (Urry 1995). McCabe and Stokoe (2004) illustrate that the identity of places (good/bad) is based on one's own and others' activities. Correspondingly, Gustafson (2001) notes that 'others' – as opposed to 'self' – play a significant role in creating a meaning of place. Likewise, Mossberg (2001, 2007b) argues that encounters with other tourists, locals, and staff are an important part of the 'experience room' where other tourists may function either as a positive or negative influencer. In that way, the presence – or the absence – of others contributes significantly to the entire atmosphere of a place (Bærenholdt *et al.* 2004; Urry 1995).

A conceptual understanding of place experience and making of place

The subjective conceptions of place are closely related to our and others' activities in a given space. The pre-conception of a place affects the choice of a particular space and the expectation we have of that location; thus, it affects our performance 'in place'. Hence, the tourist is an active partner in the making of place as conception and activities determine the character of a given place. Hence, in order to create place experience, the architectural composition necessarily has to promote activities and encounters that the individual perceives to be relevant and fulfilling for his/her purposes of being there. If the architecture of space only provides for activities that do not match the anticipation of the tourist, the meeting will consequently become a negative experience and likewise, if a given location fails to establish meaningful activities, it remains an 'empty' space that we move through without ascribing any specific images, sensations or memories to it. In contrast, unfamiliar places may arouse the curiosity of its visitors and create an experience beyond that expected by breaking the established routines; architecture may be one of the elements that can form such place (Ringgaard 2010). In brief, the physical architectural making of place may affect the subjective place experience positively if it supports or exceeds the personal conception of activities within a given space.

A tourism destination is made up of multiple physical spaces and potentially multiple places; thus, the holiday home destination may not alone be determined on the basis of its physical settings and spatial structures but must necessarily include the conception and activities of its users as not all spaces automatically turn into place experiences. Furthermore, a tourist place often involves many different users; hence, the physical and architectural structure ideally has to generate multiple conceptions and a hybrid of activities within the same space and time including both the potential of the existing landscape and the design of purpose-built interventions.

Methodology

Two cases of holiday home destinations

Denmark has a relatively high concentration of privately owned holiday homes (second homes) which, in contrast to most other countries, are not only used by their owners but are also rented out to tourists. Thus, the holiday home makes up a significant share of the Danish tourism industry, not least in North Jutland. This empirical study of place experience is a comparative case study of two characteristic holiday home destinations within this region: Blokhus on the west coast and Hals on the east coast (Figure 11.2).

Blokhus is one of the main tourist destinations within the municipality of Jammerbugt which, counted in weeks of rentals, is among the most important holiday home municipalities in Denmark (Jammerbugt 2009). Within the municipality, holiday home tourism accounts for 41 per cent of all overnight stays, equivalent to 636,100 overnight stays in 2010 (VisitNordjylland 2011).

Hals is situated in the municipality of Aalborg. Aalborg is the fourth largest city in Denmark and a considerable part of tourism within the municipality therefore relies on hotels and city breaks. However, holiday home rental is also significant, accounting for 163,600 or 19 per cent of the overnight stays in 2010 (VisitDenmark 2010) and Hals is by far the largest holiday home destination within the municipality with approximately 4,500 holiday homes.

Qualitative interviews and site registrations

During 2010 and 2011, a two-fold empirical research was conducted within the two case destinations. In order to analyse the physical structures and architecture within the holiday home destinations, field observations and site registrations were conducted by surveying the area taking photos, making notes and drawing maps.

To obtain an understanding of the renters' experience of place, qualitative methods were used. Throughout the research period, both in the main summer

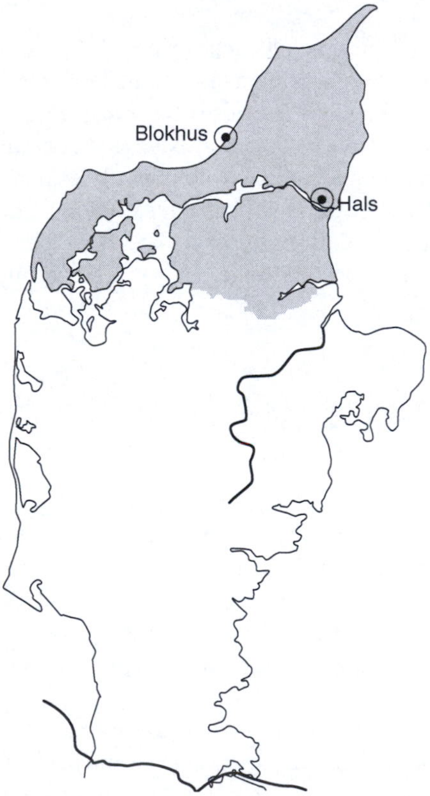

Figure 11.2 Blokhus and Hals – two destinations in North Jutland, Denmark (source: the authors).

seasons and in the off-seasons, in-depth semi-structured interviews were conducted (Kvale and Brinkmann 2009) with 26 families with dependent children in the age range 0–15 years from the three main markets (Denmark, Germany and Norway; national diversities however appeared of minor importance and will not be part of the analysis). To elicit the most immediate response on the family experiences, the interviews took place within the holiday home during the families' holiday with the participation of both children and parents. The interviewed travel units included nuclear and extended families as well as friends travelling together with children, and a total of 156 respondents were interviewed. Each interview lasted between one and two hours, was voice recorded and subsequently transcribed. To support the registration of architectural structures, the physical architecture inside and outside the interviewed families' rented holiday home was documented through photographs. Furthermore, in each destination, participant observations were made during one week of the main summer season 2010.

According to the theoretical framework, field observations and registrations sought to provide a picture of the physical architecture of spaces within the holiday home destinations while the qualitative data aimed to analyse the renters' place experiences (conception and activities) within these. This understanding of renters' place experience is the point of departure for a reflective discussion on how physical structures affect family place experiences and how architectural restructuring may enhance future place experiences within the studied holiday home destinations.

Findings

In the following section, the empirical findings are presented according to the theoretical framework: first, the physical structures and architecture of the holiday homes destinations (Blokhus and Hals) are discussed and, second, the families conceptions and activities are portrayed to scrutinise holiday home place experiences from a tourist perspective.

The physical place and architecture in Blokhus and Hals

The holiday home

A natural starting point in analysing the architectural structure of holiday home destination is the holiday home itself. Regarding architecture and appearance, the holiday homes in Hals and Blokhus are alike as most are standardised structures made of wood (Figure 11.3). They are located on a private lot which, notably in Hals, is often a garden separated from the surroundings by plants or fences which create privacy by seemingly shutting out the surrounding landscape. Similar types of houses are also present in Blokhus but, in addition, there are also houses that are more integrated into the existing coastal landscape, placed on lots in the dunes with vegetation growing freely. The gardens of many

Figure 11.3 Holiday homes in Hals (left) and Blokhus (right) (source: the authors).

rental houses in both Hals and Blokhus confirm that families with children are the dominant renters; interventions in form of play equipment (for example, sand box, swings, trampoline) and a large terrace are often installed, apparently creating a hybrid of activities.

The holiday home areas

The holiday homes are placed within holiday home areas that relate to the zonal restrictions within Danish planning law prescribing, among other things, a 'green appearance' and usage for leisure purposes only. In Hals, the planning law has resulted in a holiday home band-city stretching from Hals in the south along the coastline to the north where holiday homes are placed in clusters separated with belts of vegetation on both sides of a main road. Minor access roads connect the individual holiday home with the main road which results in an antenna structure that resembles Danish suburban areas; a structure within which the privately owned lots with holiday homes are located.

In Blokhus, the boundaries between the town and holiday home areas are not as clear as in Hals as the holiday home areas are placed in a semicircle with the town at the centre and with part of the holiday home area integrated into the town. The majority of areas have a suburban grid structure but, within the areas closest to the coastline, the topography of landscape creates a structure with roads twisting through the dunes, thus seemingly making the landscape a more active and acting partner in the architectural structure.

In general, however the holiday home areas in Hals and Blokhus are geographically demarcated locations where access roads define the structure and apparently no or very few interventions have been made with other purposes than bringing people to and from the holiday homes (Figure 11.4). The holiday home areas appear as low density, closed and 'green' enclaves with a grid or organic structure – a common type within the Danish landscape – without much relation to the surrounding coastal landscape.

Figure 11.4 Holiday home area in Hals (left) and Blokhus (right) (source: the authors).

Surrounding structural elements

Besides the holiday home and the holiday home areas, the towns of Hals and Blokhus and the natural landscape both appear as characteristic physical elements. In Hals, the nearby coastal landscape is characterised by its low water and sandy beaches, edged by small dunes, meadows and woodlands. The town of Hals is an old historic harbour town and has a living harbour environment with restaurants, shops and market activities combined with harbour-related businesses, such as a small shipyard, a fishery and a ferry. In Blokhus, the town is located directly on the shore which seemingly integrates the beach as part of the town. The centre of the town is the public square with shops, restaurants and other commercial activities. Furthermore, the natural landscape is a strong element in Blokhus; the meadow, forest, sea and beach are evident elements of the landscape, where the western wind has moulded the landscape and the weather conditions are more rough than in Hals. Further, the beach is very wide and driving and parking on the beach are allowed. In both Hals and Blokhus, most interventions with 'hedonic' tourism purposes are placed within the towns while the beach and woodlands mostly display the inherent structures of natural landscape.

The holiday home destination

Analysing the structural composition of Hals and Blokhus, it is evident that there are more similarities than differences. The findings reveal destinations consisting of three spatial elements: the holiday home, the holiday home area and the surrounding landscape of the beaches and the towns (Figures 11.5 and 11.6). These three elements are all situated in close proximity to each other and can, from an architectural perspective on the physical structures, be understood as the holiday home destination.

The overall physical structures of the two holiday home destinations imply a composition of different spaces each having several architectural structures.

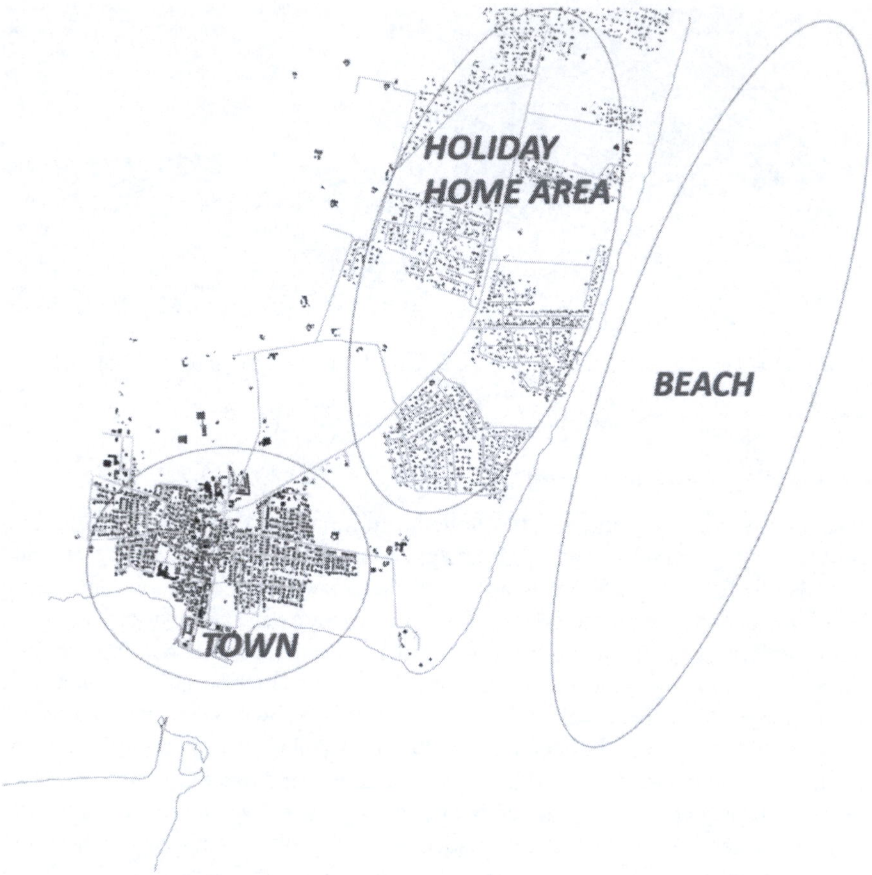

Figure 11.5 Overall structure of the holiday home destination in Hals (source: authors' own with background map from Municipality of Aalborg © kortcenter.dk).

From a theoretical standpoint, these spaces potentially make up different place experiences to the renters of holiday homes insofar as the architectural structure promotes activities that the family with children conceives as relevant and fulfilling for their purposes of spending time there. However, only a few interventions, mainly in the towns and the holiday home, offer possibilities for 'active' experiences and, in addition to the three structural elements of the holiday home destination, a fourth element, in the form of external attractions and sites, might be necessarily considered as part of the destination (we shall return to this later in the chapter). Furthermore, the destinations seem to be divided into demarcated and isolated spaces with little consistency; the holiday homes appear as closed entities separated from the holiday home area with hedges and fences and the holiday home areas appear generic, lacking an architecture that involves

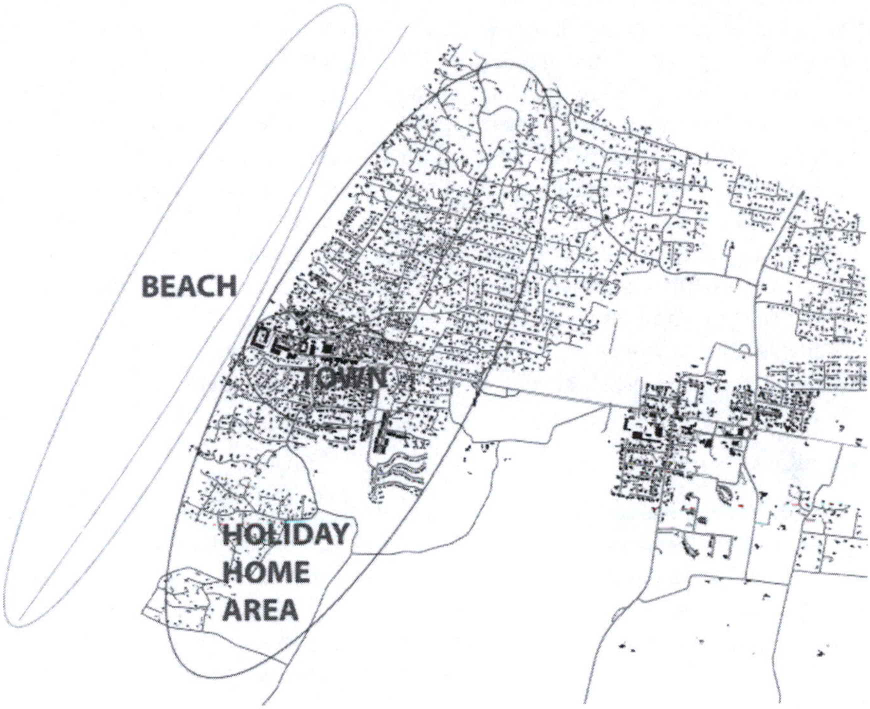

Figure 11.6 Overall structure of the holiday home destination in Blokhus (Source: authors' own with background map from Municipality of Jammerbugt © kortcenter.dk).

elements from the surrounding coastal landscape. Consequently, the physical place does not generate a relationship between the holiday home and the surrounding elements in the form of the towns, the beach and the forest. However, to fully understand the making of place within these holiday home destinations, we shall now direct attention towards the conception and activities of its renters.

The place experience within holiday home destinations

Conception of holiday home destinations

As mentioned in the preceding theoretical framework, the conception of place implies a circle of anticipation, performance and remembrance where, in particular, previous experiences contribute to the present conception of place. Bærenholdt *et al.* (2004) have previously illustrated that the holiday home often invokes associations with childhood memories or earlier holidays. Our interviews support these findings as all the interviewed families had previous experiences of holiday home destinations, several families from the same destination (12 families) and some even the same house (two families). Memories had clearly affected their expectations of this 'new' holiday home experience and the vast majority of the families seem to have created a preference for choosing holiday home destinations as a place for the family holiday (cf. Jantzen and Vetner 2007). Therefore, the holiday home destination may not in itself be anticipated to imply completely 'novel' places (cf. Snepenger *et al.* 2007) but is instead perceived as a 'social' and family-friendly place with a high degree of informality providing for 'togetherness'. The holiday home itself is, furthermore, considered a practical place that offers a context for maintaining daily routines of eating and sleeping, routines which are of course of particular importance to families with small children. A deeper consideration of the families' conception of the different spatial elements identified in the analysis above, however, reveals that not all spaces within the destinations are equally important in the making of such family place destinations.

Not all spaces make a place

The holiday home area appears as a dominant geographical territory within the destinations and is described by families in Hals as a 'forest' while the conception in Blokhus is more that of the coastal landscape, thus relating it to what in this chapter is seen as the surrounding landscape. However, although some parents claimed that 'walking through the holiday home area' is part of the holiday home experience, several families did not understand what kind of 'area' the interviewer referred to when asking about experiences in this area and, clearly, the vast majority of families did not perceive nor use the holiday home area deliberately as a place for experiences. Hence, the claim of 'walking through the area' is certainly disputed through the interviews as walking within natural landscapes appears as something primarily the adults – and only very seldom the children – conceive as a positive place experience. This notion is furthermore supported by the participant observations as they revealed family 'walks' as an activity that predominantly takes place near the town centres, with families perhaps having an ice cream while strolling around – in Blokhus going from town square to the beach while, in Hals, taking a leisure walk round the harbour. Hence, the interviews and observations unambiguously indicate that the holiday home area is not associated with the characteristics of 'place' as suggested in the theoretical framework but, rather, appears as a 'pass through space'.

What is surprising when looking at spaces and places within the two destinations is the role of the towns, Blokhus and Hals. Apart from observations that reveal families strolling through them, the results of the interviews suggest that the towns are mainly utilitarian spaces used for shopping for groceries. However, in Blokhus, families within the holiday home areas that merge with the town seem to use it slightly more actively whilst in Hals the weekly flea market appears to be a place/event worth paying a visit. Otherwise most families do not conceive of the town as a place in itself but generally use it merely as an additional choice. Hence, although the towns are a central part of the physical structure of the destinations, the families' conception and sparse use of them renders them a 'place' that is partly excluded from the families' perception of a holiday home destination. This, in turn, points towards motives for visiting relating mostly to natural landscapes.

Family experience 'in places' of the beach and the holiday home

Earlier research and market surveys (Haldrup 2004; VisitDenmark 2005) have emphasised 'nature' as a primary motive among holiday house renters; this is confirmed by our interviews in both Blokhus and Hals. Notably, the coastal landscape is conceived as 'the epitome' of a holiday home destination and activities at the beach are central for the child-friendly holiday. However, a difference between the two case destinations is in evidence; whereas the west coast in Blokhus is vital to all the interviewed families and used (more or less) actively during holidays throughout the year, the main conception regarding the beach in Hals is related to its child-friendly characteristics which means that it is used as a (safe) place for families, mainly during summer. This is confirmed explicitly by four families interviewed in Hals (during both the summer and off-season) who emphasised closeness to the beach as an important factor although they had not actually been there. Thus, place experience does not necessarily entail physical activities 'in place' but may to some extent rest on the mere *conception* of being within a particular landscape.

During the summer, the inherent potential of landscape within the beach apparently provides the opportunity for families' making use of place as water, sand and dunes appear as natural attributes for children's activities. However, describing a trip to the beach, several families explain that they have to bring a lot of equipment, suggesting that architectural interventions at the beach are partly self-structured. This structure consists of two interconnected places: a 'family camp' built of towels, windshields and folding chairs delimiting an area that offers a place for parents' relaxation while the children within a safe distance make a place of their own with activities such as bathing, playing and so on (Figure 11.7). Occasionally, the children visit the family camp and, likewise, parents shift between observing and participating in the ongoing games. This structure seems to provide a 'safety zone' within which the children can play apart from their parents. A comparison of the beaches of Blokhus and Hals shows that the structure with a narrow and calm beach in Hals provides attributes for a larger 'safety zone' – that is, the distance between parent and children being larger – than within the wider and wilder beach of Blokhus. Hence, the place experience within a family is evidently not restricted to delimited spatial boundaries but may stretch across larger areas if a 'safety zone' is provided within which parents and children feel secure though being in separate places. When the weather does not allow for sun-bathing, or in families where the parents do not enjoy this aspect of the beach, a trip to the beach is primarily made for the purpose of using it actively – taking a quick swim, gathering

Figure 11.7 Family places at the beach in Blokhus (left) and Hals (right) (source: the authors).

mussels or playing games. This is naturally the prevailing place-making of the beach outside summer season (except swimming) although most evident among the Blokhus renters who describe the wind and waves as important landscape attributes.

Another important place that creates a 'safety zone' for separate activities appears around the holiday home and, just like the beach, the holiday home is conceived by *all* interviewed families as a central 'family place'. The garden surrounding the holiday home materialises during summer as a central place for togetherness. In particular, the families describe playground equipment (sand boxes, swings, trampolines) and sufficient space for children's activity, such as badminton or football, while a terrace provides a place for the parents' more recreative activities (for example, socialising with extended family or friends, or having a glass of wine while relaxing) (see Figure 11.8). In the case of bad summer weather and during off-season holidays, the inside of the holiday home preferably has to offer the same opportunities; a living room with both a relaxing environment and opportunity for children's activities and, for some families, houses with an indoor swimming pool as an alternative to outdoor activity. Particularly for off-season renters, the holiday home is an essential place given that most of or the entire holiday is spent here. Similar to their expeditions to the beach, however, the families also bring their own equipment to provide activities for the children, such as computer games or a football, and ensure the right 'interventions' for family togetherness within the holiday home. Although place within the holiday home is structured by built interventions – available equipment and architectural design – that do not integrate much with the surrounding landscape, the parents nevertheless stress that an important part of the place experience within the holiday home is the sensation of being in a natural landscape.

Figure 11.8 Family places within the holiday home garden (source: the authors).

A place of your own

As mentioned in the theoretical framework, not only does the activity within the family determine place experience but also the presence or absence of others represents an important element of the experience of place. This is manifested by the interviewed families in the context of both the beach and the holiday home, as they unambiguously stress that having 'one's own place' is very important in both Blokhus and Hals. Even on a sunny day with lots of people on the beach, it is possible to find a place where you can be 'yourself' within a safe distance from the activities or gaze of 'others'. Similarly, the importance of privacy within the holiday home is emphasised by the parents; 'others' may be allowed within a spatially close distance as long as they cannot gaze upon the family place within the holiday home and, particularly for renters who are from larger cities, the opportunity of having a house and garden of their own is an essential element of the place experience. When not fulfilled, the experience 'in place' challenges the pre-conception of a holiday home and the private and introvert place structure which, as described in the physical place analysis, represents the holiday home as a positive counterpart to resorts as it provides the opportunity for being 'self' with one's family – at least seen from a parental perspective.

However, from the perspective of children, our interviews support a previous study (Gram and Therkelsen 2003) that shows that children on holiday like to meet new friends. Several of the interviewed children indicated that they would in fact enjoy the possibilities for meeting others. However, the holiday home does not provide space for such meetings as common playgrounds or other activity areas are not available within a short or safe distance from the holiday home. This lack of opportunities for getting together is, furthermore, the main reason for a majority of the interviewed families' choosing to travel with friends or extended families. The problem becomes even more evident when children enter their teens and during the off-season when weather conditions do not allow for beach experiences and external attractions are closed.

External places

Attractions outside the physical boundaries of the destinations are perceived by several families as a necessity for having exciting experiences and, in the case of Blokhus, a nearby fun park is visited by most families and for some is considered an essential parameter for choosing Blokhus as a holiday destination. Hence, exciting external attractions do form part of the families' overall conception of the place experience within a holiday home destination and are often included to meet with children's conception of a 'good' holiday place. However, several parents find these places rather stressful and they view the holiday home as a place where the family can feel at home and relax after a day of exciting and entertaining experiences. Moreover, comparing the experience of external attractions with those within the holiday home destination (beach and holiday home), the perceptions of several families testify that, within purpose-built environments, such as a theme park or zoo, they are more passive receivers of a planned experience; conversely, experiences within the holiday home and nearby surroundings take place as 'self-planned activities', self structure thus being part of the experience of 'togetherness'.

Discussion

Based upon the notion, within a broader analysis of the 'family place experience', that the holiday home and the beach are both fundamental elements of the holiday home destination, the potential for architectural remaking of holiday home destination places is now discussed.

The family place experience

In the theoretical framework presented earlier in this chapter, it was argued that both conception and activities may determine the character of a place and, therefore, in order to create place experience the architectural composition has to promote activities that the individual conceives as relevant and fulfilling the purposes of being there. Not surprisingly, perhaps, one particular aspect that appears repeatedly in the findings of family place experiences is the difference between children's and parents' use and conception of landscape and architectural structures. The physical architecture of these places is based on both the inherent potential of existing landscapes (the beach, the garden) and built interventions (toys, terrace, windshields) which, combined, generate children's activity (fun and exciting play) and parent recreativity (relaxation, observations of and partaking in the children's play). 'In place' children and parents are, therefore, often divided in separate places.

The structure of the family place experience was exemplified 'in place' in two central family places: the holiday home and the beach. Within the garden of the individual holiday home, the good family place experience occurs within the introvert cultural *landscape* of a holiday home, answering to the parents' wish for privacy from 'others' and generating a 'safety zone' within which *purpose-built interventions*, such as playground equipment and a terrace, generate a hybrid providing for place experience as interactions between recreativity (for example, relaxation or socialising) and activity (excitement, games). An analogous picture is evident at the beach. Here, an introvert and private 'family camp' is built as an intervention by the family in the form of towels, windshields and so on to provide a private place of recreativity within the surrounding coastal landscape, while both the existing natural landscape (sand, water, dunes) as well as interventions (toys and equipment brought along) transform it for more active experiences. Although the family – adults and children – are apart some or most of the time, performing different activities/recreativities, the families describe these places as a coherent experience of being and doing things together as a family.

Hence, within the studied holiday home destinations, the family place experience (Figure 11.9) occurs as a hybrid interaction between the *physical architecture*, spanning the existing landscape (cultural or natural) and built interventions (purposely designed elements), and *conception and performance* established on a division between activity (physically active, excitement) and recreativity (relaxation, socializing). The successful family place experience within a holiday home occurs in those providing a 'hybrid circle' embracing all four of these parameters.

The model in Figure 11.9 reflects the chapter's conceptual understanding of place experience: first, the architectural design of built interventions ideally includes the inherent capability of the landscape within which it is placed and, second, the making of place promoting a hybrid of activities that the individual conceives fulfilling for his/her purposes of being there, relating to both exciting

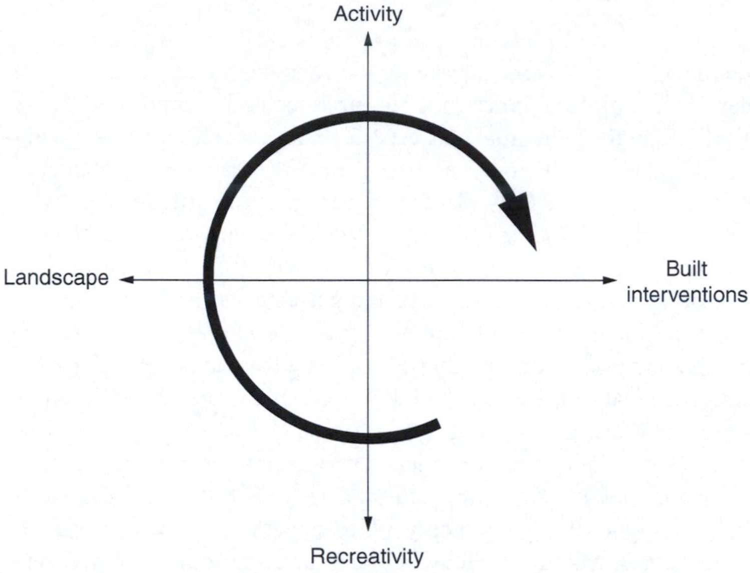

Figure 11.9 Family place experience within holiday home destinations.

experiences and more relaxing ones. In the holiday home destination, the possibility for activity is required in order to meet with children's concept of a good holiday place while recreativity place experience seems crucial for parents. At the same time, architectural structures are found to involve the existing natural and culture landscapes within the destination.

Potentials for architectural remaking of place

Looking at the overall making of places within the holiday home destination, a balance of family place experiences between parents and children seems not to be completely achieved. Thus, the need to combine places within the physical surroundings of the holiday home destination with external places of 'exciting activity', such as theme parks, arises. In particular, it appears from the research that older children's place experience suffers from a lack of possibilities for appropriate activities. The place experience at Blokhus and Hals relies predominantly on the cultural and natural landscapes of the holiday home, holiday home areas and the beach. The only interventions are equipment placed within the holiday home and the towns which leaves the overall structure of the holiday home as a place experience belonging to the lower left part of the model ('recreative landscape'). Consequently, the architectural composition of landscape and built interventions within the holiday home destination may be restructured to make a more coherent hybrid place involving both activity and recreativity.

One place that in particular seems a potential space for developing 'family place experience' is the holiday home area. Despite being a significant spatial element in the overall structure of the destination in both Blokhus and Hals, it constitutes the space between two important family places (the holiday home and the beach) and is situated within a coastal and/or forestry landscape that makes up an essential part of the conception of a holiday home landscape. The only architectural interventions within these areas are roads and paths with the strictly utilitarian purpose of bringing people to and from the holiday home. Hence, the potential for activity and recreativity is not present and, as a consequence, the holiday home area vanishes as a place; it is not part of the families' conception of the destinations but remains an 'empty space' that renters pass through on the way to other places.

The spatial structure of a holiday home area, however, appears to be strongly integrated as part of the conception of the cultural landscape conceived as a utilitarian space; owing to the renters' routines it may, therefore, only be used as such. However, a physical restructuring of the architecture – creating unfamiliar places (Ringgaard 2010) – may surprise holiday home renters and make them stop and experience it, thereby breaking with the conservative conceptions of a holiday area and arousing curiosity amongst visitors that could transform it into a place. One means of achieving this would be to integrate built interventions with respect to the natural landscapes (coast and forests) to generate possibilities for exciting activities aiming at both younger and particularly older children (maybe even parents) and, within the same space, to establish small private places fulfilling the recreative part of a family place. Furthermore, the holiday home area could be used to expand the concept of a 'safety zone' experienced at the beach and within the holiday home. Inspiration here might be sought from within other closed 'destinations', such as the theme park, resort or camping site, where a delimited and secure space creates a safe haven for children to do something on their own (cf. Gram and Therkelsen 2003; Johns and Gyimóthy 2002). Integrating activity/recreative spaces with safe access within the holiday home area would provide children with an opportunity for more extrovert experiences – for example, meeting new friends – away from their parents and would potentially provide greater interactions between the holiday home and the holiday home area, enhancing the 'active' element of the family place experience.

However, as noted in the theoretical framework, any architectural intervention has to acknowledge the potential within the existing landscape and, moreover, the restructuring of space must pay attention to the circular balance of a family place experience within the holiday home in order to make a successful place. The findings of the research revealed that parents stress private and introvert places as a very important element of the existing landscape within a holiday home and, consequently, this cannot be destroyed by new interventions. Integrating future interventions of activity within the existing landscape may therefore be adequately 'disguised' to avoid intrusions into the private spheres, yet still provide for activities that stretch beyond the demarcated settings.

Hence, based upon the model, it has been argued that spaces which are traditionally conceived as possessing a merely 'utilitarian' purpose (cf. Snepenger *et al.* 2007), of which the holiday home area is a clear example, may be augmented by a 'hedonic' layer of activity and recreativity, respectively, through an architectural structure that evolves within the cross field of landscapes and built interventions. Furthermore, the architectural remaking of family holiday places may potentially seek to break with confined places which include only experiences of either activity *or* recreativity, adding more hybrid layers that promote both activity *and* recreativity within the same space and time. By doing this the potential for a family place experience is increased as it meets with both children's and parents' wishes and needs. Finally, such restructuring of the holiday home area may create a greater interplay with other central holiday home places, such as the holiday home and the beach, thus establishing a more coherent holiday home destination.

Conclusion

Based on observations and qualitative interviews, this chapter has scrutinised the place experience of families and the making of place within two holiday home destinations, Blokhus and Hals in Northern Jutland, Denmark. Based upon Canter's three dimensions of place, a conceptual understanding of 'place experience' was established as the interplay between the physical place and its architecture, the conceptions of place, and activities 'in place'. Building on this, the empirical findings showed that 'family place experience' and the making of place within the holiday home destinations occur as a hybrid within the cross field of architectural structures (landscape–built interventions) and performance (activity–recreativity). A model of 'family place experience' was consequently developed and discussed as a potential starting point in the future (re-)making of holiday home places aimed at hybrid experience opportunities answering to both children's and parents' conception of a good holiday home place.

12 Museums as playful venues in the leisure society

Babak Taheri and Aliakbar Jafari

Leisure society

Our contemporary society – at least explicitly in more economically developed contexts in urban spaces – is becoming a leisure society. Compared to our predecessors, we are more restless. We get bored easily. We show little interest in seriousness. Serious things scare us. Nowadays, people tend to watch less television news than they do quizzes or soap operas or reality shows. Television news channels, which traditionally broadcast serious materials, are turning their studios into theatres of 'infotainment' (Brants 1998). Educators are encouraged to apply interactive methods to entertain students and to keep them engaged in the classroom. Individuals seem to become afraid of being on their own. On the train, on the bus or on foot, people are becoming more accustomed to having their earphones on, listening to music or playing with their smart phones. City councils arrange more festivals and public shows to entertain their citizens. Thanks to the online environment (for example, social media, email and blogs) and multi-application smart phones, more entertaining contents, such as jokes, amusing video clips and photographs and artistic tastes, are shared amongst people.

With the intensified pace of life in the conditions of modernity, we are becoming more aware of the value of time and self, the time that we could devote to fulfilling our own satisfaction, pleasure and peace of mind. In our everyday life situations in urban spaces, by and large, we encounter stressful moments in different areas of social life. In the midst of all the roles we hold and play in society, work in particular is becoming more stressful. Under unprecedented economic pressure, we are required to work harder and deliver more. For a majority of middle-class populations, creating balance between personal and professional spaces is becoming ever more difficult. The fear of missing a meeting at work or leaving a task unfulfilled brings more anxiety to our lives. These stressful conditions make us increasingly needier for leisure (Deem 1996).

Our society is seriously becoming a leisure society. Once signifying childhood and mental and emotional immaturity, leisure and play have become necessities for modern mankind (Gillin 1914). Based on our socio-cultural norms, economic resources and personal agendas, we pursue different forms of leisure in order to cope with the reality of life (Stebbins 2009). Through leisure, we may seek ways of transforming our less satisfactory present life conditions, such as boredom or anxiety, into more desirable modes of being (Taheri and Jafari forthcoming). Whilst some of us may proactively pursue more enduring agendas, such as personal achievement and self-actualisation, in 'serious leisure' activities, others may simply seek commonplace temporary moments of pleasure in 'casual leisure' activities (Stebbins 2009)

Our growing interest in leisure is not only driven by our 'instinctive desire' for entertainment (Gillin 1914). We are becoming more interested in leisure because our imagination is stretched out beyond the boundaries of our everyday life horizons. We are now more able to imagine a wide variety of new modes of being. We are more able to embrace leisure in different ways. With the advance of technology, the boundaries between vicarious experience and lived experience are becoming more blurred than ever. Second Life, an online virtual world, best exemplifies this scenario. People immerse themselves in virtual worlds as though they are more real than real. For Facebook users, there may be more meaning and value to their virtual communities than to the non-virtual ones.

We live in an experience economy where organisations are increasingly making efforts to engage people in memorable and extraordinary experiences (Pine and Gilmore 1999). With the rapid development of the leisure industry, we have more choices. There are more cinemas, theatres, concerts, recreational centres, holiday opportunities, online entertainment activities such as gambling, TV productions and the like. Shopping centres are also becoming leisure centres, keeping people engaged for longer hours in their experiential environments (Bendar 1989; Howard 2007; Millan and Howard 2007). In the age of pursuing desires, the lines between advertising and entertainment have also become increasingly blurred (Kenway and Bullen 2011; Moore 2004).Whilst children are born into an entertainment-driven society, adults are similarly getting more eager to experience moments of pleasure and playfulness. Adulthood is somehow becoming pre-mature and childhood is becoming extended. That is, in a society driven by passion for desire (Belk *et al.* 2003), children are pulled towards adulthood in order to experience more entertainment and adults are equally pushed to experience childhood moments of play. There seems to be no or little difference between childhood and adulthood anymore. The boundaries of reality and hyper-reality are fading away in contemporary life (Firat and Venkatesh 1995).

In such conditions, our consumption practices become particularly important as they shape our modes of being. Whether our consumption activities are regarded as ends in themselves, that is, functional instances such as eating food to resolve hunger, or instrumental means of fulfilling higher order human needs, wants or desires (for example, experiential aspects such as dining out at a restaurant), they are part of our overall strategies and activities of organising our lives (Firat 1999). As life-organising activities, they reflect broader dynamics of an ever-changing landscape of life in which our expectations and mode-making activities also change. Our consumption practices are no longer exclusively determined by functional pursuits. Instead, we are driven by multiple motives that extend ourselves (Belk 1988) and address different dimensions of our fragmented and made-up selves (Firat and Venkatesh 1995).

It is based on these premises that leisure becomes a significant part of our lives as we seek more pleasurable experiences and modes of being. Leisure activities provide us with moments of excitement, happiness, creativity, escapism, learning, socialising, fun and play and the like. And amongst a diversity of leisure production and consumption venues, museums have traditionally played an important role in creating such qualities. Museums are important institutions that fulfil many functions in today's leisure society (Carnegie 2010; Sandell 2002; Veal 2009). The self-directed form of learning and enjoyment is important to both museums and their visitors, particularly as museums are operating progressively more in the leisure sphere and leisure society (Scott 2009). Museums have the capacity to capture human imagination, augment fantasies, stimulate different feelings and sensibilities and teach a myriad of lessons about past, present and future (Carnegie 2010; Kotler *et al.* 2008; Welsh 2005). The creation of such experiences, however, depends very much on the depth and quality of 'engagement'. There are many venues (both offline and online) that competitively put a great deal of effort into winning audiences and keeping them engaged in their increasingly attractive physical or virtual environments. Shopping malls, casino hotels, Disneyfied theme parks and the like have all become 'cathedrals of consumption' (Ritzer 2001) in which consumers of goods and services are encouraged to spend longer hours and consequently more money. With its $2 trillion market, the global entertainment and media industry (see www.marketingcharts.com/television/2-trillion-in-global-entertainment-media-spending-by-2011-763/) continues to attract more and more people in all corners of the world. In the midst of such an enormous market, one would wonder how museums can remain competitive and attract visitors! A foregone conclusion is that it is only through enduring and high-quality engagement that museums can accomplish their mission and remain attractive to their evasive modern audiences who demand more different and memorable experiences.

Experiential consumption

In order to better understand how engagement can be augmented in the context of the museum, we need to examine the nature of the consumption that paves the way for engagement. Consumption can be understood in light of the way consumption objects are appropriated. Holt's (1995) typology of consumption situations provides a useful means of understanding these varying appropriations: consuming as experience (where consumers subjectively and emotionally react to objects), consuming as integration (where consumers acquire and manipulate meanings of objects), consuming as classification (where objects can classify their consumers), and consuming as play (where objects are used as means of entertainment). Although all of these four consumption situations are relevant to our present discussion, the interconnectivity of consuming as experience and consuming as play is more pivotal to understanding consumption in the museum context.

Consumers often directly engage in consumption of entities (objects or events) and use such entities as resources to interact with fellow consumers or further immerse themselves in their engagement activities. Consumption encompasses a wide range of activities and modes of being concerning leisure, things such as aesthetics, variety seeking, pleasure, creativity, engagement, interaction and emotions. These qualities are generally regarded as experiential aspects of consumption (Hirschman and Holbrook 1982). As people around the world increasingly seek desirable experiences, more and more businesses are increasing their efforts towards creating, promoting and delivering such experiences (Pine and Gilmore 1999). The money consumers spend in consumption spaces is not just the price they pay for the product or service they buy, but also for the atmospherics – that is, lighting, staging, shelving, space, smell, and so forth – of the spaces in which their purchase or consumption activities take place. Hence, the concept of experience becomes a prominent theme in contemporary consumption situations. Such an experiential approach to consumption recognises the role of

> emotions in behaviour; the fact that consumers are feelers as well as thinkers and doers; the significance of symbolism in consumption; the consumer's need for fun and pleasure; the roles of consumers, beyond the act of purchase, in product usage as well as brand choice, and so forth.
>
> (Addis and Holbrook 2001: 50)

This conceptualisation of consumption as an experience shapes the foundations of leisure and tourism. Organisations in this industry sector are becoming more aware of the importance of engaging their clients in memorable and active ways in order to create extraordinary and enjoyable experiences (Arnould and Price 1993; Carù and Cova 2007b). However, organisations' efforts in optimising consumers' experiences are not simply focused on utilising organisational resources. Such efforts also largely focus on maximising consumers' participation in co-creation of experiences (Prahalad and Ramaswamy 2004). The active role of consumers in the production and consumption of experience is substantial (Sherry *et al.* 2007). For consumers, creating an experience can sometimes be a great experience in itself. For instance, the experience of engagement in stage settings, in particular, can be more pleasurable than the resultant experience more generally. The consumption experience scene can be viewed as a playground in which players activate their imagination and creativity and set their own idea scene. Consumers, therefore, may value co-creation of the experience more than having the experience made readily available to them, in a one-way tradition, by experience providers.

Co-creation of experience

Sometimes, solutions can paradoxically be problems. Offering solutions can sometimes decrease the level of creativity and suppress imagination. In the age of experiential consumption, ready-made solutions can hamper consumers' efforts and render consumers powerless and bored audiences. This is like forcing a group of energetic teenage footballers to watch a live football match without giving them any opportunity to play themselves. In the age of theatres of consumption, consumers want to be on the stage rather than simply watching, from their seats, actors play on the stage. Disempowering consumers can, therefore, result in feelings of agitation, exclusion and alienation. In Grant's (2000: 123) words, in our modern consumption spaces, 'people expect to have a part to play and, when they don't, they feel shut out'.

Such metaphors can be extended to a majority of experiential contexts including the museum. Museum visitors are interested in co-creating their experiences (White *et al.* 2009). They want to be seen as participants and not just idle audiences who stand and watch the game take place. Consumers and organisations, as partners and not oppositions, both can benefit from this willingness to participate (Grant 2000). Whilst consumers can have better feelings and experiences in their consumption spaces, organisations can equally channel their consumer-centred activities towards enhancing such experiences and augment their brand image and value propositions. Without doubt, better utilisation of resources can also benefit organisations. Such partnership is therefore valuable for both parties. Co-creation of experience can co-create value.

Whilst the creation of value has historically been viewed as the favourable outcome of an economic transaction (Arnould *et al.* 2006; Prahalad and Ramaswamy 2004), within the realm of cultural consumption (heritage/tourism) in general, and the museum context in particular, the creation of value is principally associated with consumers' experience (Shaw *et al.* 2011). Examples are abundant. The creation of the theatre experience in Disneyland largely depends on the quality and level of interaction between consumers and producers (Payne *et al.* 2008). Similarly, there are symbiotic relationships between participants and organisers of an exhibition. For instance, a photographic exhibition's existence and success relies not only on what the exhibition exhibits but also on who visits the exhibition (Hooper-Greenhill 2007). In other words, exhibitions gain credit on account of their visitors. The quantity and quality of visitors are increasingly becoming touchstones for assessing exhibitions' performance.

This question of 'who' is crucial to the organisation and management of the museum. A key challenge for any museum can be how to synchronise its own goals with its visitors' intended experiences (Black 2009). Since co-creation of experience requires that both parties' interests be taken into account, museums need to meticulously examine their visitors' dynamic and varying expectations. Only in light of sufficient knowledge of consumers' intended experiences can museums plan to co-create such experiences. Acknowledging the difficulties of balancing the museum's goals and visitor interests, Simon (2010) suggests that museums should still prioritise co-creating with visitors in their agendas. This way, they can address their visitors' needs and interests, provide a place for dialogue, and help visitors develop skills that will support their individual and social goals. Given the differences in visitors' intrinsic motivation and personal interest, deciding the breadth and depth of activities for engagement and co-creation of experience remains a prime challenge for museum managers and marketers (Falk and Storksdieck 2010; Leinhardt *et al.* 2003).

In this regard, Misiura (2006) suggests that careful application of marketing techniques can help to resolve the problem. For instance, in heritage marketing, as long as heritage products' core value is maintained, cultural product designers can assist to create and augment the image of cultural sites in visitors' minds. Similar suggestions have been offered (Gruen *et al.* 2000; Kleinschafer *et al.* 2011) in order to enhance the image of art galleries by incorporating designers' ideas. Such suggestions imply the fact that although for cultural consumption sites, such as museums, it is very difficult to reconcile all the varying interests of their visitors, they can leverage different techniques to make their atmosphere more appealing to their visitors and hence maximise engagement and co-creation of experience. Since the quality of experience in the museum depends highly on the quality of engagement, museums' prime focus is now on enhancing the duration and quality of their visitors' engagement.

Engagement in the museum

Engagement has been described as a sense of initiative, involvement and adequate response to stimuli, participating in social activities and interacting with others or alone (Achterberg *et al.* 2003). Also, Higgins and Scholer (2009: 102) define engagement as 'a state of being involved, occupied, fully absorbed, or engrossed in something with sustained attention'. Engagement, as consumers' 'commitment to an active relationship with a specific market offering', is differentiated from involvement which describes consumers' 'interest in a product category' (Abdul-Ghani *et al.* 2011: 1061). Engagement requires more than the use of cognition; it necessitates the satisfying of both experiential value and instrumental value – that is, involvement (Mollen and Wilson 2010). Engagement is in harmony with other concepts that describe consumer interest, including involvement, flow and interactivity (Abdul-Ghani *et al.* 2011; Csikszentmihalyi 2008; Mollen and Wilson 2010).

Whatever definition we take, engagement refers to the level and type of interaction and involvement individuals undertake in their consumption situations. In the context of the museum, for instance, visitors willingly focus on artifacts and exhibits and during their visits interact with(in) the museum context. Even in the case of surreal museums, drawing on their imagination, visitors can willingly suspend their sense of disbelief[1] and engage with the museum content and context. This kind of willingness can magnify the level of enjoyment, excitement, or any other emotional uptake one can derive from the museum environment. For example, in visiting museums of simulated horror (for example, the

London Dungeon), although visitors know in advance that the atmosphere of the museum is not real and does not impose any threat on them, they willingly give up this notion of unreality and immerse themselves in the experience of horror the venue intends to create. The experience of horror is therefore partially dependent on the level of visitors' willingness to being horrified.

Given the importance of meaningful engagement to high-quality experience and visitor satisfaction, museums now strive to retain visitor attention and increase satisfaction levels by engaging visitors with innovative presentation and interpretation techniques. These methods are of course heterogeneous in nature but homogeneous in purpose. That is, although all such methods are geared towards enhancing visitor engagement, the forms of these methods vary based on the characteristics, such as demographics and psychographics, of their audiences. For instance, a family's visit to a museum may be determined by children's interests (Sterry and Beaumont 2005).

Just like any other consumption situation, cultural consumers' consumption choices and experiences are determined by many internal and external factors. Museum visitors' types and levels of engagement are associated with particular personal preferences and characteristics. Prior research (Plog 1974) has already delineated two distinct types of cultural consumers: psychocentric (those who prefer the familiar) and allocentric (those who prefer the unfamiliar). Psychocentric individuals prefer to encounter more commonplace and familiar objects and events and allocentric people have a preference for more challenging situations in which they can activate their imagination to engage with the objects and events of consumption. Such orientations towards consumption situations determine the level of engagement in cultural consumers' experiences. Those with a higher level of zest and willingness to face the unfamiliar can be more demanding and proactive in their visits to cultural sites such as museums (Pattakos 2010). They seek more exciting and challenging experiences whereby they can let their imagination fly and enact their creativity.

The level of engagement is also associated with the nature of exhibits and the physical context in which the experience is created. Physical context includes the architecture and feel of the museum building, design and layout, space, lighting, colour and sound, as well as the artifacts enclosed within (Falk and Dierking 1997). These elements have a great deal of impact on the type of engagement in the museum because they facilitate the experience. Prior work on engagement (Bilda *et al.* 2008; Edmonds *et al.* 2006) identifies four core categories of interaction between exhibits and visitors: static, dynamic-passive, dynamic-interactive and varying. These represent a hierarchy of level of engagement which can be drawn on to identify skills and knowledge visitors require in engaging with the different types of exhibits. At the highest level of interaction, dynamic-interactive relationships between the visitor and the artwork occur when the experience is influenced by both players and changes over time as a direct result of the history of interactions. Different degrees of engagement bring with them different types of rewards; that is, depending on their expectations, visitors can derive different levels of satisfaction from their cultural consumption experiences.

Driven by the motive to enhance visitors' satisfaction level, art galleries and museums now attempt to engage cultural consumers through the ways objects are displayed and the activities constructed for the multiple purposes (for example, enjoyment or learning) visitors pursue. From an educational perspective (Bourdieu and Darbel 2008; Falk and Dierking 1997; Guintcheva and Passebois 2009; Hooper-Greenhill 2007), these activities expand a variety of offerings for visitors of different age groups with various motivations. Modern museums utilise a variety of ways to engage visitors and provide them with playful venues that offer intrinsic rewards (Holt 1995; Zwick and Dholakia 2004). Activities include organised events as well as engaging the audience with visual and interactive cultural facilities (Anderson 1999; Black 2009; Kotler *et al.* 2008). These playful consumption situations create enjoyable experiential outcomes such as informal learning and pleasure, what Sherry *et al.* (2007: 17) refer to as 'ludic autotely'. Experiencing such autotelic experience requires less preparation or a low level of cultural capital (Bourdieu 2007; Hein 1998; Whitaker 2009). However, achieving this kind of experience requires two conditions to be met: rich content and efficient mechanism. Rich content provides sufficient means for different types of interpretation for any given exhibit, and an understandable and meaningful mechanism facilitates visitors' retrieval of content of interest and enjoyment (Simon 2010).

Creation of such interpretations is closely related to cultural consumers' prior experience. Individuals' own characteristics and motives largely affect their interaction with the contents and context of the museum. As Ooi (2002) reminds us, visitors interpret cultural products through their own lens and their worldviews contribute to the operant resources they use in engaging with local cultures and co-creating the experience. Mindful visitors experience greater learning and understanding as well as higher levels of satisfaction than mindless visitors who, in the absence of commitment and focus, exercise weak levels of engagement (Moscardo 1996; Pattakos 2010). Individuals with more prior knowledge and experience about the museum experience higher levels of engagement and satisfaction than those less knowledgeable (Black 2009; Fienberg and Leinhardt 2002). Regular visitors are more likely to seek deeper levels of engagement during their visit (Black 2009). Previous experience may come not from previous visits to the museum itself, but from awareness and knowledge of the exhibit itself (Goulding 1999). These characteristics also affect the way visitors personalise the museum's meanings and message(s). When seen in collective forms, prior knowledge can both influence and be influenced by others' personal agenda. For instance, most visitors go to museums in a group and even those who visit museums alone may come into contact with other visitors and museum staff; therefore, their perspective is influenced by the social context (Falk and Dierking 1997, 2002).

Playfulness

Engagement is the main part of a valuable experience and a sense of being in the scene (Higgins and Scholer 2009). That is, it is mainly through the consumption stage of the service encounter that individuals' experience is affirmed through the level of their engagement (Carù and Cova 2003). Thus, the success of exhibits is often measured in relation to the average time spent on an exhibit and the perceived level of interactivity, as well as the ease with which a visitor can use an exhibit. Such measures reflect the increasingly high-tech forms of edutainment which can effectively enhance engagement amongst museum visitors. Given the emphasis on enjoyment, therefore, 'play' becomes an important construct within the museum experience (Csikszentmihalyi and Robinson 1990; Holt 1995; Sherry *et al.* 2007).

Play is usually associated with various consumption definitions such as an act of consumption (Holt 1995) and a dimension of experiential value (Holbrook *et al.* 1984). In Zwick and Dholakia's (2004: 228) words, 'playful consumers pursue actions for their propensity to enhance the interaction among the game's participants. Thus, interaction becomes an end in itself, thereby stressing the non-instrumental character of playful consumption.' In playful situations, visitors become involved in an activity for its inherent pleasure and enjoyment rather than for some utilitarian purposes or external benefits (Huang 2006).

Play has different forms. Sometimes, it can be a simple form of entertainment. That is, individuals involve themselves in a game and feel moments of cheerfulness and amusement. For instance, playing cards with friends whist chatting creates temporary moments of fun and amusement. This kind of play may be part of one's pastime activity. One may play to pass time. But sometimes, the same action of playing cards with friends may involve more mental engagement which requires the players to mentally concentrate on the game. In this case, the actors involved in the game take the task at hand more seriously and use their skills in order to play better and possibly win. Playing the game may also require them to have moments of silence and anxiety which can indicate players' concentration and thinking. In such a situation, players may also enhance their skills and knowledge of the game. In this scenario, the passage of time is not felt because the players are deeply involved in the game. This second type of play which requires deeper levels of engagement involves moments of 'flow experience' (Csikszentmihalyi 1975).

The flow experience brings moments of enjoyment and satisfaction. In fact, enjoyment is the focal driver of the flow experience. What we wish and what we think are in harmony (Csikszentmihalyi 2008). In flow experience, mind and heart can be reconciled; that is, one can engage with the task at hand both mentally and emotionally. Such experience also needs harmony between one's challenges and the skills required to face the challenges. In the presence of this harmony, the concentrated individual can feel moments of wholly engaged sensation and experience high levels of enjoyment. This experience can be intrinsically enjoyable for its own sake, regardless of any rewards that might be relative to the knowledge achieved (Csikszentmihalyi 2008).

Research on the flow experience (see, for example, Csikszentmihalyi and Hermanson 1995; Csikszentmihalyi and Robinson 1990; Griffin 1998) indicates that museums are amongst the most powerful contexts in which optimum moments of enjoyment can be created. As visitors engage with(in) the museum, they can immerse themselves in the act of engagement to an extent that they don't feel the passage of time and experience pleasure. Such visits to museums can be highly rewarding. Learning can be mixed with fun and further skills can develop. The act of visiting can therefore be more rewarding than initially intended. For instance, whilst a museum's initial goal may be informative, such as communicating a piece of information about a scientific fact, creating the flow experience can further fructify the museum, adding enjoyment to information. That is why a large number of museums have embarked on employing highly interactive means of engaging their visitors. Such offerings can certainly help to promote the image and value of museums in an ever-changing society.

Playful engagement and its value propositions

The museum experience has shifted from the Victorian idea of education to a more 'learning for fun' aspect (Black 2009; Packer 2006; Whitaker 2009). Visitors are no longer viewed as passive individuals; they are seen as active and pro-active people (Bagnall 2003; Bourdieu 2007; Peterson 2005). Over time, museums' functions have changed. There are questions around what defines public taste, who has the right to choose collections and engage and enjoy the exhibits and social environment, and how to represent them. These questions are related to the context-dependency of the role of museums and the set of values they propose. Museums are 'social constructs, and powerful ones at that, and they need to assume their place in the mainstream of contemporary life, not sit eccentrically on the margins' (Fleming 2005: 9). No establishment can come to the forefront of society without engaging the public. Visibility needs effort. That is, in order to be visible, any entity needs not only to endeavour to make itself visually available to the public but also to insert an impact on the members of society. To achieve such a mission, museums' most crucial task is to engage the public. That is, they should influence peoples' worldviews, knowledge, experiences and private and public lives. Museums' commitment to effective engagement is beneficial from different perspectives. Playful engagement at the level of flow experience may apparently seem to be a prime objective for some visitors in their visits to museums, but this playfulness can also be instrumental. That is, through playful engagement, ultimately a range of other objectives may be met and both visitors and museums benefit in a variety of ways.

Creating fun

Play inherently involves fun. Through playful activities, we pursue pleasant moments of enjoyment. Play is fundamental to health, both physically and mentally (Millar 1968). Through play, children develop their personality, their mind and emotions (Caplan and Caplan 1973). They interact with other children and learn ways of interacting with them. Play is a powerful activity whose benefits go beyond the realm of childhood and encompass a wider life span. Adults, too, can immensely benefit from play activities (Millar 1968). Play can be an escape from the monotony of everyday life situations. It is also an escape into better experiences in which one does not have to think about serious matters. Play can take adults back to the pre-institutionalisation stages of their life, their childhood (Csikszentmihalyi 1992). As we grow older, life institutionalises us through schooling, work and other social institutions. We develop a consciousness towards all matters around us and this consciousness changes our perception of what happiness is. Play can simplify life for us by removing this consciousness and immersing us in moments of happiness and contentment (Csikszentmihalyi 1992).

Playful engagement experiences in museums can create such feelings of satisfaction, for both children and adults. Through voluntary engagement in playful activities, visitors can achieve better feelings themselves and transfer their positive feelings and moments of enjoyment to others around them. In stressful conditions of life in urban spaces, we need to find ways of reducing our stress and to play more. Play slows down the maniacal pace of life. It makes us stop to pay attention to ourselves and to those living around us and those with whom our relationships have been formalised through work and social roles. The positive impact of play can be further strengthened through its occurrence in public spaces such as museums. In public, positive energies spread faster as others watch us play and enjoy ourselves. By creating playful engagements, museums can therefore act as healing centres where people can share their fun with others in healthy ways.

Activating creativity and imagination

Playful engagement fosters creativity and imagination. Through play activities, we play roles and do our best to play them well. Since plays are often developed around a task, we work towards resolving the puzzle or problem at hand and do the task as perfectly as we can. Through engagement in a given activity, if we don't have the required skills to accomplish the task, we think of acquiring new ones. Hence, we search for new ways of handling the task. This needs us to creatively think about alternative approaches. The psychology of play (Caplan and Caplan 1973; Csikszentmihalyi 1992; Millar 1968) provides evidence that play strengthens individuals' creativity. Play also provides the grounds for enacting our imaginative power and putting into practice what we have in mind. In playful engagement there is no penalty for making mistakes. One can stretch the wings of imagination as far as they can go. In a stress-free context, one can try different ways of playing the game. And this makes a difference to applying imagination. At work and real-life situations, our imagination is restricted to the boundaries of our responsibilities. Our imaginative minds have lower ceilings because we have to think of the consequences of our imaginations. Any mistake will cost us dear.

In museums, we can let our imagination fly. Playful engagements legitimise trial and error in a cost-free manner. We have a right to try the game and fail.

We can also close our eyes and travel back in history. The atmospherics of the museum can let us imagine different modes of being for ourselves in the present. We can also be futuristic and travel ahead in time. We can play different games in a guilt-free way and watch others play too. We can also inspire others and be reciprocally inspired by them. Such qualities of museums can create stages of performance for zealous visitors who yearn for participation. Children and adults can both benefit. Those who activate their imaginations more often can enhance their performance in other areas of life, such as work, family ties and relationship with friends. Imagination in turn activates creativity.

Enhancing learning

Play can also act as a medium for learning and skill development (Bergen 1988). Play acts as a personality development workshop. Participants in playful engagements consciously or unconsciously become involved in learning, learning about objects, themselves and others. Children can develop a wide range of key skills such as seeing, analysing, thinking, identifying, calculating (Singer *et al.* 2006). As they are exposed to playful situations, they learn how to conduct the act of playing. They learn how to find their way through the play and achieve the target. In their mission, they are encouraged by parents and others around them. They feel rewarded and build a sense of self-confidence. They also learn how to be competitive. All of these qualities can apply to adults too. As adults, we can enhance our personal as well as social qualities through playful activities. Through playful activities we don't get bored, we learn things by doing.

Museums can enhance visitors' learning through playfully engaging their visitors. Research (Malone and Lepper 1987) confirms that playful learning is more effective and enduring. Museums therefore use interactive and playful means of engagement (application of sound and lighting effects, digital screens, 3D games, and mechanical tools and playgrounds) to foster their visitors' learning process (Hein 1998). This learning enhancement is also important for another significant reason. Since people's interests in things can be associated with their level of knowledge in those things, enhancing individuals' knowledge can develop in them a sense of interest in certain things they were not previously interested in (Leinhardt *et al.* 2003). Through playful engagement activities, therefore, museums can ultimately attract uninterested groups.

Nurturing social interaction

Playful activities nourish sociability and social interaction. In playful venues, people are more relaxed; they smile more and are more open to new ideas and social relationships. In playful activities, people are even more generous in sharing their feelings and thoughts. Due to such characteristics, playful engagements in museums can cultivate seeds of friendship and social interaction. Such positive human relationships influence visitors' experience. Playful engagements with objects and interactive means and equipment become excuses for visitors to talk to one another. Even those who visit museums on their own and do not actively pursue social contact may become interested in socializing with others (Debenedetti 2003; Taheri and Jafari forthcoming). Through social interaction, visitors' cultural consumption experiences can become even more enjoyable. Apart from learning faster (Hilke and Balling 1985), people can come into contact with other individuals who may share similar interests. Therefore, for visitors museums can act as social hubs in which they construct and reconstruct their social ties primarily around the playful context of the museum and also extend their relationships beyond the physical boundaries of museums (Taheri and Jafari forthcoming).

The museum and leisure society

Visitors are affected not only by the historical period in which they grew up – and hence developed certain knowledge about history, society, culture, science and life at large – but also by the present set of circumstances that shape and possibly alter their interpretation and understanding of the knowledge and experiences they hold about the past. Museums have a great capacity to develop a distinct consciousness of generations' experiences and knowledge (Hetherington 2000; López-Sintas *et al.* 2008). Ensuring that museums can sustain this significant historical role in transferring generational knowledge and experience requires that museums remain at the centre of social reality of life. An effective way of achieving this goal is to attract visitors and engage them not only in the context of the museum but also in the total sphere of life in society. That is, visitors should be able to take with them memorable experiences and knowledge and share such uptakes with others in society (Simon 2010). The offerings of museums should go beyond the museum walls (Taheri and Jafari forthcoming).

Today's leisure-driven society has forced museums not only to concentrate on the education of their visitors, but also to entertain their audiences in order to successfully compete with the growing variety of available entertainment facilities, such as computer games, smart phones, cinemas, theme parks and live shows, in the world around them (Packer 2006; van Aalst and Boogaarts 2001). This evolution means that museums should undergo constant metamorphoses. Museums are allocating more resources to participatory experiences than they had previously put towards traditional singular exhibits (Kotler *et al.* 2008; Simon 2010). For instance, Witcomb (2003) demonstrates how museums position themselves as entertaining sites through incorporating popular culture with exhibition programmes. Kotler *et al.* (2008) and Simon (2010) also provide a host of examples in which museums strategically employ marketing techniques to reposition themselves as highly valuable and entertaining socio-cultural hubs in the twenty-first century.

For many museum marketers, these processes of popularisation and commercialisation call into question their definition of a traditional museum, as they consider it to be a 'debasement' of cultural experiences (Tufts and Milne 1999).

A key question for museums is how to provide infrequent visitors with a 'wow experience' rather than concentrate on repeat visitors (Kotler and Kotler 2000; Kotler *et al.* 2008). In a time of economic hardship, budget cuts and financial crises, museums are forced to undertake commercial roles. For museum managers the focus is, therefore, on more practical considerations such as visitor numbers, education and funding and other market considerations (Genoways and Ireland 2003). The visitor is increasingly being thought of as a 'customer' and, while such a designation would have been improbable 50 years ago, today museums are actively competing for the flexible leisure time and commercial income of both residents and tourists (Chhabra 2007; Kotler *et al.* 2008).

The majority of museums are now concerned about their ability to remain competitive in the art world and the leisure-driven society. Funding, as a fundamental issue, often places museums at the centre of local development plans that require them to renew their strategy and mission statement accordingly with regards to public opinion (Stevenson *et al.* 2008; Strom 2002). Even in free market economies, such as the UK and the USA, museums are no longer autonomous institutions. Governments are increasingly intervening in museums' policies and operations (Smith 2001). Technology is another important issue to address. With the rapid growth of technology, museums are forced to install and renovate their technological systems. In a technology-driven world, this is a necessity not a cosmetic supplement. Technology's role in enhancing visitor experience is undeniable.

Museums compete for the public's leisure time, which is becoming more and more dominated by computers. Thus, sustaining cultural heritage and encouraging less interested audiences, mobilising younger technology-maniac generations, enhancing connections and cooperation among different players within the tourism, heritage and museum fields and extending event management, and rebranding and rejuvenating conventional images of museums gain importance in the museum marketing.

Conclusion

In our opening paragraphs, we argued that, in a leisure society, museums' main challenge is to compete with many well-equipped and well-resourced establishments, such as the media and game industries. Museums therefore, need to employ sophisticated marketing techniques to make them competitive enough. What we propose here is not to make museums competitive enough 'to survive'. This is a reactive or rather passive strategy. The ideal situation is to make them sufficiently competitive to outdo competition. A key strategic approach in this regard is to change the image of the museum. As discussed earlier, recent developments in this case testify the fact that museums are becoming more aware of seriously incorporating the element of entertainment into their strategic and tactical plans. However, these activities should be strategically channelled towards enhancing the image of museums as modern institutions that can play a significant role in contemporary society.

In a society which is becoming more and more leisure oriented, where the traditional boundaries of demographic segmentation are fading away, museums need to promote many of their other values that come in a package. Augmenting playful engagement for museums may not be the only, but is certainly a crucially significant, way of attracting and retaining visitors. Playful engagements should not be viewed as only activities that take place within museums; if effectively implemented, these activities can insert their impact on society even outside museums. Besides, museum marketers and managers should not see playful engagements exclusively as ends in themselves. They can serve a multitude of purposes that can collectively offer value to society. Recognition of these values by people depends highly on how museums communicate such values with their existing visitors or a large number of potential cultural consumers in society. Understanding this important task and strategising effective and efficient action plans are key priorities for museum managers and marketers to consider. In a leisure society, competition amongst leisure providers is increasing. Museums are too valuable to fall behind.

Note

1 The concept of 'willing suspension of disbelief', first coined by Samuel Taylor Coleridge in his *Biographia Literaria* in 1817, denotes the status of suspending one's belief that a piece of artwork is not real. Suspension of one's disbelief is crucial to enjoying the aesthetics and fantasies of a piece of art.

Part V

Managing tourist experiences

As discussed in the first chapter in this volume, although the tourist experience is personal and individual to the tourist, there being as many 'tourist experiences' as there are tourists, it cannot be dissociated from the supply of tourism services. In other words, it has long been recognised that tourism, as with all services, is produced and consumed instantaneously; the production and consumption of tourism services are inseparable in the context of the tourist experience. Putting it another way, the tourist experience is not only a function of the relationship between the tourist and the object of consumption; the intervention of intermediaries, such as suppliers or managers of tourist services, may make a significant contribution to the nature of the tourist experience. Thus, as others have argued (Morgan *et al.* 2010), research into the management of tourist experiences represents an important theme within the overall study of the tourist experience.

In this section, the three contributions explore the relevance of supply/management of the tourist experience in contrasting contexts. First, in Chapter 13, Peter Bolan, Stephen Boyd and Jim Bell introduce what they refer to as 'displacement theory' within the larger phenomenon of film-induced tourism, exploring the inherent implications, opportunities and challenges for economic development that this implies for film tourism destination managers. In other words, films are not always shot in the place they are portraying on screen; it is not unusual for a film to be made in a completely different country from that it portrays. This form of displacement creates issues of authenticity and implications as to where the tourist influenced by such a film will choose to visit and the experiences they have. The authors explore the motivations and experiences of film tourists at different locations and, as a consequence, propose a model that can form the basis for recommendations as to how industry can maximise future potential from film-induced tourism, especially when displacement occurs, in order to enhance the tourist experience.

In Chapter 14, Tiffanie L. Skipper, Barbara A. Carmichael and Sean Doherty consider tourists' attitudes towards hosts, and what factors influence the quality of their tourism experiences, in the thematic context of harassment. Drawing specifically on research amongst tourists in the two resorts of Montego Bay and Negril in Jamaica, they explore how and to what extent harassment by local people affects tourists' attitudes towards hosts themselves and the overall tourism experience. They found that, although a majority of tourists experienced harassment, generally their attitudes towards the island of Jamaica and its local people were positive. Indeed, none of those who experienced harassment was deterred from recommending Jamaica or returning there in the future. Consequently, the chapter offers a number of management policies for mitigating the effects of harassment on tourists.

In Chapter 15, the final chapter in this volume, Bridget Major and and Fraser McLeay look at the experience of the 'grey market' on package holidays. Their chapter commences with a review of tourist consumer behaviour and provides a summary that is relevant to this book as a whole, before going on to report on the results of an exploratory study amongst British older tourists on holiday in the Canary Islands. The findings from this study inform potential interventions by providers of package holiday experiences for this particular (and increasingly significant) market, contributing ultimately to an enhanced consumer experience.

13 'We've seen it in the movies, let's see if it's true'

Motivation, authenticity and displacement in the film-induced tourism experience

Peter Bolan, Stephen Boyd and Jim Bell

Introduction

Tourists as consumers are increasingly searching for and demanding new experiences. Film can provide such profound experiences, allowing the viewer to transcend what may be termed the shallowness of everyday life and be transported to another place, to view somewhere which may be inherently new to or different for them. Tourists may then seek to recapture or replicate the experience gained from viewing the film by actually travelling to and spending time in the place they were drawn to. Films or movies, therefore, provide us with a window into other places that broaden our knowledge and can fuel our desire to travel. What has become known as film-induced tourism has begun to gather momentum as an area of both academic research and industry interest. However, the phenomenon is wide-ranging and, according to Beeton (2005), still a largely untapped and little-understood field of tourism research. Much of the literature to date has focused on the promotional aspects and the impacts of the phenomenon, with little research into the motivations of the film-induced tourists themselves. Furthermore, films are not always shot in the place they portray on screen. This has become a common occurrence and it is not unusual for a film to be made in a completely different country from that it portrays. This form of displacement creates issues of authenticity and implications as to where the tourist influenced by such a film will choose to visit. This aspect of film tourism has been mentioned briefly by authors such as Beeton (2005), Hudson and Ritchie (2006a) and Shandley *et al.* (2006) but they have not conducted investigations themselves and to date there have been no in-depth research studies into this aspect of the phenomenon.

According to Beeton (2005), much of the more recent academic literature has not specifically added to the overall body of research, tending to focus on replicating (and supporting) earlier studies, and looking mainly at the promotional value of film in relation to tourism. This is a serious issue that this chapter addresses through the investigation of previously under-researched aspects of the film-induced tourism phenomenon. More specifically, the overall aim of this chapter is to consider what the authors have termed displacement theory (grounded in aspects of authenticity) within the larger phenomenon of film-induced tourism and to present a clearer understanding of impacts on the tourist experience and the inherent implications and opportunities for economic development this may bring. An interpretivistic research approach was adopted, utilising the power of the Internet and harnessing the use of specially created blogs, to collect qualitative data. Analysis of qualitative data from respondents was then followed up by further blog-related data from a sample of the original bloggers. Semi-structured interviews with management staff from key tourism and film organisations throughout the UK and Ireland also took place. Stemming from this, a model of displacement (the first such model in this field of study) in film tourism has been created. This is then utilised to make key recommendations as to how the tourism industry can maximise future potential from film-induced tourism, especially when displacement occurs, thus enabling the phenomenon to be better managed to enhance tourist experience and create greater economic benefit.

Film-induced tourism

Film-induced tourism can be defined as 'tourist visits to a destination or attraction as a result of the destination being featured on television, video, DVD or the cinema screen' (Hudson and Ritchie 2006a: 256). Today we can add to such a definition, Blu-ray and digital downloads as yet further ways of watching and experiencing a film. While in its widest sense the concept includes television shows and dramas, this chapter chiefly concerns itself with cinematic film and its influence through the medium of the cinema theatre, DVD/Blu-ray/digital download and public broadcast on television (the typical lifecycle through which most films progress).

Butler (1990), in his study of media influence on tourism and international tourist patterns, provided the initial impetus for the academic community to gain interest in researching the phenomenon of film and its effects on tourism. Other authors, such as Riley and van Doren (1992), Tooke and Baker (1996) and Riley *et al.* (1998,) advanced the research much further through the 1990s and established a platform for the study of film-induced tourism to grow and develop. This has continued into the twenty-first century with authors such as Beeton (2001, 2002, 2004, 2005, 2006), Tzanelli (2003, 2004, 2006), Hudson and Ritchie (2006a, 2006b), Carl *et al.* (2007), O'Connor *et al.* (2010), Croy (2011) and Hudson (2011) taking study of this field further still. Table 13.1 provides a more comprehensive review of authors who have researched the area and is broken down into a number of categories, including the impacts of film tourism, destination branding (including movie maps – that is, regional or national maps showing the locations of movies) and case-study research.

As far as the phenomenon itself is concerned, high-profile examples include *The Lord of the Rings* trilogy (2001–2003) and the impact on New Zealand tourism, *Braveheart* (1995) and its impact on tourism to Scotland and *The Sound*

Table 13.1 Categories of previous film tourism research

Film tourism categories/ themes	*Authors*
Measurement of film tourism	Busby and Klug (2001), Kim and Richardson (2003), Beeton (2005)
Impacts of film tourism	Riley *et al.* (1998), Beeton (2004, 2005), Graml (2004), Tzanelli (2006), Hudson and Ritchie (2006b), Grihault (2007), Croy (2011), Hudson (2011)
Destination branding (including movie maps)	Tooke and Baker (1996), Riley *et al.* (1998), Grihault (2003), Beeton (2004, 2005), Bolan and Davidson (2005), Hudson and Ritchie (2006a, 2006b), Bentham (2006), Bolan and O'Connor (2007, 2008), Olsberg/SPI (2007), Donald and Gammack (2007), Bolan and Williams (2008), O'Connor *et al.* (2010)
Case-study research	Grihault (2003, 2007), Tzanelli (2003, 2006), Graml (2004), Beeton (2005), Jones and Smith (2005), Hudson and Ritchie (2006a), Bolan and Crossan (2006), Carl *et al.* (2007), Iwashita (2006, 2008)
Current state of film tourism	Bentham (2006), Grihault (2007), Olsberg/SPI (2007), Oxford Economics (2007)

Source: compiled by the authors.

of Music (1965) and its impact on Austria (most notably Salzburg). Some of the earliest examples can be linked to destinations such as Ireland; John Ford's 1952 film *The Quiet Man*, according to Bolan and Crossan (2006), still draws large coach-parties of American tourists to the small village of Cong in County Mayo where the movie was filmed.

Despite a growing body of research, as indicated by Table 13.1, the concept of movies being filmed in one place but portraying somewhere else has not received much attention in the film tourism literature of either an academic or industry nature. As such, this chapter addresses this gap in the literature.

Tourist motivation and behaviour

What motivates film-induced tourists is an area that warrants more research and, indeed, tourist motivation is a crucial aspect in the field of tourism studies. According to Shepherd (2003: 133) 'the question of travel motivation, along with touristic impact on toured societies, remains a central issue among tourism theorists'. Interest in tourist motivation and decision-making has grown further out of studies of tourist behaviour both by tourism academics and particularly geographers (though many hail from both camps), such as Cooper (1981), Dann (1981), Pearce (1982b, 1992), Mathieson and Wall (1982), Iso-Ahola (1983), Gilbert (1991), Crompton (1993), Gnoth (1997) and Ryan (1997).

However, according to some commentators, such as Parinello (1996), no single theory can possibly encompass all individual travel motivations. The heterogenous nature of tourism itself and the complexities of human behaviour make this a highly challenging area of investigation. What motivates film-induced tourists is central to this chapter, especially any linkage between motivational drivers at work and the authenticity and displacement issues under investigation.

When viewing films, consumers are able to experience attractions and destinations vicariously without leaving the security of their home and without the 'hard sell' impressions inherent in specific advertising (Riley and Van Doren 1992). The motivation to visit somewhere seen in a movie (whether real or imagined) is likely to have an effect in ways which traditional advertising cannot. With the medium of film, the person is not being cajoled into choosing the destination; rather, they are making their own decision on the basis of the influence that various aspects of the movie has had upon them. Such various motivational aspects may be the scenery (natural landscape or urban) in the movie, the narrative/storyline, the music/film score, some identification with the film characters, or the actors themselves. These motivational aspects or drivers are examined and explored later in this chapter.

Authenticity and displacement

While films may act as a catalyst or motivating factor on people to visit a particular place, they may rarely offer an authentic view of that place compared to the reality of what the tourist will find there. Displacement in the film-induced tourism context refers to the situation where a movie is shot in one place but in reality is representing somewhere else entirely. Any inauthenticity is compounded further in such situations. However, what constitutes authenticity with regard to tourism is not always clear and has been the subject of much debate amongst researchers. Since MacCannell's work in the 1970s (see, for example, MacCannell 1973), others have made contributions in the field of authenticity in relation to tourism, such as Cohen (1988), Engler (1993), Hughes (1995), Fees (1996), Wang (2000), Jamal and Hill (2004), Tzanelli (2004), Steiner and Reisinger (2006) and most recently Kim and Jamal (2007). Despite many such key contributions, the authenticity concept is still arguably under-researched in some areas of the tourism domain.

Wang's (2000: 34) research on the sociology of travel and tourism proposes three 'types' of authenticity at play: 'objective', 'constructive' and 'existential'. Wang states that the concept of authenticity in tourism would strongly benefit from clearly distinguishing two key areas of study 'that of the authenticity of toured objects (that is, objective authenticity) and that of the experience of authenticity'. Both have relevance to what is addressed in this chapter, though a key objective is to examine authenticity of place in relation to what viewers see on the cinema screen (and/or repeat viewing on DVD/Blu-ray/television) and how this may affect any resulting tourism to either film location or film setting when both are different.

Researchers such as Jansson (2007: 5) believe that all forms of media, especially 'new media' 'influence perceptions of place, distance, sociality, authenticity, and other pre-understandings that frame tourism'. Butler briefly touched on the concept of displacement in film in 1990, whilst Tooke and Baker (1996) were the first to give an actual example of this in the form of the British television series Cadfael set in Shrewsbury in England but filmed in Hungary. In relation to cinematic film, other examples in previous research have included *The Fugitive* (1993), as cited by Riley *et al.* (1998), and *The Beach* (2000) as cited by Tzanelli (2006). None of these examples, however, was actually supported by any rigorous empirical research. In addition, these latter two film examples featured displacement on a small scale, with only a relatively small number of scenes filmed somewhere different from where they were 'pretending' to be. There are a great many film examples where this takes place on a much larger scale and often where the entire scope and breadth of the movie is shot in a completely different country.

Butler (1990), in his seminal paper some two decades ago, stated that we may be entering an era where people's geographical knowledge of the world is based on something inherently false that they have gleaned through various media forms, such as movies and fictional literature. Tzanelli (2004: 38) echoes this strongly in her work on *The Lord of the Rings* and New Zealand when she states that 'there is a danger that tourist consumption of simulatory landscape and cultures will overwrite specific histories of actual places and cultures'. Beeton (2005: 105) also touches on such issues, noting that

> [there] is anecdotal evidence . . . that visitors to film sites are disappointed when they do not see exactly what was portrayed on the screen. For such film-induced tourists, this presents an *inauthentic* experience as, for them, what was on screen was the *reality* they wanted to experience.

Table 13.2 illustrates that this form of displacement has been occurring for decades on a global basis with a diverse range of examples. Ireland, as can be seen from the table, has been something of a prevalent example of this, often doubling for other places around the world (particularly elsewhere in Europe) and, as such, provides a good illustration of this aspect of film-induced tourism in relation to examining the authenticity and displacement issues this chapter focuses on.

This phenomenon of course raises a number of fundamental questions, including:

- How do tourists feel if they are not aware of such displacement and then find out later?
- If they are aware before booking a holiday, will the tourists prefer to visit the setting, the actual location, or both?
- Do all such potential markets exist?
- What possible economic benefits can this bring in relation to tourism?
- What implications or threats exist?
- Is there any linkage between what motivates film-induced tourists and what they then find most authentic?

Table 13.2 Displacement film tourism examples

Film title	*Film location*	*Film setting*
A Fistful of Dollars (1964)	Spain	USA
The Spy Who Came in From the Cold (1965)	Ireland	East Germany
Excalibur (1981)	Ireland	England
Waking Ned (1994)	Isle of Man	Ireland
Braveheart (1995)	Ireland	Scotland
Seven Years in Tibet (1997)	Argentina	Tibet
Saving Private Ryan (1998)	Ireland	France
The Count of Monte Cristo (2002)	Ireland	France/Italy
Gangs of New York (2002)	Italy	USA
Cold Mountain (2003)	Romania	USA
The Last Samurai (2003)	New Zealand	Japan
King Arthur (2004)	Ireland	England
Batman Begins (2005)	England	USA
Memoirs of a Geisha (2005)	USA	Japan

Source: compiled by the authors.

These important questions in relation to film-induced tourism are central to this chapter and are addressed in the following case study.

Case study on motivation, authenticity and displacement

An interpretivistic approach was taken by the authors to this topic, utilising qualitative methods in terms of data collection and analysis. The strength of contribution the research makes to the understanding of film-induced tourism lies in the rigour and utilisation of innovative methodologies and the fact it addresses a gap in the academic (and industry) literature on the aspect of 'displacement' in relation to the phenomenon. The authors used blogs as a data collection method to gather opinion on the film tourism phenomenon. An initial dedicated blog was set up using a facility provided by www.blogger.com at the URL: http://mediatourism.blogspot.com and can be seen in Figure 13.1. The intention was to harness the opportunities of Web 2.0 applications, such as blogs and social media platforms, in order to gather attitudes and opinions on the topic under study.

Data of a qualitative nature was obtained and analysed from 161 respondents on this initial blog. A further dedicated blog was set up and a sample of respondents (19 in all) gave further detailed qualitative responses to the core issues under study. Research also took place with those in the tourism and film industry, employing the use of semi-structured interviews. Seven organisations from around the UK and Ireland were interviewed. These included national tourist bodies as well as film councils and commissions. The actual organisations were chosen through critical case sampling which is, according to Saunders *et al.* (2009: 590), 'A purposive sampling method which focuses on selecting those cases on the basis of making a point dramatically or because they are important'.

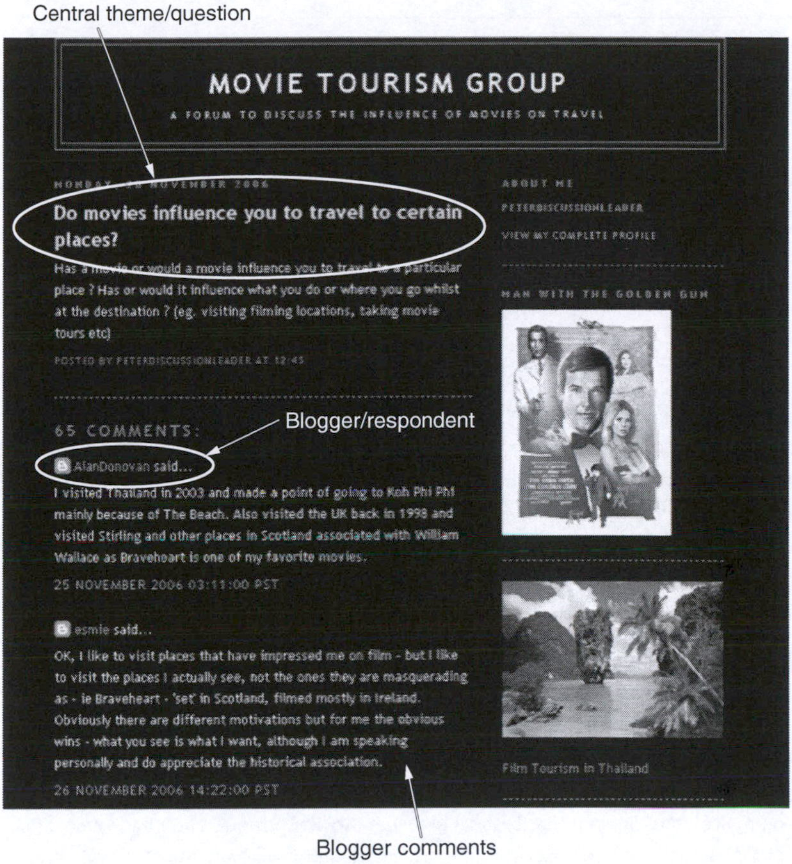

Figure 13.1 Blog screenshot explanation (source: http://mediatourism.blogspot.com).

Key findings and emergent data resulting from the blogs and industry interviews are now discussed and explained.

Research findings

Data collected and analysed through blog research revealed not only what motivates film-induced tourists, but also that the issues of displacement and authenticity are something that matters to such tourists. The dedicated blog attracted a range of nationalities over the period of data collection mentioned. This international representation is illustrated in Table 13.3.

A potential concern over using online methods of research, particularly in the early years of new innovations, is that the data might be skewed towards the young and the highly computer literate. However, the results here echo and support the work of authors such as Cohen and Krishnamurthy (2006), Schmallegger and

Table 13.3 Nationality of bloggers (respondents)

UK	(*n*=46)
USA	(*n*=38)
Ireland	(*n*=29)
Australia	(*n*=12)
Germany	(*n*=10)
Japan	(*n*=6)
New Zealand	(*n*=6)
France	(*n*=4)
Italy	(*n*=4)
Switzerland	(*n*=3)
Norway	(*n*=2)
Jamaica	(*n*=1)

Carson (2008) and Hookway (2008) who believe that people of all ages are now more comfortable with using the Internet, and especially so in a tourism related context. The age range of bloggers in this study was 23–63 years which clearly reflects this.

As Figure 13.2 illustrates, qualitative comments were obtained in relation to blogger's views on what motivated them from the medium of film to want to visit certain destinations. In these examples shown, motivational drivers such as *scenery* and *nostalgia* are coming through strongly amongst respondents.

Desert Rose (age 27, female, nationality: Australian) said

For me its very much the scenery that grabs me. Fiji looked so fabulous in the Blue Lagoon that I just had to go there . . . and Ko Samui is still very much on my list after seeing *The Beach*. I also want to visit Prague and I think part of that is that I've been exposed to many scenes of the city in lots of recent movies. So whether its natural or man-made its the scenery that gets me.

05 April 2007 02:44:00 PDT

Zeni (age 57, female, nationality: Jamaican) said

In Jamaica we get a lot of people who are interested in visiting the beach location used for '*Dr. No*' (the scene where Ursula Andress comes out of the sea). That draws far more people than more recent films that were shot here. So in this case I feel it is the Ursula Andress and James Bond connection moreso than just the beach scenery. Perhaps there is also a nostalgic apsect. Many people remember than scene from the 60's.

25 April 2007 12:28:00 PDT

Figure 13.2 Sample comments on motivational factors.

In relation to what influences film-induced tourists, Table 13.4 illustrates the findings from the blog data collected. Scenery is the dominant motivational driver but narrative/storyline and characters are also important influences, whilst emotion/romance and music also have a role to play.

Experiential aspects in film-induced tourism

Also emerging from the blog data was the fact that some bloggers were seeking, in some way to relive or recapture the experience they had whilst first viewing a particular film. The cinema experience means many things to many people, and the cinema-goer can be motivated to spend time in front of the big screen for a number of reasons. The teenager, for example, may want to remove him- or herself from the family home for a couple of hours, spending time in what parents may perceive as a 'safe' environment. For the adult, it may be 'switching off' from normality in a relatively undisturbed way. Both examples relate to the issue of escapism, specifically if one views the cinema as an opportunity to escape reality, and move away 'from the routine of everyday living' (McIntyre 2007: 115).

There is also the social element linked to the cinema experience. More often than not, the cinema-goer is sharing the experience with others in the cinema (not merely the person(s) they may have gone with); many may be laughing at the same parts of the film, feeling similar emotions or thinking similar things at the same time. It is this combination of a shared social experience and escapism which is increasingly influencing people to visit the cinema. Indeed, research conducted by SPA Research for Carlton Screen Advertising in 2006 finds that today's consumers see a trip to the cinema as a rare shared experience with family and friends, a treat and a chance to escape busy, stressful lives.

Expanding the mind and exploring different concepts can also be considered another influencing factor for cinema participation. The ever-increasing choice of film types allows people to become absorbed in a range of new and/or different thoughts, feelings and emotions. Watching an historical, science-fiction or foreign cinema film in particular provides an opportunity to do or experience

Table 13.4 Summary of film factors influencing travel decision

Film factor	*% of bloggers influenced*
Characters	10
Narrative/story	20
Scenery	43
Music/film score	7
Actors	0
Emotion/romance	8
Nostalgia	5
Combination of factors	8

Source: Blog created by author at http://mediatourism.blogspot.com.

something very different for the viewer. This latter point especially resonates with travel and tourism activities, where 'experiencing something different' is often a key aspect. Zhou (2004), for example, recognises the experience factor in relation to travel and tourism, whilst also acknowledging the escapism element that it can bring.

Through exploring examples from the blog data in terms of bloggers' views in this research, it became clear that there are parallels between the cinema experience and the tourism experience. These similarities, and others, have been summarised in Figure 13.3 below, alongside activity specific experiences.

Whilst both activities (film viewing and tourism) have a set of independent experiential factors, both can contain common experiences, such as escapism, relaxation, nostalgia, entertainment, romance and adventure. This, therefore, raises the question as to whether there are any important implications to this commonality, and invites an exploration into the extent of its relationship with film-induced tourism. Research findings from the blog data in this study strongly suggest there is important substance to this commonality between the two sets of experiences. Bloggers cited that, through their travels, they were in some cases seeking to recapture the experiences and feelings they had whilst watching a particular film; for example, blogger geoffdowl sought to experience what he felt whilst watching *Out of Africa* (1985), even taking the theme tune on his Ipod with him to help in such a regard whilst he visited the destination.

The cinema experience can, therefore, be a motivating factor in the tourist's choice of holiday destination (leading to the tourism or holiday experience). The experience the viewer has whilst immersed in a film is something which may not only prompt them to visit the place depicted but also to go there to recapture or relive that very experience. For those film-induced tourists, issues of displacement and authenticity may then be of even greater relevance.

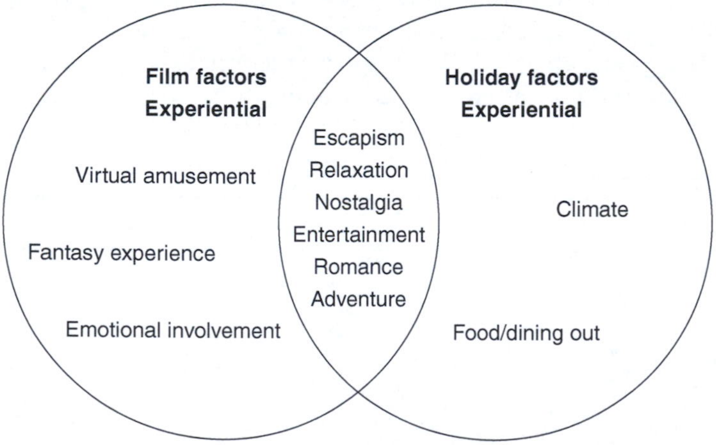

Figure 13.3 The coalescence of factors between the film experience and the holiday experience (source: Bolan 2010).

Comments in Figures 13.4 and 13.5 highlight sample comments from bloggers regarding their thoughts on displacement and authenticity which were the core aims of the study. In these examples, the respondents clearly prefer to visit the film setting rather than the actual location. However, research conducted for the study revealed that there were tourists who prefer to visit the location in such instances and indeed those who like to visit both setting and location.

marcushog (age 28, male, nationality: Australian) said

Really interesting question! Don't think its happened to me yet but I can see how it raises some issues for people. I agree with Chris somewhat in that if its a science fiction or fantasy film then the 'place' depicted doesn't really exist – so it doesn't raise the same questions over how authentic the place is. If the setting in the movie is real and yet it's filmed somewhere else – then that's very different. I read on the blog here about *Braveheart* and Ireland. I never knew that. I would have visited Scotland without thinking, never realising it wasn't Scotland I saw on film.

17 June 2007 09:53:00 PDT

Figure 13.4 Sample comments on authenticity and displacement.

Kerry (age 33, female, nationality: British) said

Well this is a really interesting aspect!

As I said elsewhere on this blog 3 movies influenced me to visit Japan: *The Last Samurai*, *Memoirs of a Geisha* and *Lost in Translation*.

Although I didn't realise at the time, only one of these films was actually made in Japan (*Lost in Translation*). I learned whilst visiting the country that *The Last Samurai* had been shot mainly in New Zealand and that *Geisha* was mostly American I think. However to me (although some people may find this disappointing) these films still made me want to experience Japan.

For me its the setting – and all the characters and story, the culture and issues surrounding it that grab me. That's what I want to experience. So for me when this happens with a film I will always visit the country that is portrayed and not where it is filmed.

30 April 2007 12:40:00 PDT

Figure 13.5 Further sample comments on authenticity and displacement.

Data collected and analysed through the blog research revealed not only what motivates film-induced tourists, but that the issues of displacement and authenticity are clearly something that matter to such tourists. Arguably, from analysis of the industry interview data, it appears to matter less to tourism bodies and film organisations (certainly as far as the UK and Ireland are concerned).

The view that when setting and location are different the setting will win (in terms of attracting tourists) was something first postulated by Tooke and Baker (1996). This view also seems to pervade the opinion of the industry bodies interviewed in this research, particularly so the tourism organisations. For example in relation to *Braveheart* (1995):

> from my experience of working with film studios, you know, you can't go with a confused message, you know, promoting Scotland and Ireland – it would just get quite confusing.'
>
> (Brand partnerships manager, VisitBritain)

> and more recently *Becoming Jane*, you know about the life of Jane Austen. That was filmed in southern Ireland, at Ardmore studios as well as numerous outdoor locations, but England received the tourism benefit from that.
>
> (Head of marketing, Northern Ireland Screen)

There appears to be a reluctance to market a film location if that is not where the story takes place, yet this research has revealed that there is a market for the location in such instances.

The model of displacement in film-induced tourism (depicted on Figure 13.6) illustrates the key factors and issues at play from the qualitative research conducted. The film and related factors influencing the tourist have been sub-divided into primary motivational drivers (closely tied to the film itself, such as scenery and narrative) and secondary motivational drivers (activities/facilities such as movie maps and location tours provided by tourist related bodies). All of these motivational drivers (primary and secondary) are at play, acting as an influence on the film viewer. The central core of the model depicts three distinct markets: A is the tourist who will ideally visit both film location and story setting; B is the tourist who will prefer to visit the film location; and C is the tourist who will prefer to visit the setting only. Qualitative research conducted and analysed for this study has shown that all three distinct markets do exist in relation to film-induced tourism. This has enabled the authors to take such findings represented on the model in Figure 13.6 and further identity three distinct tourist types that give rise to these markets, as outlined in Table 13.5.

The letters A, B and C in the table correspond to those on the displacement model in Figure 13.6 and denote the distinct film-induced tourist types which create the three markets that exist in film-induced tourism. From the research findings, this can then be linked further to authenticity. What the authors here term 'search for authenticity' is also depicted on the model and represents the fact that film-induced tourists are seeking some form or aspect of authenticity

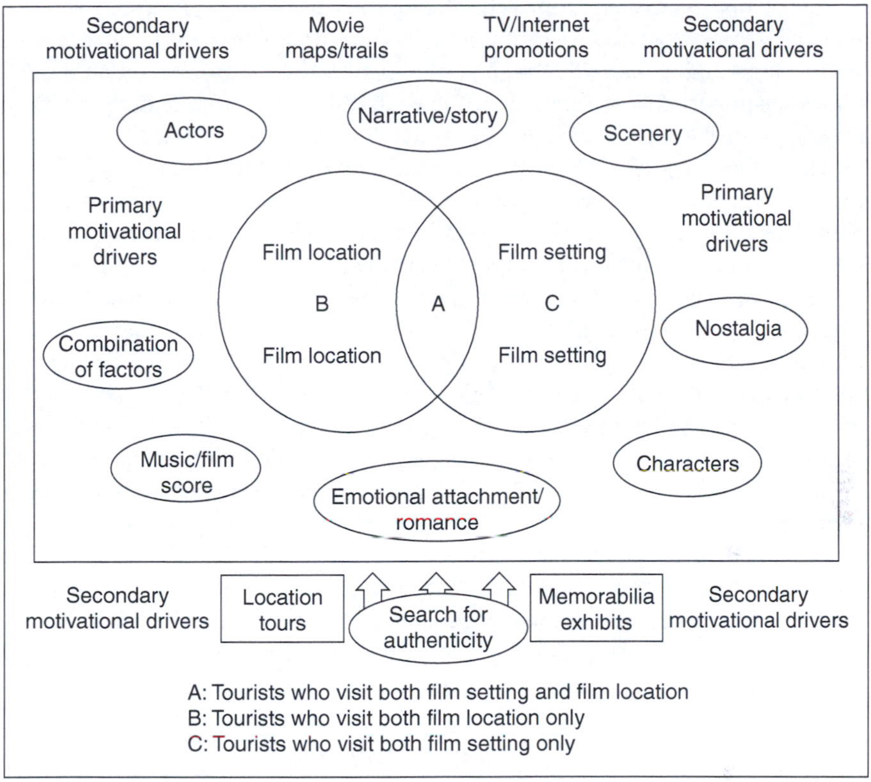

Figure 13.6 Model of displacement in film-induced tourism (source: Bolan 2010).

Table 13.5 Typology of film-induced tourists

Tourist type	*Model*	*Influences and motivations*
Scenic/visual tourist	B	Influenced by what they see – they seek out the actual location, attracted to landscape (both rural and urban)
Emotional/nostalgic tourist	C	Influenced by narrative and characters they identify with – driven to seek out the film setting connected to the story
Pure film tourist	A	Influenced by most or all factors in the film – driven to seek out both actual location and film setting

Source: Bolan (2010).

that makes sense to them, that they can relate back to the actual film and experience that first motivated them. The degree of authenticity of experience will inevitably vary from tourist to tourist and from destination to destination and will be impacted upon by the original film or films in question. Some important issues relating to this authenticity in film-induced tourism (particularly where it pertains to displacement) have been revealed through such research.

The authors have further created in Figure 13.7 a Setting/Location Model for tourism industry involvement, which illustrates the implications that have been discussed here. As depicted on the model, recognition and interest from tourist organisations are often centred on the setting (where the story in the film takes place).

Initiatives, such as movie maps/trails, Internet promotions and location tours (secondary motivational drivers for film-induced tourists), are therefore also centred on the setting. This enables the setting to become a tourist destination and to tap into the emotional/nostalgic tourist market (which, as research in this chapter has detailed, is attracted to the setting). The setting then benefits from an influx of film-induced tourists and receives an economic boost and an improved or altered image in the minds of tourists through enhancing the tourist experience.

On the other side of the model there is the opportunity for the location to be promoted and developed as a tourist destination. However, as the model depicts, the lack of tourist authority knowledge and lack of interest result in the location being overlooked. This ignores two key markets that exist: the scenic/visual

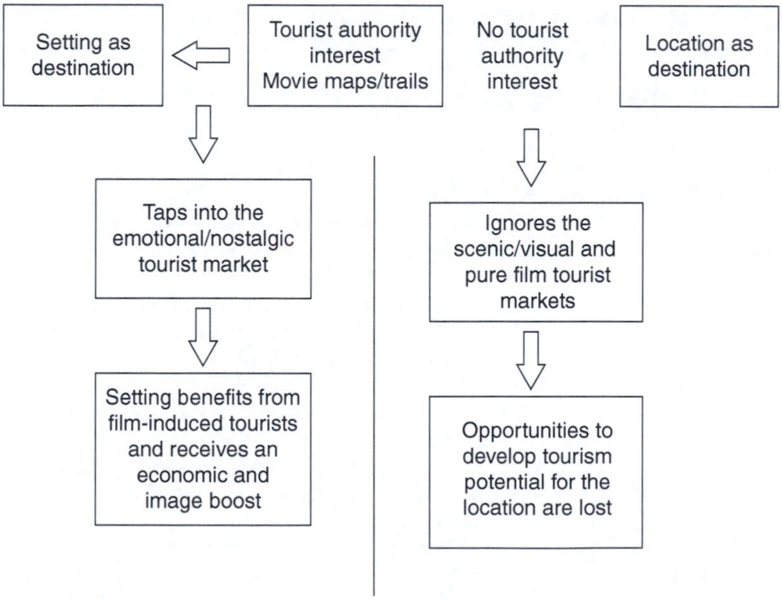

Figure 13.7 Setting/location model for tourism industry involvement (source: Bolan 2010).

tourist who prefers to visit the actual location; and the pure film tourist who likes to visit both location and setting. Valuable opportunities from tourism development that will boost the location's economy are therefore lost. Some tourists may find their way to visiting the location on their own, but the lack of tourist authority involvement and subsequent lack of activities such as movie maps/trails and location tours will mean tourist numbers are likely to be much fewer and the experience less meaningful for those who do visit. This needs to be addressed through greater collaboration between tourism bodies and film organisations (as also advocated by authors such as Hudson 2011) and between them a more thorough understanding and awareness of the different film-induced tourism markets that exist, what motivates those markets and what they find authentic when they visit film related destinations.

Conclusion

The world of film has come a long way since the Lumiere brothers held their first public film screening in the late nineteenth century at the Salon Indien du Grand Café in Paris. The significant impact such an event had on popular culture has continued to grow to this very day. Previous studies in the arena of film-induced tourism have not given any really serious attention to the concept of displacement. Despite awareness of the film tourism phenomenon becoming greater in a general sense in recent years, there is a lack of understanding of some aspects of film-induced tourism by tourism and film bodies, especially on the theme of displacement and authenticity. So, whilst awareness is there on some issues, the breadth and depth of understanding are not.

This chapter has discussed the core emergent themes and issues relating to this in light of qualitative research conducted. The model of displacement in Figure 13.6 (the first of its kind in this field) can be used to aid in the understanding of film-induced tourism in relation to displacement and the motivational drivers that influence the tourist. Stemming from this, the typology of film-induced tourists (Table 13.5) and the resulting authenticity issues provide further exploration and explanation of what is happening in such situations. Finally, in relation to opportunities and implications for economic development, the model in Figure 13.7 illustrates the most common pattern to date, who benefits and who loses out as a result. Discussion has been provided on how this might be altered in future so that the maximum potential can be gained from film-induced tourism when displacement occurs, which will benefit film location regions, tourism organisations and film-induced tourists themselves.

Finally the following recommendations for industry and future research are strongly advocated by the authors:

1. greater recognition and acceptance of film-induced tourism by industry;
2. closer collaboration between tourist authorities and film bodies;
3. greater efforts to develop and promote the film locations as opposed to the story settings/places depicted when displacement occurs;

4 retention or re-creation of film sets – building simulacra if necessary to retain more essence of film authenticity;
5 further research into motivation of film-induced tourists, particularly quantifying level of demand amongst the three tourist types identified;
6 greater use of qualitative research generally, especially through new and innovative means such as the blog techniques used in this study.

With proper recognition and attention given to the above areas, there is great potential for the phenomenon of film-induced tourism to grow and develop and for opportunities in relation to displacement to be seized upon and exploited rather than overlooked and ignored. In turn, this can aid the focused and sustainable management of the film-induced tourism phenomenon, ensuring that the resulting tourism experience is enjoyable and worthwhile and that economic and image benefit to the destination is meaningful.

14 Tourism harassment experiences in Jamaica

Tiffanie L. Skipper, Barbara A. Carmichael and Sean Doherty

Introduction

Tropical scenery, long white sandy beaches, with beach front resorts alongside deep blue waters are what await vacationers looking for a relaxing Caribbean getaway. Caribbean islands have been successful in using the natural elements of sun, sea and sand to attract tourists. This destination image has made the Caribbean region one of the most sought-after vacation spots in the world (Jayawardena 2002). Part of an island's destination image includes those welcoming faces of the local community willing to provide prompt and friendly hospitality. As observed by Dunn and Dunn (2002), it is not physical structures or even natural features that distinguish one Caribbean destination from the other, but the warmth and uniqueness of the people. Conversely, although the attractiveness of the Caribbean's landscape is undeniable, it can be undermined if the host community behaviour is not at par with tourists' expectations.

Host–guest interactions are an inevitable occurrence while on vacation, and tourists can assume their interaction with the host community will result in positive experiences. However, when tourists encounter negative experiences, conflicting attitudes may arise towards the local community and, potentially, the destination. For many Caribbean islands, the negative experience most often experienced by tourists is harassment. The Caribbean island of Jamaica struggles to maintain its favoured destination image in the face of published reports of crime and harassment against tourists. Kingsbury (2005) describes the initial communication between hosts and guests in Jamaica as uneasy and uncomfortable as guests are greeted by pimps, prostitutes, beach vendors, drug dealers and other sources of harassment. This negative behaviour is the leading cause for dissatisfaction and complaints (Kozak 2007), and is the most frequently identified negative experience conveyed by tourists (de Albuquerque and McElroy 2001). Thus, the research presented in this chapter focuses on the relationship between tourists' perceptions of, attitudes towards, and experiences with hosts in Jamaica, specifically the host behaviour of harassment.

As early as 1982, Knox stated 'The tourist may have his vacation spoiled or enhanced by the resident. The resident may have his daily life enriched or degraded by the unending flow of tourists' (cited in Ap, 1992: 669). Previous literature on the host–guest relationship is mainly concerned with understanding and measuring residents' attitudes towards tourists. Apart from the marketing literature on service quality in purchase situations, little research focuses on the flip side of this social interaction, looking more widely at tourists' attitudes towards hosts, and what factors influence the quality of their tourism experiences (Carmichael 2006). Such research is important because tourist satisfaction is influenced by the host community, and negative experiences may result in negative attitudes towards not only the hosts but also the destination. While both positive and negative attitudes towards hosts may be investigated, the harassment of tourists by hosts is a specific focus of this chapter. Attention is given to the host behaviour of harassment of tourists in Montego Bay and Negril, Jamaica, and how this negatively perceived behaviour affects tourists' attitudes towards hosts, and the overall tourism experience. The purpose of this chapter is to understand how tourist experiences are impacted by the negative host behaviour.

Negative tourism experiences: crime and safety concerns and harassment

Crime and harassment against tourists are common forms of host–guest interactions experienced while on vacation, especially in the Caribbean (Ajagunna 2006; Alleyne and Boxill 2003; Brunt *et al.* 2000; de Albuquerque and McElroy 2001; Dunn and Dunn 2002; George 2003; Kozak 2007; Ryan 1993). 'The primary concern for four out of five visitors to the Caribbean is being the target of harassment' (King 2003, cited in McElroy *et al.* 2008: 97). Criminal activity is an ongoing issue in popular tourism destinations, and seminal work has linked crime with increased mass tourism (Alleyne and Boxill 2003). Alleyne and Boxill (2003) examined the impact of crime on tourist arrivals in Jamaica between 1962 and 1999. Tourism in Jamaica has been a major source of foreign exchange earnings and employment opportunities, and because of the importance of this sector, crime against tourists has become an increasing concern. The authors found that the relationship between crime levels and tourist arrivals was mediated by increased advertising promoting a positive destination image, and various discount packages being offered by hotels to further lure tourists to the island. Furthermore, all-inclusive resorts create a great sense of safety, shielding tourists from the problems of crime, violence and harassment, whether real or perceived (Alleyne and Boxill 2003). The crime most often experienced by tourists was robbery and, although crime rates were shown to have a negative impact on tourist arrivals, the impact of crime on the overall tourism market was relatively small, due to the extensive marketing efforts by the Jamaican Tourism Board (JTB) and the growth of all-inclusive hotels (Alleyne and Boxill 2003).

Ajagunna (2006) found similar results in his study examining how crime and harassment have impacted the tourism and hospitality industry in Jamaica. Jamaica struggles with bad publicity which gives it the reputation of being an unsafe place, although most incidents of crime have been reported in Kingston, the capital of Jamaica, whereas tourist hot spots are located on the north-west coast (Ajagunna 2006). Accordingly, tourists can often avoid being victims of crime but few tourists can escape harassment, which often materialises in the form of beach boys, street vendors, art and craft vendors, taxi operators and beggars (Ajagunna 2006). Corresponding with Alleyne and Boxill's (2003) findings, Ajagunna (2006) also found the concept of the all-inclusive resorts to be important to Jamaica's tourism industry. The perception of Jamaica as a potentially dangerous place owing to the level of crime and harassment has caused many tourists to remain confined to their all-inclusive resorts, only leaving on organised tours.

Dunn and Dunn (2002) also looked at the popular perceptions of Jamaican attitudes towards crime and violence, visitor harassment, and the all-inclusive concept. They found through focus groups that while Jamaica can be described as 'a paradise', growth potential is being compromised by a number of concerns, including tourist harassment, owing to the lack of employment opportunities. For example, local talents like hair-braiding are not organised nor operated in shops with regulations, which forces braiders to harass tourists for business. As a consequence, all-inclusive resorts have become the norm in Jamaica, as tourists feel neither safe nor comfortable experiencing the island outside the boundaries of the hotels (Dunn and Dunn 2002). The survey data identified crime and violence (59.3 per cent), visitor harassment (29.1 per cent), and bad roads (28.5 per cent) as the main problems affecting the tourism industry of Jamaica. The main solutions proposed to these problems include more community education and training, brighter street lights, stiffer penalties for harassment, more police and resort patrols, and diversifying the tourism product to increase employment opportunities (Dunn and Dunn 2002).

Caribbean islands like Jamaica have seen an increase in harassment trends over the years. The Caribbean Tourism Organization defines harassment as 'conduct aimed at or predictably affecting a visitor which is (1) likely to annoy the visitor who is affected thereby and (2) an unjustified interference with the visitor's (a) privacy or (b) freedom of movement or (c) other action' (cited in de Albuquerque and McElroy 2001: 478). Harassment can certainly influence the quality of the tourist experience, as was found in a study conducted by de Albuquerque and McElroy (2001) in Barbados between 1991 and 1994. The survey content contained general questions on harassment, tourist characteristics, the location of the harassment and the nature of the harassment. The authors found that roughly 60 per cent of those surveyed reported experiencing some type of harassment, mostly taking place on the beach, and occurring from vendors. De Albuquerque and McElroy (2001) proclaim that this study was the first of its kind to gather information on harassment derived from a satisfaction survey. The authors thought that, while knowing tourists' perceptions and experiences of harassment were significant, in order to gain a complete understanding of the problem, they should also investigate harassers' perceptions. During the authors' interviews with harassers, such as vendors, it was found that the vendors did not think persistence to trying to sell their merchandise was a form of harassment.

Harassers viewed tourists as having lots of money and took the attitude of 'wanting to make a little something' (de Albuquerque and McElroy 2001). Other harassers took the attitude that the streets and beach are public property, and were going to take advantage of every opportunity to make a sales pitch. It became evident to the authors that harassment will continue to persist in tourism-dependent destinations, like the Caribbean, as long as there exists a clear divide between rich guests and poor hosts.

Kozak (2007), building and expanding on the work of de Albuquerque and McElroy (2001), defines five types of harassment. The first type of harassment arises when a tourist is shopping and is pestered to make a purchase by persistent vendors. The second type of harassment is sexual, where tourists are approached by someone soliciting an unwanted sexual relationship for a payment. The third form of harassment involves the use of obscene language in order to irritate tourists and even make them feel threatened. The fourth occurs when tourists are approached by locals in an aggressive manner resulting in physical harassment and finally, the fifth type of harassment is criminal in nature, largely dealing with the peddling of drugs. Kozak (2007) conducted a study in Marmaris, Turkey, that focused on answering such questions as where, why and how tourists are harassed, their reactions to such an experience, and what impact harassment has on one's overall holiday and likelihood of returning. It was found that those harassed were more likely to report lower satisfaction with their overall tourism experience and less likely to return in the future (Kozak 2007). These results support de Albuquerque and McElroy's (2001) findings that harassment mostly took place on the street and on the beach by vendors. Both studies have practical implications, as the results are useful for the governments of the tourism destinations in their efforts at curbing the problem of harassment.

Safety for tourists has become an increasing concern, and tourism destinations need to implement crime prevention initiatives in order to help minimise this negative impact. One solution that has been implemented for this problem is the concept of the all-inclusive resort, shielding tourists from incidents of crime and harassment (Boxill 2004). Issa and Jayawardena (2003) suggest that the idea behind the all-inclusive concept is to make travelling easier by grouping all the amenities, including flight, hotel, meals, drinks and recreational activities into one large package. Furthermore, all-inclusive resorts provide safety and for some tourists the idea of being protected within a closed area is particularly appealing. All-inclusive resorts limit the amount of host–guest interaction, which reduces the possibility of experiencing any type of criminal activity or harassment. The all-inclusive concept seems to be ideal but, as Boxill (2004) explains, it is beneficial in the short term and detrimental in the long term, as this solution fails to deal with the underlying causes of crime and harassment.

There are few published studies of harassment behaviour in the academic literature (McElroy *et al.* 2008). McElroy *et al.* (2008: 98) state that 'this is unfortunate since without an empirical examination of the specific contours of harassment types, levels and locations policy makers cannot appreciate the scope of the problem nor design effective mitigation measures'. This study was designed to describe the negative harassment experiences of visitors to Jamaica and link these experiences to the visitors' perceptions and attitudes toward the local people and the tourism destination.

Study area

There are several reasons why Jamaica was selected for this research study. Jamaica has actively pursued tourism for decades and has established itself as the fifth most popular tourist destination in the Caribbean (Caribbean Tourism Organization 2003, cited in Kingsbury 2005). As Jamaica increasingly became more popular as a tourist destination, the island became more and more dependent on tourist dollars (Kingsbury 2005). This overdependence on tourism was further reinforced as traditional means of economic development, such as agriculture and mining, declined (Singh *et al.* 2006). However, this heavy reliance on the tourism industry as the main source of income can prove to be detrimental. Jamaica has long been a popular vacation spot but, more recently, the island's image has been tarnished with claims of crime and harassment against tourists. Kingsbury (2005) claims that Jamaica has one of the worst reputations for crime, drug trafficking and harassment of any Caribbean destination; thus, it makes a very suitable location to study harassment.

According to the Minister of Tourism in Jamaica, tourism has grown so much over the years that it has surpassed expectations in all sectors of the industry. This success, however, comes at a price; 'we have also attracted to the industry, some downsides … such as harassment, which, if not managed carefully on a daily basis, can capsize the entire industry' (Jamaican Labour Party 2009a). Former Prime Minister Percival J. Patterson called harassment the single biggest problem facing Jamaica's tourism industry (McDowell 1998).

Selected quotes from a variety of news articles illustrate this problem:

- 'The Jamaican traveler's biggest problem is the vast army of hustlers who harass visitors, notably in and around major tourist centers' (*Sydney Morning Herald* 2008);
- 'Some street vendors, beggars, and taxi drivers in tourist areas aggressively confront and harass tourists to buy their wares or employ their services' (US Department of State 2009);
- 'Jamaica's unprecedented crime level is threatening to derail the Caribbean island's vital tourism industry by scaring away visitors and hurting investment' (CNN 2004);
- 'While Jamaican officials say that crime against visitors has fallen in the last couple of years, harassment is so widespread, especially in cruise ports … four cruise lines threatened to pull out of Montego Bay two years ago' (McDowell 1998);
- 'Minister of Tourism, Edmund Bartlett, has said that the Ministry was determined to stamp out harassment and other unsavory activities, which threaten the tourism sector' (Jamaican Labour Party 2009b).

The problem of harassment against tourists in Jamaica is plainly visible and internationally recognised. According to Kingsbury (2005), the Lonely Planet guidebook for Jamaica warns potential tourists about the Jamaican character, which at times can be unpredictable, sullen, argumentative and confrontational. Visitors are often shocked when they encounter 'hustlers' trying to sell souvenirs, drugs, aloe massages, hair braiding and unwanted taxi services or tours (Kingsbury 2005). 'Difficulty in dealing with people whose value system and communication style may be markedly different is a major contributor to culture shock' (Pearce 2005: 130). This may partly explain the reason for these negative encounters in cross-cultural interaction. While the street vendor may consider their loud tactics good salesmanship in gaining attention, the North American and European tourists do not respond to greetings and approaches by strangers (McElroy *et al.* 2008).

Jamaican officials have long feared that the pervasiveness of harassment against tourists could put an end to tourism's position as the dominant source of income to the island (McDowell 1998) whilst, more recently, the Minister of Tourism was quoted as saying 'we have also attracted to the industry some downsides … such as harassment, which, if not managed carefully on a daily basis, can capsize the entire industry' (Jamaican Labour Party 2009b). Furthermore, tourists' perceptions of Jamaica as a potentially dangerous destination are causing tourists to travel cautiously and even deterring them from visiting Jamaica at all. To counteract this bad publicity, the Jamaican Tourism Board has increased advertising to help promote a positive island image, along with various discount packages offered by hotels to help lure tourists back to the island (Alleyne and Boxill 2003). Also in effect are fines for harassing tourists, which is another attempt to protect this vital industry and to continue to attract visitors. Fines have been raised from previous years, as offenders used to have to pay only $27 for being caught harassing tourists, but since the late 1990s a first-time offender can be fined $2,700 whilst a repeat offender can draw fines up to $4,100 (McDowell 1998). More recently, Jamaica's Ministry of Tourism launched the

Figure 14.1 Main Jamaican tourist resorts.

Tourism Courtesy Corps (TCC) programme. This programme is designed to 'enhance the safety, service and comfort of visitors by strategically deploying courtesy officers in the resort areas of Negril, Montego Bay, Runaway Bay, Ocho Rios, Port Antonio, and Kingston' (Jamaican Labour Party 2009b). These resort locations are shown in Figure 14.1. These strategies are a confirmation that Jamaican officials are aware of the problem and are trying to resolve the issue to the best of their abilities. It can be affirmed, however, that despite the strengths of the Jamaican tourism industry, harassment remains a pressing issue. Whether or not Jamaica provides the perfect scenery for those looking for a relaxing getaway, if visitors are constantly subjected to harassment, they simply may not return.

Methodology

Data collection used a mixed method approach that included a questionnaire survey and an in-the-moment event tracking approach. Survey data collection took place between 14 and 21 June 2008. Participants were surveyed in public locations, such as the beach, thought to be prime areas for the behaviour of harassment. Some were also surveyed at the resort hotel pool. Adult participants (over 18 years old) were selected randomly and asked to participate in this study on a voluntary basis. Anonymity was stressed and their survey answers were kept confidential. The survey content was broken down into three parts, namely, tourist characteristics, general questions regarding tourists' attitudes towards host, and specific questions regarding their last harassment experience. A total of 209 questionnaires were collected (87 per cent response rate). The researcher tried to minimise response bias by sampling at both public and private locations. One hundred and eight surveys were collected on the public beaches of Doctors Cave Beach in Montego Bay and Seven Mile Beach in Negril. The remaining 101 surveys were collected in the private resort area of the Royal Decameron in Montego Bay. The survey was designed to capture participants' attitudes towards the locals of Jamaica, and whether or not the local behaviour of harassment influences participants' attitudes and/or affects their overall tourism experience.

A second exploratory method was employed by two volunteers who recorded their 'in the moment experiences' of harassment using BlackBerry hand-held devices with a custom-made event-log program. Shortly after a harassment experience, the respondents self-reported these experiences by responding to a series of open-ended questions, as shown in Figure 14.2. A total of 15 harassment experiences were recorded and they revealed in-depth audio and logged response comments about these events.

After selecting 'Add New Event' (screenshot 1 in Figure 14.2), the first steps required participants to log the type of harassment experienced and the location of where the harassment incident took place, as shown in the screenshots 3–5. The event type/location was then logged alongside the date and time of the incident on screen (screenshot 5). Participants then had the option to add details (screenshot 6) to the experience, either immediately or at a later time more

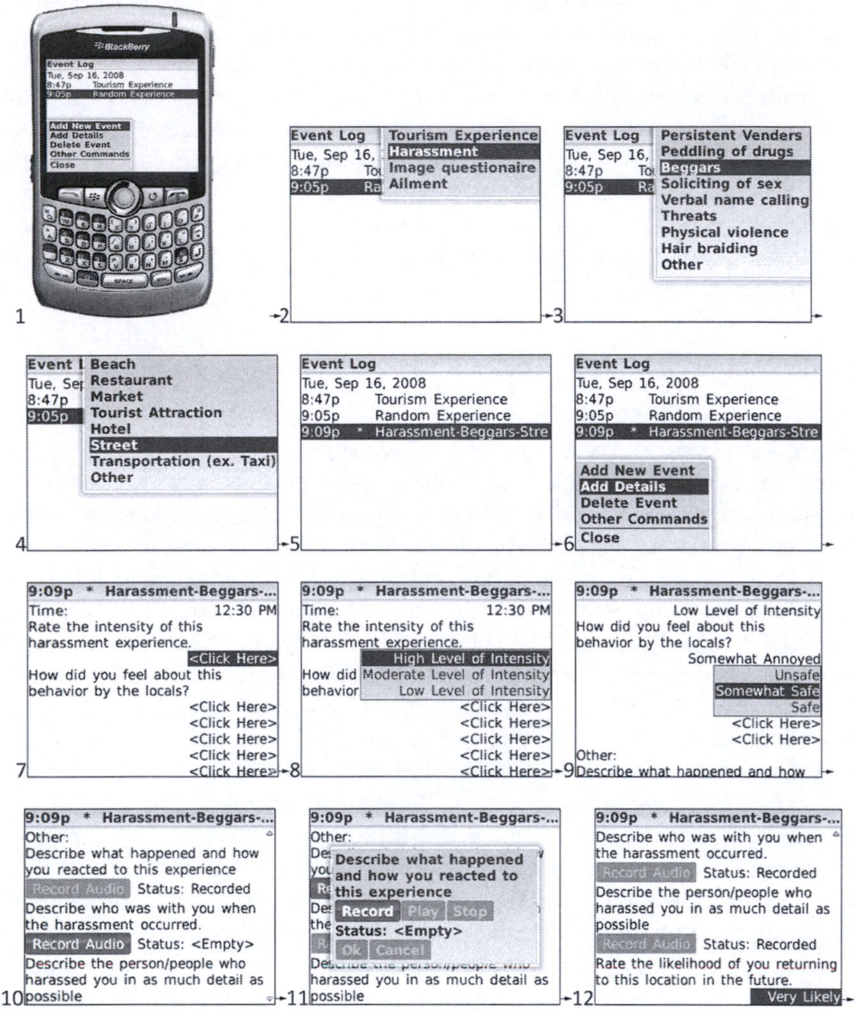

Figure 14.2 Event logging software snapshots depicting 'harassment' manual entry.

convenient to them (the intent being to at least log the basics of the event as a memory jogger for later). If participants wished to proceed at a later time, a star would appear on the screen beside the logged event to indicate that the event had yet to be completed. Clicking on the 'add details' option brings up a set of questions starting with the seventh screenshot in Figure 14.2. At the top of the screen, the harassment event type in question is displayed for reference. The first question asked participants to rate the level of intensity of the harassment experience on a three-point Likert scale (high, moderate, low), displayed in a pull-down list (screenshot 8). The next set of questions asked participants to rate how they felt about their harassment experience on a three-point Likert scale with respect to feelings of annoyance, anger, safety, threat, victimisation and amusement. An example of this process is provided in screenshot 9, as level of safety is rated as unsafe, to somewhat safe, to feeling safe.

The next three questions were designed to be answered verbally and recorded in audio format, as these questions asked more in-depth information about participants' attitudes towards harassment. To start, participants were asked to describe what happened and how they reacted to this harassment experience, as shown in screenshot 11. The 'record' and 'stop' buttons were used to make the recording. The status of the recording would remain 'empty' until recorded, as a reminder to participants. This process was repeated for two more audio questions concerning who they were with at the time of the harassment, and who harassed them (screenshot 12). The final question asked participants to rate their likelihood of returning to this location in the future on a three-point scale (very likely, somewhat likely, not at all likely).

The above process was to be repeated for every incident of harassment experienced. Note that participants had the flexibility of quickly entering the essential information into the BlackBerry (type and location) so as to not let this involvement interfere with their vacation. Considering that participants were volunteering their time while on vacation, it was important to make this experience as convenient as possible. The ideal scenario however, would be for participants to complete the entire set of questions 'in the moment', thereby enhancing the accuracy of participants' attitudinal responses towards their harassment experience. While there were only two participants in this study as this was a test launch for the methodology, interesting in-depth results were nevertheless revealed about the social contact situation and harassment feelings.

Results

Visitor characteristics

The survey data shows the sample population to be 68.6 per cent female and 31.4 per cent male, 65 per cent first-time visitors and 35 per cent repeat visitors, with 67.9 per cent staying in an all-inclusive resort and 31.8 per cent staying in non-all-inclusive accommodations. Almost 59 per cent reported experiencing harassment. Of the 114 people who were harassed, 71.1 per cent were female and 28.9 per cent were male, 69 per cent were first-time visitors and 31 per cent were repeat visitors, and 63 per cent reported staying in an all-inclusive resort while the remaining 37 per cent stayed in non-all-inclusive accommodation. Repeat visitors and those staying at an all-inclusive resort reported less harassment, whereas first-time visitors and those staying in non-all-inclusive accommodation were more likely to feel that they were being harassed.

Location and type of harassment

The areas where participants experience harassment most include the streets, the public beach, and the market (Figure 14.3). The street seems to be the area where the most harassment against tourists occurs (64 per cent), followed by the public beach (38.7 per cent) and the market (37.8 per cent). The resort beach was a location that produced surprising results. Roughly 25 per cent of participants were harassed at a resort beach, which seems fairly high. However, those who did not have an all-inclusive beach may have construed the public beach as the hotel's resort beach, which may account for the higher than anticipated harassment level at this location. Approximately 8 per cent of participants experienced harassment at hotels, tourist attractions and transportation (most notably in the form of locals pestering tourists by repeatedly asking them if they need a taxi). A small number of participants (6.3 per cent) were harassed at restaurants/cafés.

The types of harassment most often experienced were vending, peddling of drugs, and begging (Figure 14.4). Approximately 71 per cent of participants

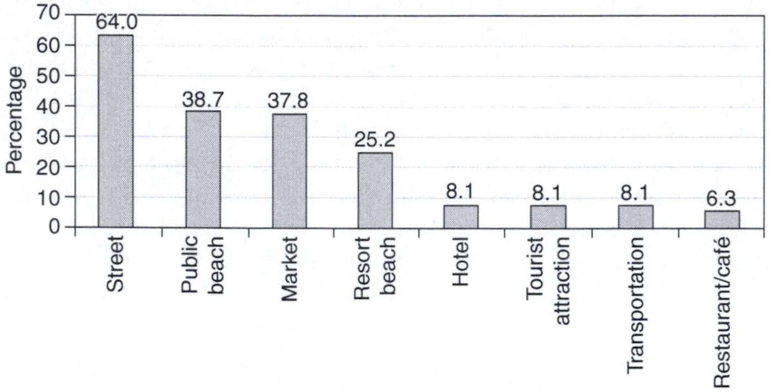

Figure 14.3 Places participants were harassed.

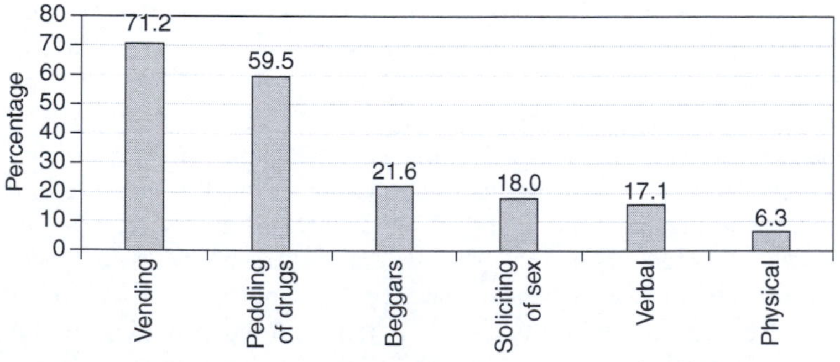

Figure 14.4 Types of harassment experienced.

experienced harassment by vendors. This result is not surprising as many local vendors are constantly seeking tourists to buy their merchandise, and vendors can be annoyingly persistent to the point of harassing. Furthermore, the market place was the third highest harassment location as indicated by those who participated, as harassment by vendors is highly prevalent here. Participants who found this local behaviour annoying and disruptive would have considered this harassment, whereas those who like to barter and interact more personally with the locals would not.

Feelings about harassment

Participants were asked how they felt about this behavior by placing an X along a semantic differential scale between bipolar adjectives. As there are many possible responses to harassment, the researcher narrowed it down to six responses that could have been elicited: annoyance, feelings of unhappiness, anger, questions of safety, feeling threatened, feeling victimised. The scale was quantified for analysis purpose; 1 represented the negative end of the scale and 10 represented the positive end of the scale. Table 14.1 shows the mean values of each response as indicated by those who participated.

Generally participants were annoyed and unhappy about this local behaviour, and expressed anger and concern for their safety, and felt slightly threatened and victimised over this experience.

Similarly, BlackBerry participants were asked to describe how they felt about each logged harassment experience. Table 14.2 below shows the frequencies, as well as the mean values for each of the six responses to harassment.

Harassment intensity

BlackBerry participants were asked to rate the intensity of each logged harassment experience. Four of the 15 cases were rated as highly intense, five cases were rated at the moderate level, and six cases were rated low intensity. A highly intense harassment experienced was described by Participant A:

> I said no and kept walking and as I was walking he started to follow me, which kind of made me nervous and I looked around and there wasn't a lot of people around so I quickly walked to where there was a crowd.

Table 14.1 Survey participants' responses to harassment

Responses (negative/positive)	N	*Mean*
Annoyed/not annoyed	105	3.9
Unhappy/happy	99	4.1
Angry/not angry	99	5.5
Unsafe/safe	101	5.6
Threatened/not threatened	100	6.0
Victimised/not victimised	99	6.6

Table 14.2 BlackBerry responses to harassment

Responses	*Frequency*	*Mean*
Annoyed	9	1.5
Somewhat annoyed	5	
Not annoyed	1	
Angry	5	2.2
Somewhat angry	2	
Not angry	8	
Unsafe	1	2.5
Somewhat safe	6	
Safe	8	
Threatened	2	2.5
Somewhat threatened	3	
Not threatened	10	
Victimized	3	2.5
Somewhat victimised	2	
Not victimised	10	
Not amusing	12	1.3
Somewhat amusing	2	
Amusing	1	

Participant A also describes a low-intensity harassment situation as just being caught off guard, as she explains,

> I was a little startled by this experience because this gentleman came up from the water, I was lying beside the sea, sun tanning and he just popped up out of the water.

Reaction to harassment

Both survey and BlackBerry respondents were asked how they reacted to their most recent harassment experience. A majority of survey participants said 'No thank you' (79.3 per cent), 45 per cent walked away from the harassment situation, a very small percentage said 'Yes' (1.8 per cent), 12.6 per cent looked the other way, 26.1 per cent ignored the harassing comments, and 16.2 per cent excused themselves from the harassment situation by saying 'Maybe another time'.

Predominately, participants were polite when approached in a harassment situation by saying 'No thank you' and walking away. Participants' reactions also varied depending on what type of harassment was experienced, which is why this question was posed for their most recent harassment encounter only. This question was posed to BlackBerry participants in audio format, allowing them to explain their reaction to the harassment situation, plus their reasons for reacting in a specific way. Table 14.3 presents the themes found within the data and how many times each participant complied with the designated theme. Three

Table 14.3 Key themes and selected quotes by participants, generated from the question, 'Describe what happened and how you reacted to this experience?'

Theme	*Participant A*	*Participant B*
Said 'No thank you' and walked away' Participant A (4) Participant B (4)	'I said no thank you and kept walking.' 'I just very politely told her no thank you and tried to move on.' 'When the gentleman started hollering at me, I did turn and look at him and I did say no thank you because he was asking me if I had a moment to spare and when I did say no thank you it was in fact another elderly woman that was sitting behind him that spoke to me in a very angry voice and said "just listen to what he has to say". I just turned and I said no thank you for about the fourth time and I walked away.'	'I said sorry and no thank you, I can't help you and just walked away.' 'I said no thank you and just turned and looked the other way and kept on walking.'
Ignored the comment and walked away Participant A (1) Participant B (2)	'I continually ignored this man that was continually hollering at me saying "hey lady, hey beautiful lady come here I want to talk to you". I tried to ignore him, definitely tried not to make eye contact with him, I proceeded to move on to another place in the market.'	'I ignored them and kept on walking.'
Interest/purchase Participant A (2) Participant B (0)	'I went along with the woman because she was showing us the way to the market and her little booth, and, umm, she insisted that I go see her booth, so once I was there she allowed me to go in and see her goods, and insisted that I pick something out so she could make a deal.' 'The woman pulled me into her shop and I felt at that point a little vulnerable, I did look at what she had and I did end up buying something.'	

themes were recovered: saying ‘No thank you’ and walking away, ignoring the comment and walking away, and showing interest and even choosing to make a purchase.

In cases when the locals were trying to sell drugs to the participants, a commanding ‘No’ was in order. Participant A was suntanning at the resort beach when a Jamaican man popped up out of the water wearing snorkel gear and asked her if she wanted to buy some drugs. Participant A responded by saying no:

> I did not want any of his marijuana, and then he tried to sell me aloe vera and then he moved on.

Similar to the survey results, for most of the logged harassment cases, Participants A and B responded politely by saying ‘No thank you’ and walking away.

Attitudes toward the local people

For the majority of survey participants, overall experience with the local people was positive and these experiences influenced their impressions of the island positively. Their description of the local people was positive, their opinions of the locals before and after travelling to Jamaica were positive, and their perceptions of quality with the tourism destination were also positive. While this sounds very positive for the destination, when comparisons were made between those who reported being harassed and those who did not, those who experienced harassment had more negative attitudes.

Table 14.4 shows the results of participants’ attitudes towards the local people based on whether or not they were harassed. As expected, those who experienced harassment portrayed slightly more negative attitudes towards the local people.

Harassed participants rated their overall tourism experience with the local people slightly more negatively in comparison to those who did not experience harassment. Also of statistical significance was the relation between harassed and non-harassed participants and their thoughts on Jamaica as influenced by the local people ($p=0.016$, $\alpha=0.05$). Although this variable was deemed significant by the chi-square test, only a few harassed participants felt more negatively about the island of Jamaica based on their experience with the local people. These participants cannot separate their feelings about the local people from their feelings about the island. Furthermore, two non-harassed participants felt their impressions of Jamaica changed in the negative direction based on their experience with the local people. As these participants did not experience harassment themselves, an explanation for their change in attitude could be attributed to witnessing others being harassed, among other factors.

Of insignificance was harassed and non-harassed participants’ opinion of the locals before travelling to Jamaica ($p=0.086$, $\alpha=0.05$). As this question required participants to recall how they felt about the local people *before* coming to

Table 14.4 Bivariate analysis between harassed and non-harassed participants' attitudes towards the locals

	Yes	*No*	χ^2	p
Overall tourism experience with the local people (n=193)				
Very good	35	48	19.983	0.000*
Good	42	19		
Satisfactory	26	13		
Poor	10	0		
Experiences with the local people influencing thoughts on Jamaica (n=194)				
More positive	46	35	8.313	0.016*
Neutral	51	43		
More negative	17	2		
Opinion of the locals before travelling to Jamaica (n=190)				
Like the locals very much	21	26	6.608	0.086
Like most of the locals	61	35		
Somewhat like the locals	26	15		
Do not like the locals	5	1		
Opinion of the locals after travelling to Jamaica (n=192)				
Feel better (more positive)	36	34	9.645	0.008*
Feel the same	62	44		
Feel worse (more negative)	15	1		

Note
* Significant at the 0.05 level.

Jamaica, thus prior to experiencing harassment, it is not surprising that there is no relationship between these two variables. There was, however, a relationship between harassed and non-harassed participants' opinions of the locals *after* travelling to Jamaica ($p=0.008$, $\alpha=0.05$). Experiencing harassment was enough to change participants' opinions about the local people from their initial thoughts prior to travelling to Jamaica.

It seems that harassment is an impressionable experience for those participants who have been subjected to this negative behaviour while on vacation in Jamaica. It has been determined that some of those who have encountered harassment rated their experience with the local people as poor, and their opinions of the locals worsened in light of this behaviour. It has yet to be determined whether or not harassment has caused those who were harassed to describe the local people negatively as well. The difference between harassed and non-harassed participants description of the local people was compared using an ANOVA (see Table 14.5).

Results show all descriptive characteristics but threatening/not threatening were statistically significant. Those who were harassed described the local people slightly more negatively than those who were not harassed, as the mean values for these participants approach the negative end of the scale (1 being least favourable and 10 being most favourable). Take, for example, the descriptive characteristic friendly/unfriendly. Those who were harassed had a mean score of $\bar{x}=7.933$ and those who were not harassed had a mean score of $\bar{x}=8.550$. It should be acknowledged however, that these mean values are still relatively high, suggesting that even though participants were harassed, they still viewed the local people favourably as friendly.

There was no significant difference found between harassed and non-harassed participants and the four variables in Table 14.6. For the majority of participants, the local people did not spoil participants' vacation, nor did harassment diminish their impressions of Jamaica. Harassed participants' experience with the local people did not put them off from returning to Jamaica in the future, and these same participants would still recommend Jamaica to others. However, there were still some participants who felt their vacation was spoiled by the local people, who felt their impression of Jamaica was diminished, who would not return in the future, and who would not recommend Jamaica to others. Overall, harassed participants' positive experiences sustained while on vacation outweigh any negative experiences, such as harassment by the local people.

The last two questions posed on the survey were open-ended, and asked participants how their experience of harassment affected their attitudes towards the local people, and how their experience of harassment influenced their overall tourism experience. Responses frequently elicited for the first question included:

> no effect, avoid contact, sad, sympathetic, empathetic, annoyed, wary, nervous, part of the local culture, locals just trying to make a living, expected this behaviour.

Table 14.5 ANOVA analysis comparing harassed and non-harassed participants on their description of the local people.

ANOVA	n	*Mean*	F	*Sig.*
Unfriendly/friendly				
Yes (harassed)	112	7.933	7.749	0.006*
No (non-harassed)	80	8.550		
Disrespectful/respectful				
Yes	111	6.775	40.568	0.000*
No	80	8.469		
Unreliable/reliable				
Yes	108	6.829	19.789	0.000*
No	78	8.077		
Dishonest/honest				
Yes	109	6.482	27.204	0.000*
No	78	8.045		
Unhappy/happy				
Yes	112	7.969	12.084	0.001*
No	80	8.738		
Impolite/polite				
Yes	111	7.396	19.141	0.000*
No	80	8.531		
Irritating/not irritating				
Yes	110	5.446	7.552	0.007*
No	73	6.493		
Annoying/not annoying				
Yes	108	5.417	12.517	0.001*
No	73	6.706		
Threatening/not threatening				
Yes	109	6.583	0.103	0.749
No	72	6.701		
Not willing to help/willing to help				
Yes	111	7.743	3.884	0.050*
No	76	8.257		

Note
* Significant at the 0.05 level.

Table 14.6 Bivariate analysis between harassed and non-harassed participants' thoughts of Jamaica

	Yes	*No*	χ^2	p
Has your trip been spoiled because of the locals? (n=131)				
Yes	10	1	0.777	0.378
No	96	24		
Has harassment diminished your impression of Jamaica? (n=134)				
Yes	26	2	2.791	0.095
No	84	22		
Has experiences with the locals put you off from returning to Jamaica? (n=134)				
Yes	14	2	0.454	0.501
No	95	23		
Would you recommend Jamaica? (n=136)				
Yes	92	24	1.261	0.262
No	18	2		

Note
* Significant at the 0.05 level.

Common responses for the second question included:

> no effect, doesn't bother me, avoid certain areas, hesitant to venture outside the compound, will not come back, minimal impact, will be prepared to handle this behavior next time, leaves a negative overall impression, not representative of the entire local community, understand the need to make money.

Management implications

This research draws attention to the hosts' ability to influence the quality of tourists' experiences and advocates the need for continued research on the important topics of visitor harassment and host–guest interactions. Insights from this research provide suggestions for theory development and management implications.

Similar to the findings of de Albuquerque and McElroy (2001), results suggest considerable harassment, since nearly 59 per cent of participants experienced harassment, most often in the form of pestering vendors with interactions taking place on the street. Generally, participants' attitudes towards the island of Jamaica and its local people were positive. The experience of harassment did make some participants cautious about visiting local markets, going out alone, and going out at night. Whether harassed or not, the majority of participants said their vacation was not spoiled by the local people, their impressions of Jamaica did not diminish, and they would still return to Jamaica in the future and recommend it to others although, when harassed and non-harassed participants were compared, those who were harassed expressed slightly more negative views. Overall, Jamaica is still one of the most popular Caribbean tourist destinations and continues to attract millions of visitors annually. Harassment is an issue in Jamaica, but seems to be regarded as an everyday occurrence, a way of life and even a social norm that is part of the tourism experience.

The findings of the present study raise important implications for tourism managers, operators and planners, as harassment, although deemed an annoying local behaviour, did not appear to negatively impact participants' tourism experience of Jamaica. When reviewing the literature on harassment, three main solutions towards mitigating the affects of tourist harassment have been put forward: law enforcement, increased education and training, and the all-inclusive concept. TCC is the newest line of law enforcement in Jamaica, working together with state security to fight against harassment (Jamaican Labour Party 2009a). The TCC are strategically located in resort areas around the island to ensure the comfort and safety of visitors, and have the right to detain, but not to arrest, unwanted locals whose intent is to harass. Former Tourism Minister, Edmund Bartlett suggests that the TCC is a 'softer and more congenial and hospitable approach to safety and security in the resort areas' (Jamaican Labour Party 2009b).

Dunn and Dunn (2002) found increased education and training opportunities would help tackle the issue of visitor harassment. The Team Jamaica programme does just that. This two-week programme provides locals working directly in the tourism sector with tourism awareness, work experience, leadership and motivational skills and customer service skills (Tourism Product Development Co. Ltd 2005). This programme is now mandatory for all workers in the tourism industry. Team Jamaica, for example, assists with the training of vendors who are occasionally accused of 'badgering' visitors (Jamaican Labour Party 2009a). One of the best ways to sell the Jamaican product and service is through well-informed workers, and uninformed workers, like vendors, present a limiting picture of quality (Tourism Product Development Co. Ltd 2005). Dunn and Dunn (2002) further suggest that training vendors will educate them on product knowledge, product diversity and product quality.

All-inclusive resorts limit the encounters between hosts and guests, therefore limiting the amount of harassment experienced while on vacation. Alleyne and Boxill (2003: 390) noted that, while all-inclusive accommodation is a short-term solution to the problem of visitor harassment, in the long term these establishments 'limit the capacity of the industry to spread benefits outside the environment controlled by the all-inclusive hotels'. This will surely lead to further frustration by locals not being able to benefit from selling their goods to the tourists.

One recommendation could be to increase local participation within the tourism sector. The Meet-the-People programme was implemented to provide visitors curious to explore Jamaican culture with an opportunity to go beyond the traditional resort and beach setting and experience the colourful realm of Jamaica's lifestyle, traditions and customs (Jamaican Tourist Board 2009).

Historical tours might also be a way for visitors to learn about the island of Jamaica, to learn about the local people and of their trials and tribulations; this may create a mutual understanding, especially for those who come to Jamaica with negative attitudes. Published reports of visitor harassment have potentially tarnished Jamaica's image as a welcoming and friendly destiantion. Potential visitors may generalise the local community based on these sources and retain negative attitudes towards the locals before even travelling to Jamaica.

Both of these strategies help create an opportunity for intimate contact to occur between hosts and guests, and promote positive attitudes towards the locals and the destination.

Participants were harassed most often on the streets and the type of harassment most often experienced was vending. Knowing this information the Government of Jamaica could implement efforts to clean up the streets, by having designated areas for vending. This was suggested by Dunn and Dunn (2002) for hair braiders, who would benefit from having a place to operate their business from, instead of harassing tourists on the street. Vendors are for the most part located in market areas, where tourists can wander round the stalls and booths and look at the local merchandise. This is one way to experience local culture and, thus, the suggestion of moving vendors into an enclosed area, like a mall, would take away from this cultural appeal. A more practical solution would be training local vendors on how to communicate more effectively with tourists, instead of forcefully trying to sell their merchandise by following tourists around and yelling at them. Harassment by drug peddlers was also a common form of harassment experience by participants. Stricter fines may need to be implemented for those who try to sell drugs to tourist.

Finally, a note on methodology is needed here. Data used in this research was mainly quantitative and a survey methodology was employed. However, a test launch of an innovative data collection methodology in the form of 'in the moment' experiences contributed additional insights into tourism experiences of harassment. This methodology proved useful and is now being used in further in-depth studies of tourism experiences in a number of different contexts and tourism settings that can be linked with GPS applications.

15 The UK 'grey' market's holiday experience

Bridget Major and Fraser McLeay

Introduction

This chapter focuses on exploring the overseas package holiday experience for UK older consumers, defined here as those over 50 years old, who make up the so-called 'grey' or senior market. Although package travel is frequently described as a mature market in which levels of product innovation are not high (Cooper *et al.* 2008), package holidays represent nearly 40 per cent of all holidays (Mintel 2010). Mintel estimates that 14.4 million package holidays were taken in 2010. The Eyjafjallajokull volcano in April 2010, in particular, led to an endorsement of the package holiday by travellers as a result of the travel protection offered within it. All-inclusive holidays within Europe in particular have risen in popularity as a result of the strong euro to the pound and the UK recession and associated uncertainties (Fearis 2011).

The 'grey' market segment was selected as the focus for this chapter. It has long been recognised as extremely important to the travel industry (Ryan 1995; Lehto *et al.* 2008) as older people place travel as a high priority in their retirement years (Lehto *et al.* 2008; Patterson and Pegg 2009; IpsosMori 2010). This is because many older people prefer to buy experiences rather than material possessions which they already have, as they feel that these will enrich their lives and make them feel young (Patterson and Pegg 2009). This segment has also been recognised as loyal (Evans *et al.* 2009) and has a growing tendency to take holidays (Mintel 2004). It is important, therefore, that the experience of tourists in this market is fully identified and explored, which is the key objective of this chapter. There has been a plethora of contemporary research produced as the concept of the tourist experience is being recognised for its value and importance. Two approaches to the literature have emerged, one from a management perspective and the other from a consumer's perspective (Morgan and Watson 2007; Jackson *et al.* 2009; Morgan *et al.* 2010). The authors of all three publications point out the considerable challenge in bringing together these two perspectives in order to understand how to best manage tourist experiences. The book, *Tourist Experience: Contemporary Perspectives* (Sharpley and Stone 2011b), demonstrates the variety of diverse tourist experiences in tourism whilst, in the same volume, Ryan (2011) provides a review of literature on how tourists experience their holiday destination. Sharpley and Stone (2011a: 3) state that 'the tourist experience is by definition, what people experience as tourists'. They make the distinction between the specific services which make up holiday experiences which are temporally defined and away from home, and those broader experiences which collectively tourists play a part in. The results presented later in this chapter specifically focus only on the consumer perspective and not the management perspective.

In this chapter, we briefly review literature on consumer behaviour in tourism and discuss the package holiday industry. Relevant experience management literature is summarised, before we focus more specifically on tourism experience management research. Characteristics of the 'grey' market are explored and the factors that influence a holiday for older tourists are discussed. Finally, a brief summary of the initial results from an on-going research project focusing on the older package holiday maker's experience is provided. The research project utilises a qualitative, inductive approach, which is particularly well suited to analysing and understanding the service experience which is 'inherently interpretative, subjective and affective' (Morgan and Xu 2009: 222). In so doing, the project adopted the method suggested by Woodside and Macdonald (1994: 32) who argue that we need to capture all temporal dimensions of travellers – that is, travelling to the resort, in the resort and leaving: 'we need thick descriptions about what, when, where, how, did what and with what outcomes in the traveler's own language and cultural interpretations'.

Consumer behaviour

It is important to understand the theoretical background to the concept of the experience before evaluating it further in the context of tourism. Not only is the experience receiving increasing academic and professional attention, but also its value as a competitive tool has come to be recognised.

This section, therefore, commences with such a discussion, setting the experience in the context of broader consumer behaviour. More specifically this section considers the concept of the experience and its relationship with consumer behaviour models.

The concept of the experience has been studied within a multitude of disciplines, such as psychology, sociology and anthropology, and literature can be drawn from several of these disciplines depending on the context of the study. The study of consumer behaviour from a psychological perspective was an early and dominant approach, and Mihaly Csikszentmihalyi in particular was the first to study the experience within the context of leisure and play (Csikszentmihalyi 1982). He introduced the concept of 'flow', which describes those exceptional moments in life, and which in the leisure context refers to those feelings arising from effortless action, such as those athletes feel (Patterson and Pegg 2009). Csikszentmihalyi's later work applied his psychological theories to marketing and consumer behaviour. He argues that experiential rewards are important; 'these refer to the temporary improvement in positive mood people experience when they are acting in goal-directed, purposeful ways' (Csikszentmihalyi 2000: 267), and that consuming is one of those ways in which such an experience can be obtained.

Consumer behaviour as a discipline is closely allied to marketing and of tremendous importance to tourism scholars (Walle 1996). It can be defined as 'those activities directly involved in obtaining consuming and disposing of products and services, including the decision processes that precede and follow these actions' (Engel *et al.* 1995: 4). Solomon (2009: 33) provides a definition which incorporates the experience element. He defines the field of consumer behaviour as 'the study of the processes involved when individuals or groups select, purchase, use, or dispose of products, services, ideas, or *experiences* to satisfy needs and desires' (emphasis added). It is apparent that some of the 'Grand Models' of consumer behaviour embrace no time dimension and, therefore, provide no guide to the practitioner as to timely moments to intervene in processes (Hudson 1999). This is particularly relevant for a service product such as travel or tourism and, in this instance the package holiday, where there may be a gap of several months between purchase and holiday uptake. Another criticism of the 'Grand Models' (upon which subsequent models of the tourist's consumer behaviour were founded) was that they were based on the purchase of goods rather than services and that they were about individual purchases rather than those made jointly, that is, by couples or families (Gilbert 1991).

Understanding consumer behaviour patterns is fundamental to managers in that they can then intervene in processes to attempt to obtain and optimise the results that they wish to. Paul Peter and Olson (2005: 5) argue that 'behaviour involves the thoughts and feelings people experience and the actions they perform in the consumption processes'. By understanding consumers' behaviour, marketers can persuade consumers to choose products which will meet their needs and wants (Swarbrooke and Horner 2007).

Moving more explicitly to an evaluation of the tourism service product, Woodside (2000: 1) states that 'the field of consumer psychology of tourism, hospitality and leisure focuses on describing, understanding, predicting and/or influencing the discretionary travel and time-use motivations, beliefs, attitudes, intentions and behaviours of individuals, households and organizations'. This rather broad definition does not refer specifically to the experience concept but it is implicit in it. Mowen and Minor (2001) developed a model of consumer behaviour evaluating three perspectives: decision-making, an experiential perspective and a behavioural influence perspective. They argue that consumers' purchases are not always a rational decision and that they may purchase products, particularly leisure products, in order to have fun and create fantasies, emotions and feelings. This stems from the seminal work by Holbrook and Hirschman (1982) which criticised previous emphasis on consumer behaviour evolving as a result of rational and logical choice as this approach neglected important consumption phenomena. 'Consumption has begun to be seen as involving a steady flow of fantasies, feelings, and fun encompassed by what we call the "experiential view"' (Holbrook and Hirschman 1982: 132). Literature focusing on consumer behaviour in tourism will now be explored and tourism behaviour models discussed.

Consumer behaviour and tourism

The purpose of this section is to build on the previous exploration of consumer behaviour theory. The travel and tourism service product and some of its features are introduced against a consumer behaviour backdrop with a specific focus on the experience element. In addition, the complex nature of a travel and tourism product is explored.

Despite the fact that the travel, hospitality and leisure sectors represent one of the largest and fastest segments of consumer spending, academic knowledge and understanding are arguably not yet commensurate with the economic and social significance of the sector (Crouch *et al.* 2004). Swarbrooke and Horner (2007) make the point that, although there have been some improvements in consumer research in tourism in recent years, there still remain some major weaknesses. They identify that one of the problems which pertains to package holiday research is: when is the best juncture to ask people questions about their holiday experience? Prior to the holiday start? While they are on holiday? On their return? The research discussed later in this chapter adopted primarily the middle approach; that is, exploring the experiences of older people whilst on holiday. It can be argued that this is the most important element of the consumer experience, involving time spent and the take-up of the purchased product.

As is well known, the features and characteristics of the travel and tourism product service and its complex nature include:

- intangibility
- inseparability
- variability
- perishability
- lack of ownership
- heterogeneity
- experiential nature.

These features are, of course, common to other service products and are not just unique to tourism. They pose distinctive marketing challenges for managers, and have been discussed widely in the literature (Mudie and Pirrie 2006; Evans *et al.* 2003; Lovelock and Wirtz 2004; Kandampully *et al.* 2001: Palmer 1994). Travel, therefore, invokes a special form of consumption behaviour which involves the purchase of an intangible, heterogeneous product which is also experiential (Mayo and Jarvis 1981; Mathieson and Wall 1982). Cai *et al.* (2003: 136) state that 'From the consumer's perspective, a vacation destination is an experience product. It is characterised by intangibility at the time of both purchase evaluation and consumption.'

The study of consumer behaviour within the field of tourism is complex. Any decision to purchase a holiday is of emotional significance in terms of high spend, high involvement and high-risk decision on an intangible product (Seaton and Bennett 1996). The cost of a holiday represents a sizeable proportion of the holiday maker's income. In addition, the fact that a prospective buyer cannot directly examine or observe what is being purchased nor try it out in advance inexpensively, adds to the uncertainty and risk (Goodall 1991). A holiday is regarded by some as the highlight of their year, but consumers do have many different influences on their decision-making process with a number of variables involved (Swarbrooke and Horner 2007).

Models of the tourism decision-making process have been accused of being guilty of neglecting consumer behaviours which occur during the vacation (Hyde 2000: 178). However, a model developed by Woodside is presented in Figure 15.1, and has been cited as an example of a model of tourism decision-making which does include the experience; that is, it embraces consumer behaviour whilst on holiday, thus leading to post-experience intentions (Woodside 2000: 6) or future purchase decisions. This tries to address the criticisms previously made

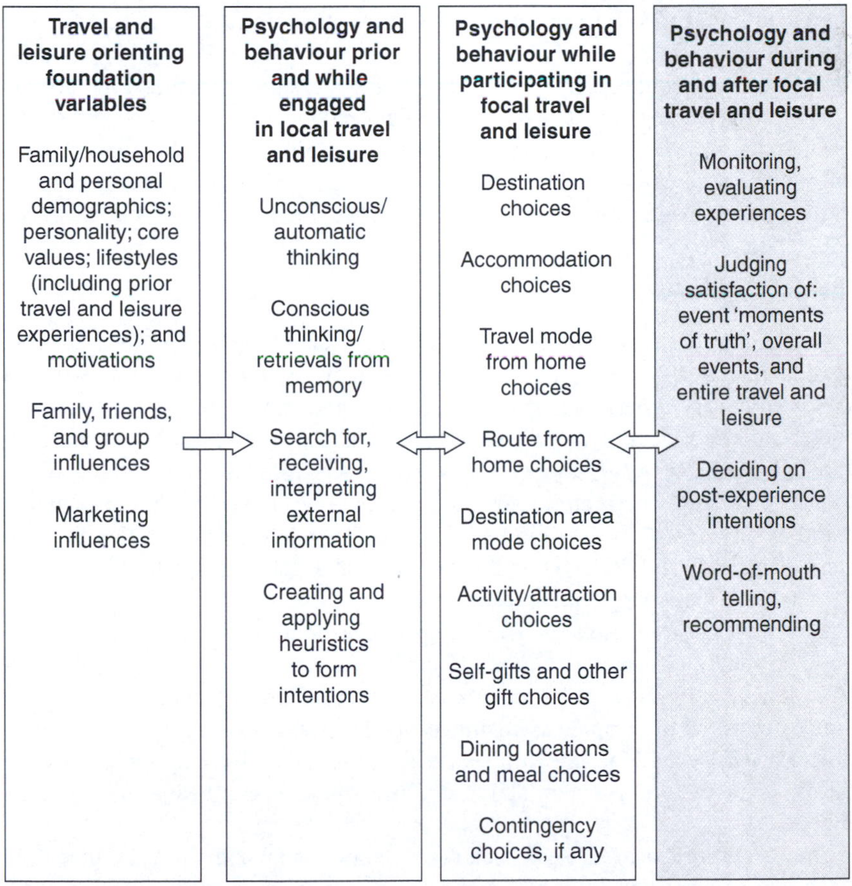

Figure 15.1 General systems framework of customer decision-making and behaviour (source: Woodside 2000: 6).

that the 'Grand Models' 'fail to capture the rich interactions of decisions and behaviours of the travel party and the destination environment experienced by the travel party' (Woodside and MacDonald 1994: 32).

A lack of coverage of consumer behaviour is, perhaps, understandable where a purchase decision and experience is short, convenient or utilitarian, for example, in a retail or other service experience, but a package holiday generally takes place over seven days or more. Moreover, there is the added complexity of the fact that the package is a combination of products sold by different service providers (Swarbrooke and Horner 2007). Figure 15.1 demonstrates how consumers make decisions about holiday purchases. Box 1 illustrates the primary variables that influence consumers' views on travel and holidays. Box 2 shows the thinking processes that are involved, whilst Box 3 illustrates some of the decisions and choices that are made. Box 4 is where the monitoring and evaluation takes place. It is here that the 'Experience' element is situated. However, Woodside's model focuses on the post-experience from a reflective basis, whereas it could also be argued that the experience actually runs horizontally across all four boxes.

We have described theory on consumer behaviour and consumer behaviour in tourism in order to contextualise the holiday experience which sits within the consumption phase. There is a lack of academic evaluation on this tourism consumption phase, which in the case of a holiday has specific features such as its length, making evaluation complex. The package holiday will now be discussed.

The package holiday

It is necessary to understand the nature of the package holiday before evaluating the older traveller's experience. A complexity in managing package holidays and associated tourist experiences is that the fragmented experience takes place over several months and, in some cases, years, as well as over several different geographical area (Ryan 2002c). Complex travel decisions are made about many separate elements which are interrelated and may be made over a considerable period of time, thus offering marketing and management opportunities for suppliers (Dellaert *et al.* 1998; Baum 2002). This makes the package holiday unique in terms of service management.

As a concept, the modern overseas package holiday is widely credited to Vladimar Raitz, a Russian emigrant to the UK (Evans *et al.* 2003; Bray 2001). In 1950, Raitz chartered a plane to Corsica and provided accommodation in the form of tents with camp beds to make up the package (Bray 2001). Raitz's company was called Horizon Holidays, which was taken over by the Thomsons Holidays Travel Group (now TUI Travel plc) in the late 1980s, but now no longer exists.

The basic tourism model has been considerably enhanced since the inception of the package holiday by Raitz, and now encompasses a wide range of additional services which add to the consumer's perception of the product and experience. Examples stem from the inclusion of basic transfers (for example, coach to the destination) to a variety of leisure, cultural, sporting or entertainment activities (Laws 1991). Urquhart (2006) comments that the 'package' is now a merely literal description, incorporating a wide variety of products and, therefore, experiences. As noted earlier, the growth in all-inclusive holidays for the UK market has been seen recently as a result of the strength of the euro and the UK recession, as a large majority of the expenditure is pre-paid, allowing consumers to budget carefully their spending in the destination.

Package holidays vary as to what is included, although will typically consist of transport and accommodation as stipulated in the legal definition (UK Government 1992). They may also, however, include some excursions and the meal basis may be bed and breakfast, half-board or fully inclusive (Rewtrakunphaiboon and Oppewal 2004). Package holidays are a type of bundling; this is where two or more products and/or services are put together in a single package and at a special price (Rewtrakunphaiboon and Oppewal 2004; Guiltinan 1987). Sheldon and Mak (1987) and Ryan (1995) argue that the main reasons why tourists purchase package holidays are convenience and price. Rewtrakunphaiboon and Oppewal (2004) maintain that research into bundling has mostly been from an economic perspective, focusing on a change of profits, and that only a few studies have examined consumer behaviour in relation to bundling. Ryan (1995) cites Laing (1987) who claims that the primary reason for consumers taking package holidays was that little planning was needed. The results from his research showed that 16 per cent of respondents felt that there was 'no risk involved'. Laing (1987), however, also stated that the reasoning behind taking package holidays was not necessarily clear, and that it could be regarded as a habitual action with consumers rarely considering their reasoning behind this preference. Laing (1987: 179) concludes by saying 'A closer grasp is needed of the individual's perception of package tours and their associated meaning'.

To understand the operations of a package holiday, Leiper's well-known tourism system model (Leiper 1979), which demonstrates the fragmented nature of the experience is presented in Figure 15.2. The three geographical areas through which the traveller passes also present challenges to management in managing the experience across all three areas.

The traveller-generating region is where consumers will purchase their package holiday and this is, arguably, where the experience first commences. Baum (2002) argues that the customer believes that they are purchasing the product from one company when, in fact, the experience is delivered by and made up of contact with a variety of intermediaries, over whom the principal agent company has little control. Examples of these are retail travel agents, airlines, local ground transportation and hoteliers, to name but a few (Baum 2002). Limited research has been conducted on the tourist experience in this area (Cliff and Ryan 2002). Van Rekom (1994) refers to these intermediaries as the production chain and he queries as to how skilful the companies in the chain are at delivering customers their desired travel experience. He also suggests that vertically integrated companies may be a solution in that they build a chain identity, which comprises aspects like holiday booking, flights, transfer and the hotel.

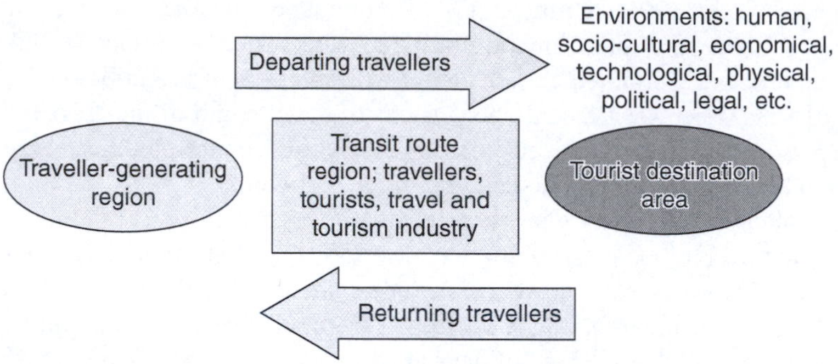

Figure 15.2 A basic tourism system (source: adapted from Leiper 1979).

These are important to the tourist's travel experience. The chain as a whole can help deliver the experience. The tourist destination area is the core service product and arguably where the most important 'moment of truths' (Carlson 1987) are evaluated.

The transit route region may be the area where the shortest duration of time is spent; however, the experience of, for example; the airport, airport hotel, restaurants or stopover can still be of importance to a holistic judgement of the overall experience. The air travel experience clearly includes the flight, or other mode of transport, but also check-in, waiting to board and so on, and this period provides time for changes in the consumer's mood (Gountas and Gountas 2004). The tourist destination area is generally seen as the most fundamental to the experience and this is the major focus of this chapter.

Ryan (2002c) produced a model which is presented in Figure 15.3, and provides the context to what motivates tourists and how they assess the tourism experience. The propositions are based on marketing paradigms in which satisfaction results from an evaluation of experience in comparison to expectations or tourists' perceptions of what is of importance on their holidays. He states that the model shows the consequences of choice: 'the confirmation of the choice begins with the closing of the door of the family home as holiday makers set out on their holiday' (Ryan 2002c: 65). This model draws from a motivational and assessment perspective and demonstrates the factors preceding the actual holiday experience and it is these factors against which the actual experience is gauged.

Quality and satisfaction clearly impact upon a consumer's evaluation of experience which may lead to loyalty, and any discussion without them would be incomplete. A tourist experience involves interactions with service deliverers, other guests and the wider host society and satisfaction is seen as a consequence of the tourist experience (Hanefors and Mossberg 1999; Bowen and Schouten 2008; Crouch *et al.* 2004). The value of the experience is also closely linked to the brand, which in this case is the tour operator (Mitchell and Orwig 2002).

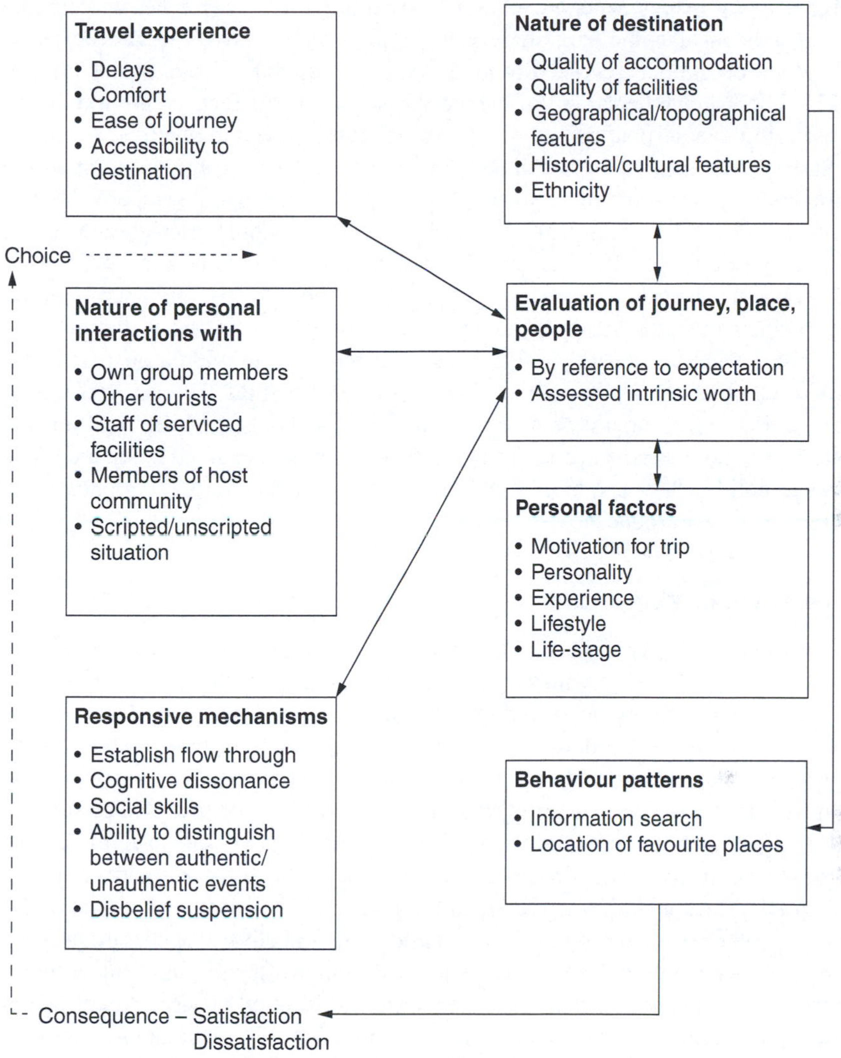

Figure 15.3 The tourist experience (Ryan 2002c: 63).

Frochot and Kreziak (2009) discuss the complexities of understanding satisfaction in an experiential context and over a long stay which is relevant to the package holiday. Arnould and Price (1993) also discuss the extended service encounter and the delivery of extraordinary experiences in river-rafting trips. Satisfaction clearly shares many characteristics related to a desirable experience but its relationship with behavioural intention and repeat booking have been questioned. Palmer (2010: 199), for example, sees satisfaction and quality as 'parallel or contributory constructs' to the experience. Consumer perceptions and judgements of events experienced and an evaluation of experiences can also be regarded as an outcome variable which affects satisfaction and future purchase behaviour of similar service products (Woodside 2000; Yuksel and Yuksel 2002). These judgements will influence the sense of satisfaction, the likelihood of returning to a destination and the 'word of mouth' given to others.

Satisfaction and quality are linked to loyalty. Given the highly competitive marketplace that tourism and hospitality organisations operate in, loyalty has become a key focus with providers seeking to continuously design and create enhanced experiences (Pullman and Gross 2003). Pine and Gilmore (1998, 1999) argue that successful experiences are those that the customer finds unique and memorable and that are sustained over a period of time. This means that the consumer will want to repeat the experience and will also provide a positive feedback to others on their experience. Wickens (2002) defined the characteristic of the 'Lord Byron' tourist type as one who has an annual ritual of revisiting the same place and the same accommodation this demonstrates loyal behaviour. The package holiday has been briefly examined and the concept of experience management is now introduced.

Experience management

The pioneering work by Pine and Gilmore stated that an economist's perspective was to put experiences in with services. They argued that 'experiences are a distinct economic offering, as different from services as services are from goods' (1998: 97). Pine and Gilmore's work has not been above criticism, however, as subsequent literature moved to the second strand, the consumer focus (see also Chapter 1 in this volume). Staging performances came to be regarded as superficial and product-centred (Holbrook 2001; Prahalad and Ramaswamy 2004). There was a move to adopt a more strategic approach to the experience, based on shared values and allowing consumers to create their own experiences thus allowing them personal growth (Morgan and Watson 2009). The change in focus to consumers wanting to 'buy experiences' and to spend time engaging in memorable events has resulted in an adaptation in the way tourism organisations view their customers and meet their needs and desires. This can be thought of as a shift from a product-centric mindset to a customer-centred one (Patterson and Pegg 2009; Gilmartin 2007). Scott *et al.* (2009) argue that in some fields such as marketing, academics have only recently discovered the importance of incorporating experiences into products, although leisure and tourism providers have always recognised the significance of these.

The tourist experience

Research focusing on the tourist experience has classified tourists into 'Raver Types', 'Escapers' and 'Heliolatrous types' and other categories. Indeed, Cohen (1979) presented five different types of tourist experiences. Hedonism is found to be prevalent on holidays and Wickens (2002) classifies the 'Raver Type', with an emphasis on sexual activities, clubbing and alcohol whilst on holiday, as a clear example of the hedonistic traveller. Ryan (2002c) claims that holidays are periods of play and social irresponsibility, with the escape from home being fundamental to the experience. Although individual tourists can be hedonistic or self-actualising in behaviour, collectively their actions create what we call 'tourism' (Ryan 2002c). Wickens (2002) develops the theme of 'escape', defined by Cohen (1979), as a need for rest and recovery. Wickens (2002) found that a common theme amongst her research participants was 'to forget about work' or to forget about everyday life. Although these can be construed as motivating factors, they clearly make up an important part of the tourist experience. Van Rekom (1994: 22) also regards tourism as providing consumers with an escape from everyday life. The tourism industry, and particularly the tour operator, are responsible for providing the means for the journey. Van Rekom (1994: 22) states that the tourism industry's 'societal function lies in making the non-ordinary experience accessible to the stressed customer'. Van Raaij and Crotts (1994) add to this, contending that consumers partake in travel and tourism in order to increase their stimulation in case of boredom.

Ryan (2002c) argues that as tourism is an experience that occurs as a result of travel, it happens outside normal settings. Therefore, attempting to understand the holiday experience solely by describing, for example, tourist interactions with other tourists, representatives, etc., provides only a partial analysis for the very reason that the interaction takes place away from 'normality' (Ryan 2002c). It could be argued, however, that it is the very fact of this displaced activity which gives it its unique value to consumers and makes up the important elements of the experience. It is evident that one of the main motivators for leisure travel in northern Europe is to have some sunshine. For example, Ryan (1995) found that the main reason given for visiting Majorca by UK visitors was to escape the British winter. Wickens (2002) in her typology of the 'Heliolatrous type' emphasised the importance of sun: 'The sun definitely is one of the main reasons that I'm here' and 'I love the sun' (Wickens 2002: 840). She found that this cluster of holiday makers spent the largest part of their holiday (more than seven hours per day) lying on the beach and tanning. Ryan (1995: 210) suggests that relaxation motivation was specifically referred to as 'the holiday meeting a need to relax or in the sense of getting away from it all'. Wickens (2002) concludes that 'ontological security' was a common theme amongst tourists; that is 'a package holiday makes you feel safe if anything goes wrong' (Wickens 2002: 843). She puts it another way, stating that 'institutionalized tourists' can 'feel secure' and still enjoy the 'strangeness' of the resort, particularly so against the backdrop of the security provided by a package holiday Ontological security refers to the security that humans have in their self-identity and the environment that they are in; it is closely related to routine.

Wickens' suggests that for many holiday makers, their holiday is underlined by minor health problems and that, in such cases, they choose to take a pre-packaged holiday as they see it as free from health risks and physical hardships.

An elderly respondent she interviewed endorsed this by saying that there are many advantages to returning to the same place and the same hotel, more than once. She commented on the security that this provides and that familiarity is extremely important, as is being made to feel welcome.

For some tourists, particularly those taking package holidays, the actual choice of destination was not as important as factors such as price, timing, departure airport and general convenience factors. This was particularly the case when the break in question was a getaway/sun break. The results from Ryan (1995) suggest that older travellers rated their past holiday experience and destination experience as more important in destination selection than other age groups. He argued that older travellers used their past experience as a basis for what provides a satisfactory holiday and vice versa, and also to judge where risks can and cannot be taken. He concludes that a high number of repeat visits are associated with loyalty and that holiday makers had a strong identification with a destination and what it had to offer without apparently considering alternative destinations. Socialising and social interaction have been found to be important in the tourism experience; this could include interactions with staff and other holiday makers in social settings (Quinlan Cutler and Carmichael 2010; Andereck *et al.* 2006; Mossberg 2007a; Trauer and Ryan 2005). Andereck *et al.* (2006) claim that social interaction experiences will influence the perception of quality.

Changes of scene were found to be important by older travellers in Ryan's (1995) study; they enjoyed the chance to stroll around, albeit slowly – and safely. He states that 'the perception of friendly shop-owners, smiling waiters and a feeling of safety was something that was sensed, appreciated and something perhaps felt lacking in their home, UK environment.' Ryan (1995: 213) concludes from this that, for these older travellers, the minimisation of risk is highly important. He found that quiet, reflexive and relaxing activities, often not taken at home, were important. 'Such things included sitting at restaurants taking time reading the Sunday paper, going for a stroll in the sunshine, taking a trip to a favourite place, viewing the scenery, people watching.' He reflects that his perception was that these activities were not normally undertaken at home. Ryan points out that the perception of 'safety' to this category of holiday makers needs to be explored further. The concept of friendliness was highlighted as important but in many differing contexts, making it difficult to evaluate.

The 'grey' market

We now explore literature on the descriptive experiences of the 'grey' market's package holiday experience. The 'grey' market is defined and characteristics relevant to travel and holidays are explored. It is the particular characteristics of this market segment which led to it being the selected demographic segment upon which to focus this chapter, and, in particular, its importance to the travel industry.

It has been necessary to select a demographic market segment on which to evaluate the tourism experience, as all package travel market segments differ fundamentally in terms of the experience offered by the service provider and the manner in which the consumer undergoes the experience. The 18–30-year-old segment, for example, is clearly radically different, in terms of product offering and therefore experience, from the 'grey' market. One problem encountered is absolute definitions of age segments. Littrell *et al.* (2004) comment that, in many studies, researchers failed to agree on what constitutes an older traveller. Some studies set 50 as the age of demarcation and other studies used research respondents 55 or 60 or older; 'Clearly, the need for a common definition of the senior traveller is apparent in order to make cross-study comparisons' (Littrell *et al.* 2004: 350). Categories include those born before 1946 (Gilmartin 2007) or depicting those aged 50 and over or 55 and over (Shoemaker 2000) and these are also called the 'mature' market, the 'older' market and the 'muppie' market (mature, upscale, post-professional) (Shoemaker 2000). For the purposes of this chapter, older or 'senior' travellers are categorised as those aged 50 or over at the time of the research in 2011. The reasoning behind this was that it covered ages that a majority of definitions had applied. There is a small overlap with the 'younger seniors' and also baby boomers, those born between 1946 and 1964 (Lehto *et al.*, 2008).

Evans *et al.* (2009) state that people over 50 do not like to be portrayed as 'old'. They suggest that they see through marketing attempts to portray them as young and that they would rather be referred to as 'youthful'. Importantly, Evans *et al.* recognise that people over 50 can be more loyal, which is extremely important for organisations offering products to this segment. They suggest that the 55–64-year-old segment takes more holidays than average and that more than half of them plan to have two or more holidays in the next 12 months. Mintel (2004) refer to the 'grey' market, which they categorise as those aged 45 plus, and state that today's 'grey' market is younger in outlook than previous generations and is also expanding and affluent. However, other research also found that some older tourists were concerned with security, illness, danger avoidance and the smooth operation of travel plans (Littrell *et al.* 2004), The number of holidays taken each year by the average older consumer is growing and Mintel (2004: 2) suggests that 'holiday companies may wish to devote more marketing effort towards existing customers, perhaps through relationship marketing schemes in order to encourage the reuse of holiday services'. This claim is still valid today. Consumers aged 45–74 are the most likely to take a package holiday break, with one in four consumers being aged between 55 and 64 and 15 per cent of adults aged 75 plus taking a package holiday (Mintel 2010). Important characteristics of the 'grey' market are presented in Table 15.1.

An examination of the features and characteristics of older travel consumers reveals how well suited they are in principle to the buying of holidays. However, despite being a promising segment on account of size and potential for future growth, older travellers are often overlooked in the tourism literature; (Littrell *et al.* 2004). Shoemaker (2000) comments that people aged 55 or over are one of the fastest growing market segments. By 2050, it is estimated that over two billion people will be aged 60 or over, representing 22 per cent of the world's

Table 15.1 Important characteristics of the 'grey' market

• Preference for buying experiences rather than material possessions • More discretionary time in retirement • Preference to travel in off season or shoulder season • Tendency to spend longer periods on holiday in a resort than other vacationers • Loyal customers to tour operator	• Growing size of segment • Fastest growing market segment • Higher discretionary income than other segments • Less consumer debt • Inflation-proof pensions • Inherited wealth often received • Empty nesters • Greater holiday propensity than other segments

Sources: Adapted from Mintel (2010); Evans *et al.* (2009); Mintel (2004); Littrell *et al.* (2004); Shoemaker (2000); Patterson and Pegg (2009); and Ryan (1995).

population; in 2000, it was 10 per cent (United Nations 2000). The aging population of the UK is set to grow – those aged between 75 and 84 by 8.6 per cent by 2015, and those aged over 85, by 15.6 per cent (Mintel 2010).

Results and discussion

This section presents the preliminary findings from the ongoing research project and describes the 'grey' market's package holiday experience. Access was provided by Thomson Holidays, part of TUI Travel PLC and the largest tour operator in Europe in terms of revenue. Semi-structured interviews were conducted in the resorts. A pilot study was initially undertaken in Majorca and then, after adapting the interview style and questions to elicit richer data, 12 interviews were undertaken in Los Gigantes in the Canaries before saturation point was reached. The interview questions were derived from practitioner knowledge and a review of the literature on the package holiday and the experience. The interviews ranged in length from half an hour to an hour, and both couples and single people were interviewed. Template analysis was used to analyse the findings, 'a related group of techniques for thematically organizing and analysing textual data' (King 2004) and particularly suitable for phenomenological and experiential research (King and Horrocks 2010). Results are summarised in Table 15.2.

Holiday booking

Older travellers are Internet-savvy, using the Internet to find out holiday prices. Some then book through their local travel agent who will match the Internet price (more often than not Thomson). Trust is important; one respondent stated, 'I tend to go with the big boys; I am not worried that Thomson's will go bust ... if Thomson's went down there probably wouldn't be much left of the economy anyway!' This security provided by the brand (Mitchell and Orwig 2002) is also linked to the concept of 'no risk' being involved in terms of planning the holiday (Laing 1987; Ryan 1995) and concerns about the use of paid holiday and disposable

Table 15.2 The 'grey' market's package holiday experience

Theme	*Quotations from interviewed customers*
Holiday booking	
Often consumers used the Internet for price comparison and then booked through their local travel agent although some did book online. Convenience was a strong theme and the provision of the transfer was found to be an important element.	'I will look it up [the holiday] but I wouldn't book it [on the internet].' 'I always book mine on the internet … cos it's a lot cheaper.' 'They [the tour operator] just sort everything, the tickets, the transfers, the room.'
Holiday activities	
Socialising, meeting up with friends from previous years, walking, strolling, relaxing in the sun, British evening entertainment.	'We make friends wherever we go.' 'We always meet loads of people.' 'We like to have a walk after dinner.'
Quality, satisfaction and loyalty	
Consumers rated quality and satisfaction highly. Loyalty was found to be very high amongst these consumers with many repeat bookers, particularly to the same familiar destination, hotel and staff.	'They [Thomson] have never let us down.' 'When you arrive at the hotel it's like coming home.' 'We come here every year … for at least 25 years … maybe twice a year.'
Security	
Grey consumers were concerned over health issues and the security provided by the tour operator and the reps was very important to them.	'We've had people here that have got seriously ill and in hospital and Thomsons sort of get them sorted out and get them home, we even had a lady die here, didn't we?'
The brand	
Security of a well known brand was found to be important	[On the package] 'It gives you security.' 'I mean with Thomson I think you'd feel more secure than with some outlandish company you'd never heard of.'

income (Seaton and Bennett 1996). Convenience is important: one respondent commented on package holidays, 'Well, I think especially now, I mean as we've got older we want as least hassle as possible' and another stated 'They [the tour operator] just sort everything, the tickets, the transfers, the room.'

Holiday activities

Socialising is important to package holiday makers who stated 'We always meet loads of people' and 'We make friends wherever we go.' This concurs with previous findings (Mossberg 2007a; Quinlan Cutler and Carmichael 2010; Andereck *et al.* 2006; Trauer and Ryan 2005). Guests come to relax, which is aided by the sun, a particularly important benefit to the older traveller (Ryan 1995). They also like to walk, stating 'We do a lot of walking' and 'We like to have a walk after dinner'.

Quality, satisfaction and loyalty

Positive evaluation of quality and satisfaction is essential to the holiday experience. This is clearly a subjective area but holiday makers made the following comments: 'As a matter of fact the hotel has exceeded our expectations' and 'they [Thomson] have never let us down … of course they run their own airline which helps'. No children under 16 were allowed in the hotel. 'We like the fact, it sounds awful, but there aren't any little children.' The link between quality, satisfaction and loyalty was evident with holiday makers often returning to the same destination, invoking destination and supplier loyalty. Holiday makers made comments such as 'Some people have been here 50 times'; 'When you arrive at the hotel it's like coming home'; and 'We come here every year … for at least 25 years … maybe twice a year'. This concurs with research on satisfaction and future purchases (Woodside 2000; Yuksel and Yuksel 2002) and satisfaction and its link to the tourist experience (Crouch *et al.* 2004; Bowen and Schouten 2008; Hanefors and Mossberg 2003).

Security

Risk has already been discussed but the allied concept of security came through strongly as very important to these older consumers in the findings. Quotations from holiday makers explain its significance: 'When you get to our age … you want to know where you are and you never know if something's going to go wrong and you haven't got the capacity you might have if it went wrong, you panic more I think' and 'Any of us can be taken seriously ill and you know, if one person is left on their own, they would need somebody to help them get back.' A comment on the package was 'It gives you security'. These findings are very much in accordance with Wickens (2002) and her concept of ontological security.

To conclude, it must be emphasised that this is an exploratory piece of research which used non-probability convenience sampling on account of time and cost factors. Only preliminary findings are presented and the study is still on-going. It is appreciated that a much larger study could have been undertaken in several countries and resorts. Moreover, although the research method employed here is qualitative, a positive, quantitative approach could be employed at a later stage, building onto these preliminary, qualitative, rich findings. These findings cannot be generalised and are restricted to the context in which they were collected.

Nevertheless, in the chapter and the accompanying research project, we have revealed new insights into an area of significant importance in the UK travel industry which has however until now, had a very limited academic research focus.

References

Abdul-Ghani, E., Hyde, K. and Marshall, R. (2011) Emic and etic interpretations of engagement with a consumer-to-consumer online auction site. *Journal of Business Research* 64(1), 1060–1066.

Achterberg, W., Pot, A., Kerkstra, A., Ooms, M., Müller, M. and Ribbe, M. (2003) The effect of depression on social engagement in newly admitted Dutch nursing home residents. *The Gerontologist* 43(2), 213–218.

Addis, M. and Holbrook, M. (2001) On the conceptual link between mass customisation and experiential consumption: An exploration of subjectivity. *Journal of Consumer Behaviour* 1(1), 50–66.

Adler, J. (1989) Origins of sightseeing. *Annals of Tourism Research* 16(1), 7–29.

Aho, S. K. (2001) Towards a general theory of touristic experiences: Modelling experience process in tourism. *Tourism Review* 56 (3–4), 33–37.

Ajagunna, I. (2006) Crime and harassment in Jamaica: Consequences for sustainability of the tourism industry. *International Journal of Contemporary Hospitality Management* 18(3), 253–259.

Alleyne, D. and Boxill, I. (2003) The impact of crime on tourist arrivals in Jamaica. *International Journal of Tourism Research* 5(5), 381–91.

Alluri, R. (2009) *The Role of Tourism in Post-Conflict Peacebuilding in Rwanda.* Working Paper. Bern: Swisspeace.

Al-Sabbahy, H., Ekinci, Y. and Riley, M. (2004) An investigation of perceived value dimensions: Implications for hospitality research. *Journal of Travel Research* 42(3), 226–234.

Ambrosie, L. (2010) Regulatory space and child sex tourism: The case of Canada and Mexico. In N. Carr and Y. Poria (eds). *Sex and the Sexual During People's Leisure and Tourism Experiences*, pp. 81–101. Newcastle: Cambridge Scholars Publishing.

Andereck, K., Bricker, K., Kerstetter, D. and Nickerson, N. (2006) Connecting experiences to quality: Understanding the meanings behind visitors' experiences. In G. Jennings and N. Nickerson (eds), *Quality Tourism Experiences*, pp. 81–98. Oxford: Elsevier Butterworth-Heinemann.

Anderson, M. (1999) Museums of the future: The impact of technology on museum practices. *Daedalus* 128(3), 129–162.

Ap, J. (1992) Residents' perceptions of tourism impacts. *Annals of Tourism Research* 19(4), 665–690.

Apostolakis, A. (2003) The convergence process in heritage tourism. *Annals of Tourism Research* 30(4), 795–812.

Aremberri, J. (2010) *Modern Mass Tourism*. Bingley: Emerald.

Arendt, H. (1958) *The Human Condition*. Chicago: University of Chicago Press.

Ariès, P. (1981) *The Hour of Our Death*. Trans. H. Weaver. Oxford: Oxford University Press.

Aristotle (1941) *Politica* (Politics). In R. McKeon (ed.), *The Basic Works of Aristotle*, pp. 1127–1316. New York: Random House.

Armstrong, K. (2002) Race and sport consumption motivations: A preliminary investigation of a black consumers' sport motivation scale. *Journal of Sport Behavior* 25(4), 309–330.

Arnould, E. and Price, L. (1993) River magic: Extraordinary experience and the extended service encounter. *Journal of Consumer Research* 20(1), 24–45.

Arnould, E., Price, L. and Malshe, A. (2006) Toward a cultural resource-based theory of the customer. In R. Lusch and S. Vargo (eds), *The Service-Dominant Logic of Marketing*, pp. 91–104. London: Sharp.

Ashworth, G. (1996) Holocaust tourism and Jewish culture: The lessons of Kraków-Kazimierz. In M. Robinson, N. Evans and P. Callaghan (eds), *Tourism and Cultural Change*, pp. 1–12. Sunderland: Business Education Publishers.

Ashworth, G. (2002) Holocaust tourism: The experience of Kraków-Kazimierz. *International Research in Geographical and Environmental Education* 11(4), 363–367.

Ashworth, G. (2004) Tourism and the heritage of atrocity: Managing the heritage of South Africa for entertainment. In T. V. Singh (ed.), *New Horizons in Tourism: Strange Experiences and Stranger Practices*, pp. 95–108. Wallingford: CABI.

Ashworth, G. and Hartmann, R. (2005) *Horror and Human Tragedy Revisited: The Management of Sites of Atrocity for Tourism*. New York: Cognizant.

Austin, N. K. (2002) Managing heritage attractions: Marketing challenges at sensitive historical sites. *International Journal of Tourism Research* 4(6), 447–457.

Avery, J., Beatty, S., Holbrook, M., Kozinets, R., Mittal, B., Raghubir, P. and Woodside, A. (2010) *Consumer Behavior: Human Pursuit of Happiness in the World of Goods*, 2nd edn. Cincinnati: Open Mentis.

Babin, B., Darden, W. and Griffin, M. (1994) Work and/or fun: Measuring hedonic and utilitarian shopping value. *Journal of Consumer Research* 20(4), 644–656.

Badone, E. and Roseman, R. (2004) Approaches to the anthropology of pilgrimage and tourism. In E. Badone and S. Roseman (eds), *Intersecting Journeys. The Anthropology of Pilgrimage and Tourism*, pp. 1–23. Chicago: University of Illinois Press.

Bærenholdt, J. and Simonsen, K. (2004) *Space Odysseys: Spatiality and Social Relations in the Twenty-First Century*. Aldershot: Ashgate.

Bærenholdt, J., Haldrup, M., Larsen, J. and Urry, J. (2004) *Performing Tourist Places*. Aldershot: Ashgate.

Bagnall, G. (2003) Performance and performativity at heritage sites. *Museum and Society* 1(2), 87–103.

Bakir, A. and Baxter, S. (2011) 'Touristic fun': Motivational factors for visiting Legoland Windsor Theme Park. *Journal of Hospitality Marketing and Management* 20(3–4), 407–424.

Barroso, C. and Martín, E. (1999) *Marketing Relacional*. Madrid: ESIC.

Barthes, R. (1972) *Mythologies*. Trans. Annette Lavers. New York: Noonday Press.

Baum, T. (2002) Making or breaking the tourist experience. In C. Ryan (ed.), *The Tourist Experience*, 2nd edn, pp. 94–111. London: Continuum.

Bauman, Z. (2001) *The Individualized Society*. Cambridge: Polity Press.

Bayton, J. (1958) Motivation, cognition, learning: Basic factors in consumer behavior. *Journal of Marketing* 22(3), 2822–89.

BBC (2008) Rwanda: How the genocide happened. BBC News. Online, available at http://news.bbc.co.uk/2/hi/1288230.stm (accessed 28 September 2010).

BBC. (2009) On This Day – 26 February 1993: World Trade Center bomb terrorises New York. BBC News. Online, available at http://news.bbc.co.uk/onthisday/hi/dates/stories/february/26/newsid_2516000/2516469.stm (accessed 7 July 2009).

Beech, J. (2009) Genocide tourism. In R. Sharpley and P. Stone (eds), *The Darker Side of Travel: The Theory and Practice of Dark Tourism*, pp. 207–223. Clevedon: Channel View Publications.

Beeton, S. (2001) Smiling for the camera: The influence of film audiences on a budget tourism destination. *Tourism, Culture and Communication* 3(1), 15–26.

Beeton, S. (2002) reCAPITALizing the image: Demarketing undesired film-induced images. Paper presented at the Travel and Tourism Research Association 33rd Conference, CAPITALizing on Tourism Research, Arlington, Virginia, 23–26 June.

Beeton, S. (2004) Rural tourism in Australia: Has the gaze altered? Tracking rural images through film and tourism promotion. *International Journal of Tourism Research* 6(3), 125–135.

Beeton, S. (2005) *Film-Induced Tourism*. Clevedon: Channel View Publications.

Beeton, S. (2006) Understanding film-induced tourism. *Tourism Analysis* 11(3), 181–188.

Belhassen, Y., Caton, K., and Stewart, W. (2008) The search for authenticity in the pilgrim experience. *Annals of Tourism Research* 35(3), 668–689.

Belk, R. (1988) Possessions and the extended self. *Journal of Consumer Research*, 15(2), 139–168.

Belk, R., Ger, G. and Askegaard, S. (2003) The fire of desire: A multisited inquiry into consumer passion. *Journal of Consumer Research* 30(3), 325–351.

Bendar, M. (1989) *Interior Pedestrian Places*. New York: Whitney Library of Design.

Bentham, J. (2006) The Set-Jetters. *The Guardian*, 17 February 2006.

Ben-Yehuda, N. (1990) Positive and negative deviance: More fuel for a controversy. *Deviant Behavior* 11(3), 221–243.

Berdichvisky, L., Poria, Y. and Uriely, N. (2010) Casual sex and the backpacking experience: The case of Israeli women. In N. Carr and Y. Poria (eds), *Sex and the Sexual during People's Leisure and Tourism Experiences*, pp. 105–118. Newcastle: Cambridge Scholars Publishing.

Bergen, D. (1988) *Play as a Medium for Learning and Development: A Handbook of Theory and Practice*. Portsmouth, NH: Heinemann.

Berry, L. (1983) Relationship marketing of services. Growing interest, emerging perspectives. *Journal of the Academy of Marketing Science* 23(4), 236–245.

Bhardwaj, S. (1973) *Hindu Places of Pilgrimage in India. A Study in Cultural Geography*. Berkeley: University of California Press.

Bhardwaj, S. and Rinschede, G. (1988) Pilgrimage: A worldwide phenomenon. *Geographia Religionum* 4, 11–19.

Bilda, Z., Edmonds, E. and Candy, L. (2008) Designing for creative engagement. *Design Studies* 29(6), 525–540.

Bilyeu, J. and Wann, D. (2002) An investigation of racial differences in sport fan motivation. *International Sports Journal* 6(2): 93–106.

Binkhorst, E. (2002) Holland, the American way: Transformations of the Netherlands into US vacation experiences. PhD thesis, Tilburg University.

Binkhorst, E. (2005) The co-creation tourism experience. *Whitepaper Co-creations*, Sitges. Online, available at www.esade.edu/cedit2006/pdfs2006/papers/esther_binkhorst_paper_esade_may_06.pdf (accessed 15 October 2011).

Biran, A., Poria, Y. and Oren, G. (2011) Sought experiences at (dark) heritage sites. *Annals of Tourism Research* 38(3), 820–841.

Bird, S. E. (2002) It makes sense to us: Cultural identity in local legends of place. *Journal of Contemporary Ethnography* 31(5), 519–547.

Bitner, M. J. (1995) Building service relationships: It's all about promises. *Journal of the Academy of Marketing Science* 23(4), 246–251.

Black, G. (2009) *The Engaging Museum: Developing Museums for Visitor Involvement*. London: Routledge.

Blair, J. (2002) Tragedy turns to tourism at Ground Zero. *The Age*, 29 June 2002. Online, available at www.theage.com.au/articles/2002/06/28/1023864657451.html (accessed 31 July 2008).

Bogari, N., Crowther, G. and Marr, N. (2003) Motivation for domestic tourism: A case study of the Kingdom of Saudi Arabia. *Tourism Analysis* 8(2), 137–141.

Bolan, P. (2010) Film-induced tourism: Motivation, authenticity and displacement. PhD thesis, University of Ulster.

Bolan, P. and Crossan, M. (2006) The influence of film induced tourism on Ireland's Dingle Peninsula: A case-study of *Ryan's Daughter*. Paper presented at 2nd Annual Tourism and Hospitality in Ireland Conference, Waterford Institute of Technology, Waterford, June 2006.

Bolan, P. and Davidson, K. (2005) Film-induced tourism in Ireland: Exploring the potential. Paper presented at Tourism and Hospitality in Ireland Conference, University of Ulster, Coleraine, June 2005.

Bolan, P. and O'Connor, N. (2007) Northern Ireland and *The Chronicles of Narnia – The Lion, the Witch and the Wardrobe*: An innovative destination branding partnership. In N. O'Connor, M. Keating, J. Malone and A. Murphy (eds), *Tourism and Hospitality Research in Ireland – Concepts, Issues and Challenges*, pp. 125–146. Waterford: WIT Publications.

Bolan, P. and O'Connor, N. (2008) Creating a sustainable brand for Northern Ireland through film-induced tourism. *Tourism, Culture and Communication* 8(3), 147–158.

Bolan, P. and Williams, L. (2008) The role of image in service promotion: Focusing on the influence of film on consumer choice within tourism. *International Journal of Consumer Studies* 32(4), 382–390.

Boorstin, D. (1964) *The Image: A Guide to Pseudo-events in America*, New York: Harper and Row.

Boswijk, A., Thijssen, J. and Peelen, E. (2005) *A New Perspective on the Experience Economy: Meaningful Experiences*. Amsterdam: Pearson Education.

Bourdieu, P. (2007) *Distinction: A Social Critique of the Judgement of Taste*. London: Routledge.

Bourdieu, P. and Darbel, A. (2008) *The Love of Art: European Art Museums and Their Public*. Cambridge: Polity Press.

Bowen, D. and Clarke, J. (2009) *Contemporary Tourist Behaviour: Yourself and Others as Tourists*. Wallingford: CABI.

Bowen, D. and Schouten, A. (2008) Tourist satisfaction and beyond: Tourist migrants in Mallorca. *International Journal of tourism Research* 10(2), 141–153.

Bowman, M. and Pezzullo, P. (2009) What's so 'dark' about 'dark tourism'? Death, tours, and preference. *Tourist Studies* 9(3), 187–202.

Boxill, I. (2004) Towards an alternative tourism for Jamaica. *International Journal of Contemporary Hospitality Management* 16(4), 269–272.

Boyd. S. (1991) *Towards a Typology of Tourism: Setting and Experiences Presented at the Association of America Geographers*. Youngstown, OH: East Lakes Division.

Brants, K. (1998) Who's afraid of infotainment? *European Journal of Communication* 13(3), 315–335.
Bray, R. (2001) *Flight to the Sun: The Story of the Holiday Revolution*. London: Continuum.
Bright, A. (2008) Motivations, attitudes, and beliefs. In H. Oh and A. Pizam (eds), *Handbook of Hospitality Marketing Management*, pp. 239–265. Oxford: Butterworth-Heinemann.
Bruner, E. (1991) Transformation of self in tourism. *Annals of Tourism Research* 18(2), 238–250.
Brunt, P., Mawby, R. and Hambly, Z. (2000) Tourist victimisation and the fear of crime on holiday. *Tourism Management* 21(4), 417–424.
Bryant, F. and Veroff, J. (2007) *Savoring: A New Model of Positive Experience*. Mahwah, NJ: Lawrence Erlbaum.
Burns, P. (1999) *An Introduction to Tourism and Anthropology*. London: Routledge.
Busby, G. and Klug, J. (2001) Movie-induced tourism: The challenge of measurement and other issues. *Journal of Vacation Marketing* 7(4), 316–332.
Butler, R. (1990) The influence of the media in shaping international tourist patterns. *Tourism Recreation Research* 15(2), 46–53.
Buttle, F. (1996) Relationship marketing. In F. Buttle, (ed.), *Relationship Marketing. Theory and Practice*, pp. 1–16. London: Paul Chapman Publishing.
Cai, L., Feng, R. and Breiter, D. (2003) Tourist purchase decision involvement and information preferences. *Journal of Vacation Marketing* 10(2), 138–148.
Canter, D. (1977) *The Psychology of Place*. London: Architectural Press.
Caplan, F. and Caplan, T. (1973) *The Power of Play*, New York: Anchor Books.
Carl, D., Kindon, S. and Smith, K. (2007) Tourists' experiences of film locations: New Zealand as 'Middle Earth'. *Tourism Geographies* 9(1), 49–63.
Carlson, J. (1987) *Moments of Truth*. Cambridge, MA: Ballinger.
Carmichael, B. (2006) Linkages between residents' quality of life and quality tourist experiences. In G. Jennings and N. Nickerson (eds), *Quality Tourism Experiences*, pp. 115–135. Oxford: Butterworth Heinemann.
Carnegie, E (2010) Museums in society or society as a museum? In D. O'Reilly and F. Kerrigan (eds), *Marketing the Arts: A Fresh Approach*, pp. 231–239. London: Routledge.
Carneiro, M. and Crompton, J. (2010) The influence of involvement, familiarity, and constraints on the search for information about destinations. *Journal of Travel Research* 49(4), 451–470.
Carr, N. (2002) The tourism-leisure behavioral continuum. *Annals of Tourism Research* 29(4), 972–986.
Carù, A. and Cova, B. (2003) Revisiting consumption experience: A more humble but complete view of the concept. *Marketing Theory* 3(2), 267–286.
Carù, A. and Cova, B. (2004) How can services elements help the consumer in immersing himself in the experience? The case of Auditorium – Giuseppe Verdi Milan Symphony Orchestra. *Finanza Marketing e Produzione* 2, 5–28.
Carù, A. and Cova, B. (2006) How to facilitate immersion in a consumption experience: Appropriation operations and service elements. *Journal of Consumer Behavior* 5(1), 4–14.
Carù, A. and Cova, B. (2007a) *Consuming Experience*. London: Routledge.
Carù, A. and Cova, B. (2007b) Consuming experiences: An introduction. In A. Carù and B. Cova (eds), *Consuming Experience*, pp. 3–16. London: Routledge.

Chhabra, D. (2007) Research note: Exploring market influences on curator perceptions of authenticity. *Journal of Heritage Tourism* 2(2), 110–119.

Chon, K. (1990) The role of destination image in tourism: A review and discussion. *Tourist Review* 45(2), 2–9.

Clawson, M. and Knetsch, J. (1966). *Economics of Outdoor Recreation*. Baltimore, MD: Johns Hopkins University Press.

Cliff, C. and Ryan, C. (2002) Vital encounters: When tourists contact travel agents. In C. Ryan (ed.), *The Tourist Experience*, 2nd edn, pp. 78–93. London: Continuum.

Clift, J. and Clift, B. (1996) *The Archetype of Pilgrimage*. New York: Paulist Presas.

CNN (2004) Minister: Jamaican crime hurting tourism. Online, available at www.latinamericanstudies.org/jamaica/hurting.htm. (accessed 30 November 2007).

Cofer, C. and Appley, M. (1964) *Motivation: Theory and Research*. New York: John Wiley & Sons.

Cohen, E. (1972) Toward a sociology of international tourism. *Social Research* 39: 164–172.

Cohen, E. (1974) Who is a tourist? A conceptual clarification. *Sociological Review* 22(4), 527–555.

Cohen, E. (1979) A phenomenology of tourist experiences. *Sociology* 13(2), 179–201.

Cohen, E. (1985) Tourism as play. *Religion* 15(3), 291–304.

Cohen, E. (1988) Authenticity and commoditization in tourism. *Annals of Tourism Research* 15(3), 371–386.

Cohen, E. (1992a) Pilgrimage and tourism: Convergence and divergence. In A. Morinis (ed.), *Sacred Journeys*, pp. 47–64. Westport, CT:Greenwood Press,

Cohen, E. (1992b) Pilgrimage centers, concentric and excentric. *Annals of Tourism Research*, 19(1), 33–50.

Cohen, E. (2001) Who is a tourist? A conceptual clarification. In E. Cohen (ed.), *Contemporary Tourism. Diversity and change*, pp. 17–36. Oxford: Elsevier Science.

Cohen, E. (2008) The changing faces of contemporary tourism. *Society* 45(4), 330–333.

Cohen, E. (2010) Educational dark tourism at an *in populo* site: The Holocaust Museum in Jerusalem. *Annals of Tourism Research* 38(1), 193–209.

Cohen, E. and Krishnamurthy, B. (2006) A short walk in the Blogistan. *Computer Networks* 50(5), 615–630.

Cohen, J. W. (1988) *Statistical Power Analysis for the Behavioral Sciences*. Hillsdale, NJ: Lawrence Erlbaum Associates.

Cole, T. (1999) *Selling the Holocaust. From Auschwitz to Schindler: How History is Bought, Packaged and Sold*. New York: Routledge.

Coleman, S. and Eade, J. (2004) Introduction: Reframing pilgrimage. In S. Coleman and J. Eade (eds), *Reframing Pilgrimage: Cultures in Motion*, pp. 1–25. London: Routledge.

Coleman, S. and Elsner, J. (1995) *Pilgrimage: Past and Present in the World Religions*. Cambridge, MA: Harvard University Press.

Collins-Kreiner, N. (2010) Researching pilgrimage: Continuity and transformations. *Annals of Tourism Research* 37(2), 440–456.

Connell, J. and Meyer, D. (2009) Balamory revisited: An evaluation of the screen tourism destination–tourist nexus. *Tourism Management* 30(2), 194–207.

Cooper, C. (1981) Spatial and temporal patterns of tourist behaviour. *Regional Studies* 15(5), 359–371.

Cooper, C., Fletcher, F., Fyall, A., Gilbert, D. and Wanhill, S. (2008) *Tourism: Principles and Practice*. Harlow: Pearson Education.

Crawford, G. (2004) *Consuming Sport: Fans, Sport and Culture*. London: Routledge.

Crompton, J. (1979). Motivations for pleasure vacation. *Annals of Tourism Research* 6(4), 408–424.

Crompton, J. (1993). Choice set propositions in destination decisions. *Annals of Tourism Research* 20(3), 461–477.

Crompton, J. and McKay, S. (1997) Motives of visitors attending festival events. *Annals of Tourism Research* 24(2), 426–439.

Cronin, J., Brady, M. and Hult, T. (2000) Assessing the effects of quality, value and customer satisfaction on consumer behavioural intentions in service environments. *Journal of Retailing* 76(2), 193–218.

Crouch, G., Perdue, R. and Timmermans, H. (2004) Building foundations for understanding the consumer psychology of tourism, hospitality and leisure. In G. Crouch, R. Perdue and H. Timmermans (eds), *Consumer Psychology of Tourism, Hospitality and Leisure*, volume 3, pp. 1–10. Wallingford, CABI.

Croy, W. G. (2011) Film tourism: Sustained economic contributions to destinations, *Worldwide Hospitality and Tourism Themes* 3(2), 159–164.

Csikszentmihalyi, M. (1975) *Before Boredom and Anxiety*. San Francisco: Jossey-Bass.

Csikszentmihalyi, M. (1982) Toward a psychology of optimum experience. In L. Wheeler (ed.), *Review of Personality and Social Psychology*, pp. 13–36. Thousand Oaks, CA: Sage.

Csikszentmihalyi, M. (1992) *Flow: The Psychology of Happiness*. London: Rider.

Csikszentmihalyi, M. (1997). *Finding Flow: The Psychology of Engagement in Everyday Life*. New York: Basic Books.

Csikszentmihalyi, M. (2000) The costs and benefits of consuming. *Journal of Consumer Research* 27(2), 267–272.

Csikszentmihalyi, M. (2008) *Flow: The Psychology of Optimal Experience*. New York: Harper Perennial Modern Classics.

Csikszentmihalyi, M. and Hermanson, K. (1995) Intrinsic motivation in museums: Why does one want to learn? In E. Hooper-Greenhill (ed.), *The Educational Role of the Museum*, pp. 146–160. London: Routledge.

Csikszentmihalyi, M. and Robinson, R. (1990). *The Art of Seeing: An Interpretation of the Aesthetic Encounter*. Los Angeles: Getty Publication.

Dale, C. and Robinson, N. (2011) Dark tourism. In P. Robinson, S. Heitmann and P. Dieke (eds), *Research Themes in Tourism*, pp. 205–217. Wallingford: CABI.

Danmarks Statistik (2011) Overnatninger for alle overnatningsformer efter overnatningsform, område, nationalitet og periode (1992–2011) *Statistikbanken*. Online, available at www.statistikbanken.dk (accessed 16 October 2011).

Dann, G. (1977) Anomie, ego-enhancement and tourism. *Annals of Tourism Research* 4(4), 184–194.

Dann, G. (1981) Tourist motivation: An appraisal. *Annals of Tourism Research* 8(2), 187–219.

Dann, G. (1998) *The Dark Side of Tourism*. Etudes et rapports, série L. Aix-en-Provence: Centre International de Recherches et d'Etudes Touristiques.

Dann, G. and Parrinello, G. (2009) *The Sociology of Tourism: European Origins and Developments*. Bingley: Emerald Group Publishing.

Dann G. and Seaton, A. (eds), (2001) *Slavery, Contested Heritage and Thanatourism*. New York: Haworth Hospitality Press.

de Albuquerque, K. and McElroy, J. L. (2001) Tourism harassment: Barbados survey results. *Annals of Tourism Research* 28(2), 477–492.

Debenedetti, S. (2003) Investigating the role of companions in the art museum experience. *International Journal of Arts Management* 5(3), 52–63.

Deem, R. (1996) Woman, the city and holidays. *Leisure Studies* 15(2) 105–119.

DeLeire, T. and Kalil, A. (2009) Does consumption buy happiness? Evidence from the United States. *International Review of Economics* 57(2), 163–176.

Dellaert, B., Ettema, D. and Lindh, C. (1998) Multi-faceted tourist travel decisions: A constraint-based conceptual framework to describe tourists' sequential choices of travel components. *Tourism Management* 19(4), 313–320.

Destination Forks: The Real World of Twilight (2010) DVD documentary, Summit Entertainment.

Dirckinck-Holmfeld, K. and Selmer, F. (2006) *Arkitekternes sommerhuse*. Copenhagen: Arkitektens Forlag.

Dixon, J. (2008) Dr John Dixon's homepage. Online, available at www.psych.lancs.ac.uk/people/JohnDixon.html (accessed 3 June 2008).

Dodge, D. (1985) The over-negativized conceptualization of deviance: A programmatic exploration. *Deviant Behavior* 6(1), 17–37.

Donald, S. and Gammack, J. (2007) *Tourism and the Branded City: Film and Identity on the Pacific Rim*. Aldershot, Ashgate.

Douglas, M. (1986) *How Institutions Think*. Syracuse, NY: Syracuse University Press.

Douthwaite, R. (1999) *The Growth Illusion*, revised edn. Dublin: Lilliput Press.

Duman, T. and Mattila, A. (2005) The role of affective factors on perceived cruise vacation value. *Tourism Management* 26(3), 311–323.

Dunn, H. and Dunn, L. (2002) Tourism and popular perceptions: Mapping Jamaican attitudes. *Social and Economic Studies* 51(1), 25–45.

Dunne, J. (1997) *Back to the Rough Ground: Practical Judgment and the Lure of Technique*. Notre Dame, IN: University of Notre Dame Press.

Durkheim, E. (1912) *Elementary Forms of Religious Life*. London: Allen & Unwin.

Dutt, A. K. (2006) Consumption and happiness: Alternative approaches. Rough draft prepared for the conference on New Directions in the Study of Happiness, University of Notre Dame. Online, available at www.nd.edu/~adutt/activities/documents/DuttConsumptionandhappiness.pdf (accessed 15 December 2011).

Dwyer, L., Forsyth, P., Spurr, R. and VanHo, T. (2006) Economic effects of the world tourism crisis on Australia. *Tourism Economics* 12(2), 171–186.

Eade, J. and Sallnow, J. (2000) *Contesting the Sacred: The Anthropology of Christian Pilgrimage*. Chicago: Urbana.

Easterlin, R. (1975) Will raising the incomes of all increase the happiness of all? *Journal of Economic Behavior and Organization* 27(1), 35–47.

Edensor, T. and Kothari, U. (2004) Sweetening colonialism: A Mauritian themed resort. In D. Lasansky and B. McLaren (eds), *Architecture and Tourism: Perception, Performance and Place*, pp. 189–206. Oxford: Berg.

Edmonds, E., Müller, L. and Connell, M. (2006) On creative engagement. *Visual Communication* 5(3), 307–322.

Ek, R., Larsen, J., Hornskov, S. and Mansfeldt, O. (2008) A dynamic framework of tourist experiences: Space-time and performances in the experience economy. *Scandinavian Journal of Hospitality and Tourism* 8(2), 122–140.

Engel, J., Blackwell, R. and Miniard, P. (1995) *Consumer Behavior*. Forth Worth, TX: The Dryden Press.

Engler, M. (1993) Drive-thru history: Theme towns in Iowa. *Landscape* 32(1), 8–18.

Evans, M., Jamal, A. and Foxall, G. (2009) *Consumer Behaviour*. Chichester: John Wiley & Sons.

Evans, N., Campbell, D. and Stonehouse, G. (2003) *Strategic Management for Travel and Tourism*. Oxford: Butterworth-Heinemann.

Evans, P. (1975) *Motivation*. London: Methuen & Co Ltd.

Facaros, D. and Pauls, M. (1986) *Turkey*. London: Cadogan Guides.

Falk, J. and Dierking, L. (1997) *The Museum Experience*. Washington, DC: Whalesback Books.

Falk, J. and Dierking, L. (2002) *Lessons Without Limit: How Free-Choice Learning is Transforming Education*. Walnut Creek, CA: AltaMira Press.

Falk, J. and Storksdieck, M. (2010) Science learning in a leisure setting. *Journal of Research in Science Teaching* 47(2), 194–212.

Faulkner, B., Fredline, E., Larson, M. and Tomljenovic, R. (1999) A marketing analysis of Sweden's Storsjöyran musical festival. *Tourism Analysis* 4(3–4), 157–171.

Fearis, B. (2011) Strong UK performance boosts TUI profits. Online, available at www.travelmole.com (accessed: 10 August 2011).

Fees, C. (1996) Tourism and the politics of authenticity in a north Cotswold town. In T. Selwyn (ed.), *The Tourist Image: Myths and Myth Making in Tourism*, pp. 121–146. Chichester: John Wiley & Sons.

Feifer, M. (1985) *Going Places*. London: Macmillan.

Ferrari, S., Adamo, G. and Veltrí, A. (2005). Creative tourism, experiential holidays and multisensority. Paper presented at ATLAS Annual Conference. Tourism, Creativity and Development. Barcelona, 2–4 November.

Field, A. (2009) *Discovering Statistics Using SPSS*, 3rd edn. London: Sage.

Fienberg, J. and Leinhardt, G. (2002) Looking through the glass: Reflections of identity in conversations at a history museum. In G. Leinhardt, K. Crowley and K. Knutson (eds), *Learning Conversations in Museums*, pp. 167–211. Mahwah, NJ: Lawrence Erlbaum Associates.

Fink, J., Trail, G. and Anderson, D. (2002) An examination of team identification: Which motives are most salient to its existence? *International Sports Journal* 6(2), 195–207.

Firat, F. A. (1999) Rethinking consumption. *Markets and Culture* 3(4), 283–296.

Firat, F. A. and Venkatesh, A. (1995) Liberatory postmodernism and the reenchantment of consumption. *Journal of Consumer Research* 22(3), 239–268.

Fleming, D. (2005) Managing change in museums. Paper presented at The Museum and Change International Conference, Prague, November.

Fodness, D. (1992) The impact of family life cycle on the vacation decision-making process. *Journal of Travel Research* 31(2), 8–13.

Fodness, D. (1994) Measuring tourist motivation. *Annals of Tourism Research* 21(3), 555–581.

Foley, M. and Lennon, J. (1996) JFK and dark tourism: A fascination with assassination. *International Journal of Heritage Studies* 2(4), 198–211.

Formica, S. and Uysal, M. (1998) Market segmentation of an international cultural-historical event. *Journal of Travel Research* 36(4), 16–24.

Frey, L. (1998) *Pilgrim Stories: On and Off the Road to Santiago*. Berkeley: University of California Press.

Frochot, I. and Kreziak, D. (2009) Tourist experience: An in-depth analysis of satisfaction in the long encounter of a skiing holiday. Paper presented at the Tourism and Hospitality Ireland Conference, Dublin Institute of Technology, 16–17 June.

Frost, W. (2006) From backlot to runaway production: Exploring location and authenticity in film-induced tourism. Working Paper Series ISSN 1327–5216, presented at Second International Tourism and Media Conference in Melbourne, Monash University, Department of Management, Australia.

Frost, W. (2009) From backlot to runaway production: Exploring location and authenticity in film-induced tourism. *Tourism Review International* 13(2), 85–92.

Frow, J. (2008) Kitsch politics. *Cultural Studies Review*, 14(2), 200–204.

Gadamer, H.-G. (1981) *Reason in the Age of Science*. Cambridge, MA: MIT Press.

Gadamer, H.-G. (1986a) The festive character of theatre. In R. Bernasconi (ed.), *The Relevance of the Beautiful and Other Essays*, pp. 57–65.Cambridge: Cambridge University Press.

Gadamer, H.-G. (1986b) The relevance of the beautiful. In R. Bernasconi (ed.), *The Relevance of the Beautiful and Other Essays*, pp. 3–56. Cambridge: Cambridge University Press.

Gadamer, H.-G. (2003) *Truth and Method*. New York: Continuum Publishing Company.

Galbraith, M. (2000) On the road to Czestochova: Rhetoric and experience on a Polish pilgrimage. *Anthropological Quarterly* 73(2), 61–73.

Gammon, S. (2011) 'Sporting' new attractions? The commodification of the sleeping stadium. In R. Sharpley and P. Stone (eds), *Tourist Experience: Contemporary Perspectives*, pp. 115–126. Abingdon: Routledge.

Gartner, W. (1993). Image formation process. In M. Uysal, and D. R. Fesemaier (eds), *Communication and Channel Systems in Tourism Marketing*, pp. 191–217. New York: Haworth Press.

Genoways, H. and Ireland, L. (2003) *Museum Administration: An Introduction*. Walnut Creek, CA: AltaMira Press.

Gentile, C., Spiler, N. and Noci, G. (2007) How to sustain the customer experience: An overview of experience components that co-create value with the costumer. *European Management Journal* 25(5), 395–410.

George, R. (2003) Tourist's perceptions of safety and security while visiting Cape Town. *Tourism Management* 24(5), 575–585.

Getz, D. (2007) *Event Studies: Theory, Research and Policy for Planned Events*. Oxford, Butterworth-Heinemann.

Gibson, H. and Yiannakis, A. (2002) Tourist roles needs and the lifecourse. *Annals of Tourism Research* 29(2), 358–53.

Giddens, A. (1991) *Modernity and Self-identity: Self and Society in the Late Modern Age*. Cambridge: Polity Press.

Gilbert, D. (1991) An examination of the consumer decision process related to tourism. In C. Cooper (ed.), *Progress in Tourism, Recreation and Hospitality Management*, vol. 3, pp. 78–105. London: Belhaven Press.

Gilbert, D. and Abdullah, J. (2004) Holidaytaking and the sense of well-being. *Annals of Tourism Research* 31(1), 103–121.

Gillin, J. (1914) The sociology of recreation. *American Journal of Sociology* 19(6), 825–834.

Gilmartin, J. (2007) Challenge your current marketing approach. Online, available at www.comingofage.com/wp-content/themes/coa/articles/Challenge-Your-Marketing-Approach.pdf (accessed 5 January 2011).

Glanz, J. and Lipton, E. (2003) *City in the Sky: The Rise and Fall of the World Trade Center*. New York: Times Books.

Gnoth, J. (1997) Tourism motivation and expectation formation. *Annals of Tourism Research* 24(2), 283–304.

Gonzalez, M., Hidalgo, C. and Albert-Laszlo, B. (2008) Understanding individual human mobility patterns. *Nature* 453, 779–782.

Goodall, B. (1991) Understanding holiday choice. In C. Cooper and A. Lockwood (eds), *Progress in Tourism, Recreation and Hospitality Management*, pp. 58–77. London: Belhaven Press.

Goode, E. (1991) Positive deviance: A viable concept. *Deviant Behavior* 12(3), 289–309.

Goss-Turner, S. (2000) Accommodation. In J. Jafari (ed.), *Encyclopedia of Tourism*, pp. 2–4. London: Routledge.

Gottlieb, A. (1982) Americans' vacations. *Annals of Tourism Research* 9(2), 165–187.

Goulding, C. (1999) Contemporary museum culture and consumer behaviour. *Journal of Marketing Management* 15(7), 647–671.

Gountas, S. and Gountas, J. (2004) The influence of consumer's emotions on their service product evaluation. In G. Crouch, R. Perdue, H. Timmermans and M. Uysal (eds), *Consumer Psychology of Tourism, Hospitality and Leisure*, vol 3, pp. 21–32. Wallingford: CABI.

Graburn, H. (1989) Tourism: The sacred journey. In V. Smith (ed.). *Hosts and Guests: The Anthropology of Tourism*, pp. 21–36. Philadelphia: University of Pennsylvania Press.

Graburn, N. (2001). Secular ritual: A general theory of tourism. In V. Smith and M. Brent (eds), *Hosts and Guests Revisited: Tourism Issues of the Twenty-First Century*, pp. 42–50. New York: Cognizant Communication Corporation.

Graham, C. (2009) *Happiness around the World: The Paradox of Happy Peasants and Miserable Millionaires*. Oxford: Oxford University Press.

Gram, M. and Therkelsen, A. (2003) *Børnefamilieferie – en kvalitativ undersøgelse af tyske og danske børnefamiliers idealer for og beslutninger om ferie med særlig fokus på Danmark som ferieland.* Aalborg University: Tourism Research Unit.

Graml, G. (2004) (Re)mapping the nation: *Sound of Music* tourism and national identity in Austria. *Tourist Studies* 4(1), 137–159.

Grant, J. (2000) *The New Marketing Manifesto: The 12 Rules for Building Successful Brands in the Twenty-First Century*. London: Thomson.

Grayling, A. C. (2008) Happiness is the measure of true wealth. *Daily Telegraph*, 10 April. Online, available at www.telegraph.co.uk/comment/3557112/Happiness-is-the-measure-of-true-wealth.html (accessed 29 December 2011).

Grecevičius, P. (2002) *Turizmas*, Klaipėdos Universitetas, Kauno Kolegija.

Gretzel, U., Mitsche, N., Hwang, Y.-H. and Fesenmaier, D. (2004) Tell me who you are and I will tell you where to go: Use of travel personalities in destination recommendation systems. *Information Technology and Tourism* 7(1), 3–12.

Griffin, J. (1998) *School–Museum Integrated Learning Experiences in Science: A Learning Journey*. Sydney: University of Technology.

Grihault, N. (2003) Film tourism – the global picture. *Travel and Tourism Analyst*, October, 1–22.

Grihault, N. (2007) *Set-jetting Tourism – International*. Mintel Reports, March, 1–45.

Grondin, J. (2003) *The Philosophy of Gadamer*. Montreal, McGill-Queen's University Press.

Grönroos, C. (1996) Relationship marketing: Strategic and tactical implications. *Management Decision* 34(3), 5–14.

Grosspietsch, M. (2006) Perceived and projected images of Rwanda: Visitor and international tour operator perspectives. *Tourism Management* 27(2), 225–234.

Gruen, T., Summers, J. and Acito, F. (2000) Relationship marketing activities, commitment, and membership behaviors in professional associations. *Journal of Marketing* 64(3), 34–49.

Guiltinan, J. (1987) The price of bundling services: A normative framework. *Journal of Marketing* 51(2), 74–85.

Guintcheva, G. and Passebois, J. (2009) Exploring the place of museums in European leisure markets: An approach based on consumer values. *International Journal of Arts Management*, 11, 4.

Gunn, C. (1989). *Vacationscape: Designing Tourist Regions*, 2nd edn. New York: Van Nostrand Reinhold.

Gustafson, P. (2001) Meanings of place: Everyday experience and theoretical conceptualizations. *Journal of Environmental Psychology* 21(1), 5–16.

Hair, J., Black, W., Babin, B. and Anderson, R. (2010) *Multivariate Data Analysis*. 7th edn. Upper Saddle River, NJ: Prentice Hall.

Hajer, M. (2005) Rebuilding Ground Zero: The politics of performance. *Planning Theory and Practice* 6(4), 445–464.

Haldrup, M. (2004) Laid-back mobilities: Second-home holidays in time and space. *Tourism Geographies* 6(4), 434–454.

Haldrup, M. and Larsen, J. (2006) Material cultures of tourism. *Leisure Studies* 25(3), 275–289.

Hall, C. M. (2006) Travel and journeying on the Sea of Faith (perspectives from religious humanism). In D. Timothy and D. Olsen (eds), *Tourism, Religion and Spiritual Journeys*, pp. 64–77. London: Routledge.

Hall, C. M. (2011) Consumerism, tourism and voluntary simplicity: We all have to consume, but do we really have to travel so much to be happy? *Tourism Recreation Research* 36(3), 298–303.

Hanefors, M. and Mossberg, L. (1999) Package tourism and customer loyalties. In A. Pizam and Y. Mansfeld (eds), *Consumer Behavior in Travel and Tourism*, pp. 185–204. Binghampton, NY: The Haworth Press.

Hanefors, M. and Mossberg, L. (2003) Searching for the extraordinary meal experience. *Journal of Business and Management,* 9(3), 249–270.

Harrison, R. (2003) *The Dominion of the Dead.* Chicago: Chicago University Press.

Heelas, P. and Woodhead, L. (2005) *The Spiritual Revolution: Why Religion is Giving Way to Spirituality*. Oxford: Blackwell Publishing.

Heidegger, M. (1962) *Being and Time*. San Francisco: Harper & Row.

Hein, G. (1998) *Learning in the Museum*. London: Routledge.

Henning, G. (2006) Understanding the guided hiking experience: A theatrical model of organizational performance and hiker reception. PhD thesis, University of Calgary.

Henning, G. (2008) The guided hike in Banff National Park: A hermeneutical performance. *Journal of Sustainable Tourism* 16(2), 182–196.

Henning, G. (2011a) Corporation and polis. *Journal of Business Ethics* 103(2), 289–303.

Henning, G. (2011b) I–Thou relationships in tourism: The case of cross-cultural interaction between Okinawan locals and Japanese tourists. *Tourism, Culture and Communication* 11(1), 43–54.

Hepburn, S. (2010) Shades of darkness: Silence, risk and fear among tourists and Nepalis during Nepal's civil war. *Journeys* 11(1), 133–155.

Hetherington, K. (2000) Museums and the visually impaired: The spatial politics of access. *Sociological Review* 48(3), 444–463.

Higgins, T. and Scholer, A. (2009) Engaging the consumer: The science and art of the value creation process. *Journal of Consumer Psychology* 19(2), 100–114.

Hilke, D. and Balling, J. (1985) *The Family as a Learning System: An Observational Study of Families in Museums*. Washington, DC: Smithsonian Institution Press.

Hirschman, E. and Holbrook, M. (1982) Hedonic consumption: Emerging concepts, methods and propositions. *Journal of Marketing* 46(3), 92–101.

Holbrook, M. (1996) Customer value – a framework for analysis and research. In K. Corfman and J. Lunch (eds), *Advances in Consumer Research* 23, pp. 138–142. Provo, UT: Association for Consumer Research.

Holbrook, M. (1999a) *Consumer Value: A Framework for Analysis and Research*. London: Routledge.

Holbrook, M (1999b). Introduction to consumer value. In M. Holbrook (ed.). *Consumer Value: A Framework for Analysis and Research*, pp. 1–28. London: Routledge.

Holbrook, M. (2001) Times Square, Disneyphobia, hegemickey, the Ricky Principle, and the downside of the entertainment economy: It's fun-dumb-mental. *Marketing Theory* 1(2), 139–163.

Holbrook, M.(2006) 'ROSEPEKICECIVECI versus CCV', in R. Lusch, and S. Vargo (eds), *The Service-Dominant Logic of Marketing: Dialog, Debate, and Direction*, pp. 208–223. Armonk, NY: M. E. Sharpe.

Holbrook, M. and Hirschman, E. (1982) The experiential aspects of consumption: Consumer fantasies, feelings, and fun. *Journal of Consumer Research* 9(2), 132–140.

Holbrook, M., Chestnut, R., Oliva, T. and Greenleaf, E. (1984) Play as a consumption experience: The roles of emotions, performance, and personality in the enjoyment of games. *Journal of Consumer Research* 11(9), 728–739.

Holt, D. B. (1995) How consumers consume: A typology of consumption practices. *Journal of Consumer Research* 22(1), 1–16.

Hookway, N. (2008) Entering the blogosphere: Some strategies for using blogs in social research. *Qualitative Research* 8(1), 91–113.

Hooper-Greenhill, E. (2007) *Museums and Education: Purpose, Pedagogy, Performance (Museum Meanings)*. London: Routledge.

Howard, E. (2007) New shopping centres: Is leisure the answer? *International Journal of Retail and Distribution Management* 35(8), 661–672.

Howarth, G. (2007) *Death and Dying: A Sociological Introduction*. Cambridge: Polity Press.

Hsu, C. and Huang, S. (2008) Travel motivation: A critical review of the concept's development. In A. Woodside and D. Martin (eds), *Tourism Management: Analysis, Behaviour and Strategy*, pp. 14–27. Wallingford: CABI.

Huang, M.-H. (2006) Flow, enduring, and situational involvement in the web environment: A tripartite second-order examination. *Psychology and Marketing* 23(5), 383–411.

Hudson, S. (1999) Consumer behavior related to tourism. In A. Pizam and Y. Mansfeld, (eds), *Consumer Behavior in Travel and Tourism*, pp. 7–32. Binghampton, NY: The Haworth Press.

Hudson, S. (2011) Working together to leverage film tourism: Collaboration between the film and tourism industries. *Worldwide Hospitality and Tourism Themes* 3(2), 165–172.

Hudson, S. and Ritchie, J. (2006a) Film tourism and destination marketing: The case of *Captain Corelli's Mandolin*. *Journal of Vacation Marketing* 12(3), 256–268.

Hudson, S. and Ritchie, J. (2006b) Promoting destinations via film tourism: An empirical identification of supporting marketing initiatives. *Journal of Travel Research* 44(4), 387–396.

Hughes, G. (1995) Authenticity in tourism. *Annals of Tourism Research* 22(4), 781–803.

Hughes, R. (2008) Dutiful tourism: Encountering the Cambodian genocide. *Asia Pacific Viewpoint* 49(3), 318–330.

Hvattum, M. (2010) Stedets tyranni. *Arkitekten* 2, 34–43.

Hyde, K. (2000) A hedonic perspective on independent vacation planning, decision-making and behaviour. In A. Woodside, G. Crouch, J. Mazanec, M. Oppermann and M. Sakai (eds), *Consumer Psychology of Tourism, Hospitality and Leisure*, pp. 171–191. Wallingford: CABI.

Hyde, K. and Harman, S. (2011) Motives for a secular pilgrimage to the Gallipoli battle-fields. *Tourism Management* 32(6), 1343–1351.

Interviews (2009) Visitor interviews at the Tribute WTC Visitor Center and Ground Zero. 17–23 February, Lower Manhattan, New York, USA, in Stone 2010b.

Ipsos Mori (2010) Grey power: The grey ahead. Online, available at www.ipsos-mori.com/newsevents/ca/ca.aspx?oItemId=74 (accessed 3 December 2010).

Iso-Ahola, S. (1982) Toward a social psychological theory of tourism motivation: A rejoinder. *Annals of Tourism Research* 9(2), 256–262.

Iso-Ahola, S. (1983) Towards a social psychology of recreational travel. *Leisure Studies* 2(1), 45–56.

Issa, J. and Jayawardena, C. (2003) The 'all-inclusive' concept in the Caribbean. *International Journal of Contemporary Hospitality Management* 15(3), 167–171.

Iwashita, C. (2006) Media representation of the UK as a destination for Japanese tourists. *Tourist Studies* 6(1), 59–77.

Iwashita, C. (2008) Roles of films and television dramas in international tourism: The case of Japanese tourists to the UK. *Journal of Travel and Tourism Marketing* 24(2 and 3), 139–151.

Jackowski, A. (1996) *Przestrzen i sacrum: Geografia kultury religijnej w Polsce i jej przemiany w okresie od XVII do XX w. na przykladzie osrodkow kultu i migracji piel-grzymkowych*, Krakow: Instytut Geografii Uniwersytetu.

Jackowski, A. (1998) *Pielgrzymowanie*, Wroclaw: Wydawnictwo Dolnoslaskie.

Jackowski, A. (2000) Religious tourism – problems with terminology. *Peregrinus Cracoviensis* 10, 63–74.

Jackson, C., Morgan, M. and Hemmington, N. (2009) Extraordinary experiences in tourism: Introduction to the special edition. *International Journal of Tourism Research* 11(2), 107–109.

Jacobs, K. (2008) Normalizing Ground Zero? *Metropolis Magazine*, 18 June. Online, available at www.metropolismag.com/story/20080618/normalizing-ground-zero (accessed 26 July 2009).

Jacobsen, J. (2002) Southern comfort: A study of holiday style patterns of northernness in coastal Mallorca. *Scandinavian Journal of Hospitality and Tourism Research* 2(1), 49–78.

Jacobsen, J. and Dann, G. (2009) Summer holidaymaking in Greece and Spain: Exploring visitor motive patterns. *Anatolia: An International Journal of Tourism and Hospitality Research* 20(1), 5–17.

Jamaican Labour Party (2009a) Bartlett warns drug peddlars in tourist capital. Online, available at www.jamaicalabourparty.com/base/content/bartlett-warns-drug-peddlars-tourist-capital (accessed 27 April 2009).

Jamaican Labour Party (2009b) Government determined to stamp out visitor harassment. Jamaica Information Service. Online, available at www.jamaicalabourparty.com/base/content/govt-determined-stamp-out-visitor-harassment (accessed 27 April 2009).

Jamaican Tourist Board (2009) About Jamaica: Meet the People. Online, available at www.visitjamaica.com/about-jamaica/meet-people.aspx (accessed 24 July 2009).

Jamal, T. and Hill, S. (2004) Developing a framework for indicators of authenticity: The place and space of cultural and heritage tourism. *Asia Pacific Journal of Tourism Research* 9(4), 353–371.

Jamal, T. and Lee, J.-H. (2003) Integrating micro and macro approaches to tourist motivations: Toward an interdisciplinary theory. *Tourism Analysis* 8(1), 47–59.

Jamal, T. and Lelo, L. (2011) Exploring the conceptual and analytical framing: From darkness to intentionality. In R. Sharpley and P. Stone (eds), *Tourist Experience: Contemporary Perspectives*, pp. 29–42. Abingdon: Routledge.

James, J. and Ridinger, L. (2002) Female and male sport fans: A comparison of sport consumption motives. *Journal of Sport Behavior* 25(3), 260–278.

Jammerbugt Kommune (2009) *By- og egnsbeskrivelser- planområde Hune, Helhedsplan09*. Online, available at www.jammerbugt.dk/Helhedsplan_09/By-_og_egnsbeskrivelser.aspx (accessed 30 September 2011).

Jammerbugt Kommune (2011) *Strukturer og Politikker – Helhedsplan 11, Kommuneplantillæg nr.2 til Kommuneplan 2009–21 (Helhedsplan)*. Online, available at www.jammerbugt.dk/Helhedsplan_09.aspx (accessed 30 September 2011).

Jang, S. and Cai, L. A. (2002) Travel motivations and destination choice: A study of British outbound market. *Journal of Travel and Tourism Marketing* 13(2), 111–133.

Jansson, A. (2007) A sense of tourism: New media and the dialectic of encapsulation/decapsulation. *Tourist Studies* 7(1), 5–24.

Jantzen, C. (2007). Mellem nydelse og skuffelse. Et neurofysiologisk perspektiv på oplevelser. In C. Jantzen, and T. A. Rasmussen (eds), *Oplevelsesøkonomi. -inkler på forbrug*, pp. 135–165. Aalborg: Aalborg Universitetsforlag.

Jantzen, C. and Vetner, M. (2007). Design for en affektiv økonomi. In C. Jantzen, and T. A. Rasmussen (eds), *Oplevelsesøkonomi. -inkler på forbrug*, pp. 201–219. Aalborg: Aalborg Universitetsforlag.

Jantzen, C., Rasmussen, T. A. and Vetner, M. (2006). Bag om dillen. Oplevelsesøkonomiens aktive forbrugere. In C. Jantzen, and J. F. Jensen (eds), *Oplevelser. Koblinger og transformationer*, pp. 177–189. Aalborg: Aalborg Universitetsforlag.

Jayawardena, C. (2002) Mastering Caribbean tourism. *International Journal of Contemporary Hospitality* 14(2), 88–93.

Jenkins, R. (2008) *Social Identity*, 3rd edn. London: Routledge.

Jennings, G. and Nickerson, N. (eds) (2006) *Quality Tourism Experiences*. Burlington, MA: Elsevier Butterworth-Heinemann.

Jensen, S. (2005) Promoting the known and the unknown of cities and city regions. In T. O'Dell and P. Billing (eds), *Experiencescapes: Tourism, Culture, and Economy*, pp. 147–161. Copenhagen: Copenhagen Business School Press.

Johns, N. and Gyimóthy, S. (2002). Mythologies of a theme park: An icon of modern family life. *Journal of Vacation Marketing* 8(4), 320.

Johnston, T. (2011) Thanatourism and commodification of space in post-war Croatia and Bosnia. In R. Sharpley and P. Stone (eds), *Tourist Experience: Contemporary perspectives*, pp. 43–55. London: Routledge.

Jones, D. and Smith, K. (2005) Middle Earth meets New Zealand: Authenticity and location in the making of *The Lord of the Rings*. *Journal of Management Studies* 42(5), 923–945.

Kandampully, J., Mok, C. and Sparks, B. (eds) (2001) *Service Quality Management*. Binghampton, NY: Haworth Hospitality Press.

Kang, E., Scott, N., Lee, T. and Ballantyne, R. (2011) Benefits of visiting a 'dark tourism' site: The case of the Jeju April 3rd Peace Park, Korea. *Tourism Management* 33(2), 257–265.

Kaplan, A. (2003) Homeland insecurities: Transformations of language and space. In M. Dudziak (ed.), *September 11 in History: A Watershed Moment?* (pp. 55–69), Durham, NC: Duke University Press.

Kearl, M. (2009) Kearl's guide to sociological thanatology: Sociology of death and dying. Trinity University website, San Antonio, TX. Online, available at www.trinity.edu/mkearl/death.html (accessed 8 May 2009).

Kellehear, A. (2007) *A Social History of Dying.* Cambridge: Cambridge University Press.

Kelley, T. and Littman, J. (2006) *The Ten Faces of Innovation: Strategies for Heightening Creativity*. London. Profile Books.

Kelly, J. (1987) *Freedom to Be: A New Sociology of Leisure*. New York, Macmillan.

Kendle, A. (2008) Grief tourism: Straddling the boundary between sympathy and snooping. *Vagabondish.* Online, available at www.vagabondish.com/grief-tourism-dark-travel-tours/ (accessed 16 November 2011).

Kenway, J. and Bullen, E. (2011) *Consuming Children: Education-Entertainment-Advertising*. Milton Keynes: Open University Press.

KGMC (2010) *Kigali Genocide Memorial Centre: Education*. Online, available at www.kigalimemorialcentre.org/old/index.html (accessed 6.10.10).

Kim, H. and Jamal, T. (2007) Touristic quest for existential authenticity. *Annals of Tourism Research* 34(1), 181–202

Kim, H. and Richardson, S. (2003) Motion picture impacts on destination images. *Annals of Tourism Research* 30(1), 216–237.

Kim, N.-S. and Chalip, L. (2004) Why travel to the FIFA World Cup? Effects of motives, background, interest, and constraints. *Tourism Management* 25(6), 695–707.

King, N. (2004) Using templates in the thematic analysis of text. In C. Cassell and G. Syman (eds), *Essential Guide to Qualitative Methods in Organisational Research*, pp. 256–270. London: Sage.

King, N. and Horrocks, C. (2010) *Interviews in Qualitative Research*. London: Sage Publications.

Kingsbury, P. (2005) Jamaican tourism and the politics of enjoyment. *Geoforum* 36(1), 113–132.

Kleinschafer, J., Dowell, D. and Morrison, M. (2011) Doing more with less: Understanding the contributions of regional art gallery members through marketing segmentation. *Arts Marketing: An International Journal* 1(1), 39–55.

Klenosky, D. (2002) The 'pull' of tourism destinations: A means–end investigation. *Journal of Travel Research* 40(2), 385–395.

Knowles, T. and Curtis, S. (1999) The market viability of European mass tourist destinations. A post-stagnation life-cycle analysis. *International Journal of Tourism Research* 1(2), 87–96.

Kotler P., Bowen, J. and Makens, J. (2004) *Marketing para turismo*. Madrid: Pearson.

Kotler, N. and Kotler, P. (2000). Can museums be all things to all people? Missions, goals, and marketing's role. *Museum Management and Curatorship* 18(3), 271–287.

Kotler, N., Kotler, P. and Kotler, W. (2008) *Museum Marketing and Strategy: Designing Missions, Building Audiences, Generating Revenue and Resources*, 2nd edn. San Fransisco: Jossey-Bass.

Kozak, M. (2002) Comparative analysis of tourist motivations by nationality and destinations. *Tourism Management* 23(3), 221–232.

Kozak, M. (2007) Tourism harassment: A marketing perspective. *Annals of Tourism Research* 34(2), 384–399.

Krakover, S. (2005) Attitudes of Israeli visitors towards the Holocaust remembrance site of Vad Yashem. In G. Ashworth and R. Hartmann (eds), *Horror and Human Tragedy Revisited: The Management of Sites of Atrocities for Tourism*, pp. 108–117. New York: Cognizant.

Krippendorf, J. (1987) *The Holiday Makers*. Oxford: Heinemann.

Kvale, S. (1996) *Interviews: An Introduction to Qualitative Research Interviewing*. Thousand Oaks, CA: Sage Publications.

Kvale, S. and Brinkmann, S. (2009) *InterView*. Copenhagen: Hans Reitzels Forlag.

Ladwein, R. (2002) Voyage à Tikidad: De l'accès à l'expérience de consommation. *Decisions Marketing* 28(1), 53–63.

Laing, A. (1987) The package holiday participant: Choice and behaviour. PhD thesis, Hull University.

Larsen, J. R. K. and Therkelsen, A. (2011). Udviklingspotentialer i det danske feriehusprodukt. et efterspørgselsperspektiv på samspillet mellem feriehus, feriehusområde og attraktioner. *Økonomi and Politik*, 84(4), 40–55.

Larsen, S. (2007) Aspects of a psychology of the tourist experience. *Scandinavian Journal of Hospitality and Tourism* 7(1), 7–18.

Lasalle, D. and Britton, T. (2003) *Priceless: Turning Ordinary Products into Extraordinary Experiences*. Boston, MA: Harvard Business School Press.

Laursen, L. H. (forthcoming) Enhancing the landscape: Small architectural installations in the landscape. In V. Andrade, S. Smith and D. B. Lanng (eds), *The Urban Design Book*. Aalborg: Aalborg University Press. Expected publication 2012.

Laursen, L. H. (2011) *Stedsspecifikke potentialer i fremtidens feriehus og feriehusområde*. Scientific report. Aalborg: Architecture, Design and Media Technology, Aalborg University.

Laws, E. (1991) *Tourism Marketing: Service and Quality Management Perspectives*, Cheltenham: Thornes.

Lee, G., O'Leary, J., Lee, S. and Morrison, A. (2002) Comparison and contrast of push and pull motivational effects on trip behavior: An application of a multinominal logistic regression model. *Tourism Analysis* 7(2), 89–104.

Lee, S. Scott, D. and Kim, H. (2008) Celebrity fan involvement and destination perceptions. *Annals of Tourism Research* 35(3), 809–832.

Lee, Y. and Dattilo, J. (1994) The complex and dynamic nature of leisure experience. *Journal of Leisure Research* 26(3), 195–211.

Lehto, X., Soocheong, J., Achana, F. and O'Leary, J. (2008) Exploring tourism experience sought: A cohort comparison of Baby Boomers and the Silent Generation. *Journal of Vacation Marketing* 14(3), 237–252.

Leinhardt, G., Knutson, K. and Crowley, K. (2003) Museum learning collaborative redux. *Journal of Museum Education* 28(1), 23–31.

Leiper, N. (1979) The framework of tourism: Towards a definition of tourism, tourist, and the tourist industry. *Annals of Tourism Research* 6(4), 390–407.

Lennon, J. and Foley, M. (2000) *Dark Tourism: The Attraction of Death and Disaster*. London: Continuum.

Levitt, T. (1980) Marketing success through differentiation of anything. *Harvard Business Review* 58(1), 83–91.

Lindgren, S. (2005) *Populärkultur: Teorier, metoder och analyser*, Malmö: Liber.

Lisle, D. (2004) Gazing at Ground Zero: Tourism, voyeurism and spectacle. *Journal for Cultural Research* 8(1), 3–21.

Littrell, M., Paige, R. and Song, K. (2004) Senior travellers: Tourism activities and shopping behaviours. *Journal of Vacation Marketing* 10(4), 348–362.

Liutikas, D. (2003) Katalikiškosios piligrimystės sociologiniai aspektai. *SOTER* 9, 117–132.

Liutikas, D. (2009) *Piligrimystė. Vertybių ir tapatumo išraiškos kelionėse*, Vilnius: Lietuvos piligrimų bendrija.

Logan, W. and Reeves, K. (2009) Introduction: Remembering places of pain and shame. In W. Logan and K. Reeves (eds), *Places of Pain and Shame: Dealing with 'Difficult Past'*, pp. 1–14. London: Routledge.

López-Sintas, J., Garcia-Alvarez, M. E. and Filimon, N. (2008) Scale and periodicities of recorded music consumption: Reconciling Bourdieu's theory of taste with facts. *Sociological Review* 56(1), 78–101.

Lovelock, C. and Wirtz, J. (2004) *Services Marketing, People, Technology, Strategy*. Upper Saddle River, NJ: Pearson Education.

Lundberg, C., Lexhagen, M. and Mattsson, S. (2011) *I populärkulturturismens spår: Twilight + Vacation = Twication©*, Östersund: Jengel Förlag AB.

Lundberg, D. (1971) Why tourists travel. *Cornell Hotel and Restaurant Administration Quarterly* 11(4), 75–81.

Luongo, M. T. (2011) 9/11 Memorial: Ground Zero as dark tourist site. *Miller-McCune*, 5 September. Online, available at www.miller-mccune.com/culture/9–11-memorial-ground-zero-as-dark-tourist-site-34277/ (accessed 15 November 2011).

MacCannell, D. (1973) Staged authenticity: Arrangements of social space in tourist settings. *American Journal of Sociology* 79(3), 589–603.

MacCannell, D. (1989) *The Tourist: A New Theory of the Leisure Class*, 2nd edn. New York: Schocken Books.

MacCannell, D. (1999) *The Tourist: A New Theory of the Leisure Class*, 3rd edn. Berkeley: University of California Press.

Maffesoli, M. (1996) *The Time of the Tribes. The Decline of Individualism in Mass Society*. London: Sage Publications.

Malabou, C. (2008) Addiction and grace: Preface to Felix Ravaisson's *Of Habit*. London: Continuum International Publishing Group.

Malone, T. and Lepper, M. (1987) Making learning fun: A taxonomy of intrinsic motivations for learning, in R. Snow and M. Farr (eds), *Aptitude, Learning and Instruction: Cognitive and Affective Process Analysis*, pp. 223–254. Hillsdale, NJ: Lawrence Erlbaum.

Mannell, R. (1980) Social psychological techniques and strategies for studying leisure experience. In S. Iso-Ahola, (ed.), *Social Psychological Perspectives on Leisure and Recreation*, pp. 62–88. Springfield, IL: Charles C. Thomas.

Mannell, R. (1984) Personality in leisure theory: The self-as-entertainment construct. *Society and Leisure* 7, 229–242.

Mannell R. and Iso-Ahola, S. (1987) Psychological nature of leisure and tourism experience. *Annals of Tourism Research* 14(3), 314–331.

Mannell, R. and Kleiber, D. (1997) *A Social Psychology of Leisure*. State College, PA: Venture Publications.

Manzo, L. (2003) Beyond house and heaven: Toward a revisioning of emotional relationships with places. *Journal of Environmental Psychology* 23(1), 47–61.

Margry, J. (ed.) (2008a) *Shrines and Pilgrimage in the Modern World: New Itineraries into the Sacred*. Amsterdam: Amsterdam University Press.

Margry, P. J. (2008b) Secular pilgrimage: A contradiction in terms? In P. J. Margry (ed.), *Shrines and Pilgrimages in the Modern World*, pp. 13–48. Amsterdam: Amsterdam University Press.

Marling, K. (1997) *Designing Disney's Theme Parks: The Architecture of Reassurance.* New York: Flammarion.

Marson, D. (2011) From mass tourism to niche tourism. In P. Robinson, S. Heitmann and P. Dieke (eds), *Research Themes for Tourism*, pp. 1–15. Wallingford: CABI.

Maslow, A. (1943) A theory of human motivation. *Psychological Review* 50(4), 370–396.

Maslow, A. H. (1970) *Motivation and Personality*, 2nd edn. New York: Harper and Row.

Mathieson, A. and Wall, G. (1982) *Tourism: Economic, Physical and Social Impacts*. Harlow: Longman.

Mayo, E. and Jarvis, L. (1981) *The Psychology of Leisure Travel: Effective Marketing and Selling of Travel Services.* Boston, MA: CBI Publishing Co.

McCabe, S. (2000) Tourism motivation process. *Annals of Tourism Research* 27(4), 1049–1052.

McCabe, S. and Foster, C. (2006) The role and function of narrative in tourist interaction. *Journal of Tourism and Cultural Change*, 4(3), 194–215.

McCabe, S. and Stokoe, E. (2004). Place and identity in tourists' accounts. *Annals of Tourism Research* 31(3), 601–622.

McCain, G. and Ray, N. (2003) Legacy tourism: The search for personal meaning in heritage travel. *Tourism Management* 24(6), 713–717.

McClellan, T. (1998) Tourism marketing: A question of perception. *Journal of Vacation Marketing* 4(4), 408–414.

McDonald, S. and Murphy, P. (2008) Utilizing and adapting leisure constraints models to enhance 'short break' vacations: Case study of Melbourne, Australia. *Journal of Vacation Marketing* 14(4), 317–330.

McDowell, E. (1998) Jamaica prepares to put troops on patrol at resorts to help ease tourists' fears of crime. *New York Times*, 21 June. Online, available at www.nytimes.com/1998/06/21/travel/travel-advisory-correspondent-s-report-jamaica-sweeps-off-its-welcome-mat.html (accessed 4 December 2007).

McElroy, J., Tarlow, P. and K. Carlisle, K. (2008) Tourist harassment and responses. In A. Woodside and D. Martin, (eds), *Tourism Management: Analysis, Behaviour and Strategy*, pp. 94–106. Wallingford: CABI.

McGehee, N. and Andereck, K. (2008) 'Pettin' the critters': Exploring the complex relationship between volunteers and the voluntoured in McDowell County, West Virginia, USA and Tijuana, Mexico. In K. Lyons and S. Wearing (eds), *Journeys of Discovery in Volunteer Tourism: International Case Study Perspectives*, pp. 12–24. Wallingford: CABI.

McIntyre, C. (2007) Survival theory: Tourist consumption as a beneficial experiential process in a limited risk setting. *International Journal of Tourism Research* 9(2), 115–130.

Mehmetoglu, M., Hines, K., Graumann, C. and Greibrokk, J. (2010) The relationship between personal values and tourism behaviour: A segmentation approach. *Journal of Vacation Marketing* 16(1), 17–27.

Mellor, P. (1993) Death in high modernity: The contemporary presence and absence of death. In D. Clarke (ed.), *The Sociology of Death*, pp. 11–30. Oxford: Blackwell.

Mellor, P. and Shilling, C. (1993) Modernity, self-identity and the sequestration of death. *Sociology* 27(3), 411–431.

Metcalf, P. and Huntington, R. (1991) *Celebrations of Death: The Anthropology of Mortuary Ritual*, 2nd edn. Cambridge: Cambridge University Press.

Miles, W. (2002) Auschwitz: Museum interpretation and darker tourism. *Annals of Tourism Research* 29(4), 1175–1178.
Millan, E. and Howard, E. (2007) Shopping for pleasure? Shopping experiences of Hungarian consumers. *International Journal of Retail and Distribution Management* 35(6), 474–487.
Millar, S. (1968) *The Psychology of Play*. Oxford: Penguin Books.
Milman, A. (1998) The impact of tourism and travel experience on senior travelers' psychological well-being. *Journal of Travel Research* 37(2), 166–170.
Mintel (2004) *Grey Market Ireland*. London: Mintel International.
Mintel (2010) *Package Holidays – UK – July 2010*. London: Mintel International.
Misiura, S. (2006) *Heritage Marketing*. Oxford: Elsevier.
Mitchell, M. and Orwig, R. (2002) Consumer experience tourism and brand bonding. *Journal of Product and Brand Management.* 11(1), 30–41.
Mohr, K., Backman, K., Gahan, L. and Backman, S. (1993) An investigation of festival motivations and event satisfaction by visitor type. *Festival Management and Event Tourism* 1(2), 89–98.
Mohsin, A. and Ryan, C. (2007) Exploring attitudes of Indian students toward holidaying in New Zealand using the Leisure Motivation Scale. *Asia Pacific Journal of Tourism Research* 12(1), 1–18.
Mollen, A. and Wilson, H. (2010) Engagement, telepresence and interactivity in online consumer experience: Reconciling scholastic and managerial perspectives. *Journal of Business Research* 63(9–10), 919–925.
Montes, J. and Butler, D. (2008) Debating race through the tourist plantation: Analyzing a *New York Times* conversation. *Southeastern Geographer* 48(3), 303–315.
Moore, E. (2004) Children and the changing world of advertising. *Journal of Business Ethics* 52(2), 161–167.
Moore, K. (1997) Tourism: Escape or virtual escape. Paper presented at the Australian Tourism and Hospitality Research Conference, Sydney, Australia.
Morgan, M. and Watson, P. (2007) *Resource Guide in Extraordinary Experiences: Understanding and Managing the Consumer Experience in Hospitality, Leisure, Events, Sport and Tourism*. Online, available at www.heacademy.ac.uk/assets/hlst/documents/resource_guides/extraordinary_experiences.pdf.
Morgan, M. and Watson, P. (2009) Unlocking the shared experience. In M. Kozak and A. Decrop (eds), *Handbook of Tourist Behaviour*, pp. 116–132. New York: Routledge.
Morgan, M. and Xu, F. (2009) Student travel experiences: Memories and dreams. *Journal of Hospitality Marketing and Management* 18(2–3), 216–236.
Morgan, M., Lugosi, P. and Ritchie, J. (eds) (2010) *The Tourism and Leisure Experience: Consumer and Managerial Perspectives*. Clevedon: Channel View Publications.
Morinis, A. (1992) Introduction: The territory of the anthropology of pilgrimage. In A. Morinis (ed.), *Sacred Journeys*, pp. 1–28. Westport, CT: Greenwood Press.
Morris, D. (1981) *The Soccer Tribe*. London: Jonathan Cape.
Mort, G. and Rose, T. (2004) The effect of product type on the means–end chain: Implications for theory and method. *Journal of Consumer Behaviour* 3(3), 221–234.
Moscardo, G. (1996) Mindful visitors, heritage and tourism. *Annals of Tourism Research* 23(2), 376–397.
Mossberg, L. (2001) *Upplevelser och marknadsföring*. Göteborg: Studenterlitteratur.
Mossberg, L. (2003) *Att skapa upplevelser: Från OK til WOW!* Lund: Studenterlitteratur.
Mossberg, L. (2007a) A marketing approach to the tourist experience. *Scandinavian Journal of Hospitality and Tourism* 7(1), 59–74.

Mossberg, L. (2007b) *Å Skape opplevelser – fra OK til WOW!*. Bergen: Fagbogforlaget Vigmostad & Bjørke.
Mossberg, L. and Nissen Johansen, E. (2006) *Storytelling: Marknadsföring i upplevelseindustrin*. Lund: Studentlitteratur AB.
Mowatt, R. and Chancellor, C. (2011) Visiting death and life: Dark tourism and slave castles. *Annals of Tourism Research* 38(4), 1410–1434.
Mowen, J. and Minor, M. (2001) *Consumer Behavior: A Framework*. Upper Saddle River, NJ: Prentice Hall.
Mudie, P. and Pirrie, A. (2006) *Services Marketing Management*. Oxford: Butterworth-Heinemann.
Müller, D. (2006) Unplanned development of literary tourism in two municipalities in rural Sweden. *Scandinavian Journal of Hospitality and Tourism* 6(3), 214–28.
Müller, T. (1991) Using personal values to define segments in an international tourism market. *International Marketing Review* 8(1), 57–70.
Munt, I. (1994) The 'other' postmodern tourism: Culture, travel and the new middle classes. *Theory, Culture and Society* 11(3), 101–123.
Murray, N., Lynch, P. and Foley, A. (2010) Addressing the gap in understanding the tourist experience: Towards an integrated perspective. Online, available at http://repository.wit.ie (accessed 15 June 2011).
Muzaini, H., Teo, P. and Yeoh, B. (2007) Intimations of postmodernity in dark tourism: The fate of history at Fort Siloso, Singapore. *Journal of Tourism and Cultural Change* 5(1), 28–44.
Neulinger, J. (1980) *The Psychology of Leisure*. Springfield, IL: Charles C. Thomas.
Nielson, H. and Spenceley, A. (2010) The success of tourism in Rwanda: Gorillas and more. World Bank/SNV. Online, available at http://siteresources.worldbank.org/AFRICAEXT/Resources/258643–1271798012256/Tourism_Rwanda.pdf (accessed 4 October 2010).
Nijs, D. and Peters, F. (2002) *Imagineering: Het crëren van belevingswerelden*. Amsterdam: Boom.
NISR (2010) Visitor arrivals in Rwanda. National Institute of Statistics of Rwanda. Online, available at http://statistics.gov.rw/index.php?option=com_content&task=view&id=270&Itemid=310 (accessed 4 October 2010).
Nolan, L. and Nolan, S. (1989) *Christian Pilgrimage in Modern Western Europe*. Chapel Hill: University of North Carolina Press.
Nørgaard, V. and Clausen, F. (2004) *Sommerhuse*. Copenhagen: Lindhardt og Ringhof.
Noy, C. (2004) 'This trip really changed me': Backpackers' narratives of self-change. *Annals of Tourism Research* 31(1), 78–102.
Nyaupane, G. and Andereck, K. (2008) Understanding travel constraints: Application and extension of leisure constraints model. *Journal of Travel Research* 46(4), 433–439.
Obenour, W., Patterson, M., Pedersen, P. and Pearson, L. (2006) Conceptualization of a meaning-based research approach for tourism service experiences. *Tourism Management* 27(1), 34–41.
Observations (2009) Participant observations: Tribute WTC Visitor Center and Ground Zero. 17–23 February, Lower Manhattan, New York, in Stone 2010b.
O'Connor, N., Flanagan, S. and Gilbert, D. (2010): A film marketing action plan for film induced tourism destinations: Using Yorkshire as a case study. *European Journal of Tourism Research* 3(1), 80–82.
O'Dell, T. (2007) Tourist experiences and academic junctures. *Scandinavian Journal of Hospitality and Tourism* 7(1), 34–45.

Olsberg/SPI (2007) *Stately Attraction: How Film and Television Programmes Promote Tourism in the UK*. London: Olsberg/SPI Publications.

Ooi, C. (2002) *Cultural Tourism and Tourism Cultures: The Business of Mediating Experiences in Copenhagen and Singapore*. Denmark: Copenhagen Business School Press.

Ooi, C. (2005). A theory of tourism experiences: The management of attention. In T. O'Dell and P. Billing (eds), *Experiencescapes: Tourism, Culture, and Economy*, pp. 53–69. Copenhagen: Copenhagen Business School Press.

Østergaard, P. and Jantzen, C. (2000) Shifting perspectives in consumer research: From buyer behaviour to consumption studies. In S. Beckmann and R. Elliott, *Interpretive Consumer Research. Paradigms, Methodologies and Applications*, pp. 9–23. Copenhagen: Handelshøjskolens Forlag, Copenhagen Business School Press.

Oswald, A. (1997) Happiness and economic performance. Warwick Economic Research Papers 478. Online, available at http://wrap.warwick.ac.uk/335/1/WRAP_Oswald_happecperf.pdf (accessed 3 January 2012).

Otto, J. and Ritchie, J. (1996) The service experience in tourism. *Tourism Management* 17(3), 165–174.

Overby, J. and Lee E.-J. (2006) The effects of utilitarian and hedonic online shopping value on consumer preferences and intentions. *Journal of Business Research* 59(10–11), 1160–1166.

Oxford Economics (2007) *The Economic Impact of the UK Film Industry*. Oxford: Oxford Economics.

Packer, J. (2006) Learning for fun: The unique contribution of educational leisure experiences. *Curator* 49(3), 320–344.

Palmer, A. (1994) *Principles of Services Marketing*. Maidenhead: McGraw-Hill.

Palmer, A. (2010) Customer experience management: A critical review of an emerging idea. *Journal of Services Marketing* 24(3), 196–208.

Pan, S. and Ryan, C. (2007) Mountain areas and visitor usage-motivations and determinants of satisfaction: The case of Pirongia Forest Park, New Zealand. *Journal of Sustainable Tourism* 15(3), 288–308.

Papatheodorou, A., Rosselló, J. and Xiao, H. (2010) Global economic crisis and tourism: Consequences and perspectives. *Journal of Travel Research* 49(1), 39–45.

Parinello, G. (1993) Motivation and anticipation in post-industrial tourism. *Annals of Tourism Research* 20(2), 233–249.

Parinello, G. (1996) Motivation and anticipation in post-industrial tourism. In Y. Apostolopoulos, S. Leivadi and A. Yiannakis (eds), *The Sociology of Tourism*, pp. 75–89. London, Routledge.

Paris, C. and Teye, V. (2010) Backpacker motivations: A travel career approach. *Journal of Hospitality Marketing and Management* 19(3), 244–259.

Pattakos, A. (2010) Discovering the deeper meaning of tourism. In R. Wurzburger, T. Aageson, A. Pattakos and S. Pratt (eds), *Discovering the Deeper Meaning of Creative Tourism: A Global Conversation*, pp. 53–62. Santa Fe, NM: Sunstone Press.

Patterson, I. and Pegg, S. (2009) Marketing the leisure experience to baby boomers and older tourists. *Journal of Hospitality Marketing and Management* 18(2–3), 254–272.

Paul Peter, J. and Olson, J. (2005) *Consumer Behavior and Marketing Strategy*. New York: McGraw-Hill International.

Payne, A., Storbacka, K. and Frow, P. (2008) Managing the co-creation of value. *Journal of the Academy of Marketing Science* 36(1), 83–96.

Pearce, P. (1982a) Perceived changes in holiday destinations. *Annals of Tourism Research* 9(2), 145–164.

Pearce, P. (1982b) *The Social Psychology of Tourist Behaviour*. Oxford: Pergamon.

Pearce, P. (1988) *The Ulysses Factor: Evaluating Visitors in Tourist Settings.* New York: Springer-Verlag.

Pearce, P. (1992) The fundamentals of tourist motivation. In D. Pearce and R. Butler (eds), *Tourism Research: Critiques and Challenges*, pp. 113–134. London: Routledge.

Pearce, P. (2005). *Tourist Behaviour: Themes and Conceptual Schemes.* Clevedon: Channel View Publications.

Pearce, P. (2011a) *Tourist Behaviour and the Contemporary World.* Clevedon: Channel View Publications.

Pearce, P. (2011b) Travel motivation, benefits and constraints to destinations. In Y. Wang and A. Pizam (eds), *Destination Marketing and Management*, pp. 39–52 Wallingford: CABI.

Pearce, P. and Caltabiano, M. (1983) Inferring travel motivation from travelers' experiences. *Journal of Travel Research* 22(2), 16–20.

Pearce, P. and Lee, U. (2005) Developing the travel career approach to tourist motivation. *Journal of Travel Research* 43(3), 226–237.

Pearce, P., Filep, S. and Ross, G. (eds) (2011) *Tourists, Tourism and the Good Life.* Abingdon: Routledge.

Pennington-Gray, L. and Kerstetter, D. (2002) Testing a constraints model within the context of nature-based tourism. *Journal of Travel Research* 40(1), 416–423.

Peppers, D. and Rogers, M. (1995) A new marketing paradigm: Share of customer, not market share. *Managing Service Quality* 5(3), 48–51.

Peterson, R. (2005) Problems in comparative research: The example of omnivorousness. *Poetics* 33(5–6), 257–282.

Petri, H. (2005) Four motivational components of behavior. *Revista Electrónica de Motivación y Emoción* 8(20–21), 1–24.

Petrick, J. (2002) Development of a multi-dimensional scale for measuring the perceived value of a service. *Journal of Leisure Research* 34(2), 119–134.

Pezzullo, P. C. (2009a) 'This is the only tour that sells': Tourism, disaster, and national identity in New Orleans. *Journal of Tourism and Cultural Change* 7, 99–114.

Pezzullo, P. (2009b) Tourists and/as disasters: Rebuilding, remembering and responsibility in New Orleans. *Tourism Studies* 9(23), 23–40.

Pike, S. (2008) *Destination Marketing: An Integrated Marketing Communication Approach*. Oxford: Butterworth-Heinemann.

Pine, B. and Gilmore, J. (1998) Welcome to the experience economy. *Harvard Business Review* 76, 97–105.

Pine, B. and Gilmore, J. (1999) *The Experience Economy: Work is Theatre and Every Business a Stage*. Boston, MA: Harvard Business School Press.

Plog, S. (1974) Why destination areas rise and fall in popularity. *Cornell Hotel and Restaurant Administration Quarterly* 14, 55–58.

Plog, S. (2001) Why destination areas rise and fall in popularity: An update of a *Cornell Quarterly* classic. *Cornell Hotel and Restaurant Administration Quarterly* 42(3), 13–24.

Pocock, C. (2006). Sensing place, consuming space: Changing visitor experiences of the Great Barrier Reef. In K. Meethan, A. Anderson and S. Miles (eds), *Tourism, Consumption and Representation: Narratives of Place and Self*, pp. 94–112. Wallingford: CABI.

Pocock, D. (1992) Catherine Cookson Country: Tourist expectation and experience. *Geography* 77, 236–243.

Pons, P., Crang, M. and Travlou, P. (2009) Introduction: Taking Mediterranean tourists seriously. In P. Pons, M. Crang and P. Travlou (eds), *Cultures of Mass Tourism: Doing the Mediterranean in the Age of Banal Mobilities*, pp. 1–20. Farnham: Ashgate.

Poria, Y. (2007) Establishing co-operation between Israel and Poland to save Auschwitz concentration camp: Globalising the responsibility for the massacre. *International Journal of Tourism Policy* 1(1), 45–57.

Poria, Y., Butler, R. and Airey, D. (2001) Tourism sub-groups: Do they exist? *Tourism Today* 1(1), 14–22.

Poria, Y., Butler, R. and Airey, D. (2003) The core of heritage tourism: Distinguishing heritage tourists from tourists in heritage places. *Annals of Tourism Research* 30(1), 238–254.

Poria, Y., Butler, R. and Airey, D. (2004) The meaning of heritage sites for tourists: The case of Masada. *Tourism Analysis* 9(1/2), 15–22.

Poria, Y., Reichel, A. and Biran, A. (2006) Heritage site management: Motivations and expectations. *Annals of Tourism Research* 33(1), 1172–1188.

Porter, M. (1985) *Competitive Advantage: Creating and Sustaining Superior Performance.* New York: The Free Press.

Prahalad, C. and Ramaswamy, V. (2004) *The Future of Competition: Co-creating Unique Value with Customers*. Boston, MA: Harvard Business School Press.

Prayag, G. and Ryan, C. (2011) The relationship between the 'push' and 'pull' factors of a tourist destination – the role of nationality: An analytical qualitative research approach. *Current Issues in Tourism* 14(1), 121–143.

Prebensen, N. (2005) Country as destination: Norwegian tourists' perceptions and motivation. *Journal of Hospitality and Leisure Marketing* 12(5), 63–85.

Prebensen, N., Skallerud, K. and Chen, J. S. (2010) Tourist motivation with sun and sand destinations: Satisfaction and the wom-effect. *Journal of Travel and Tourism* 27(8), 858–873.

Prentice, R. (2004) Tourist motivation and typologies. In A. Lew, C. M. Hall and A. Williams (eds), *A Companion to Tourism*, pp. 261–279. Oxford: Blackwell.

Pretes, M. (1995) Postmodern tourism: The Santa Claus industry. *Annals of Tourism Research* 22(1), 1–15.

Pullman, M.and Gross, M. (2003) Welcome to your experience: Where you can check out anytime you'd like, but you can never leave. *Journal of Business and Management* 9, 215–232.

Quinlan Cutler, S. and Carmichael, B. (2010) Dimensions of the tourist experience. In M. Morgan, P. Lugosi and J. Ritchie (eds), *The Tourism and Leisure Experience: Consumer and Managerial Perspectives*, pp. 3–26. Clevedon: Channel View Publications.

Ravaisson, F. (2008) *Of Habit*. London, Continuum.

Raymore, L. (2002) Facilitators to leisure. *Journal of Leisure Research* 34(1), 37–51.

Reader, I. (2003) Review: *Dark Tourism: The Attraction of Death and Disaste*r by John Lennon and Malcom Foley. *Cult Media*. Online, available at http://cult-media.com/issue2/Rreade.htm (accessed 11 June 2003).

Reader, I. and Walter, T. (eds) (1993) *Pilgrimage in Popular Culture*. Basingstoke: Macmillan.

Reeve, J. (2005) *Understanding Motivation and Emotion*. 4th edn. Hoboken, NJ: John Wiley and Sons.

Rewtrakunphaiboon, W. and Oppewal, H. (2004) Effects of holiday packaging on tourist decision making: Some preliminary results. In G. Crouch, R. Perdue, H. Timmermans and M. Uysal, (eds), *Consumer Psychology of Tourism, Hospitality and Leisure*, pp. 181–188. Wallingford: CABI.

Richards, G. and Raymond, C. (2000) Creative tourism. *ATLAS News* 23, 16–20.

Ricoeur, P. (1966) *Freedom and Nature: The Voluntary and the Involuntary*. Evanston, IL: Northwestern University Press.

Ricoeur, P. (1991) *From Text to Action: Essays in Hermeneutics, II*. Evanston, IL: Northwestern University Press.

Riley, R. and van Doren, C. (1992) Movies as tourism promotion: A 'pull' factor in a 'push' location. *Tourism Management* 13(3), 267–274.

Riley, R., Baker, D. and van Doren, C. (1998) Movie induced tourism. *Annals of Tourism Research* 25(4), 919–935.

Ringgaard, D. (2010). *Stedssans*. Aarhus: Aarhus Universitetsforlag.

Rinschede, G. (1986) The pilgrimage town of Lourdes. *Journal of Cultural Geography* 7(1), 21–23.

Rinschede, G. (1990) Religious tourism. *Geographische Rundschau* 42: 14–20.

Rinschede, G. (1992) Forms of religious tourism. *Annals of Tourism Research* 19(1), 51–67.

Ritchie, J. and Hudson, S. (2009) Understanding and meeting the challenges of consumer/tourist experience research. *International Journal of Tourism Research* 11(2), 111–126.

Rittichainuwat, N. (2008) Responding to disaster: Thai and Scandinavian tourists' motivation to visit Phuket, Thailand. *Journal of Travel Research* 46(4), 422–432.

Ritzer, G. (2001) *Explorations in the Sociology of Consumption: Fast Food, Credit Cards and Casinos*. London: Sage.

Robb, E. (2009) Violence and recreation: Vacationing in the realm of dark tourism. *Anthropology and Humanism* 34(1), 51–60.

Robledo, M. (1998): *Marketing relacional hotelero: El camino hacia la lealtad del cliente*. Madrid: Ediciones Profesionales y Empresariales.

Rojek, C. (1993) *Ways of Escape*. Basingstoke: Macmillan.

Rotgers, F., Morgenstern, J. and Walters, S. (eds) (2003) *Treating Substance Abuse: Theory and Technique*. New York: Guilford Press.

Rufino Rus, J. (1995). *Gestión de la calidad en las empresas de servicios*. Seville: Caja San Fernando.

Rufus, A. (1999) *Magnificent Corpses*. New York: Marlowe & Company.

Ryan, C. (1993) Crime, violence, terrorism and tourism: An accidental or intrinsic relationship? *Tourism Management* 14(3), 173–183.

Ryan, C. (1995) Learning about tourists from conversations: The over-55s in Majorca. *Tourism Management* 16(3), 207–215.

Ryan, C. (1997). *The Tourist Experience: A New Introduction*. London, Cassell.

Ryan, C. (2002a) From motivation to assessment. In C. Ryan (ed.), *The Tourist Experience*, 2nd edn, pp. 58–77. London: Continuum.

Ryan, C. (2002b) Motives, behaviours, body and mind. In C. Ryan (ed.), *The Tourist Experience*, 2nd edn, pp. 27–57. London: Continuum.

Ryan, C. (ed.) (2002c) *The Tourist Experience*, 2nd edn. London: Continuum.

Ryan, C. (2003) *Recreational Tourism: Demand and Impacts*. Clevedon: Channel View Publications.

Ryan, C. (2011) Ways of conceptualising the tourist experience: A review of literature. In R. Sharpley and P. Stone (eds), *Tourist Experience: Contemporary Perspectives*, pp. 9–20. Abingdon: Routledge.

Ryan, C. and Glendon, I. (1998) Application of leisure motivation scale to tourism. *Annals of Tourism Research* 25(1), 169–84.

Ryan, C., Shuo, Y. and Huan, T. (2010) Theme parks and a structural equation model of determinants of visitor satisfaction: Janfusan Fancyworld, Taiwan. *Journal of Vacation Marketing* 16(3), 185–99.

Sáinz de Vicuña, J. (2006). *El plan de marketing en la práctica*, 10th edn. Madrid: ESIC.

Sánchez, J., Callrisa, L., Rodriguez R. and Moliner, M. (2006) Perceived value of the purchase of a tourism product. *Tourism Management* 27(3), 394–409.

Sánchez, M., Gil, I. and Mollá, A. (2000) Estatus del marketing de relaciones. *Revista Europea de Dirección y Economía de la Empresa* 9(3), 47–64.

Sandell, R. (ed.) (2002) *Museums, Society, Inequality*. New York: Routledge.

Sather-Wagstaff, J. (2011) *Heritage that Hurts: Tourists in the Memoryscape of September 11*. Walnut Creek, CA: Left Coast Press Inc.

Saunders, M., Lewis, P. and Thornhill, A. (2009) *Research Methods for Business Students*, 5th edn. Harlow: Prentice Hall.

Schaller, D. (2007) Genocide tourism: Educational value or voyeurism? *Journal of Genocide Research* 9(4), 513–515.

Schmallegger, D. and Carson, D. (2008) Blogs in tourism: Changing approaches to information exchange. *Journal of Vacation Marketing* 14(2), 99–110.

Schmitt, B. (2000) *Experiential Marketing*. Bilbao: Ediciones Deusto.

Schwandt, T. (2000) Three epistemological stances for qualitative inquiry. In N. Denzin and Y. Lincoln (eds), *Handbook of Qualitative Research*, 2nd edn, pp. 189–213. Thousand Oaks, CA: Sage Publications, Inc.

Scott, C. (2009) Exploring the evidence base for museum value. *Museum Management and Curatorship* 24(3), 195–212.

Scott, D. (1996) A comparison of visitors' motivations to attend three urban festivals. *Festival Management and Event Tourism* 3(3), 121–28.

Scott, D. and Usher, R. (1999) Observation. In D. Scott and R. Usher (eds), *Researching Education: Data, Methods and Theory*, pp. 15–30. Boston, MA: Kluwer Academic Publishers.

Scott, N., Laws, E. and Boksberger, P. (2009) The marketing of hospitality and leisure experiences. *Journal of Hospitality Marketing and Management* 18(2–3), 99–110.

Seaton, A. (1996) Guided by the dark: From thanatopsis to thanatourism. *International Journal of Heritage Studies* 2(4), 234–244.

Seaton, A. (1999) War and thanatourism: Waterloo 1815–1914. *Annals of Tourism Research* 26(1), 130–158.

Seaton, A. (2009) Purposeful otherness: Approaches to the management of thanatourism. In R. Sharpley and P. R. Stone (eds), *The Darker Side of Travel: The Theory and Practice of Dark Tourism*, pp. 75–108. Clevedon: Channel View Publications.

Seaton, A. and Bennett, M. (1996) *Marketing Tourism Products*. London: International Thomson Business Press.

Seaton, A. and Lennon, J. (2004) Thanatourism in the early twenty-first century: Moral panics, ulterior motives and alterior desires. In T. V. Singh (ed.), *New Horizons in Tourism: Strange Experiences and Stranger Practices*, pp. 63–82. Wallingford: CABI.

Segrave, J. and Chu, D. (1996) The modern Olympic Games: An access to ontology. *Quest*, 48(1), 57–66.

Shandley, R., Jamal, T. and Tanase, A. (2006) Location shooting and the filmic destination: Transylvanian myths and the post-colonial tourism enterprise. *Journal of Tourism and Cultural Change* 4(3), 137–158.

Sharpley, R. (2003) *Tourism, Tourists and Society*. 3rd edn. Huntingdon: ELM Publications.

Sharpley, R. (2005) Travels to the edge of darkness: Towards a typology of dark tourism. In C. Ryan, S. Page and M. Aicken (eds), *Taking Tourism to the Limit: Issues, Concepts and Managerial Perspectives*, pp. 215–226. London: Elsevier.

Sharpley, R. (2008) *Tourism, Tourists and Society*. 4th edn. Huntingdon: ELM Publications.

Sharpley, R. (2009a) Dark tourism and political ideology: Towards a governance model. In R. Sharpley and P. R. Stone (eds), *The Darker Side of Travel: The Theory and Practice of Dark Tourism*, pp. 145–163. Clevedon: Channel View Publications.

Sharpley, R. (2009b) Shedding light on dark tourism. In R. Sharpley and P. R. Stone (eds), *The Darker Side of Travel: The Theory and Practice of Dark Tourism*, pp. 3–22. Clevedon: Channel View Publications.

Sharpley, R. (2011) Does consumerism necessarily promote bad tourism? *Tourism Recreation Research* 36(3), 293–297.

Sharpley, R. and Jepson, D. (2011) Rural tourism: A spiritual experience? *Annals of Tourism Research* 38(1), 52–71.

Sharpley, R. and Stone, P. R (eds) (2009a) *The Darker Side of Travel: The Theory and Practice of Dark Tourism*. Clevedon: Channel View Publications.

Sharpley, R. and Stone, P. R. (2009b) Life, death and dark tourism; Future research directions and concluding comments. In R. Sharpley and P. R. Stone (eds), *The Darker Side of Travel: The Theory and Practice of Dark Tourism*, pp. 247–251. Clevedon: Channel View Publications.

Sharpley, R. and Stone, P. R (2009c) Representing the macabre: Interpretation, kitschification and authenticity. In R. Sharpley and P. R. Stone (eds), *The Darker Side of Travel: The Theory and Practice of Dark Tourism*, pp. 109–128. Clevedon: Channel View Publications.

Sharpley, R. and Stone, P. R. (2011a) Introduction: Thinking about the tourist experience. In R. Sharpley and P. R. Stone (eds), *Tourist Experience: Contemporary Perspectives*, pp. 1–8. Abingdon: Routledge.

Sharpley, R. and Stone, P. R. (eds) (2011b) *Tourist Experience: Contemporary Perspectives*. London: Routledge.

Shaw, G. and Williams, A. (2004) *Tourism and Tourism Spaces*, London: Sage Publications.

Shaw, G., Bailey, A. and Williams, A. (2011) Aspects of service-dominant logic and its implications for tourism management: Examples from the hotel industry. *Tourism Management* 32(2), 207–214.

Shedroff, N. (2008) *Making Meaning: How Successful Businesses Deliver Meaningful Customer Experiences*. Berkeley, CA: New Riders.

Shedroff, N. (2009). *Experience Design 1.1*. New York: Rosenfeld Media.

Sheldon, P. and Mak, J. (1987) The demand for package tours: A mode choice model. *Journal of Travel Research* 25(3), 13–17.

Shepherd, R. (2003) Fieldwork without remorse: Travel desires in a tourist world. *Consumption, Markets and Culture* 6(2), 133–144.

Sherry, J., Jr., Kozinets, R. and Borghini, S. (2007) Agents in paradise: Experiential co-creation through emplacement, ritualisation, and community. In A. Carù and B. Cova (eds), *Consuming Experience*, pp. 17–33. London: Routledge.

Shoemaker, S. (2000) Segmenting the mature market: 10 years later. *Journal of Travel Research* 39(1), 11–26.

Silva, O. and Correia, A. (2008) Facilitators and constraints in leisure travel participation: The case of southeast of Portugal. *International Journal of Culture, Tourism and Hospitality Research* 2(1), 25–43.

Simic, O. (2008) A tour to the site of genocide: Mothers, bones and borders. *Journal of International Women's Studies* 9(3), 320–330.

Simon, N. (2010) *The Participatory Museum*. San Francisco: Museum 20.

Sin, H. (2009) Volunteer tourism: Involve me and I will learn. *Annals of Tourism Research* 36(3), 480–501.

Singer, D., Golinkoff, R. and Hirsh-Pasek, K. (2006) *Play Equals Learning*. Oxford: Oxford University Press.

Singh, D., Birch, A. and McDavid, H.(2006) Impact of the hospitality-tourism sector on the Jamaican economy, 1974–1993: An input–output approach. *Social and Economic Studies* 55(3), 183–207.

Sirakaya, E., Uysal, M. and Yoshioka, C.(2003) Segmenting the Japanese tour market to Turkey. *Journal of Travel Research* 41(3), 293–304.

Slade, P. (2003) Gallipoli thanatourism: The meaning of ANZAC. *Annals of Tourism Research* 30(4), 779–794.

Smed, K. M. (2009) Tourism and identity: Accumulated tourist experience and travel career narratives in tourists' identity construction. PhD thesis, Aalborg University.

Smith, A. and Stewart, B. (2007) The travelling fan: Understanding the mechanisms of sport fan consumption in a sport tourism setting. *Journal of Sport and Tourism* 12(3–4), 155–181.

Smith, C. S. (2001) The nation's museums: Politics and policies. *Museum Management and Curatorship* 19(2), 187–196.

Smith, M. (2003) Holistic holidays: Tourism and the reconciliation of body, mind and spirit. *Tourism Recreation Research* 28(1), 103–108.

Smith, N. and Croy, W. (2005) Presentation of dark tourism: Te Wairoa, the Buried Village. In C. Ryan, S. Page and M. Aicken (eds), *Taking Tourism to the Limits: Issues, Concepts and Managerial Perspectives*, pp. 199–213. Oxford: Elsevier.

Smith, S. and Wheeler, J. (2002) *Managing the Customer Experience: Turning Customers into Advocates*. Harlow: FT Prentice Hall.

Smith, V. (1977) Introduction. In V. Smith (ed.), *Host and Guests: The Anthropology of Tourism*, pp. 1–14. Philadelphia: University of Pennsylvania Press.

Smith, V. (1992) Introduction: The quest in guest. *Annals of Tourism Research* 19(1), 1–17.

Snepenger, D., Snepenger, M., Dalbey, M. and Wessol, A. (2007) Meanings and consumption characteristics of places at a tourism destination. *Journal of Travel Research* 45(3), 310–321.

Solá-Morales, I. (1997) Place: Performance or production. In *Differences: Topographies of Contemporary Architecture*, pp. 93–103. Cambridge, MA: MIT Press.

Solomon, M. (2009) *Consumer Behavior: Buying, Having, and Being*. Upper Saddle River, NJ: Prentice Hall.

Squire, S. (1994). Accounting for cultural meanings: The interface between geography and tourism studies re-examined. *Progress in Human Geography* 18(1), 1–16.

Stebbins, R. (1996) *Tolerable Differences: Living with Deviance*, 2nd edn. Toronto: McGraw-Hill Ryerson.

Stebbins, R. (2009) *Leisure and Consumption: Common Ground/Separate Worlds*. Basingstoke: Palgrave Macmillan.

Steenkamp, J.-B. and Geyskens, I. (2006) How country characteristics affect perceived value of web sites. *Journal of Marketing* 70(3) 136–150.

Steiner, C. and Reisinger, Y. (2006) Understanding existential authenticity. *Annals of Tourism Research* 33(2), 299–318.

Stenbro, R. and Christoffersen, L. (2008) Stedets ånd – eller steder der ånder? Arkitektoniske arbejdsmetoder og deres mellemværende med steder. Conference paper given at Architectural Inquiries, Göteborg. Online, available at http://tintin.arch.chalmers.se/aktuellt/PDFs/Stenbro_Stedets%20and%20eller%20steder%20der%20ander.pdf (accessed 14 October 2011).

Sterry, P. and Beaumont, E. (2005) Methods for studying family visitors in art museums: A cross-disciplinary review of current research. *Museum Management and Curatorship* 21(3), 222–239.

Stevenson, N., Airey, D. and Miller, G. (2008) Tourism policy making: The policy-makers' perspectives. *Annals of Tourism Research* 35(3), 732–750.

Stone, P. R. (2005) Consuming dark tourism: A call for research. *eReview of Tourism Research*, 3(5), 109–117. Online, available at http://ertr.tamu.ed/appliedresearch.cfm?articleid=90.

Stone, P. R. (2006) A dark tourism spectrum: Towards a typology of death and macabre related tourist sites, attractions and exhibitions. *Tourism: An Interdisciplinary Journal* 54(2), 145–160.

Stone, P. R. (2009a) Morality and new moral spaces. In R. Sharpley and P. R. Stone (eds), *The Darker Side of Travel: The Theory and Practice of Dark Tourism*, pp. 56–72. Clevedon: Channel View Publications.

Stone, P. R. (2009b) 'It's a bloody guide': Fun, fear and a lighter side of dark tourism at The Dungeon visitor attractions, UK. In R. Sharpley and P. R. Stone (eds), *The Darker Side of Travel: The Theory and Practice of Dark Tourism*, pp. 167–185. Clevedon: Channel View Publications.

Stone, P. R. (2009c) Making absent death present: Consuming dark tourism in contemporary society. In R. Sharpley and P. R. Stone (eds), *The Darker Side of Travel: The Theory and Practice of Dark Tourism*, pp. 23–38. Clevedon: Channel View Publications.

Stone, P. R. (2010) Death, dying and dark tourism in contemporary society: A theoretical and empirical analysis. PhD thesis, University of Central Lancashire,. Online, available at http://works.bepress.com/philip_stone/34/

Stone, P. R. (2011a) Dark tourism and the cadaveric carnival: Mediating life and death narratives at Gunther von Hagens' Body Worlds. *Current Issues in Tourism* 14(7), 685–701.

Stone, P. R. (2011b) Dark tourism experiences: Mediating between life and death. In R. Sharpley and P. R. Stone (eds), *Tourist Experiences: Contemporary Perspectives*, pp. 21–27. Abingdon: Routledge.

Stone, P. R. (2011c) Dark tourism: Towards a new post-disciplinary research agenda. *International Journal of Tourism Anthropology* 1(3/4), 318–332.

Stone, P. R. and Sharpley, R. (2008) Consuming dark tourism: A thanatological perspective. *Annals of Tourism Research* 35(2), 574–595.

Strinati, D. (2004) *An Introduction to Theories of Popular Culture*. New York: Routledge.

Strobe, M. and Schut, H. (1999) The dual process model of coping with bereavement, rational and description. *Death Studies* 23(3), 197–224.

Strom, E. (2002) Converting pork into porcelain: Cultural institutions and downtown development. *Urban Affairs Review* 38(1), 3–21.

Sturken, M. (2004) The aesthetics of absence: Rebuilding Ground Zero. *American Ethnologist* 31(3), 311–325.

Sturken, M. (2007) *Tourists of History: Memory, Kitsch, and Consumerism from Oklahoma City to Ground Zero.* Durham, NC: Duke University Press.

Sutton, W., McDonald, M., Milne, G., and Cimperman, A. (1997) Creating and fostering fan identification in professional sport. *Sport Marketing Quarterly* 6(1), 15–29.

Suvantola, J. (2002) *Tourists' Experience of Place*. Aldershot: Ashgate.

Swarbrooke, J. and Horner, S. (2007) *Consumer Behaviour in Tourism*, 2nd edn. Oxford: Butterworth-Heinemann.

Swatos, H. and Tomasi, L. (eds) (2002) *From Medieval Pilgrimage to Religious Tourism: The Social and Cultural Economics of Piety*. Westport, CT: Praeger Publishers.

Sweeney, J. and Soutar G. (2001) Consumer perceived value: The development of a multiple item scale. *Journal of Retailing* 77(2), 203–20.

Sydney Morning Herald (2008) Jamaica – health and safety. Travel fact sheet: Dangers and annoyances. Online, available at www.smh.com.au/travel/travel-factsheet/jamaica–health-amp-safety-20081128–6l6z.html. (accessed 28 April 2009).

Tabachnick, B. and Fidell, L. (2007) *Using Multivariate Statistics*. Boston, MA: Pearson Education.

Taheri, B. and Jafari, A. (forthcoming) Socializing through cultural consumption. Paper presented at the Association of Consumer Research Conference, St Louis, MO, October 2011. *Advances in Consumer Research* 39.

Tajfel, H. and Turner, J. (1979) An integrative theory of intergroup conflict. In W. Austin, and S. Worchel, *The Social Psychology of Intergroup Relations*, pp. 33–47. Monterey, CA: Brooks-Cole.

Tanaka, H. (1984) Landscape expression of the evolution of Buddhism in Japan. *Canadian Geographer* 28(3), 240–257.

Tanaka, H. (1988) On the geographic study of pilgrimage places. *Geographia Religionum* 4: 21–40.

Tercier, J. (2005) *The Contemporary Deathbed: The Ultimate Rush*. Basingstoke: Palgrave Macmillan.

Teye, V. and Timothy, D. (2004) The varied colours of slave heritage in West Africa. *Space and Culture* 7(2), 145–155.

Therkelsen, A. and Gram, M. (2008) The meaning of holiday consumption: Constructing of self among mature couples. *Journal of Consumer Culture* 8 (2), 269–292.

Thi Le, D. and Pearce, D. (2011) Segmenting visitors to battlefield sites: International visitors to the former Demilitarized Zone in Vietnam. *Journal of Travel and Tourism Marketing* 28(4), 451–463.

Thornton, P., Shaw, G. and Williams, A. (1997) Tourist group holiday decision-making and behaviour: The influence of children. *Tourism Management* 18(5), 287–297.

Thrane, C. (1997) Values as segmentation criteria in tourism research: The Norwegian monitor approach. *Tourism Management* 18(2), 111–113.

Tilley, C. (1994) Space, place, landscape and perception: Phenomenological perspectives. In *A Phenomenology of Landscape: Places, Paths and Monuments*, pp. 7–34. Oxford: Berg.

Timothy, D. and Boyd, S. (2003) *Heritage Tourism*. Harlow: Prentice Hall.

Timothy, D. and Olsen, D. (eds) (2006) *Tourism, Religion and Spiritual Journeys*. Abingdon: Routledge.

Tinsley, H. and Tinsley, D. (1986). A theory of attributes, benefits and causes of leisure experience. *Leisure Sciences* 8(1), 1–45.

Toffler A. (1970) *Future Shock*. New York: Random House.

Tomasky, M. (2003) Battleground Zero. *USA Today*. Online, available at www.usatoday.com/travel/vacations/destinations/2002–08–30-disaster-tourism.html (accessed 8 June 2004).

Tooke, N. and Baker, M. (1996) Seeing is believing: The effect of film on visitor numbers to screened locations. *Tourism Management* 17(2), 87–96.

Tourism Product Development Co. Ltd (2005). Team Jamaica. Online, available at www.tpdco.org/dynaweb.dti?dynasection=tourismenhancement&dynapage=tj&dynawebSID=6d8. Accessed 24 July 2009.

Towner, J. (1996) *An Historical Geography of Recreation and Tourism in the Western World 1540–1940*. Chichester: John Wiley & Sons.

Trail, G. and James, J. (2001) The motivation scale for sport consumption: Assessment of the scale's psychometric properties. *Journal of Sport Behaviour* 24(1), 108–127.

Trail, G., Anderson, D. and Fink, J. (2000) A theoretical model of sport spectator consumption behavior. *International Journal of Sport Management* 1(3), 154–180.

Trauer, B. and Ryan, C. (2005) Destination image, romance and place experience: An application of intimacy theory in tourism. *Tourism Management* 26(4), 481–491.

Tribe, J. (2009) (ed.) *Philosophical Issues in Tourism*. Clevedon: Channel View Publications.

Tuan, Y.-F. (1977) *Space and Place: The Perspective of Experience*. London: Edward Arnold.

Tufts, S. and Milne, S. (1999) Museums: A supply-side perspective. *Annals of Tourism Research* 26(3), 613–631.

Tumarkin, M. (2005) *Traumascapes: The Power and Fate of Places Transformed by Tragedy*. Carlton: Melbourne University Press.

Tunbridge, J. and Ashworth, G. (1996) *Dissonant Heritage: Managing the Past as a Resource in Conflict*. Chichester: John Wiley & Sons.

Tung, V. and Ritchie, J. (2011) Exploring the essence of memorable tourism experiences. *Annals of Tourism Research* 38(4), 1367–86.

Turnbull, D. and Uysal, M. (1995) An exploratory study of German visitors to the Caribbean. *Journal of Travel and Tourism Marketing* 4(2), 85–92.

Turner, L. and Ash, J. (1975) *The Golden Hordes*. London: Constable.

Turner, V. (1967) *The Forest of Symbols*. Ithaca, NY: Cornell University Press.

Turner, V. (1969) *The Ritual Process*. Chicago: Aldine.

Turner, V. (1973) The center out there: Pilgrim's goal. *History of Religions* 12(3), 191–230.

Turner, V. and Turner, E. (1978) *Image and Pilgrimage in Christian Culture*. New York: Columbia University Press.

Tzanelli, R. (2003) 'Casting' the neohellenic 'other': Tourism, the culture industry, and contemporary Orientalism in *Captain Corelli's Mandolin*. *Journal of Consumer Culture* 3(2), 217–244.

Tzanelli, R. (2004) Constructing the 'cinematic tourist': The 'sign industry' of *The Lord of the Rings*. *Tourist Studies* 41(1), 21–42.

Tzanelli, R. (2006) Reel western fantasies: Portrait of a tourist imagination in *The Beach*. *Mobilities* 1(1), 121–142.

UK Government (1992) The Package Travel, Package Holidays and Package Tours Regulations. Online, available at www.legislation.gov.uk/uksi/1992/3288/contents/made.

United Nations (2000) *United Nations World Population Prospects. The 2000 Revision Highlights*. New York: United Nations.

Uriely, N. (2005) The tourist experience: Conceptual developments. *Annals of Tourism Research* 32(1), 199–216.

Uriely, N., Ram, Y. and Malach-Pines, A. (2011) Psychoanalytic sociology of deviant tourist behaviour, *Annals of Tourism Research* 38(3), 1051–1069.

Urquhart, C. (2006) *The Ultimate Holiday Handbook*. London: The Times.
Urry, J. (1995) *Consuming Places*. London: Routledge.
US Department of State (2009) Jamaica: Country Specific Information. Online, available at http://travel.state.gov/travel/cis_pa_tw/cis/cis_1147.html. (accessed 27 April 2008).
Uysal, M. (1998) The determinants of tourism demand. In D. Ioannides and K. Debbage (eds), *The Economic Geography of the Tourist Industry: A Supply-Side Analysis*, pp. 79–95. London: Routledge.
Uysal, M., Backman, K., Backman, S. and Potts, T. (1991) An examination of event tourism motivations and activity. Paper presented at the New Horizons Conference, Calgary, Canada, July 1991.
Uysal, M., Gahan, L. and Martin, B. (1993) An examination of event motivations. *Festival Management and Event Tourism* 1(1), 5–10.
Uysal, M., Li, X. and Sirakaya-Turk, E. (2008) Push–pull dynamics in travel decisions. In H. Oh and A. Pizam (eds), *Handbook of Hospitality Marketing Management*, pp. 412–439. Oxford: Butterworth-Heinemann.
Uzzell, D. (1989) The hot interpretation of war and conflict. In D. Uzell (ed.), *Heritage Interpretation*, vol. I. *The Natural and Built Environment*, pp. 33–47. London: Bellhaven Press.
van Aalst, I. and Boogaarts, I. (2001) From museum to mass entertainment: The evolution of the role of museums in cities. *European Urban and Regional Studies* 9(3), 195–209.
van Egmond, T. (2007) *Understanding Western Tourists in Developing Countries*. Wallingford: CABI.
van Harssel, J. (1994) *Tourism: An Exploration*. Englewood Cliffs, NJ: Prentice Hall.
van Raaij, W. and Crotts, J. (1994) Introduction: Economic psychology of travel and tourism. In J. Crotts and W. van Raaij (eds), *Economic Psychology of Travel and Tourism*, pp. 1–20. London: The Haworth Press.
van Rekom, J. (1994) Adding psychological value to tourism products. In J. Crotts and W. van Raaij (eds), *Economic Psychology of Travel and Tourism*, pp. 21–36. London: Haworth Press.
Vargo, S. and Lusch, R. (2004) Evolving to a new dominant logic for marketing. *Journal of Marketing* 68(1), 1–17.
Vargo, S. and Lusch, R. (2008) Service-dominant logic continuing the evolution. *Journal of the Academy of Marketing Science* 36(1), 1–10.
Veal, A. (2009) *The Elusive Leisure Society*. School of Leisure, Sport and Tourism Working Paper 9. Sydney: University of Technology.
Vestby, G. (2009) *Stedsutvikling I Eidfjord – sosiokulturell stedsanalyse*. NIRB-rapport 2009: 22. Oslo: Norsk institutt for by- og regionforskning.
VisitDenmark (2005) *Feriehusundersøgelse. Efterår 2005*. Copenhagen: VisitDenmark.
VisitDenmark (2010) *Turismen i region Nordjylland i tal*. Copenhagen: VisitDenmark.
VisitNordjylland (2011) *Nordjysk turisme. Overnatninger 2001–2010*. Skeelslund: VisitNordjylland.
Wallace, R. (1999) Addiction as defect of the will: Some philosophical reflections. *Law and Philosophy* 18(6), 621–654.
Walle, A. (1996) Habits of thought and cultural tourism. *Annals of Tourism Research* 23(4), 874–890.
Walter, T. (2005) Mediator deathwork. *Death Studies*, 29(5), 383–412.
Walter, T. (2009) Dark tourism: Mediating between the dead and the living. In R. Sharpley and P. Stone (eds), *The Darker Side of Travel: The Theory and Practice of Dark Tourism*, pp. 39–55. Clevedon: Channel View Publications.

Wang, N. (1999) Rethinking authenticity in tourism experience. *Annals of Tourism Research* 26(2), 349–370.

Wang, N. (2000) *Tourism and Modernity. A Sociological Analysis*. Oxford: Elsevier Science.

Wann, D. (1995) Preliminary validation of the sport fan motivation scale. *Journal of Sport and Social Issues* 19(4), 377–396.

Wann, D., Melnick, M., Russel, G. and Pease, D. (2001) *Sport Fans: The Psychology and Social Impact of Spectators*. New York: Routledge.

Wearing, S. and Ponting, J. (2009) Breaking down the system: How volunteer tourism contributes to new ways of viewing commodified tourism. In T. Jamal and M. Robinson (eds), *The Sage Handbook of Tourism Studies*, pp. 254–268. Thousand Oaks, CA: Sage Publications.

Weed, M. and Bull, C. (2004) *Sports Tourism: Participants, Policy and Providers*. Oxford: Elsevier.

Weick, K. (1995) *Sensemaking in Organizations*. Thousand Oaks, CA: Sage Publications.

Welsh, P. (2005) Re-configuring museums. *Museum Management and Curatorship* 20(2), 103–130.

West, B. (2003) Synergies in deviance: Revisiting the positive deviance debate. *Electronic Journal of Sociology* 17(4), 1–18.

Whitaker, A. (2009) *Museum Legs*. Tucson, AZ: Hol Art Books.

White, T., Hede, A.-M. and Rentschler, R. (2009) Lessons from arts experiences for service-dominant logic. *Marketing Intelligence and Planning* 27(6), 775–788.

Wickens, E. (1999) Tourists' voices: A sociological analysis of tourists' experiences in Chalkidiki, northern Greece. Unpublished PhD thesis: Oxford Brookes University, UK.

Wickens, E. (2002) The sacred and the profane: A tourist typology. *Annals of Tourism Research* 29(3), 834–851.

Wickens, E. (2006) Tourists, motivations and experiences: A theoretical and methodological critique. In A. Aktas, M. Kesgin, E. Cengiz and E. Yenialp (eds), *Turk–Kazakh International Tourism Conference 2006. Proceedings* Book 1, pp. 66–76. Alanya, Turkey 20–26 November. Akdeniz University Alanya Faculty of Business. Ankara: Detay.

Wight, C. (2005) Philosophical and methodological praxes in dark tourism: Controversy, contention and the evolving paradigm. *Journal of Vacation Marketing* 12(2), 119–129.

Williams, P. (2004) Witnessing genocide: Vigilance and remembrance at Tuol Sleng and Choeng Ek. *Holocaust and Genocide Studies* 18(2), 234–255.

Williams, P. (2007) *Memorial Museums: The Global Rush to Commemorate Atrocities*. Oxford: Berg.

Willmott, H. (2000) Death. So what? Sociology, sequestration and emancipation. *Sociological Review* 48(4), 649–665.

Wilson, N. (2011) *Seduced by Twilight: The Allure and Contradictory Messages of the Popular Saga*. Jefferson, NC: McFarland and Company Inc.

Witcomb, A. (2003) *Re-Imagining the Museum: Beyond the Mausoleum*. London: Routledge.

Witt, C. and Wright, P. (1993) Tourist motivation: Life after Maslow. In P. Johnson and B. Thomas (eds), *Choice and Demand in Tourism*, pp. 33–55. London: Mansell.

Woodruff, R. (1997) Customer value: The next source of competitive advantage. *Journal of the Academy of Marketing Science* 25(2), 139–153.

Woodruff, R. and Gardial, S. (1996) *Know Your Customer: New Approaches to Understanding Customer Value and Satisfaction*. Cambridge, MA: Blackwell Publishing.

Woodside, A. (2000) Introduction: Theory and research on the consumer psychology of tourism, hospitality and leisure. In A. Woodside, G. Crouch, J. Mazanec, M. Oppermann and M. Sakai (eds), *Consumer Psychology of Tourism, Hospitality and Leisure*, pp. 1–17. Wallingford, CABI Publishing.

Woodside, A. and Macdonald, R. (1994) General systems framework of customer choice processes of tourism services. Paper presented at the Institute of Tourism and Service Economics International Conference at the University of Innsbruck. Vienna: Kultur Verlag.

World Tourism Organization (2009) *Tourism Highlights* 2008 edition. Online, available at www.unwto.org/facts/eng/pdf/highlights/UNWTO_Highlights08_en_HR.pdf (accessed 7 May 2009).

Yiannakis, A. (1992) Roles tourists play. *Annals of Tourism Research* 19(2), 287–303.

Yuksel, A. and Yuksel, F. (2002) Measurement of tourist satisfaction with restaurant services: A segment-based approach. *Journal of Vacation Marketing* 9(1), 52–68.

Zeithaml, V. (1988) Consumer perceptions of price, quality and value: A means–end model and synthesis of evidence. *Journal of Marketing* 52(1), 2–22.

Zhou, Z. (2004) *E-commerce and Information Technology in Hospitality and Tourism*. New York: Thomson Delmar Learning.

Zwick, D. and Dholakia, N. (2004) Consumer subjectivity in the age of Internet: The radical concept of marketing control through customer relationship management'. *Information and Organization* 14(3), 211–236.

Index